Course Management Systems for Learning:
Beyond Accidental Pedagogy

Patricia McGee
The University of Texas at San Antonio, USA

Colleen Carmean
Arizona State University, USA

Ali Jafari
Indiana University-Purdue University Indianapolis (IUPUI),
USA

 Information Science Publishing

Hershey • London • Melbourne • Singapore

Acquisitions Editor: Renée Davies
Development Editor: Kristin Roth
Senior Managing Editor: Amanda Appicello
Managing Editor: Jennifer Neidig
Copy Editor: Alison Smith
Typesetter: Kristin Roth
Cover Design: Lisa Tosheff
Printed at: Yurchak Printing Inc.

Published in the United States of America by
        Information Science Publishing (an imprint of Idea Group Inc.)
        701 E. Chocolate Avenue, Suite 200
        Hershey PA 17033
        Tel: 717-533-8845
        Fax: 717-533-8661
        E-mail: cust@idea-group.com
        Web site: http://www.idea-group.com

and in the United Kingdom by
        Information Science Publishing (an imprint of Idea Group Inc.)
        3 Henrietta Street
        Covent Garden
        London WC2E 8LU
        Tel: 44 20 7240 0856
        Fax: 44 20 7379 3313
        Web site: http://www.eurospan.co.uk

                Library of Congress Cataloging-in-Publication Data

Course management systems for learning : beyond accidental pedagogy / Patricia McGee, Colleen Carmean, and Ali Jafari, editors.
        p. cm.
  Summary: "This book provides a comprehensive overview of standards, practices and possibilities of course management systems in higher education"--Provided by publisher.
  Includes bibliographical references and index.
    ISBN 1-59140-512-2 (h/c) -- ISBN 1-59140-513-0 (s/c) -- ISBN 1-59140-514-9 (ebook)
  1. Universities and colleges--Curricula. 2. Education, Higher--Computer-assisted instruction. 3. Student-centered learning. I. McGee, Patricia, 1953- II. Carmean, Colleen, 1955- III. Jafari, Ali.
  LB2361.C68 2005
  378.1'99--dc22
                                2004030902

British Cataloguing in Publication Data
A Cataloguing in Publication record for this book is available from the British Library.

Course Management Systems for Learning:
Beyond Accidental Pedagogy

Table of Contents

SECTION II: RESEARCH IMPLICATIONS AND
CREATIVE INNOVATIONS FOR FUTURE DESIGN OF CMS

Section III: Next-Generation CMS

Foreword

This book is about consequences and possibilities. Some chapters report the results of the intentional and directed efforts of serious scholars, dreamers, and practitioners. Others describe outcomes of spontaneous creativity of faculty, students, technologists, vendors, administrators, designers, and visionaries. All have been working for a number of years now to shape and define the phenomenon that we know as a *course management system* (CMS).

Faculty members were motivated to learn how to use the CMS because they quickly realized that the tool provided time-saving capabilities and the functionality to make course materials, grades, and other resources available to students electronically. The CMS was attractive to college and university administrators because it provided a means of meeting students' expectations regarding the electronic accessibility of course-related information and services. An unanticipated consequence of this facilitating technology was that faculty members and students began to use the CMS as a learning management tool. However, in pursuing functionality — indeed, in attempting to redefine the philosophy behind the CMS — faculty and student pioneers did face some frustration.

To surface the issues and to provide a vehicle to encourage rapid vendor response to the developing inadequacies of CMS, in 2003, the EDUCAUSE Learning Initiative (ELI), formerly known as the National Learning Infrastructure Initiative (NLII), held a focus session on the topic of next-generation course management systems. Those who participated came away with a sense that there was a collective voice in articulating the desired features of new releases and that there was also a desire on the part of vendors to move the CMS toward LMS (learning management systems). The editors of this energetically pragmatic yet visionary volume, along with a number of the authors, participated in that focus session. The chapters in this volume envision a new environment based on standards, creating anytime/anywhere access and ownership, and encouraging deep, meaningful learning. All of these characteristics surfaced at the focus session as essential components of the next-generation CMS.

Cynics focus on the limitations of course management systems, choosing to view the CMS as originally designed and intended to assist faculty in dealing with the burdens associated with the administrative details of managing their courses. It remains arguable whether the CMS/LMS is a tool for transformation in higher education. The next-generation CMS may serve as the model to provide a familiar context for adjusting to the destabilizing forces associated with the presence of the digital generation on campus. Owing to its widespread acceptance and use, the CMS could provide the foundation of a known and "safe" environment to ground and integrate the tools that afford the ability for faculty and students to manage learning.

Carole A. Barone
EDUCAUSE
August, 2004

Preface

The remarkable Amazon™ online retail store remembers what we like and all our purchases, eBay™ lets us bid on anything and keeps us posted on our progress, Google™ finds what we were looking for, Mapquest™ gets us wherever we wish to go, and our banks now pay our bills. Why then do course management systems (CMS), the fastest growing enterprise systems in higher education, remain unresponsive and somewhat amnesic when it comes to what we know, need, prefer, or have accomplished? Where are the functional elements and best practices that could support learning across disciplines and the diverse needs of learners? Throughout this book, authors have explored the pieces and parts of the jigsaw puzzle of CMS now before us, presenting a picture of what is and what could be. Previously, much of the focus on future developments for CMS had been on the organizational, managerial (see Gallagher, 2003), or technical (IMS Global Learning Consortium, Inc. standards and corporate white papers). What's missing from the conversation is *teaching* and *learning*. The strategic heart of the question is most directly concerned with how these systems can support learning that is substantial, meaningful, and relevant for the vast continuum of learners.

Although faculty can implement online and hybrid courses from "cookie-cutter" implementation models in CMS with a newfound ease, the structurally rigid CMS container across the curriculum creates an "accidental pedagogy" (Morgan, 2003) comprised of predefined content units, consistency of instruction, and an imposed organization on previously independent pedagogical choices. The implications for higher education are significant, transformational, and largely unaddressed in the research and literature. Based on what we now know about meaningful, engaged learning, CMS must improve support for diverse ways of teaching and learning. This next-generation CMS must work with, look like, and interact with other systems very differently than current systems do. This book provides a vision of the next-generation CMS through the voices of international experts, designers, instructors, and visionary thinkers who share their knowledge about how CMS can best support learning, teaching, instructional and library services, and the institution.

Conceptual Framework

Course management systems are used in a variety ways, in a variety of settings, for a variety of purposes. In order to produce useful descriptions for future development, it is critical to provide a common conceptual framework for learning. Although some readers may disagree with various epistemological and pedagogical approaches to teaching and learning, the framework provided here serves as the foundation for conceiving how CMS functions could work to support specific principles.

For years, the EDUCAUSE Learning Initiative (ELI), formerly NLII, has been exploring meaningful practices for teaching and learning in higher education. The NLII 2002 research fellows, Colleen Carmean and Jeremy Haefner, reviewed theory and research on developments in learning theory and identified NLII's five learner-centered principles for deeper learning. According to the principles they identified[1], deeper learning occurs when the learning experience is social, active, contextual, engaging, and student-owned. It is the deeper learning principles that guide the ideas articulated in this book. In 2003, NLII fellow Patricia McGee followed up on this work by applying deep learning principles to the evaluation of learning objects and CMS. NLII hosted a focus session on next-generation CMS in 2003, focused on consensus-building on new tools, practices, and understandings. A number of the chapter authors of this book contributed to the body of knowledge that came from that work.

How were deeper learning principles applied to what we know of CMS? *Active* learning involves real-world problems through which learners practice and receive reinforcement for their efforts by peers and experts. Images, language, and scenarios should look and feel real and utilize processes in which learners interact. Learning that is *contextual* requires a learner-centric design as opposed to a content-centric one in which the learner proceeds in a lock-step fashion through content with little or no adaptation or deviation from a content-driven script. Deeper learning requires that the learning design take into consideration the learner's context of practice, ways of learning, and experience in the world. What is learned or understood in one context may not be readily transferable to another, which holds implications on how the CMS interface, tools, and content look, act, and operate. Learning that is *social* requires feedback and interaction between learners and instructor and, in the case of learning objects, feedback may be situated in the technology as well. For learning to be *engaging*, it must be individualized to consider the learner's preferences and styles in order to motivate and challenge. Individualized learning provides the learner with multiple paths, multiple representations of content, multiple strategies, and multiple options for engagement and motivation to meet one objective. For students to have *ownership* over learning, they must have some independence or a degree of self-control that permits them to explore and evaluate new knowledge, and this necessitates higher-order thinking. Learning that gives learners ownership allows them to make decisions and provides opportunities for independent thinking and reflection. The deeper learning principles indicate a higher degree of learner control, decision-making, and organization than exists in current CMS.

The relationship between technology and organizational culture is interdependent and iterative; policy decisions may result in changes in how technology operates or is represented (Thomas, 1994). If this is the case, then the end users (instructors and students) must be deeply involved not just in the design of CMS, but in the manipulation of its functions as they create their own cultural understanding of the technology in which their shared learning and teaching experience takes place.

Teaching and learning in today's learning environment requires consideration of the roles, perspectives, and needs of many people. Instructors must utilize pedagogy that addresses the needs of a changing population with diverse learning needs in an environment with multiple means of connecting learners and instructors. Instructors are required to manage resources in new ways.

Instructional designers must consider how tools within a system can be supported, provide opportunities for collaboration, and give access to resources within and across systems, while making sure that users are not burdened by unreasonable demands on their time. Instructional support models and templates must reflect best practices and standards. Information technology systems wrestle with issues of security, changing systems and standards, structures of centralized support, and demands of providing quickly accessible tools and resources. Libraries are evolving into virtual centralized systems that support anytime/anywhere access.

Administration must find ways to balance economic realities with institutional assessment and the requisites for ensuring desired earning outcomes. Nontraditional students are now the norm and need access to peers, instructors, and course materials while being provided feedback and opportunities to develop.

Vendors look carefully at the tug between effort and outcome while attempting to design sustainable innovations and make a profit.

The conceptual framework illustrated in Carmean's (2002) learner-centered principles (*www.educause.edu/nlii/lcp*) ties all of these perspectives together through deeper learning and a common vocabulary. It is critical that we set priorities with *an authority of consensus* based on the input of all stakeholders who are fully informed on the issues and consequences. If key stakeholders such as faculty members, instructional designers, and learners do not get creatively involved in solving the deep structural problems in online learning, structural changes in higher education will be imposed on them without being informed by their values and professional wisdom.

Next-generation tools must reflect what is valuable across the curriculum and be accessible to all learners and through a variety of systems. New ways of operating require new instructional strategies and designs that include support and guidance for faculty. The research that stipulates there is no significant difference between online and brick-and-mortar learning suggests that either we're doing it wrong, we're measuring it wrong, or we could be doing it better (Twigg, 2001).

Deeper learning means learning how to learn; we must let go of the "coverage anxiety" that was so prevalent at the turn of the 21st century. It is critical that we develop a shared vocabulary across systems and disciplines. NLII has developed a CMS glossary that provides a common ground for discussion and has been included in this book as a starting place for all stakeholders to adopt a language that describes CMS form and function in terms of teaching and learning.

Book Organization

This book is organized in three sections, summarized in the following text. Section one describes standards, foundations, and developments in CMS use and current best practices. Section two focuses on the application of theory to CMS environments and how current developments are bridging the gap between current functionality and theory-based design. Section three envisions future CMS designs.

Chapter authors represent the breadth of roles that contribute to and interact with CMS in higher education: instructional designers, faculty members, academic technology staff and administrators, information technology staff and administrators, teaching and learning center staff, students, and vendors. The style of each chapter reflects the point of view of the authors and their roles within higher education in order to best portray the voice of each unique and indispensable point of view. NLII and the editors feel that representing the voices of next-generation CMS is critical as theorists and systems designers build responsive and effective functionalities.

Section I: History, Practices, and Design of Current CMS

As caretakers within the landscape of teaching and learning, educators can look no further than their classrooms and note the rapid embrace of technology that has changed the learning environment seemingly overnight. Distance learning, hybrid courses, computer-infused curricula, the virtual library, learning objects, copy-and-paste plagiarism, and to "Google™ it" are familiar landmarks of the current landscape. Of the many ways computers and the Internet have directly influenced the field before us, none has been more rapid or transformational than course management systems, or CMS.

What began as a sleepy electronic road traveled by a few on small departmental servers soon grew, morphed, and exploded into the enterprise freeways we use today. But where do these freeways go? Why did travelers choose this interface over so many other options, and why do the prevailing systems we know as "course management" look so similar? Could better pedagogical choices have been made along the way?

By exploring the history of the CMS, its inception, design choices, successes, and failures, we better understand where CMS began and where it is now. Knowing history can help us better understand the technology, avoid repeating efforts, and plan for the future. The chapters in this first section of the book cover the following topics:

Chapter I: Carmean and Brown examine CMS as an enterprise and the questions that should be asked by each of its stakeholders.

Chapter II: Long and Tansey offer the reader a specifications and standards primer, explaining meaning and importance in layman's terms (OKI, IMS, Dublin Core, etc.) as well as why these standards are so important to the development of CMS.

Chapter III: Lippincott explores libraries and the changing role of digital content delivery via the CMS.

Chapter IV: Apedoe examines teaching conceptions and their influence on adoption and innovation in CMS.

Chapter V: Britto offers a framework of pedagogical models that can be used to evaluate CMS and understand course design.

Chapter VI: Lomas and Rauch provide case studies of course design based on the WebCT™ implementation at the University of British Columbia.

Chapter VII: Bender explores his own choices in years of teaching with CMS.

Chapter VIII: O'Brien, Campbell, and Earp document how the thoughtful implementation of Blackboard™ at Duke University led to meaningful curricular change.

Chapter IX: Liu provides best practices in teaching and instructional support within the use of CMS and technology-enhanced learning.

Section II: Research Implications and Creative Innovations for Future Design of CMS

In the late 20th century, interface design developments struggled to keep pace with the voluminous CMS-delivered courses often conceived and implemented by institutional initiatives that forced faculty members into new media and new roles for which they were generally unprepared. Often rationalized as a cost-saving measure, the adoption of campus-wide CMS fails to produce learning cost benefits. Although there is substantial anecdotal and research literature providing guidelines for course design and delivery, this is often contextually situated and difficult to generalize across disciplines, systems, programs, or institutions. Most CMS courses are designed through "accidental pedagogy" (Morgan, 2003) as traditional courses are transferred to the online environments. However, as course offerings and student populations increase and the CMS becomes a fixture in the landscape, it is critical that instructional designers and faculty members reference not only best practices, but also make informed decisions about CMS functions that can best support learning outcomes.

This section draws research literature and innovative practices that have been informed by learning theory and intentional pedagogical design in the following chapters:

Chapter X: McGee, Suter, and Gurrie envision a next-generation system in which functionality is inspired by learning. They describe how stakeholders enter into and interact within a CMS to support deeper learning.

Chapter XI: Dabbagh explains a pedagogically oriented classification of the features and components of CMS and describes a framework that explicitly demonstrates how to design authentic learning tasks using the features and components of CMS to create course designs and distributed learning interactions that engage students in meaningful learning.

Chapter XII: Weigel presents four student-focused core capabilities that should be prominent in our instructional designs: the development of skill sets related to critical thinking, self-confidence, peer learning, and knowledge management capabilities. Using this foundation, Weigel describes a next-generation CMS by exploring four basic curricular capabilities (or services) that learning systems of the future will require.

Chapter XIII: Shaw and Venkatesh describe the limitations of CMS and the advantages of moving toward Learning Content Management Systems (LCMS) that can support emergent notions of content re-use and generation in an open knowledge community that nurtures a next-generation CMS that gives autonomy to the learner and instructor.

Chapter XIV: Kaltenbaek explains the process of CMS adoption through which functionality comes to support deeper learning across disciplines.

Chapter XV: Caladine examines how database-driven Web tools support a variety of learning activities in which learners engage and contribute to course content.

Chapter XVI: Lanestedt and Stokke explain how ePortfolios can become integrated to both formative and summative assessment within the CMS.

Chapter XVII: The future CMS may be something we have not yet conceptualized, as Robson proposes in this analysis of what a CMS does and how it should be designed with learning in mind.

Section III: Next-Generation CMS

In the late 1990s, the founding architects of the CMS designed their environment to meet the requirements of the early adopters, those faculty members and university visionaries who saw that a tool such as the CMS could complement classroom instruction with limited use. Today, CMS is playing a more active role in our day-to-day teaching and learning needs. As CMS have become increasingly sophisticated, it has become more apparent that the current CMS software framework and navigational scheme do not meet the functional and user interface requirements of some current and the near-future CMS users. It is necessary, therefore, that the architects of CMS technology go back to the drawing table to design a new conceptual framework that meets the evolving requirements of the next generations of CMS users.

The focus of this section is defining and designing the next generations of CMS software environment. It includes the following chapters written by visionaries and architects of the CMS software environment, both from leading software industry and educational institutions:

Chapter XVIII: Ross envisions a future CMS that inspires as well as supports individual learning through enterprise-level strategies and a commitment to learning outcomes.

Chapter XIX: Mills analyzes the needs of CMS stakeholders and offers solutions.

Chapter XX: Kumar and Merriman provide an overview and rationale for the Open Knowledge Initiative and how it serves a purpose in the development of next-generation systems.

Chapter XXI: Jafari paints a clear picture of the characteristics, requirements, and framework of next-generation CMS and how they support the needs of the users, the courses, and the software.

Chapter XXII: Alexander takes us through the historical reasons for current CMS and examines social, knowledge, and governmental challenges and trends that he believes can shape and drive innovation towards a new system that supports communities of learners.

The editors are deeply grateful to the EDUCAUSE Learning Initiative (ELI) for its support and encouragement, and to the thoughtful, talented visionaries that contributed so willingly to this fascinating, maddening, complex endeavor. The NLII has brought together a community of curious and visionary minds that have inspired and brought to fruition such lasting and far-reaching initiatives as MERLOT, IMS, and now, this book.

References

Carmean, C. (2002). Learner-centered principles. Retrieved March 11, 2004, from *http://www.educause.edu/MappingtheLearningSpace/2594*

Gallagher, S.R. (2003). The new landscape for course management systems. *ECAR Report.*

Morgan, G. (2003). Faculty use of course management systems. Educause Center for Applied Research (ECAR). Retrived from *http://www. educause.edu/ir/library/pdf/ecar_so/ers/ERS0302/ekf0302.pdf*

Thomas, R. (1994). *What machines can't do: Politics and technology in the industrial enterprise.* University of California Press.

Twigg, C.A. (2001). Innovations in online learning: Moving beyond no significant difference. The Pew Learning and Technology Symposium.

Endnotes

[1] Mapping the Learning Space: *http://www.educause.edu/nlii/ MappingtheLearningSpace/2954*

Acknowledgments

The editors are deeply grateful to the EDUCAUSE Learning Initiative (ELI), formerly known as National Learning Infrastructure Initiative (NLII), for its support and encouragement, and to the thoughtful, talented visionaries that contributed so willingly to this fascinating, maddening, complex endeavor. The ELI has brought together a community of curious and visionary minds that have inspired and brought to fruition such lasting and far-reaching initiatives as MERLOT, IMS, and now, this book.

Patricia McGee, The University of Texas at San Antonio, USA

Colleen Carmean, Arizona State University, USA

Ali Jafari, Indiana University-Purdue University Indianapolis (IUPUI), USA

Section I

History, Practices, and Design of Current CMS

Chapter I

Measure for Measure:
Assessing Course
Management Systems

Colleen Carmean, Arizona State University, USA

Gary Brown, Washington State University, USA

Abstract

The authors examine CMS as a new enterprise technology. Using a model of transformative assessment that frames value within alignment of institutional goals and mission, they define the questions that should be asked of each of the CMS stakeholders: teachers, learners, support services, leadership and the CMS vendor.

> *No more evasion...*
> *Our haste from hence is of so quick condition*
> *That it prefers itself and leaves unquestion'd*
> *Matters of needful value.*
> > Duke Vicentio (Act 1), *Measure for Measure*

Introduction

A few brief years ago, we knew not course management systems (CMS). Technology-enhanced learning often meant expensive initiatives developed by instructional designers and computer programmers. Those faculty incorporating technology into their curricula were usually entrepreneurs, risk-takers, or generously funded and safely tenured. Funding was for narrow science applications, research repositories, or large course redesign. Liberal arts faculty members were left to a few PowerPoint® workshops and the guilt-inducing notion that they really *should* develop some Web pages — though exactly *why* was, and probably remains, unclear. Few incentives were offered to do more, do better, or take the risks associated with a technology-infused curriculum.

Hagner (2001) reports that only a few faculty "entrepreneurs" were willing to take on the hard work and risk of failure associated with technology when the needed shift in institutional reward, collaboration, support, and expectation was missing. Then, something happened.

Across public and private institutions large and small, faculty embraced course management systems. In a short period of time, small departmental installations over-extended capacity and quickly gave way to institutional enterprise applications. Faculty development centers became CMS support sites. University technology staff became CMS experts. Instructional designers wrote thousands of best practices handbooks for effective discussion boards and online learning. Students began to ask if there was a CMS site for the course before registering. Universities began to create notation, policy, and process for technology-enhanced, hybrid, and online courses. In a culture where change never happens, something happened. What happened? What were faculty members doing within the CMS framework?

Did we find a tool that promotes deeper learning and better teaching? Did the CMS make mundane tasks easier for the instructor? Did the student engage in the material in a more direct or engaged way? Most anyone associated with the use of CMS will tell you that they don't know the answers, haven't asked, and aren't sure what to measure. Common thought is that if so many faculty are using CMS, this must be good for teaching. If the students are embracing the new modes of delivery, something about the CMS must be effective for learning.

This common thought is based on a pinch of intuition and a dab of hunch, but not data. Others express the hunch that technology alone is not enough, and perhaps less "enhanced learning" is happening within the CMS space than assumed. In both camps, assumptions guide current thinking about reasons for the quick and widespread adoption of CMS. What is missing is assessment.

With CMS now an integral part of much of our teaching, learning, and support endeavors, we must begin to seriously examine its value to the institution. While higher education continues to embrace the CMS in enterprise technology, and in faculty development and support, the work to determine, understand, and justify its place and value to the institution's strategic mission is still seriously missing. Questions of cost/benefit, function, and usage have yet to be addressed. In this chapter, we hope to refine some of these questions by examining the roles and needs of each of the stakeholders in CMS: teachers, students, support services, leadership, and vendors.

Seen from a model of "transformative assessment," assessment is the purposeful gathering and use of data to ensure that the application of findings and the dissemination of results will substantially change and enrich the *learning* experience. Transformative assessment strategies are based on institutional goals and missions and are implemented in an integrated way for all levels (the course, the program, and the institution). It is evident that consistent and consensus-driven goals of the stakeholders of CMS are not yet defined and that quality evidence still needs to be gathered to inform strategies for meeting these goals. Transformative assessment requires an awareness of the need for *alignment* on the part of the institution. Within each of the stakeholder sections of this chapter, we offer possibilities for this alignment. We also examine the CMS issues facing those who define and steward the missions of the university as they apply to CMS: teaching goals, learning outcomes, fiscal value, intellectual property rights, and enterprise values. Finally, transformative assessment also calls for improving the dissemination of findings to include, as much as possible, our governing constituencies — where a need for understanding and good will increases with each passing day.

Teaching and CMS

What attracts faculty to CMS? What features made it possible for such widespread adoption so quickly? What evidence exists that those features satisfy original expectations and aid in teaching? In what ways? Time saving? Reaching diverse students? Better engagement? Easier access to materials?

The literature is unclear regarding the known factors that continue to drive the increasingly costly delivery of CMS. We know faculty are requesting course shells, and to some degree, we have self-reporting data on the most frequently adopted tools within the CMS. But, we have no evidence of the teaching and learning value attributable to faculty use. Despite the prevalence of CMS as a *presumed enhancement* to face-to-face courses, we see little evidence in the literature on what is being enhanced.

Where included in studies of online learning, we see again and again that tying technology to grades alone suggests no significant difference in assessment of teaching and learning (Russell, n.d.). In the past, *no significant difference* (NSD) was enough, demonstrating twenty years of evidence that learning (as assessed by tests, grades, and measures of short-term demonstrations of memorizing course materials) does not suffer when done online or through technology mediation. Perhaps more pointedly, the NSD phenomenon suggests the myriad variables defy any kind of causal generalization. It is now understood that online instructional methods neither, in general, hinder nor help learning, but the widespread adoption of CMS in traditional instruction — and the costs in faculty time, technology resources, support services, and demands on the student — suggest that it is now crucial we ask more focused questions of CMS and the technology-enhanced model: how does it help, and what, exactly, does "help" mean?

If the value is not in the grade but depends on some measure of faculty engagement, student satisfaction, ubiquitous access, or incorporation of deeper learning theory, where is the evidence that strategic goals for these measures are being articulated, let alone reached? For instance:

- How do we know that our students know what we hope they will know?
- How are the tools in CMS changing the ways faculty teach and students learn, and how, subsequently, does that change how well and what they learn?
- How do those changes impact the services being reallocated to support CMS? What was given up to bring these new services into information technology (IT), teaching and learning centers, faculty development programs, and the library?
- How do we ensure that the changes are justified?

Within this book, you'll find much discussion of changes, features, and improvements desired for next-generation CMS. Many of the ideas are based on hard, collaborative work by EDUCAUSE and the National Learning Infrastructure Initiative (NLII) to bring vendors, faculty, researchers, administrators, innovators, IT, and instructional designers together to determine consensus on what is needed in the next generation. *If we build it, they will come*. We did, they did. Now what?

Alignment: Teaching and CMS

As the CMS community continues to work on better technology, reports on current usage suggest that faculty currently use few of the features available. The ease of use associated with a template-driven, cookie-cutter implementation is often where course development within CMS stop. Faculty must move beyond intuitive value and explore ways the CMS permits faculty to serve the mission of engaged teaching and learning.

Very few higher education institutions build incentives, rewards, or course release time into the implementation equation. Faculty members embraced CMS independent of institutional support, but now struggle to find the time or resources to examine the role of CMS in better pedagogy. Innovation and adaptation to the changing landscape will not happen without institutional commitment to change. For the next-generation systems to be truly effective learning environments, faculty must move from easy-to-use online organizers to effective pedagogical tools for assisting and assessing desired learning outcomes.

Learning and CMS

Evidence from the literature of the last ten years suggests agreement on a number of conditions that, when in place, contribute to the learner's deep, engaged understanding of the content. Carmean and Haefner (2002) examined some of the core research available on deeper learning, summarizing these conditions by suggesting that deeper learning takes place when it: 1) is social, 2) is active, 3) is contextual (related back to the conditions and understandings of the learner), 4) requires learner ownership, and 5) engages the learner.

They used these conditions to examine the tools commonly present in CMS and suggest practices for the tools that could allow the conditions that manifest in deeper learning. Theirs were merely suggestions on how the tools might be used in relationship to necessary conditions for deep learning, not evidence that the tools are being used effectively or that deep, engaged, lasting learning is taking place.

Is there evidence that the CMS tools are used to provide an environment where inquiry, not delivery, is promoted? Why should we expect any technology to improve learning? What salient features or sets of features would help students learn, especially as we avoid the harder question: What do we mean by "improve learning"? In what context, and for whom? Can we apply these deeper learning conditions to a structured, anytime/anywhere, and independently navigated environment? Does it allow for faculty members to assist students in exploring, questioning, and researching course content in ways that support diverse learning?

Alignment: Learning and CMS

How could one *measure* whether CMS usage contributes to features of authentic learning? We suggest a two-fold approach:

1. Compare the features available against a set of agreed-upon, known conditions that need to be met for the learning outcomes established. For instance, is the learning activity designed to be social, active, relevant, engaging, or creating learner ownership?

2. Observe student engagement as well as collect student responses to the use of CMS features in relationship to meeting those conditions. Did the discussion board provide opportunity for rich exchange of ideas? Did the announcement board allow for better navigation and ownership of the tasks at hand? Was the immediate quiz feedback used to encourage self-assessment and mastery of the material?

It is not an empty course shell that improves learning, so we now must ask under what conditions the features available in standard CMS lend themselves to informed design of an engaging learning environment. Did the usage of a CMS allow for recreating a more flexible course experience through online or hybrid offerings? Does less seat time and more independent inquiry make for more engaged learning, or merely fewer obstacles to getting a degree? Assessing learning should begin by clearly articulating learning outcomes and asking the students what they have learned. And, finally, learning assessment might also include simple satisfaction surveys and focus groups that explore the experience of being a student. We will never know that our students know what we want them to know until we *ask* them, and, correspondingly, we may never know what our students want to know unless we *listen* to them.

Support Services for CMS

In technology use in teaching and learning, the strategic mission of university support services is to provide the resources to help faculty help their students. Some of these resources include stable systems, in-time training, and available assistance. With the growth of CMS, many services are being reworked to provide these resources. As instructional support (in IT, the library, teaching and learning centers, and faculty development areas) is increasingly reallocated in support of CMS, what are these support units giving up to bring new CMS-related services online? Are the right people and tools in place to effectively offer these services, both to faculty and to students? Are instructional support services ensuring that use of CMS is being deployed in alignment with institutional goals and in the support of best practices? Are support services implementing enterprise CMS with full consideration of stakeholders and are they being asked to assess return on investment?

Responsive instructional support tends to align with faculty demand, and the realignment of resources to CMS has been as rapid as faculty adoption. A chicken and egg approach to institutional change took place, without assessment. Is there evidence that the change in services has been an appropriate response that has resulted in greater adoption? To what end and with what success are new services being offered and with what loss to previous services expected? And what about learning?

In this adoption, were the skills of less technology-ready students considered? Technology literacy is a valuable goal for student learning outcomes, but what services need to be in place campus-wide to assure that students are comfortable with CMS use, when not anticipated in course delivery? What is being done to bring students that need assistance with the technology up to speed? How is fear of technology hampering students and faculty from moving forward in the use of CMS, and what can support services do to mitigate the risk of technology failure in production usage of CMS?

Alignment: Support Services and CMS

The role of support is complicated by the pace of change we see in student expectations. New students want and expect better use of technology in their coursework. Calhoun (2004) addresses this pressure, acknowledging the difficulty faculty experience in keeping up, without reward and with numerous barriers to thoughtful implementation. The culture shock often leaves faculty feeling, as one faculty member puts it, "like a Pony Express rider just as the telegraph comes along" (Gustafson, 2003-2004, p. 40). In implementing technology, much responsibility for access, implementation, authentication, performance, data security, and instructional and pedagogical consulting now rests in the hands of system and instructional support services.

Delivery of these services must be evaluated in alignment with clearly understood needs of the institution. Despite the pace of change, successful implementation and support for next-generation systems will depend on clear goals, thoughtful planning, and objective assessment of service to academic strategic plans.

Leadership and CMS

As we discovered earlier in this chapter, other institutional stakeholders have been quick to respond to faculty interest in CMS. Great resources have been reallocated to allow any and every course a shell on the system. Simple servers have been converted to enterprise systems and integrated into portals. It would be rare to find such a large initiative taken on by another type of institution with no evidence of the value to bottom line, productivity, or mission. Why did leadership of academia move forward so quickly without evidence of value? How many, long removed from teaching, took a hands-off approach only to now wonder what was wrought? Were rash purchases and support decisions made as a nod to the oft-neglected teaching role in the faculty mission or, perhaps more heretically, because institutions tend to affirm a pedagogy that is uncritically faculty-centered? Is leadership prepared to suggest negative return on investment is simply not a sustainable strategy?

Technology units had previously been more comfortable supplying resources for research when suddenly a simple solution across the curriculum appeared. CIOs could now please the teaching constituency without the expenses previously associated with technology-enhanced learning. Before the effects of rapid implementation could be seriously measured, IT leaders were moving forward to choose enterprise CMS. They would soon hire or reallocate system administrators, course creation staff, faculty trainers and application support staff. The commitment to support of CMS is now considerable, as is the unanticipated cost. And what about learning?

Libraries, faculty development centers, and teaching and learning sites soon joined on. Did the campus leadership ever understand the consequences to the institution? Were they consulted? Without careful assessment or consensus, institutions often committed great resources to a new support enterprise, not to mention to one or more course management systems from which it would be very difficult to disentangle themselves. In fact, a recent argument for investing in stock in a well-known CMS stated: "Since such a migration is typically a complicated and tedious task, customers have considerable motivation to stick with a given solution.... Consequently, Blackboard has a nice moat against competitors and the potential to raise prices as the product becomes indispensable to customers" (Gibbons, 2004, p. 1). Based on decisions made with good intentions and little sense of consequence, course management systems became a part of the administrative cost within the technology and support services infrastructures.

Serious concerns now facing administrators include:

- The increasing cost of CMS licenses.
- The costs of switching to open-source solutions, problematic for a host of reasons, not the least of which are code documentation, systems integration, reliability, and migration from systems that have established a loyal, even fanatic, user base.
- The support infrastructure needs that continue to grow as faculty increase use, questions, sophistication, and demand.

- The ownership of material when faculty develop content within the shell of a course they may have difficulty accessing later, due to authentication or archiving. The issue becomes more pressing when considering the high percentage of adjunct faculty now teaching in higher education. Does the administration have an obligation to make it clear to these individuals that it might be difficult, even impossible, to take their material with them when leaving the institution?

Alignment: Leadership and CMS

How do we measure the value of these new enterprise CMS? How do we balance value against the current and often unknown inability of faculty to remove their own material from the course shell? Who is measuring the cost of the exclusion of the library from the electronic learning experience? Where are the policies outlining the rights of students to intellectual property on online work and discussion contributions from years before? What would we do if assessment showed harm from loss of intellectual property as well as no significant difference, no greater satisfaction, and no worthwhile value from the change?

It is imperative to the success of next-generation learning that university administrators step forward and do their job. Ask CIOs, deans, department chairs, and teaching support units to be responsible for assessment, return on investment, and a demonstrated commitment to meet clear, consensual, and measurable goals.

The Vendor

The CMS market is narrowing, with most institutions having settled on one of three to five vendors, though there are still about 1,000 by a recent count (CMS Watch, 2004). Within these vendors, as with the few open-source alternatives being developed, there is a base set of features that are expected, relatively uniform, and functionally indistinguishable. Are they the right feature set? Are they well used? Are there best practices for the features that can inform us on better teaching and learning? As experts argue for more sophisticated features, mainstream faculty argue for ease of use and a more intuitive, simple interface.

Morgan's (2003) EDUCAUSE Center for Applied Research (ECAR) report on *Faculty Use of Course Management Systems* surveyed 730 faculty members across the Wisconsin system and concluded that very few of the features within CMS are regularly used. This does not mean that the features being used (storing syllabus, posting announcements, course document functionality) are not of value, but what would evidence of greater value look like? If faculty members are not using many of the current features (or use a few features to achieve multiple functions), what incentives exist for the vendor to continue building more features into increasingly complex systems? As new systems like ePortfolios emerge to address increasingly similar functions, when does feature-creep become system overlap?

The CIO pays the bill, instructional designers argue for system-integration of theory, faculty plea for simplicity, futurists ask for tools now used by the younger generation of students, and learning theorists ask for better integration of modules for outcome assessment. Ignored on all sides are the students that must weigh time-demand over required use.

Vendors work to locate consensus, common practice, and consistent feedback. But they are torn by the competing requirements of a diverse set of constituencies and wonder where the profit lies in an increasingly saturated market.

Alignment: The Vendor and CMS

Vendors must understand their constituents, not just the CIO wallet, and work diligently to collaborate with higher education to define the next-generation system. Higher education, in turn, must assess value and features and reach consensus on what is needed. Enterprise systems will grow larger and more expensive as portals, features, tools, and processing power improve. What choices will we make on implementation?

Summary

Change happens as a response to stimulus. This response can be reactive or a studied and sometimes difficult choice. The studied, institutional response to this change (transformative assessment) must carefully be implemented if the academy is to make decisions that radically affect so many stakeholders, as well as the direction and mission of the institution and the future of higher education. John Tagg (2004) writes in a recent issue of *About Campus*,

> *Kellogg and Post aim to make cereal, Ford and General Motors aim to make cars, hospitals aim to make people healthier. Colleges, judged by the same standards and by the evidence of their own documentation, aim to have people take classes. It is as if Kellogg saw its function as grinding up great amounts of corn, or the RAND Corporation sought to fill as many pages as possible with reports. Kellogg knows what the corn is for. RAND knows what the reports are for. What are the classes for?* (p. 3)

It is time to ask what we're doing, whether we're doing it well, and whether the tools we're purchasing to do it serve the goals associated with getting it done. The fundamental purpose of transformative assessment is to improve student learning outcomes, and it is clear that across the academy CMS is seen as a positive tool for doing so. Based on the commitment to CMS now in place across the institution, careful assessment and inquiry should help us determine its value to teaching, learning, and the changes needed in higher education.

To achieve transformation that will be responsive to the new student, new economy, and struggling academy, we must examine the design, planning, implementation, and evaluation of CMS for each of the constituencies involved: teachers, learners, support services, leadership, and vendors. To be useful in transforming the institution, assessment of the CMS must be studied in a new way — as a tool for learning. By asking the right questions and being willing to act on the answers, we create the possibility of graduating engaged, successful, and diverse learners.

References

Calhoun, T. (2004). Feeling like a Pony Express? Uh oh, here comes the telegraph. *Syllabus*. Retrieved on January 3, 2005, from *http://info.101com.com/default.asp?id=7136*

Carmean, C. & Haefner, P. (2002). Mind over matter: Transforming course management systems in effective learning environments. *EDUCAUSE Review,* (Nov/Dec), 26-34.

CMS Watch. (2004). Retrieved from *http://www.cmswatch.com/Content Management/Products/*

Gibbons, R. (2004). Our take: Blackboard's screeching IPO. *The Motley Fool,* June 24. Retrieved on January 3, 2005, from *http://www.fool.com/ news/mft/2004/mft04062445.htm*

Gustafson, K. (2003-2004). The impact of technologies on learning. *Planning for Higher Education, 32*(2), 37-43.

Hagner, P. (2001). Interesting practices and best systems in faculty engagement and support. *EDUCAUSE Review, 35*(5), 27-37.

Morgan, G. (2003). *Faculty use of course management systems.* Boulder, CO: ECAR Research Publication.

Russell, T.L. (n.d.). The "no significant difference" phenomenon Web site. Retrieved on January 3, 2005, from *http://www.nosignificantdifference. org/*

Tagg, J. (2004). Why learn? What we may really be teaching students. *About Campus, 9*(1). Retrieved on January 3, 2005, from *http://media.wiley. com/assets/253/46/jrnls_ABC_JB_tagg901.pdf*

Chapter II

Standards?
What and Why?

Phil Long, Information Services and Technology, USA

Frank Tansey, Technology Consultant, USA

Abstract

Specifications define the nature of the interconnections between the distinct parts of complex learning systems, but not their boundaries. Next generation CMS tools are emerging from standards discussions that challenge current e-learning systems design boundaries. They raise the prospect of a complex but smoothly functioning set of components and services that aggregate in ways that best serve individual communities of users. Users need to engage in the process to express their requirements for e-learning software. These building blocks, produced by a small number of organizations, are establishing the framework that will enable CMS environments to become vastly different than the CMS you might now be using.

Introduction

Our exploration of next-generation course management systems begins with the important and somewhat hidden efforts to develop e-learning specifications and standards. These building blocks, produced by a small number of organizations, are establishing the framework that will enable CMS environments to become vastly different than the CMS you might now be using. The environment that emerges from well-defined specifications is a landscape that makes the current boundaries set by course management systems both artificial and limiting. The logical outcome of this work is a complex but smoothly functioning set of components and services that aggregate in ways that best serve individual communities of users. Specifications define the nature of the interconnections between these distinct parts of a complex learning system but not their boundaries. The result is a future world where we'll look back on this discussion of CMS software as a quaint footnote in the development of more robust educational technologies for teaching.

Common Needs

Specifications and standards arise from the need to promote technical, syntactical, and semantic interoperability. This need is important in relation to metadata, content, databases, or repositories, designs for learning, vocabularies, learner profiles, assessment, expression of competencies, and networking protocols. Standards and specifications make the "abilities" (Nissi, 2003) of e-learning possible. These abilities include:

- *Interoperability*: Systems work with other systems, within and between institutions or organizations. Content developed in one system is not restricted to that system by proprietary encoding or protocols.
- *Reusability*: Learning objects or resources are easily used in different curricula, learning settings, and for different learner profiles.
- *Manageability*: The system tracks information about the learner and the content.

- *Accessibility*: A variety of learners, with different learner profiles such as educational and physical needs, easily access and assemble the content at the appropriate time.

- *Sustainability*: The technology evolves with the standards to avoid obsolescence.

Why Are Specifications Important?

Specifications enable people to focus on a problem by providing a shared vocabulary of words and ideas. They represent a current "state of the art" consensus among developers and architects of educational software about a particular data structure, functional behavior, or service that is important for an online learning system. They are intended to capture agreement in the face of change. As such, they provide a hedge against the risks of this volatile environment. To achieve the best return on investment, these systems must be sustainable, flexible, scalable, and interoperable with new learning technologies.

Specifications and Standards Live in the Background

A key advantage of an effective standard or specification is that, with proper implementation, the standard becomes largely invisible. In this state, the standard is a building block for features that differentiate one product from another.

Take, for example, a typical electronic device you use every day. When you purchase a clock radio or a microwave oven, you focus on the features of the device. You want good sound from your radio or a small size for your microwave. You don't think about the plug that you will insert into the wall to power the device. Plugs and electrical sockets have been standardized, as have voltages and currents. You are not expected to think about these factors to use each device you have purchased. If you needed an adapter for each electrical item, you would think twice about every purchase.

The same advantage of key standards applies to CMS systems. If your content had a standard "plug" for all CMS systems, your world of content choice would be greatly expanded. Similarly, if all CMS systems could communicate with the system used by the registrar's office to exchange key student information, your class roll would always be up to date, and grade submission would be virtually finished when you posted your grades to the CMS. Such is the promise of specifications, yet unrealized.

A Closer Look at Specifications and Standards

Laying the Foundation

Specifications lay a foundation on which learning technologies should be built. They represent common agreement among communities with expert knowledge in a particular domain. Specifications are the first step on the road to standards. Standards are created by accredited bodies that give their stamp of approval to specifications placed before them. Standards represent in some sense an end point in the process. The expectation is that by the time a specification is recognized by an accrediting body, such as the Institute of Electrical and Electronics Engineers (IEEE), it has achieved a degree of stability in which change is measured and modifications follow a strictly delineated process.

What Type of Specifications?

The world of specifications is complicated in educational software because it is often viewed from differing and contradictory perspectives. This complication results in breaking down the problems that course management systems are supposed to address in wildly different ways. It's no wonder that the outcome is expressed in incompatible, divergent, and generally impoverished models for software-enabled e-learning. The problem is exacerbated by the fact that course management systems don't exist in a vacuum. They must integrate with other systems that provide necessary services for students, including library systems, student information systems, and authentication systems. Without considering the ecology of the whole e-learning landscape, there is little likelihood that these related services can be efficiently leveraged or well-integrated into course management system environments.

Software architects call this process of breaking a complex system down into its logical parts "factoring" the problem space. If the functional domains that need to be represented in the course management system are clearly identified, then it becomes easier to describe the components of the system. Describing the components carefully results in a model, and only then can important specifications be mapped to the e-learning system.

Smyth, Evdemon, Sim, and Thorne (2004) have provided a set of principles on which course management systems, or any technology-mediated learning system, should be built. They identify three patterns that appear commonly in the design of e-learning systems. These represent a consistent factoring of the educational domain for online learning. These three elements are: 1) data representation, 2) communications, and 3) interfaces.

Data Representation

The most well-defined area of specifications in the course management world applies to the description of data used by it. This makes sense, as describing the data in a learning system is essential to being able to move data from place to place. This need drove early specifications activity under the rubric of data exchange. Having agreed-upon data representations permits information to move between course management systems in such a way as to preserve meaning and structure.

Without defined and agreed-upon specifications for data, interoperability is impossible. Creating these specifications means achieving agreement in the structure, meaning, and language used to describe the data in e-learning systems. The specifications that have been developed to date for defining data include, for example, the Dublin Core metadata suite, IMS Content Packaging, and the ADL Shareable Courseware Object Reference Model (SCORM).

Communications

Course management systems are frequently self-contained, stand-alone, or at best, hand-tailored to fit into an existing enterprise environment. Defining how two or more systems communicate to achieve generic agreement on the framework to be used is a critical step to facilitate systems integration.

Examples of the problem and benefits of an agreed-upon solution are on your desktop and used every day. You select an e-mail client that has features you find useful. Regardless of your e-mail client, you can send and receive mail successfully because the programs follow common e-mail protocol specifications, such as POP or IMAP. This process works because both the mail client and the mail server have implemented a common protocol. Additional functionality, such as specifying a method of authenticating mail, might be added, but this is only an enhancement to the specification that is the basis of e-mail exchange.

Interfaces

The most striking contribution of Smyth, Evdemon, Sim and Thorne's (2004) work is the clarity they provide in defining the roles of interfaces. Interfaces can be thought of as a contract between system components that describes what a given component does and what it expects of the other components. The authors describe two fundamental approaches to establishing the responsibilities for either providing a service to an e-learning application, or using a service provided from somewhere else, either within an e-learning system, or from another system entirely (e.g., a campus authentication system).

Applications that are in the category of service consumers tend to be dependent on programming language. An interface between service consumers and providers insulates the consuming application from details that are specific to the service provider. This allows the service provider to choose technologies that are optimal for it, leaving the service consumer unaffected by such changes. This approach also permits the consuming application to select among different implementations of a service.

Let's look at an example. Most e-learning systems don't permit the option to store files in multiple locations, for example, locally, centrally, or remotely. If an e-learning application implemented multiple file interfaces, it could store files locally if not attached to a network, or centrally and mirrored to a remote server if it were. The user then might be able to select where the data should be stored, if preferred. These multiple interfaces coexist and provide functionality as well as abstraction between the consuming application and the service provider. The Open Knowledge Initiative (OKI) has developed a suite of such consumer-oriented, open-source interface definitions (OSIDs) as candidate specifications for e-learning developers.[1]

Provider-oriented interfaces are independent of language choices, often implemented over networks where the interface is not on a local user's machine. Web services are built using these interfaces to maximize the availability of the service with minimal dependence on the local consuming application. Web Service Definition Language (WSDL) is an example of a provider-oriented interface to an application that might be incorporated in an e-learning system.

Smyth, Evdamon, Sim and Thorne (2004) make the crucial observation that these interfaces are not mutually exclusive — they offer specific capabilities that can be leveraged by the builders of e-learning systems. Interfaces of either type may be implemented within an application on a single machine or across a complex network topology. What's important to the observer is this framework of data structures, communications protocols, and interfaces. e-learning system developers should be able to describe their work and their systems from this perspective, and the corresponding specifications or specification candidates that they are implementing. It should be clear from the above that proprietary implementation of service interfaces (Web services or any other) should be avoided.

Specifications Are Not Standards

More often than not, you hear about standards (rules or models) rather than specifications (detailed descriptions of work to be done). We hear about Web "standards" when referencing the World Wide Web Consortium, or W3C. There are W3C standards (for example, the standards for using URL and HTTP), but many of W3C's contributions are closer to specifications and guidelines. In the CMS world, there are few standards but many specifications, some of which are evolving to standards. Because the CMS world is evolving so rapidly, there has yet to be sufficient time to mature many specifications into standards.

The function of a specification is to provide a sufficiently detailed initial description to implement a defined scope of work. It is based upon and promotes early implementations but is a bit of a moving target. As implementation and technologies progress, specifications evolve to respond to detailed requirements.

Standards, on the other hand, are more static and become the rule. That is not to say that the standards never change. They do, by becoming a new standard, not just a new version of the same standard. The granular review involved in the standard process theoretically eliminates the need for multiple versions of standards. To call a specification a standard is a premature freezing of work. It is important not to propose a standard until the work is fully matured and accepted.

A Closer Look at Specifications

Specifications Address Real Issues

Successful specifications or standards address real issues. It is unlikely that any specification group would devote limited resources to trivial or nonconsequential work. There must be substantial consensus that an issue is worthy of a specification for the process to begin. Specifications may address a seemingly small part of a larger issue; if one considers a single specification within a larger context, then each specification is a building block.

Specification development is hard work. It is rarely done in isolation; in fact, competitors frequently sit at the same table. It requires strong technical skills, a deep understanding of topic area, the capability to reduce extensive requirements to essential features, and willingness to compromise. On top of this, it is frequently necessary to produce results in a short time frame. This is the backdrop for most specification efforts.

Let's examine a single specification as an example. The IMS Content Packaging Specification details a set of rules for packaging course material and identifying the material in the package. It is not concerned with how the content will run on another system, what the content is, or how it is sequenced in a course. The scope of the specification is limited, but packaging is a real problem that virtually all course management systems must address.

A course consists of content that is packaged for a particular need. For example, content packaging takes content material, exercises, and exams and bundles them into a course. All items cited are examples; there is no rule on what should be included in a content package. An implementation of this specification operating within a single CMS would be an improvement over a proprietary implementation since it provides the opportunity for future interoperability. However, it may be of limited value if the CMS remains isolated.

However, the impact of the content packaging specification is greatly enhanced when a content package can be exchanged from one CMS to another. Packaging and exchange is a real issue, especially on campuses that support more than one CMS and should be of crucial importance to any faculty member thinking of changing institutions. Any potential vendors or developers should be called upon to explain how their implementation addresses this need. While some vendors may view this as creating an undesirable exit strategy for a potential customer, the real point is that it can hinder access to one's own intellectual property and should be a prerequisite for considering the system's acquisition in the first place.

Specifications Help Avoid Reinventing the Wheel

The development of course management systems has followed the pattern common to early-stage technology innovations. There is a period of wide and rapid development, when diverse strategies are pursued, emphasizing differentiating feature sets and unique underlying designs. Commonly agreed specifications, if acknowledged at all, are implemented with unique "extensions" that further distinguish a given product. Course management systems developers, faculty and student users, instructional technologists, and information systems professionals have lived through this period of exhilarating change and frustration. It's important to recognize that implementing new functionality as proprietary interpretations of specifications impedes interoperability and slows progress in e-learning development.

Real value will be derived from paradigm-shifting processes that, like systems theory, look at a new level of integration to provide benefits otherwise not possible but fundamentally resting on work that has already been done at lower levels. Specifications need refinement, which can be achieved only through use and feedback. It's important, as new ideas and people engage in this work of building better and more robust course management technologies, to focus these efforts not only on the right level of abstraction, but also in the right direction.

Specifications Promote Opportunities for Adoption

The consensus process involved in specification development and standard setting promotes the opportunity for adoption in multiple implementations.

Once vendors or in-house developers become aware of, or involved in, an open specification or standard effort, the advantages of implementing such an approach quickly overwhelm proprietary solutions. While there may initially be resistance to dropping a solution developed in-house, specifications and standards promote adoption of key technologies. In the CMS world, if key underlying common needs are addressed through specifications and standards, developers are free to focus on key features and services that address the significant needs of users. Standards and specifications enable wider adoption of e-learning.

Specifications Create Flexibility

If we started our exploration of specifications with common needs, we end it with flexibility. In the beginning, we had a series of common problems that needed to be addressed. Take just two of the common issues encountered — course portability and the two-way exchange of enterprise information. Initial solutions to these challenges are often unique, requiring comparable effort to repeatedly solve the same problems across the universe of CMS implementations.

As specifications are developed to address the problem of moving course content from one system to another, or exchanging selected data between different CMS packages, limited resources can be liberated. These limited resources can then be better used, for example, to develop new content or to expand the range of services supported on the CMS. Greater flexibility is created, and, in turn, the CMS effectiveness is increased.

Similarly, if it becomes necessary to move to a new CMS environment, carefully implemented content packaging specifications already in place offer the flexibility to pack instructional materials and transfer them to a newly procured CMS. The key to this flexibility is a set of underlying specifications that provide solutions to common needs. If, however, the CMS used had yet to implement broad specification support, flexibility is limited, and once again it's necessary to create or procure tools for a specialized migration. Addressing underlying common needs with specification-based approaches is a critical component for next-generation course management systems.

Specifications Need Not Be Perfect

In the specification development world, technical perfection is low on the list of priorities. That is not to say specification working groups don't strive for this goal, but perfection in the midst of rapid technological change is unrealistic and fleeting, at best, and unnecessary. What is more important is a specification that can be implemented by the largest group of developers, a specification that provides the basic functionality required in a particular area. A necessary goal of a successful specification is the ability to develop future capabilities without losing prior capabilities. It must be backwards-compatible to be forward-looking.

Specification development frequently requires compromise from firmly held positions. In some cases, a vendor may believe that the right solution has already been reached and that anything less than its solution is inappropriate. Unless the vast majority of participants are willing and able to accept a single solution, then compromises must be made to achieve broad-based acceptability of the specification.

Specifications Can Be Good Enough

If a specification does not need to be perfect, what is "good enough"? Following our consensus model, most specifications focus on workable, acceptable solutions. Let's examine the concept of "good enough" in the context of a theoretical specification.

Involved in the process are a number of developers, each with his or her own particular set of development tools. As the specification is scoped, it is agreed that the issue is a core function for most e-learning environments. Several developers advance potential solutions to this issue. Developer A proposes an extremely elegant solution that takes full advantage of a proprietary technology. Developer B advances its own proprietary approach that, while not as elegant as Developer A's, is more inclusive of other developers. Developer C proposes a new approach that is more technology agnostic.

In this specification process, the key factor is finding a solution that all developers can implement that will permit development of a usable and scalable implementation on all platforms. The specification process must reach consensus on an acceptable solution to all — a solution that is good enough.

Resulting compromises may initially seem to decrease functionality. However, with this specification in place, developers can turn their attention to building on top of the specification to differentiate their CMS, knowing that the core need has been addressed.

Specification Development

The Specification Cycle

The specifications development process is essentially one of iterative work. The model in Figure 1 is followed by one of the central specifications development bodies, IMS Global Learning Consortium, and is illustrative of this work.

Creating specifications is a community process. Once a need has been identified, there are at least three strategies by which a new specification can be derived: adopt the work of others as is, modify an existing specification to better meet current needs, or start from scratch and create something new. Rarely does the first strategy, adopting others' work without modification by the community, make sense, as specifications are a response to a problem of one sort or another identified by a community.

Figure 1. Generic specifications development process

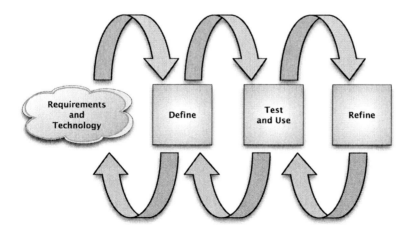

Modify Existing Specifications

Groups within a larger community often work on a common local approach to a problem with the expectation that other groups will see the value of their perspective and adopt it as their own. This approach to adoption and its challenges is often a driving force behind larger efforts to push for a common specification. A good example is Education Modeling Language, or EML.

EML was developed at the Open University of the Netherlands and released in December of 2000. The goal of EML is to address differences in the ways that learning processes are described by creating a common approach to the documentation of teaching strategies and materials. This process then facilitates consistency, comparability, and reuse of learning materials distributed and "played" in electronic environments.

Like many similar efforts within a large and diverse community, the creators of EML found that adoption of their approach to describing learning activities failed to reach a critical mass, and overall progress toward a common method to describe learning designs was stymied.

To push for wider adoption for a learning design specification, the EML team engaged in an international specifications development forum, the IMS Global Learning Consortium, through the work group formed therein called the IMS learning design work group. They contributed their 1.0 version of EML as a candidate for consideration toward a new specification. Use case scenarios were written and compared. Through this community process, the original EML candidate specification was modified, in some ways substantially, and was ultimately released as the IMS Learning Design (see *www.learningnetworks.org*, for example), and the improvement of the specification itself (see *www.imsglobal.org/learningdesign/*) in February of 2003.

Standing on the Shoulders of Specifications

Arriving at an agreed specification for a part of the e-learning puzzle sets the stage for important subsequent work. The outcome of achieving the learning design specification has spawned a wide range of projects extending the design toward tools that use it. This is a benefit from achieving consensus in a specification; it generates practical tools that advance the discipline through broader engagement of the community of developers, instructors, faculty, and students. The experiences gained from these projects will generate valuable information to guide the next iteration of the specifications development process.

There are a number of "players" in the specification community that deserve mention here. The IMS Global Learning Consortium is the successor to the IMS Project, formed by the National Learning Infrastructure Initiative of Educause in 1997. After its initial three-year charge was fulfilled, the project spun off into an independent organization. IMS produces a range of specifications to support critical e-learning infrastructure needs. Key IMS specifications include content packaging, question and test interoperability, learner information package, enterprise specification, and simple sequencing. IMS has an active development process, and new specifications, as well as enhancement to released specifications, are produced on a regular basis. The organization includes vendors and consumers of e-learning products with a significant representation from academia. IMS specifications are developed within the organization and are then freely distributed to the public. Several IMS specifications have been adopted as key components of other initiatives such as ADL/SCORM and the Open Knowledge Initiative (OKI). In addition to specification development, IMS offers workshops and developer support. They also conduct briefing on their efforts and the general state of e-learning specifications.

OKI defines an open and extensible architecture for general-purpose infrastructure with a specific focus on learning technology targeted to the higher education community. OKI provides detailed specifications for interfaces among components of a learning management or other environment and open-source examples of how these interfaces work. The OKI architecture is intended for both commercial product vendors and higher education product developers. It provides a stable, scalable base that supports the flexibility needed by higher education, as learning technology is increasingly integrated into the education process. OKI defines an architecture that precisely specifies how the components communicate with each other and with other systems. The architecture offers a standardized basis for development with proven, scalable technologies encouraging the development of specialized components that integrate into larger systems. OKI service interface definitions (OSIDs) make up the basic elements of the architecture. OKI is building a base XML generation, or "gen," code that can emit various object-oriented language bindings, as well as providing Java versions of these application programming interfaces (APIs) for use in Java-based systems. OKI's partners and developer community are providing open-source examples and reference implementations that use the APIs. OKI began as an independent project funded by the Andrew W. Mellon Foundation and continues through engagements with IMS, Centre For Educational Technology Interoperability Standards (CETIS), and other organizations worldwide.

The Aviation Industry CBT Committee (AICC) is an industry consortium that focuses on the development of computer-based training specification. With its roots in the aviation industry, the organization has narrower focus than other specification initiatives. However, the organization is mindful that it is important to create specifications that have broader application across the e-learning environment. Thus, AICC has produced a number of important specifications, referred to as "AICC Guidelines and Recommendations" (AGR), that have been adopted by other e-learning segments. The AICC offers both a self-regulated and independently certified compliance program for products against one or more of the nine AGRs.

The Advanced Distributed Learning (ADL) Initiative is an initiative lead by the U.S. Department of Defense in collaboration with other government agencies, industry, and academia. The primary goal of the project is to develop the framework for a learning environment that supports the interoperability of learning tools and course content meeting the needs of all initiative participants. One such reference implementation is the Sharable Content Object Reference Model (SCORM). To create the SCORM, the ADL documents, validates, promotes, and sometimes funds the creation of specifications and standards from other sources. Through a series of "co-labs," a wide range of SCORM implementations are tested. A principle of the initiative is to promote collaboration in the development and adoption of tools, specifications, guidelines, policies, and prototypes. The SCORM is a reference model that defines the interrelationship of course components, data models, and protocols so that learning content objects are sharable across systems that conform with the same model. The SCORM contains a collection of specifications adapted from global specification bodies and consortia to provide a comprehensive suite of e-learning capabilities enabling interoperability, accessibility, and reusability of Web-based learning content.

The Dublin Core Metadata Initiative focuses on a single goal, making it easier to find information. Through a series of working groups, Dublin Core develops interoperable online metadata standards that support a broad range of purposes and business models including specialized vocabularies that are defined to meet the needs of specific populations. Through a metadata registry and educational outreach, Dublin Core metadata is promulgated to and between the various metadata communities.

A Further Exploration of Standards

If standards are different from specifications, where are the differences? A key difference is the maturity of a specification. Specifications reflect an initial early consensus on an approach to addressing a technical issue. It is possible that multiple specifications might be developed to address a similar issue. That was the case with metadata, as several groups developed varying specifications to address the discovery of learning objects. The feedback loop is a key component to moving a specification to a standard. As specifications are implemented, issues emerge that require refinement of the specification. Sometimes these issues require changes in the actual specification; other times, issues force changes to the implementation. In either case, the specification is progressing through a maturation process, the end point of which is a declared standard.

When a specification is proposed as a standard, the submission may be from a specification body, or it may be from one of the developers who have implemented the specification. In either case, standards review is the final polishing of a single specification or the melding of multiple specifications into an agreed-upon whole.

Standards Trail the Marketplace

By the time a specification reaches a standards body, it may significantly trail implementations and acceptance in the marketplace as the standards process is a more deliberative process than specification development. Specifications are frequently developed in six months or less from the initial proposal to the adoption of version one of the specification. As specification implementations occur, the developer community is validating the specification through implementations. Over time, successful early adoption spurs more extensive adoption of specifications. The key for any specification is to promote early adoption and validation of the approach to a perceived problem the specification addresses.

Customers and developers often feed off each other in the early phases. As we pointed out earlier, specifications are developed in response to customer and developer needs. If customers are aware of a specification that addresses their particular needs, they frequently press their developer to implement a solution that has a specification-backed approach. Similarly, developers frequently find commonly adopted specifications a market advantage.

Thus, in fairly short order, the marketplace may coalesce around an implemented specification long before any standards body is ready to review the proposed solution. Going back to our electrical plug analogy, the plug has been specified, developers are including it in their products, and customers have grown to expect a common plug, but there is not yet the universal acknowledgment of our plug as the solution. At this point, the specification is running ahead of a standard in the marketplace.

Standards Reflect Further Consensus

Standards organizations are well aware of the specification development process. They understand that specifications are rooted in early agreement on approaches to key issues. For a standards organization, there is a responsibility to make sure that an adopted standard is more than a consensus — it must be a comprehensive solution. During the standards review process, the boundary of a submitted specification may expand to encompass related specifications, or the scope of the standard may be pared down.

As the standards body moves through its process, a primary outcome is the promotion of final consensus. Participants who have yet to implement a proposed standard are now taking a closer look at the details of the proposal. Issues are being clarified, and in some cases, further implementations are being validated. No proposal moves through a standards body quickly, without protracted inspection and consensus building.

The Role of Standards

Standards play an important role when multiple specifications address essentially the same issue. The International Organization for Standards (ISO) and IEEE are representative standards bodies at the end of our continuum. Frequently, specification organizations submit proposals to organizations like IEEE or ISO after the marketplace has had some time to implement and fully exercise a specification. The typical standards process will involve the review of any existing specifications and the formulation of a draft standard from the range of available options. Sometimes this draft standard will refine one selected specification; other times, the draft may include pieces of multiple specifications. Only after extensive deliberation will a standard be approved.

Melding Specification and Standards Development

Trying to accelerate the standards process, IEEE's Learning Technology Standards Committee (LTSC) began working on a metadata standard while several specification groups were still developing competing metadata specifications. In this role, the LTSC became another specification effort rather than waiting for the marketplace to settle out. The LTSC began to develop its own standard after efforts to combine the work of Dublin Core, IMS, and ARIADNE failed. Eventually, LTSC, IMS, and ARIADNE contributed their work to the LTSC. From these contributions and the standards process, the Learning Object Metadata standard was forged. Sometimes it is better to let the specification community do its work; sometimes the standards process needs a jump-start.

Implications for Users

It is easy to think specifications are for technical staff members, who focus on arcane details deep within a CMS. In most cases, however, the requirements of users drive the specification process. This can be seen by exploring a number of user issues and their implications for specification- or standards-based solutions in next-generation course management systems.

To some, it might seem that the CMS marketplace is coalescing into just a few vendors. The reality is that there are still a significant number of solutions available. One should anticipate next-generation course management systems will be more plentiful. Whether one believes that the market is contracting or expanding, portability is a key issue for most users. Unless one wants to rely on a single vendor to continue to meet e-learning requirements, the ability to move content easily from one solution to another is a high priority. Understandably, at procurement time, looking to your next CMS is not a high priority, but it should be a consideration in any procurement.

Maintaining Multiple Course Management Systems

In the early days of course management systems, it was not uncommon for a CMS to simply appear running on computers in faculty offices or on departmental servers. In this period, the proliferation of e-learning systems on campuses was significant. Low initial costs, high enthusiasm among new online learning advocates, and rapid development were major drivers of this proliferation. Where there were commercial offerings, they were characterized by proprietary solutions, with each CMS implementing key features in its own specialized fashion.

As course management systems moved from the early adoption stage to broader campus usage, the need to maintain multiple solutions became a serious problem. Instructional technology services were frequently flooded with requests to implement similar content and resources on multiple CMS platforms. Soon the bloom of excitement from new and evolving technology faded. Those actively utilizing a CMS in this period will remember the issues it presented.

There were decidedly different responses to this situation. On some campuses, the selection and support of the CMS became an enterprise-wide issue. Many campuses limited the choices and support to one or perhaps two solutions. Departments that were satisfied with their prior choice were sometimes forced to abandon their option.

EDUCOM's National Learning Infrastructure Initiative (NLII) observed this problem and concluded that there was another way to address the issue through the development of e-learning specifications. NLII created the IMS Project, which evolved into the independent IMS Global Learning Consortium. One of its early goals was to create specifications that facilitate the interoperability of key components within course management systems.

Specialized Needs

To some, implementing specifications and standards is a limitation on choice, forcing all to implement the same capabilities. However, specifications organizations recognize that there are specialized needs, and further recognize that there may be more than one specification in the same domain that must be supported. Thus, specifications and standards need not only restrict but can also support specialized needs.

Sometimes the specialized needs of a constituency or constituencies result in more than one specification addressing a particular need. One example of this is metadata, or information to describe the development and uses of particular data. There are several widely recognized metadata specifications and standards. For example, Dublin Core Metadata, the LTSC's Learning Object Metadata (LOM), and the Metadata Encoding and Transmission Standard (METS) all offer different approaches to metadata specification.

To an individual not interested in metadata, the functional abilities of these approaches look similar. When procuring a CMS, multiple implementations for metadata specifications should be supported. This will provide the greatest likelihood that future systems will support the needs of your community.

Specification Groups Want to Respond to Real Needs

Specification development efforts are dependent on good user input. Widely implemented specifications begin with user requirements and well-documented use cases. These two inputs become the benchmark for the specification development process. Think carefully about this. The technical staff developing a specification is critically dependent on users to describe their needs. If users skip this important opportunity for input, they may doom themselves to receiving technically sound specifications that misunderstand their needs. Similarly, the limited resources available for specification development may be misdirected to issues that do not address user needs.

Consequently, most specification development efforts are constantly seeking user input as they cannot effectively perform their task without user participation. Some of the most valuable specification development efforts extend user participation throughout the specification creation process. That way users can validate approaches as they surface. As a specification is released in draft form, both technology developers and users are critical to the validation of the proposed specification.

Users Have a Forum for Input

Developing a specification involves a variety of roles. These include system architects and developers as well as users. A common comment from user constituencies, especially academia, is that specifications are not fully addressing the needs of the constituency. One of the most frequently heard pleas from specification groups is for requirement documents and use cases. This circular reference problem is broken when users provide their active input into the process. It is important to emphasize that users focus their contributions on the requirements and use cases rather than on architectural or technical solutions.

Compliance

Before we launch into some of the key players in specification development, it is important to add a word about specification compliance. As specifications are developed and then adopted or supported by a vendor, there is an expectation that someone has certified these specifications. This concept, known as compliance testing, is a costly process. Frequently, specifications have no formal compliance process, so care must be taken to clearly understand claims of compliance. While it is possible for a vendor to fully conform to a specification, there may not be full compliance certification because of a lack of testing.

This lack can lead to significant problems during implementation when the scope of the compliance is tested against real-world needs. Imagine, for example, that a company has implemented a specification that is fully operational and functions as expected within the test system. However, during implementation, it is discovered that the specification, as implemented, fails to scale to the volume of the transactions the system generates. A similar problem can develop in a multivendor environment when all vendors indicate compliance with a specification but the various implementations do not interoperate. System one cannot exchange information with system two even though the specification indicates that information and data exchange is required. These problems can be addressed in formal compliance testing. However, if there is no formal compliance testing, it is essential to define the expectations and to understand a vendor's implementation of the specification. Ways to resolve specification compliance issues should be clearly spelled out in any procurement.

Specification development groups are mindful of these issues and do work to promote solutions to these problems. However, consumers of course management systems that rely on these specifications should be prepared to pressure vendors and specification development efforts to clearly define reasonable expectations for self-claims of compliance. In the case of the specifications groups, active participation in the process will be key to pressuring for accurate claims of compliance.

The Role of Specifications and Standards in the RFP Process

The importance of a well-thought-out request for proposal (RFP) cannot be emphasized enough. When it comes to specifications and standards, it is not sufficient to include only simple statements such as "must support the XYZ specification." This vague requirement leads to an evaluation process that is little more than checking boxes for proclaimed specification compliance. In this scenario, vendors can respond to such a requirement in the affirmative with only minimal implementation.

This is not a criticism of the vendor community. A user may ask for support of the XYZ specification, the vendor may have implemented it, but the implementation may not meet the user's needs. Or, in some cases, specification support is available, but the core product may largely ignore the specification, and there may be significant expenses to having a meaningful implementation of the specification.

While the vendor may be technically meeting the bid requirements, it is the campus or user that will suffer the consequences. The fault in a vague RFP is a lack of understanding on the part of the campus as to the full implications of required specifications. Failing to fully understand the implication of the specifications leads to a lack of specificity in the RFP. The fiscal, time, and functional penalties for this approach are significant. Properly articulating both the scope of the requirement and the importance of the specifications and standards compliance is critical to a successful RFP.

To overcome this potential problem there are some important details to include in an RFP. In a general sense, and particularly in the case of specifications and standards, it is helpful to build a use case for the key aspects of an RFP. The use case should include functionality and scaling metrics to illustrate use patterns. For example, a campus might need to use the same content on more than one CMS, or there might be a need to assure an easy transition of content to a next-generation CMS. A thorough use case would help the campus and the vendor understand the scope of the users' expectations and needs.

Especially in the latter case, moving to a next-generation CMS and adopting a specification-based approach would provide the greatest probability of packaging and moving content. Remember, while the new vendor is likely to support the import of content from a competing CMS, they are less likely to be interested in helping move it to the next system.

A second improvement to any RFP would be the careful selection of key specifications and standards. In some cases, a particular organization is addressing a range of e-learning issues via specifications, while other organizations are specializing in a single specification. It is important to do your homework to understand the various specifications available to you and the vendor community. Most specification organizations will point to vendors that have implemented a particular specification. A sample implementation may also be available to help you evaluate a specification for inclusion in your RFP.

Later we will be suggesting some specifications that should be high on a user's list of potential specifications, but even that list should only be a starting point for consideration. For example, there are multiple metadata specifications with slightly different approaches. Users should take the time to understand the implications of choosing a particular specification. This includes functional and technical implications, as well as the integration between specifications and the new CMS.

Consider an RFP to be an opportunity to communicate to the vendor community about which specifications are important. This is important with existing specifications, but is also critical to the development of emerging specifications.

Early on, vendor support of specification efforts was influenced by the simple inclusion of the "must support XYZ specification" statements. Both the vendor and user community should be well beyond these types of simple statements. Inclusion of detailed use statements and awareness of current and emerging specifications demonstrates to the vendor community the importance of supporting bedrock specification efforts.

Key Specifications and Standards

The specifications and standards shown in Table 1 should be considered during the procurement of a next-generation course management system. Specifications and standards are under continual development. It is important that users track the specifications and standards under active development.

Table 1. Specifications and standards

Specification	URL
Dublin Core Metadata	*http://dublincore.org/documents/*
EduPerson	*http://www.educause.edu/eduperson/*
IEEE Learning Object Metadata	*http://ltsc.ieee.org/wg12/index.html*
IMS Specifications	*http://www.imsglobal.org/*
Metadata Object Description Language	*http://www.loc.gov/standards/mods*
MPEG	*http://www.chiariglione.org/mpeg/standards.htm*
OKI Authentication, Authorizations, Filing, and Digital Repository	*http://sourceforge.net/project/showfiles.php?group_id=69345 &package_id=68278*
MPEG7	*http://www.chiariglione.org/mpeg/standards/mpeg-7/mpeg-7.htm*
SOAP	*http://www.w3.org/TR/soap/*
WSDL	*http://www.w3.org/TR/wsdl*

Conclusions

E-learning specification and standards organizations are setting the stage for the next generation of course managements systems. Users need to engage in the process to express their requirements for e-learning software. Users who rely solely on the vendor community to integrate specifications and standards into proprietary course management systems are likely to remain in the current realm of course management systems.

Institutions and users interested in next-generation systems have a number of opportunities to both advance their progress and assure themselves and their institutions that they are investing in the future rather than the past. Tracking key specification efforts as an observer is a first step. Understanding the issues being addressed and matching them to user needs provides an important benchmark. During the procurement of the next CMS at an institution, users should take extra care to have potential vendors fully articulate their positions on adopting and complying with key e-learning specifications and standards. Users should develop their own use cases and compare them against the vendor's implementation. Users must fully understand how the vendor will address these issues.

Institutions capable of more fully engaging in the specification effort are encouraged to join the key organizations described in this chapter, providing requirements and use cases as the basis for development. These institutions should also participate in the work groups that create the specifications and standards that will enable next-generation course management systems.

References

DIN (German Institute for Standardization). (2004). Learning sequence. Available at *http://eduplone.net/products/learningsequence/*

DIN. (2000). Economic benefits of standardization: Summary of results final report and practical examples. Available at *http://www.din.de/set/aktuelles/benefit.html*

Duval, E. (2004). Learning technology standardization: Making sense of it. *Computer Science and Information Systems*, 133-143. Available at *http://www.comsis.fon.bg.ac.yu/ComSISpdf/Volume01/InvitedPapers/ErikDuval.pdf*

elive Learning Design. LD-Suite. Available at *http://learningnetworks.org/forums/showthread.php?s=&threadid=202*

European Committee for Standardization. *http://www.cenorm.be/cenorm/index.htm*

Nissi, M. (Ed). (2003) *Making sense of learning specifications and standards: A decision maker's guide to their adoption.* 2nd ed. The Masie Center, Learning Technology & e-Lab Thinktank. Available at *http://www.masie.com/standards/s3_2nd_edition.pdf*

Reload: Reusable eLearning Object Authoring and Delivery. *http://www.reload.ac.uk/*

Smythe, C., Evdemon, J., Sim, S., & Thorne, S. (2004). *Basic architectural principles for learning technology systems* (DRAFT). Available from Alt-i-Lab Topical Working Sessions, *http://www.imsglobal.org/architecture.pdf*

Why e-Learning Standards? *http://careo.prn.bc.ca/losc/mod3t1.html*

Endnote

[1] *http://sourceforge.net/okiproject*

Chapter III

Libraries, Information, and Course Management Systems

Joan K. Lippincott, Coalition for Networked Information, USA

Abstract

Content owned or licensed by academic libraries, such as electronic journals, art image databases, and digital videos, provides a means to enhance curricula and allow for deeper learning by students. Lack of interoperability between library systems and course management systems (CMS) limits the use of library content within CMS. Learning environments, CMS, and institutional repositories must all interoperate since content can be used in many ways in both research and learning. Librarians can also add value to CMS if their virtual services — such as reference and information literacy — are integrated into the CMS. The content of CMS raises many policy issues which must be addressed by institutions.

Introduction: A Scenario

For his Civil War history class, a professor at a university prepares his syllabus for the coming semester. He uses both the library's online catalog and a Web browser to locate materials he wishes to include in his reading list for the semester and provides links to the materials so that all will be accessible by one "click." For one week's class, he pulls archival excerpts from the four newspapers (two from the North, two from the South) available in the University of Virginia's "Valley of the Shadow" Civil War-era archive (*http://valley.vcdh.virginia.edu/*). He will use these in class to describe reaction to the advance of Sherman's army in the South. For their homework assignment, students will be asked to find other sources, which may include newspapers from other cities, diaries, maps, or photos from the same period. The professor has always emphasized an end-of-semester project in which students must use primary and secondary sources to write a paper on some aspect of the Civil War, ranging from military to political to societal topics. Now that his university has a cutting-edge course management system (CMS), he is able to work with a librarian to develop a guide (structured bibliography) for his students that will be integrated into the CMS and lead students to some of the best resources on the Civil War. Since there are many amateur Civil War buffs, understanding what makes a Web site appropriate for academic research is something the professor wants to emphasize, and in collaboration with a reference librarian, he has developed a brief tutorial describing how to evaluate a Web site for use in historical research. In addition, he employs a standard button in the CMS that provides a link to an online chat with a reference librarian. For secondary sources, he wants to make sure that students use appropriate journals, and he and the library provide links to Historical Abstracts, a key service for locating refereed journal articles in the field, and to JSTOR, a collection of the major journals in humanities and social sciences disciplines. Both of these resources are accessible via licenses negotiated by the library. When the students develop their end-of-course projects, they will submit them via the CMS. After revision, they will have the opportunity to submit their work to their e-portfolio.

This scenario illustrates the outcome of an environment in which an institution's CMS and its library information system (LS) interoperate in a seamless manner for both faculty course creators and student learners in a way that does not exist today. This scenario does not illustrate innovations in teaching and learning. It does describe typical use of information in courses. Since the electronic locus of many courses is increasingly in the CMS environment, what is needed is a more seamless integration of these types of information resources, generally accessible through the LS, into the CMS.

The library and library-licensed or library-owned content have been at the periphery of developments related to course management systems (CMS) for the last few years. Librarians have raised concerns that the institutional investment in scholarly digital content is being marginalized by the structure of course management systems and that freely available Web content is more heavily used by faculty as they build a Web presence for a course. Some CMS companies market packages of digital content that can be used from within their CMS systems, but those packages may include materials that the library has already paid for through its own licenses. Further, the technical structures of library systems and course management systems do not interoperate seamlessly, and there is no simple "fix" for this problem. It appears that the focus of conversations and presentations related to libraries and course management systems is on how the library can have a presence in course management systems, as if they must be invited in as special guests. Instead, the genuine central concern of librarians is an underlying assumption that needs clear statement, namely that the use of a wide variety of information resources, beyond assigned course readings, is a key element of deeper learning and an integral part of many existing curricula in higher education.

Course Management Systems, Libraries, and Deeper Learning Principles

Providing seamless access from within the CMS environment to a wide variety of information resources helps achieve the goals of deep learning. Those who value the pursuit of deeper learning in the context of teaching and learning with technology are wary of the trend towards self-contained, packaged courses that is one vision of online learning, particularly in the distance education context. In the "packaged" environment, students can complete a course by working at their own pace on a logical series of modules in which they read textbooks or other materials bundled into the CMS, complete a series of exercises, and take exams without ever going beyond the confines of the materials presented in the CMS. While this type of self-contained environment may be useful in some courses that emphasize mastery of a given body of knowledge, it is not an environment that in general promotes critical thinking or scholarship. Students who merely do exercises within a CMS and take exams based solely on a textbook and required readings are not encouraged to explore the wide world of information resources, which include many points of view and perspectives on related topics.

The CMS environment can be a tool for promoting engaging and student-centered learning experiences. In an exploration of how a CMS can be used to provide an effective learning environment, Carmean and Haefner (2003) synthesize the work of a number of leading educational researchers to delineate five principles of deeper learning. They conclude that deeper learning occurs when it is social, active, contextual, engaging, and student-owned. Appropriate and creative incorporation of library resources into learning, made more visible through the integration of CMS and LS, can help achieve the principles of deeper learning. While it is possible to find examples of how integration of LIS into CMS could address each of the five principles of deeper learning, the evidence is strongest in support of two of the principles: "engaging" and "student-owned." Some of the characteristics of an "engaging" learning environment include respect for "diverse talents and ways of learning" and emphasis on "motivators and natural curiosities" (Carmean & Haefner, 2002). Providing opportunities for students to use a wide variety of information resources in assignments allows students to capitalize on their learning strengths and encourages them to pursue a specialized interest within the course structure. For example, in an American studies course on popular culture, visual learners could explore posters from a particular historical era and a student with aural skills could use the library of the spoken word to investigate speeches and oral history interviews. The faculty member can provide links to a range of appropriate resources into the CMS, including resources licensed by the library and freely available Web resources, or a librarian can provide a guide to many high-quality digital resources. Librarians from some institutions are making available such guides that can be easily integrated into courses (Reeb & Gibbons, 2004).

Some characteristics of "student-owned" learning also relate well to the opportunities that can be provided when integration of library and information resources is made seamless through integration into CMS. By providing a variety of links to appropriate, high-quality information resources in connection with course assignments, students are encouraged to take control of their own learning as they follow up and explore more deeply some aspects of the topics covered in the class. In the sciences, giving students assignments in which they must explore and utilize large data sets such as those gathered by government agencies like NASA or the USGS and then present data to illustrate an aspect of the topic provides students with practice in organizing knowledge in ways that facilitate retrieval and application, one of the deeper learning characteristics. Providing students with assignments in which they independently explore a topic emphasizes learner independence and choice, characteristics of deeper learning. Assigning students to complete papers or projects on topics of their choice emphasizes higher order thinking, which includes synthesis and reflection, also characteristics of deeper learning.

A study using data from the College Student Experiences Questionnaire supports the view that use of library and information resources promotes deeper learning. Kuh and Gonyea (2003) write that:

> ...*institutions that set high standards for academic work seem to impel students to use a variety of intellectual resources actively, including the library. As a result, students who frequently use library resources are also more likely to work harder than they thought they could to meet a faculty member's expectations and in response to instructor feedback; and they are assigned projects that require integrating ideas, putting different facts and ideas together, and applying class material to other areas in life* (p. 26).

Making information resources more accessible to students from within the CMS in order to promote deeper learning principles is a learner-centered view of the relationship between the CMS and LS. However, McLean and Lynch (2004) report that:

> ...*much of the current thinking is based on a fairly library-centric view of being able to "push" information resources into the LMS [learning management system]. There has been little thought given to the learner activity perspective where the learner may wish to draw on any number of information resources either prescribed, or of his or her choosing, at any given moment in the learning activity* (p. 6).

In addition to providing access to digital resources, librarians can be part of online learning communities, playing an active role in classes that emphasize student assignments that require information discovery, access, and analysis (Cox, 2002; Lippincott, 2002). However, this type of embedded role is not realistic for broad implementation in an institution because of the limited number of librarians compared to the number of courses offered in a higher education institution. The CMS should include standard mechanisms at the opening page for each course that provide access to such functions as library reference service via e-mail or chat, electronic reserves, standard guides or pathfinders by discipline, and information literacy modules. This could be conceived as a CMS-based "library reference area" where library resources and services that support teaching and learning are readily accessible and available for every course offered via the CMS.

One step in this direction is being taken by the Online Computer Library Center (OCLC), which is doing a pilot e-learning project with faculty at eight universities who are implementing links on their online course home pages to QuestionPoint, the digital collaborative reference service coordinated by OCLC (QuestionPoint, 2004). On a broader scale, librarians and information technologists have collaborated at Penn State to enable their CMS software ANGEL to "push" resources for discipline-specific library materials into individual courses." Functions have been implemented to provide subject guides to content, to generate links to e-reserves, and to link directly to online reference services from within the CMS environment. They noted, "The Library no longer will live outside the CMS. Instead, the CMS will serve as a door to the library — a most important campus resource" (Pyatt & Snavely, n.d.).

Interoperability

The general lack of seamless interoperability between CMS and LS has been the focus of most articles and presentations on the relationship between CMS and LS. Stated simply, the current problem is that there are too many steps needed for faculty or students to have access to library resources when they are operating from within a CMS, and this discourages the use of library resources. Creating links to freely available Web content is currently much easier than providing access to resources licensed by the library. Library systems and CMS are developed on different tracks and operate in silos within the institution. Librarians are concerned that the necessity to access library resources from outside the CMS, using a separate authentication process, discourages their use and instead encourages students to use Web resources that may not have the quality of licensed resources selected by the library (often with faculty input). Reliance on freely available Web resources, rather than on library-selected content, is wasteful of the very large investments libraries make in licensing content (Cohen, 2003).

If a student or faculty member is working within the CMS environment, he or she is often required to exit that environment or open a new window to access the library's electronic reserve system or online catalog. Access to licensed material means yet another login to the same account and password used in the CMS. Alternatively, the faculty member might obtain or make a Hyper Text Markup Language (HTML) or Portable Document Format (pdf) document to mount within the CMS, taking considerably more time than if he or she were able to easily create a link to the full text in the LS. If a faculty member is building a reading or e-reserves list within the CMS, it would be a timesaver if he or she could query the catalog without having too many extra steps. In addition, faculty may want to incorporate content available through the LS and the library's licensed resources directly into course units within the CMS. For example, the faculty member might want to incorporate or embed spectrum data, art images, video clips, or text into a class assignment or lecture.

Many of the electronic resources licensed by academic libraries — typically scholarly journals but also other materials, such as collections of art representations — require authentication by users so that the company providing the resources can track the amount of use of the material by a particular institution. Adding information resources into the CMS is not an easy process, often requiring a multistep process of copying the resource and then adding it to the CMS or providing access through electronic reserves, which also may require an access procedure separate from the CMS. An OCLC task force concluded that:

> ...*a successful strategy must allow faculty easily to find and integrate resources and services from multiple environments into their unique course. Libraries must find strategies for making their resources and services readily available in the environments faculty use to create and manage their courses* (McLean & Sander, 2003, p. 9).

This represents a user-centric rather than a library-centric view of the trajectory of future development. In order to realize a future of an integrated learning and information environment, an "underlying infrastructure for access management encompassing issues of authentication, authorization and directory services" will need to be established (McLean, 2002). A project at Indiana University is using the Sakai[1] environment to develop a solution to easy interoperability between CMS and licensed library resources. The goal of the project is to allow users to search the library database from within the CMS and then use a "drag-and-drop" mechanism to transfer articles from research journals and other library content into the CMS. As part of this project, Indiana University will explore faculty needs and preferences for including library content within the CMS. As library director Suzanne Thorin noted in a presentation, library content can include a broad array of materials (Wheeler & Thorin, 2004). She cited the example of the library's Hoagy Carmichael collection, which includes scores, audio, photos, and online interviews with Carmichael family members. Currently, the library makes this content available for use within CMS through a "kluge" via electronic reserves.

Discussions of interoperability often use examples that focus on content that the faculty member selects and develops as part of the syllabus of the course. However, as Massachusetts Institute of Technology's Phil Long (2004) points out, interoperability of CMS and LS is also important for student exploration and unstructured use, and it is not yet available. He states, "What do learners need? They should be able to draw on digital assets from any resource, or repository, that strikes them as useful — even if the rationale is serendipity — at the exact moment when the learning activity calls for it. Today they can't do that." Some solutions to this issue include icons that directly link students to recommended resources for the course or embedded guides to subtopics related to the course.

An alternative to interoperability between CMS and LS is to bring related but disparate resources together in a way that will be convenient to users and provide value-added connectivity of information. At the University of California, San Diego, a campus partnership of Academic Computing Services, the library, the registrar, the bookstore, and other departments developed a mechanism to bring together for each course in a "course details" menu the links to the course Web site, campus bookstore's text list for the course, library reserves for the course, and course materials and lecture notes available from a campus duplicating service (Gold, 2003).

CMS, Repositories, and Learning Environments

"Library issues" related to the CMS may, on some campuses, be limited to what have been traditional library interests, such as course reserves, librarian-developed guides to quality information resources, and electronic reference services. However, in institutions developing infrastructures for the intellectual assets of the college or university, the library may play a much broader role in the stewardship of information resources. This broader set of intellectual assets could include faculty-created data sets of scientific or other information, nontext and multimedia objects, such as sound recordings, slides, and simulations, Web sites on the faculty member's area of research, learning objects, whole courses or curricula, e-prints or preprints, and articles, chapters, and monographs. The development of repositories for such information is slowly being adopted by major universities (Lynch, 2003). What is important in the consideration of next-generation course management systems is to understand that the focus of interoperability between this emerging institutional repository infrastructure and the CMS may become as important or more important than interoperability between the traditional library system and the CMS.

Institutions are becoming increasingly aware that various units on campus are developing rich information resources that could have wider value as institutional assets if they were developed and made available in the framework of a coherent information infrastructure. For example, there are many departments in addition to an art department that could make use of digitized collections of art objects, such as the history, area studies, anthropology, classics, and religion departments. These collections can be used both for research and for teaching and learning. However, the digitized objects developed by the art department may be housed in a content management system that does not interoperate with collections of slides maintained by the classics department.

Faculty are developing data sets in conjunction with major research projects. In the sciences, let us use the example of the faculty member developing a set of data for his research related to water temperature in the Chesapeake Bay. He may want to use that data as part of a course assignment integrated into a CMS, and if it becomes an important resource for other scientists, he may also wish to develop an arrangement with his home institution to house the data permanently in a repository accessible to others. How will the data be housed and maintained for these various uses? What kinds of institutional infrastructure can be developed to make access of various types more seamless for users? What interface is more in daily use by faculty and students than the CMS? Linking content and repository systems to the CMS, or developing them within the CMS so that faculty can grab objects or sets of digital objects for use in their courses, will be a similar issue to providing transparent interoperability with LS.

While early discussions of library integration with CMS focused largely on interoperability issues, especially for content such as course reserves, online catalogs, and guides to specialized information resources, the territory has quickly expanded. The emerging emphasis of interactions of CMS with library resources is in a much broader context, one that includes discussion of licensed library resources, content management systems, faculty-created learning objects, institutional repositories, and infrastructure issues (Long, 2004; McLean & Lynch, 2004).

An important project that is examining the structure of a cohesive information environment — from laboratory data to research publication to teaching and learning — is being developed in the United Kingdom. The eBank UK project[2] is looking at how a common information infrastructure could serve the needs of research and teaching (Lyon, 2004). In a separate development, UK information specialists and Australian counterparts collaborated on a white paper to provide an overview of issues related to institutional repositories, including the relationship of educational assets to institutional repositories (*Repository Management*, 2004). A project coordinated by Harvard's Dale Flecker and Neil McLean of IMS Australia, funded by the Mellon Foundation, has created a checklist that outlines both essential and desirable interoperability functionality between repositories and learning applications, which include CMS (*Digital library content*, 2004).

In the next-generation CMS, faculty should be able to easily share a course module or learning object that they have developed — perhaps a simulation or an assignment — that has worked particularly well. One possibility would be to have a button on the CMS that he or she can choose to contribute learning objects to an institutional content management system or institutional repository so that others can access the content from that location. A pop-up screen would ask the user to use a provided template to enter basic metadata, or information about the project, such as when it was created, terms of use, etc. Information on the creator of the submitted learning object would be embedded into the metadata that surrounds the entry so that the source of the content would be accessible to future users.

Some leading technology thinkers believe that we need a new overall examination of the campus technology architecture and a new vision of the teaching, research, and information digital environment. Long believes that the "institutional infrastructure must share functional and technical services" among a wide variety of units and applications. He, McLean, and Lynch believe that this architecture will likely develop in a Web services environment (Long, 2004, para. 13; McLean & Lynch, 2004). Atkins (2004) suggests that we not build barriers between scholarship, teaching, and learning as we create information infrastructures. He envisions new information infrastructures that bridge research information and teaching and learning contexts as special cases of collaborative environments.

Preservation and Long-Term Access

Another aspect of the connection between CMS and repositories is the long-term preservation of faculty-created course content or student-produced content in connection with courses. Libraries have traditionally had the responsibility for long-term access to information on campuses (along with archivists), but this is a new area for them. Generally, libraries have not provided overall stewardship for instructional materials (except on a temporary basis on reserve) nor do they generally collect student work with the exception of theses and dissertations. However, there is increasing interest in institutions providing mechanisms for long-term access to the intellectual assets of the university, including course-related materials, via the mechanism of an institutional repository. A leading example of this is MIT's Open Courseware initiative.[3] Some higher education institutions are also developing e-portfolio services that are intended to survive long after students have left the institution so that they can be used by the alumni as a continuing repository of their intellectual work.

Some question whether course content or learning objects are appropriate candidates for full-fledged preservation in the context of an institutional repository. As more courses are developed within the CMS and more student assignments, projects, and portfolios are being submitted within the CMS, we must more seriously examine both preservation and intellectual property rights of student and faculty work. Long (2004) proposes a different genre of repository for learning objects that are lightweight digital repositories (DR-Lite) intended for ephemeral use and with fewer requirements or parameters than library-controlled institutional repositories. On the other hand, Gold (2003) provides a rationale for the preservation of the content of a CMS; it represents a context for understanding instruction, a key part of the institution's mission, and also represents a community that has developed in the context of a course. It is possible that institutions will want to selectively include some courses in their institutional repositories, but extraction, intellectual property issues, and how those selections will be made will have to be guided by institutional policy.

In the future, it is likely that many higher education institutions will develop short-term and long-term homes for content, such as the CMS for short-term instructional use and the institutional repository for long-term access. The infrastructures will allow faculty to easily transfer materials from one system to the other. These information infrastructures will need to be developed in the context of an institutional, long-term planning processes.

Policy Issues

Intellectual Property Issues

A wide variety of intellectual property issues affect the production of course materials, the types of materials that can be used in technology-enabled courses, and the way that student products can be used in these courses. Although it is not clear to what extent software can alleviate problems associated with intellectual property issues, the way that the next generation of CMS are developed has the potential to help clarify what intellectual property rights apply to a particular digital object. New systems may also educate creators of course materials and users of those materials about their rights and obligations.

One specific concern in the intellectual property arena is whether faculty can transfer whole courses to an institutional repository if they include materials that are under license to the institution. If institutions develop mechanisms whereby whole articles, chapters, and other copyrighted materials can be incorporated directly into the CMS, the licensing provisions for those materials may not permit that they be housed, in a sense as separate copies, for the long-term in an institutional repository. This will create challenges for the transfer to an institutional repository of courses developed within a CMS.

CMS, Faculty and Student Rights, and Institutional Policies

In the future, the CMS may assist users in identifying the rights holders of particular digital content. A CMS will not be able to intuit this information but may provide fields in its data structure that allow clear rights information to be attached to digital content or interface with a digital rights management (DRM) system. A wide-ranging study commissioned by the Joint Information Systems Committee (JISC) in the UK provides many specific examples, gleaned from higher education user communities, of the ways in which DRM could facilitate use and re-use of digital information in the context of research, teaching, and learning (Intrallect, Ltd, 2004).

Still, the issue of who owns what digital content will always be complex. For example, when a faculty member creates new course material in close collaboration with his or her institution's instructional technology unit, who owns the rights? The faculty member or the university? Higher education institutions must create policies to deal with these issues. Some model policies have been developed at the University of Texas.[4] Carol Twigg's *Who owns online courses and course materials? Intellectual property policies for a new learning environment*[5] (2002) provides a good discussion of the issues.

To further complicate the ownership issue, students are the rights holders of the intellectual property that they contribute to a course, unless they have specifically signed over those rights to an instructor or institution. Under current U.S. law, individuals do not have to register intellectual products in order to be considered rights holders, so students who contribute term papers to a course Web site are — without taking any additional action — the copyright holders of those papers. Cliff Lynch has contributed an excellent discussion of faculty and student rights in his ECAR/CNI paper, "The afterlives of courses on the network: Information management issues for learning management systems."[6]

Reuse and retention of intellectual property is as complex as its production. If a faculty member holds the rights to particular course content, which is also used by others in his or her department, what happens to that content when he or she leaves the institution? If a faculty member incorporates copyrighted material created by someone else into course materials (e.g., a poem or a photograph), does he or she have permission to retain that content for use in later courses or for preservation purposes? If a student contributes a paper to a course Web site, does the institution have permission to use the paper as a model in future offerings of the course without express permission from the student? Lynch's ECAR/CNI paper, cited above, elaborates on these issues. He frames the concerns as both legal and institutional policy issues. For example, while requiring students to give permission for public access to their content in specific courses or in every course in which they are enrolled may provide legal protection for the institution, the relevant constituencies must also make policy decisions to clarify what is appropriate for their community.

Librarians raise an additional concern related to CMS and intellectual property. Some companies market and sell packages of content to higher education institutions specifically for use within the CMS. The institution may already own or license those materials through its library or other units and therefore may end up paying twice for the same content.

Privacy

If course content is made available outside the confines of a particular course taught for a particular time period, the institution needs to make sure that policies and procedures are in place that safeguard the privacy of all of those individuals who participated in the course. For example, a faculty member may think that the class members of a course had a particularly good discussion of one of the course topics and wants to make this available as a learning object in an institutional repository for use in future classes. Without the express permission of all students involved, this would likely be considered a violation of the privacy of the class members. New generations of CMS may build in various types of permissions software to assist faculty in collecting and documenting permissions for sharing products of the course, both informal products, such as discussions, and formal products, such as course projects. But, this effort must also be implemented within the framework of institutional policy.

Next Steps

Developing mechanisms to enable easy access to the wide range of information resources and services offered by libraries from within CMS is ultimately about providing the means to enrich learning experiences for students. Learner-centered goals should drive the technical work that is needed to increase interoperability between LS and CMS. Many faculty members already incorporate into their courses some assignments that require students to seek, evaluate, and use a wide variety of information resources, including those available under the auspices of the library. Currently, faculty face barriers to the easy incorporation into CMS of guides to quality information sources, digital content provided under license to the library, and services such as easy access to reference librarians. Students who are using a CMS as the digital "home" for a course also face barriers in easily roaming from that home to the rich digital resources provided via the library when they wish to fulfill an assignment or explore a subject on their own.

Members of an OCLC task force "agreed unequivocally that the faculty, the library, and the IT and instructional design departments need to collaborate in developing sustainable and seamless infrastructure." They further reported, "Evidence suggests, however, that very few institutions have systemically attained such a coherent strategic approach" (McLean & Sander, 2003, p. 7). Planning for a campus information infrastructure should become a top priority at higher education institutions today, and the planning team should involve collaboration among all relevant sectors. Ideally, we will see the development of integrated information infrastructures that are seamless and driven by user needs. This service model will have an intuitive interface, be Web-driven, and rest on a single user authentication. Widely deployed CMS are now available to enable Web delivery of course materials, and rich digital content is readily available through college and university libraries. We must now build bridges to unite these two important institutional resources.

Acknowledgments

The author expresses her appreciation to Clifford Lynch, Executive Director of the Coalition for Networked Information, for his comments and perspectives on this paper.

References

Atkins, D. E. (2004). The cyberinfrastructure movement and the potential for revolutionizing science-engineering research and education. Presentation at the *JISC/CNI Meeting 2004: The Future of Scholarship in the Digital Age*. Brighton, England.

Carmean, C. & Haefner, J. (2003). Next generation course management systems, *EDUCAUSE Quarterly*, *26*(1), 10-13.

Cohen, D. (2003). Course-management software: Where's the library? *Educause Review, 10*, 12-13.

Cox, C. (2002). Becoming part of the course: Using Blackboard to extend one-shot library instruction. *C&RL News, 63*, 11-13, 39.

Digital library content and course management systems: Issues of interoperation. Report of a study group co-chaired by D. Flecker & N. McLean. Digital Library Federation: July, 2004. *http://www.diglib.org/pubs/cmsdl040 7/*

Gold, A. K. (2003). Multilateral digital library partnerships for sharing and preserving instructional content and context. *Portal: Libraries and the Academy, 3*(2), 269-291.

Intrallect, Ltd. (2004). Digital rights management study: Interim report. JISC. Available at *http://dewey.intrallect.com/drm-study/Interim_Report. pdf*

Kuh, G. D. & Gonyea, R. M. (2003). The role of the academic library in promoting student engagement in learning. *C&RL News, 64*, 256-282.

Lippincott, J. K. (2002). Developing collaborative relationships: Librarians, students, and faculty creating learning communities. *C&RL News, 63*(3), 190-192.

Long, P. D. (2004). Learning object repositories, digital repositories, and the reusable life of course content. *Syllabus.* Available at *http://www.campus-technology.com/article.asp?id=9258*

Lynch, C. (2002). The afterlives of courses on the network: Information management issues for learning management systems. *Educause Center for Applied Research Bulletin, 23.* Available at *http://www.cni.org/ staff/clifford_publications.html*

Lynch, C. (2003). Institutional repositories: Essential infrastructure for scholarship in the digital age. *ARL Bimonthly Report, 226*, 1-7. Available at *http://www.arl.org/newsltr/226/ir.html*

Lyon, L. (2004). Realizing the scholarly knowledge cycle: The experience of eBank UK. Presentation at *Coalition for Networked Information Spring Task Force Meeting*, Alexandria, VA. Available at *http:// www.cni.org/tfms/2004a.spring/abstracts/PB-realizing-lyon.html*

McLean, N. (2002). Libraries and e-Learning: Organisational and technical interoperability. Available at *http://www.colis.mq.edu.au/ news_archives/demo/docs/lib_e_learning.pdf*

McLean, N. & Lynch, C. (2004). Interoperability between information and learning environments—Bridging the gaps. A joint white paper on behalf of the IMS Global Learning Consortium and the Coalition for Networked Information. Available at *http://www.imsglobal.org/digitalrepositories/CNIandIMS_2004.pdf*

McLean, N. & Sander, H. (Eds.). (2003). Libraries and the enhancement of e-learning. OCLC E-Learning Task Force. Dublin, Ohio. Available at *http://www5.oclc.org/downloads/community/elearning.pdf*

Online Computer Library Center (OCLC). (2002). How academic librarians can influence students' Web-based information choices. OCLC White Paper on The Information Habits of College Students. Available at *http://www5.oclc.org/downloads/community/informationhabits.pdf*

Pyatt, E. & Snavely, L. (n.d.). No longer missing: Tools for connecting the library with the course management system. *Syllabus.* Available at *http://www.syllabus.com/print.asp?ID=9094*

QuestionPoint: Collaborative Reference Service. OCLC links virtual reference, course management software and libraries. OCLC Abstracts. Available at *http://www5.oclc.org/downloads/design/abstracts/04192004/questionpoint.htm*

Reeb, B. & Gibbons, S. (2004). Students, librarians, and subject guides: Improving a poor rate of return. *Portal: Libraries and the Academy, 4*(1), 123-130.

Repository Management and Implementation (2004). A white paper for alt-I-lab prepared on behalf of DEST (Australia) and JISC-CETIS (UK). Available at *http://www.imsglobal.org/altilab/*

Twigg, C. A. (2000). Who owns online courses and materials: Intellectual property policies for a new learning environment. Rensselaer Polytechnic Institute: Center for Academic Transformation. Available at *http://www.center.rpi.edu/PewSym/mono2.html*

Wheeler, B. & Thorin, S. (2004). Sakai project update: Connecting libraries and the CMS/LMS. Presentation at *Coalition for Networked Information Spring Task Force Meeting*, Alexandria, VA. Available at *http://www.cni.org/tfms/2004a.spring/abstracts/PB-sakai-wheeler.html*

Endnotes

---

[1]   *http://www.sakaiproject.org/about.html*

[2]   *http://www.ukoln.ac.uk/projects/ebank-uk*

[3]   *http://ocw.mit.edu/index.html*

[4]   *http://www.utsystem.edu/ogc/intellectualproperty/cprtpol.htm*

[5]   *http://www.center.rpi.edu/PewSym/mono2.html*

[6]   *http://www.cni.org/staff/cliffpubs/ECARpaper20024.0.pdf*

Chapter IV

The Interplay of Teaching Conceptions and Course Management System Design:
Research Implications and Creative Innovations for Future Designs

Xornam S. Apedoe, The University of Georgia, USA

Abstract

The purpose of this chapter is to explore the relationship between instructors' conceptions of teaching and the design and use of course management systems in instruction. Understanding this relationship helps us to understand why instructors are using course management systems in the ways they do. Subsequently, we can use our understanding to help define what future generations of course management systems look like and how we as instructors might use them.

Introduction

Remembering that we shape our tools and our tools shape us underscores the need for being proactive and thoughtful about the design of these tools. (Boettcher, 2003, Future CMSes, ¶1)

Course management systems (CMS) are promoted as an easy way for higher education faculty to integrate technology into their instruction. Along with the claims of cost savings and administrative efficiency (Cohn & Stoehr, 2003), proponents of CMS suggest that they can be used to create student-centered learning environments that actively engage students in learning. These learning environments are purported to provide students with opportunities to experience "deeper learning", or learning where the outcome is meaningful understanding of material and content (Carmean & Haefner, 2002). The emphasis in a student-centered learning environment is on helping students construct personal meaning and draw connections between new knowledge and existing conceptions and understandings (Hannafin & Land, 1997), while deeper learning environments are characterized as being social, active, contextual, engaging, and student-owned (Carmean & Haefner, 2002). While CMS have the potential to be used to create opportunities for deeper learning, decisions related to the best use of the tools within a course are often left in the hands of the individual instructor (McCray, 2000). Unfortunately, research suggests that CMS are typically not used in ways consistent with deeper learning principles, but rather are primarily used as a means of information dissemination (Oliver, 2001). Research on conceptions of teaching can help us understand why the potential of CMS for creating deep learning environments has yet to be realized extensively in higher education today, while also helping us begin to imagine what future generations of CMS should look like.

Conceptions of Teaching and Course Management Systems

An often overlooked but significantly important influence on the teaching and learning process is an instructor's belief or conception about teaching and learning. These conceptions have a significant influence on the instructional practices or strategies they employ (Kember, 1997). Yet, it would seem that the implications of the research on teaching conceptions has largely been ignored by those interested in the integration and use of technology, such as CMS, in higher education.

Higher education instructors' conceptions of teaching are categorized as belonging to one of two orientations: teacher-centered/content-centered or student-centered/learning-centered (e.g., Kember, 1997; Kember & Kwan, 2002; Samuelowicz & Bain, 2001). A teacher-centered orientation focuses on the communication of defined bodies of content or knowledge, while a student-centered orientation focuses on student learning and taking a developmental approach to students' conceptions of knowledge. Each orientation can be further categorized into *conceptions* of teaching. The term "conception," which is often used interchangeably with the term "belief," can be defined as the:

> *...specific meanings attached to phenomena which then mediate our response to situations involving those phenomena. We form conceptions of virtually every aspect of our perceived world, and in so doing, use those abstract representations to delimit something from, and relate it to, other aspects of our world. In effect, we view the world through the lenses of our conceptions, interpreting and acting in accordance with our understanding of the world.* (Pratt, 1992, p. 204)

Thus, conceptions of teaching may be envisioned as being the lens through which the process of teaching and learning is viewed and shaped. Based on the literature, Kember (1997) proposed the following five conceptions of teaching:

1. *Imparting information.* This is the most teacher-centered conception, and has a focus on delivering information to students. In this conception, teaching is viewed merely as the presenting of information, and the focus is on the lecturer.

2.   *Transmitting structured knowledge.* As with the conception of impart-
     ing information, the emphasis is on delivering information to the students
     but in a structured way so that students have a better chance of receiving
     the knowledge. Much more emphasis is placed on how the information is
     presented, and it may be viewed as a stage performance.

3.   *Student-teacher interaction.* This is a transitional conception that rec-
     ognizes the importance of student-teacher interactions. There is less
     emphasis on the lecturers' knowledge base and more emphasis on student
     understanding. Often, there is a "tension between not taking everything at
     face value and telling them the (right) outcome" (p. 267).

4.   *Facilitating understanding/learning facilitation.* This conception falls
     under the student-centered orientation. The role of the teacher is to help
     the student reach specific learning goals. The desired outcome of the
     teaching process under this conception is student understanding, which is
     demonstrated by applying knowledge, not regurgitating it.

5.   *Conceptual change/intellectual development.* This conception is the
     most student-centered. It may have two facets, changing student concep-
     tions and holistic developmental processing, resulting in interpersonal
     relationships between teacher and student.

According to Kember and Kwan (2002), instructors tend to have a predomi-
nant or preferred teaching approach, which is largely determined by their
conception of teaching. However, instructors are also likely to adopt an
alternative teaching approach if the teaching or learning environment demands
it. Factors such as institutional influence, curriculum design, and student
demands may alter an instructor's teaching approach (Kember & Kwan,
2002). One might argue that technology, specifically the characteristics,
limitations, or affordances of the technology, is another factor that may
influence teaching approaches.

This research on teaching conceptions brings to the fore two important issues
that can help provide insight into how and why instructors are using CMS in the
ways they do. Firstly, if an instructor does not value a particular teaching
approach (e.g., collaborative group learning), he or she is unlikely to choose
to use a CMS to engage students in such activities (Ehrman & Gilbert, 2003).
Secondly, the research suggests that environmental factors can influence an
instructor's choice of teaching approach. Therefore, there may be an interplay
between the design (considered as an environmental factor) of a CMS and an
instructor's conception and approach to teaching.

Design of CMS: Influences and Use

Course management systems were originally designed specifically for faculty who lacked experience with Web development or file management on Web servers, and thus they provide tools and features that instructors can easily integrate into their current teaching practices (e.g., Brown, 2000). Among these tools and features is the inclusion of templates for developing course Web pages and tools for faculty to upload course material to be accessed by students using a Web browser. Provision and use of these templates ensures that each course has a very similar layout and design. A typical template for developing a course Web site in a CMS may suggest including links to a course syllabus, an announcements page, a course notes page, or an assignments page. Templates for features such as discussion boards, chat rooms, and perhaps electronic work group areas are also typically provided.

Unfortunately, it has often been assumed that because CMS were originally developed by faculty working in higher education, they must reflect sound teaching and learning principles (Boettcher, 2003). However, it must be remembered that instruction in higher education has traditionally followed a teacher-centered model (Twigg, 1994) in which teaching and learning is viewed as the "transmission" of knowledge from the instructor to the student (Howard, McGee, Schwartz, & Purcell, 2000). Consequently, it would seem that these less than innovative views of learning (e.g., transmissionist models as opposed to student-centered learning models) were transported with the tools and features made available in CMS. Critics of CMS have expressed concern that they may promote an information dissemination pedagogy primarily by emphasizing instructor dissemination tools over student processing tools (e.g., Oliver, 2001). The implications of these design decisions are evident if we examine the ways that instructors are using CMS in their instruction.

With the introduction of CMS into higher education (the first wave), instructors initially began using CMS as an extension of their existing teaching practices for activities such as organizing the elements of a course or for communicating with students (Boettcher, 2003). While more and more instructors have moved into what Boettcher calls the second wave of CMS use in which the hybrid course (a Web-enhanced campus course) is common, critics express concern about the nature of CMS use in such courses. Critics of CMS are quick to point out that with the proliferation of CMS the focus seems to be on reproducing in an online environment what is currently done in traditional instruction (e.g., Kuriloff, 2001). Indeed, research on the use of CMS by instructors in the

University of Wisconsin System (UWS) suggests that much of the CMS use revolves around the content presentation tools (Morgan, 2003). Faculty have been slow to take advantage of the more complex or interactive elements of CMS, supporting the notion that CMS are being used primarily for supporting traditional instructional methods.

Course management systems provide a great deal of support to the teacher-centered view of teaching and learning, focusing on providing tools for faculty to develop and deliver content (Oliver, 2001), such as online readings, while the needs of the students are seemingly less important (Carmean & Haefner, 2003). While the automation of creating course Web sites has been useful, and was probably necessary during the early stages of Web use in higher education, consideration now needs to be given to the pedagogical implications of the tools and features provided in a CMS. Since pedagogical theories coded into a tool or application often cannot be differentiated from the tools (Boettcher, 2003), they likely have a significant influence on the subsequent use of the tool. As our understanding of learning and teaching processes continues to evolve, so must the design of CMS.

Emerging Conceptions of Teaching and Learning in Higher Education

The research university model, in which faculty create knowledge and deliver it to students via lecture, has become outdated and is based upon old assumptions about teaching and learning (Twigg, 1994). We are now witnessing a shift from teacher-centered to more student-centered approaches, and this is playing out in CMS usage as well. This change is the result of the combination of a number of factors, including our changing definition of *what* students should learn, *how* people learn, and the role of technology in education (Twigg, 1994).

Our ideas about *what* students need to learn, and what it means to learn, have evolved over time. According to Twigg (1994), higher education has traditionally been viewed as the mastery of a body of knowledge, but the information and knowledge explosion has sparked a reconsideration of this perspective. There has now been a move towards helping students acquire skills such as critical thinking, effective communication, and the ability to find information (Twigg, 1994).

In addition to changing conceptions of what students should learn, research in psychology and educational psychology on *how* people learn has been a driving force behind the changing conceptions and teaching practices in higher education. The importance of context for understanding, experience for learning, and the construction of knowledge have all been derived from psychological research and form the basis of student-centered learning environments (Hannafin & Land, 1997).

The explosion in information technology has also been a catalyst for change in the vision of teaching and learning in higher education over the past decade. Although for years there have been promises of technology revolutionizing education at all levels, it was not until information technology became more affordable and usable by the average consumer that the possibilities of offering instruction to anyone, anytime, and anywhere began to be explored (Twigg, 1994). Technology such as the Internet, where professors and researchers were among the first primary audience (Hafner & Lyon, 1996), has allowed educators to think about new ways to respond to changing ideas about *when, where,* and *how* students learn. With the creation of the World Wide Web and the mass propagation of Web browsers and Internet access, the capacity to use Internet technologies for teaching was opened up to the larger population of faculty who were not among the early adopters. Finally, the development of numerous CMS (e.g., WebCT™, BlackBoard™, Desire2Learn™, Angel™) represented an easy and efficient way for instructors to explore the possibilities of technology for revolutionizing instruction.

Despite the pedagogical concerns about current CMS, there are instructors who are using CMS in innovative and creative ways to foster deep learning for their students. Current CMS contain discussion boards and other communication tools that can require complex, contextual learning (Boettcher, 2003), and some, but not all, instructors are taking advantage of these features. Although CMS have come a long way in a short span of time, there is always room for improvement. With evolving views on teaching and learning, CMS need to evolve to reflect current understandings of appropriate pedagogical approaches.

CMS for Creating Deep Learning Environments: Research Implications, Design, and Use

Although the number of options has increased, we are still only at the beginning. For the most part, the tools that exist [in current CMS] are designed to support the generic activities of teaching with technology (i.e., quizzing). Among technologies missing are tools that support the varied subjects and teaching styles that comprise the full constellation of instruction that exists (Pittinsky, 2003, p. 206).

To take steps toward the holodeck, course management systems will need to become more robust and flexible and to enable, in customizable form, students and faculty to choose among pedagogies embedded in their structure (Katz, 2003, p. 56).

When we consider the implications of the design decisions made in current CMS and the interplay these design decisions have with instructors' conceptions of teaching, we are presented with at least two possible scenarios.

Firstly, CMS may be perpetuating the myth that information dissemination is the only appropriate method for teaching. Consequently, for instructors who hold a teacher-centered orientation to teaching, and thus prefer to take a content-centered approach to their instruction, CMS reinforce their notions of teaching by providing sufficient support for their pedagogical goals. Providing information to students and delivering content in an organized and understandable manner are easy tasks to accomplish using CMS. For instructors who embrace imparting information and transmitting structured knowledge conceptions of teaching, the tools available in many CMS support their notion that good teaching can be characterized as doing just that. The lack of more student-centered tools provides no incentive for instructors to explore alternative approaches to teaching or to engage their students any further than as recipients of content.

Secondly, for instructors who hold conceptions of teaching that are not in line with the information dissemination approach, CMS may not be helpful in facilitating their teaching and, subsequently, student learning. CMS can be difficult to use for instructors whose visions of teaching are not in tune with those underlying pedagogical assumptions found in CMS (Kuriloff, 2001). Indeed, higher education instructors report that a major obstacle to their use of CMS is its inflexibility and overly structured nature (Morgan, 2003). Although instructors who hold more student-centered conceptions of teaching may still use a CMS, they may be forced to seek out external tools to support their learning goals, greatly increasing the time and energy they devote to their course.

Course management systems need to become more flexible, being able to provide structure for those who need it, but also providing instructors with the freedom (and support) to use a variety of pedagogical approaches. Future CMS should provide tools that support and encourage teaching and learning away from "imparting information" and toward facilitating students' "conceptual change."

How can this be done, and what types of tools should be integrated into the CMS of the future? A greater emphasis on student-centered tools would transform current CMS into technological tools that are not only effective for managing a course, but also for the creation of deep learning environments. Current CMS have already made nods towards including such tools as discussion boards and chat tools. Instructors can use these communication tools to create activities that support the deeper learning principles of social, active, engaged, student-centered learning. Future CMS should include more tools that support the types of student engagement that can be created using the communication tools provided in current CMS. Among the features and capabilities suggested by other authors (see Carmean & Haefner, 2003; Boettcher, 2003), future CMS should include tools that support what Oliver (2001) calls Web-engaged activity. Web-engaged activities are activities that are tailored based on learning goals and require instructors to provide students with supports and tools to actively engage with course content.

For example, if a learning goal was to collaboratively create a class resource or learning object, tools such as Web annotation software or Swikis might be used. Web annotation software, such as the Annotation Engine (*http://cyber.law.harvard.edu/projects/annotate.html*), can be used by students to annotate online documents, posing questions or comments directly tied to the document. Peers or the instructor can then respond to these questions or comments, creating an annotated document that the whole class can review and share. Swikis perform functions similar to Web annotation software, except they provide the added capability of allowing users to modify a document (e.g., *http://coweb.cc.gatech.edu/csl/9*). Thus, students working collaboratively on a report can edit and refine the same document online, while preserving older versions of the document in case they need to go back. While these tools are available as stand-alone software, currently instructors who wish to make use of these tools as well as a CMS are required to manage and monitor student learning in two different learning environments. By including student-oriented processing tools such as Swikis or Web annotation software directly within a CMS, instructors can easily monitor and guide student learning. Additionally, including such student processing tools directly within CMS provides additional support, exposure, and opportunities for adopting new instructional approaches.

Conclusion

As the use of CMS becomes ubiquitous in higher education environments, it is imperative that we consider their impact and influence on teaching and learning. The move to modify existing teaching practices in higher education by moving towards more student-centered learning models is a worthwhile goal; however, as has been argued in this chapter, creation of deep learning environments using CMS is unlikely to be successful without understanding the interplay between instructors' teaching conceptions and the design and use of CMS. As we move towards more student-centered models of teaching and learning, we must begin to reconsider the design of future CMS to include more tools to facilitate student learning. Not only will the redesign of CMS support instructors who are seeking tools to create deep-learning environments, but it may also encourage information and content-centered instructors to consider alternative teaching approaches. Without these changes, CMS may be doomed to remain merely a content-delivery tool.

References

Boettcher, J.V. (2003). Course management systems and learning principles: Getting to know each other. *Syllabus*, July. Retrieved Jul. 10, 2004, from *http://www.syllabus.com/article.asp?id=7888*

Brown, G. (2000). Where do we go from here? *The Technology Source*. January/February. Retrieved June 19, 2004, from *http://horizon.unc.edu/ TS/default.asp?show=article&id=667*

Carmean, C., & Haefner, J. (2002). Mind over matter: Transforming course management systems into effective learning environments. *Educause Review, 37*(6), 27-34.

Carmean, C. & Haefner, J. (2003). Next-generation course management systems. *Educause Quarterly, 26*(1), 10-13. Available online: *http:// www.educause.edu/ir/library/pdf/eqm0311.pdf*

Cohn, E. R. & Stoehr, G.P. (2003). Multidisciplinary applications of CourseInfo course management software to motivate students in traditional course settings. *Interactive Multimedia Electronic Journal of Computer-Enhanced Learning, 2*(1). Retrieved July 10, 2004, from *http:// imej.wfu.edu/articles/2000/1/index.asp*

Ehrman, S.C. & Gilbert, S.W. (2003). Better off with or without your CMS? 5 kinds of assessment that can really help. *Syllabus*. Retrieved July 10, 2004, from *http://www.syllabus.com/article.asp?id=7889*

Hafner, K. & Lyon, M. (1996). *Where wizards stay up late: The origins of the Internet*. New York: Simon & Schuster.

Hannafin, M.J., & Land, S.M. (1997). The foundations and assumptions of technology-enhanced student-centered learning environments. *Instructional Science, 25*, 167-202.

Howard, B.C., McGee, S., Schwartz, N., & Purcell, S. (2000). The experience of constructivism: Transforming teacher epistemology. *Journal of Research on Computing in Education, 32*, 455-465.

Katz, R.N. (2003). Balancing technology and tradition: The example of course management systems. *Educause Review, 38*(4), 48-59.

Kember, D. (1997). A reconceptualisation of the research into university academics' conceptions of teaching. *Learning and Instruction, 7*, 255-275.

Kember, D. & Kwan, K. (2002). Lecturers' approaches to teaching and their relationship to conceptions of good teaching. In N. Hativa & P. Goodyear, (Eds.). *Teacher thinking, beliefs and knowledge in higher education* (pp. 219-239). Boston: Kluwer Academic Publishers.

Kuriloff, P.C. (2001). One size will not fit all. *The Technology Source,* July/ August. Retrieved June 19, 2004, from *http://ts.mivu.org/default .asp?show=article&id=899*

McCray, G. (2000). An introduction to special section. *Interactive Multimedia Electronic Journal of Computer-Enhanced Learning, 2*(1). Retrieved July 10, 2004, from *http://imej.wfu.edu/articles/2000/1/intro01/index.asp*

Morgan, G. (2003). *Faculty use of course management systems.* Boulder, CO: ECAR Research Publication.

Oliver, K. (2001). Recommendations for student tools in online course management systems. *Journal of Computing in Higher Education, 13,* 47-70.

Pittinsky, M.S., (Ed.). (2003). *The wired tower: Perspectives on the impact of the Internet on higher education.* Upper Saddle River, NJ: Prentice Hall.

Pratt, D.D. (1992). Conceptions of teaching. *Adult Education Quarterly, 42*(4), 203-220.

Samuelowicz, K. & Bain, J.D. (2001). Revisiting academics' beliefs about teaching and learning. *Higher Education, 41,* 299-325.

Twigg, C.A. (1994). The need for a national learning infrastructure. *Educom Review, 29*(4, 5, 6). Retrieved June 19, 2004, from *http://www.educause.edu/ir/library/html/nli0001.html*

Chapter V

Frameworks for CMS Design and Evaluation

Marwin Britto, Central Washington University, USA

Abstract

In recent years, institutions of higher education have been migrating to the Web for instruction in record numbers. While Web-based course management systems (CMS) offer many exciting possibilities for instructors and students, their efficacy in terms of teaching and learning has not been thoroughly evaluated. This chapter explores the inherent capabilities and limitations of five models of conceptual frameworks for the design of CMS. The chapter concludes with a discussion of CMS evaluation instruments, advice for instructors transitioning to CMS, and a call for more research in this growing area.

Introduction

The next big killer application for the Internet is going to be education. Education over the Internet is going to be so big it is going to make e-mail usage look like a rounding error (John Chambers, reported by Friedman, 1999, p. A25).

John Chambers, the chief executive officer of Cisco Systems, made this prophetic statement six years ago. Although his prediction has not yet come to be in any sector of education, there has certainly been movement in this direction in higher education. The use of the Internet to deliver instruction at all levels of education has increased steadily from the beginnings of the Web but has recently exploded partly due to the advent and proliferation of CMS in the last few years.

Part of the popularity of CMS is due to the simplicity with which instructors can create and deliver digital content online, administer tests online, manage student data, engage students in interactive activities, and provide opportunities for students to participate in meaningful asynchronous and real-time conversations without needing knowledge of programming or Web development skills.

Over the years, a number of frameworks have emerged to guide the design of CMS. A few models have been borrowed from other fields, others have new roots, and there may be others still that have value and potential in consideration for CMS design. The fourth wave of CMS (Boettcher, 2003) spurred by the formation of the Open Knowledge Initiative (OKI) boasts even more design standards and flexibility, and future generations of CMS hold even greater design promises as described in other chapters in this book.

The combination of escalating costs and increasing use of CMS has renewed interest in examining the return on investments (ROI) issue as university administrators search for solid evidence to justify and support their decisions to invest so heavily in CMS. These significant instructional costs have helped focus attention on the important question: *How effective are CMS in impacting teaching and learning?* In turn, these costs have also sparked some research in the development of CMS evaluation instruments.

One of the reasons for a paucity of research in CMS evaluation instruments may be the absence of robust theory and rigorous research in Web-based instruction (WBI) and the resulting lack of appropriate WBI models on which to base these instruments. As a result, educators and researchers have turned to other sources, borrowing and adapting existing research and models for use in this context. This chapter explores conceptual frameworks for the design and evaluation of CMS. In addition, it provides examples of how these frameworks can be used to support instructional activities in course management systems. It is important to note that the CMS tools that are listed in this chapter as supporting components of each model are not meant to represent an exclusive list, nor do they necessarily support model components as is suggested. Ultimately, the manner and strategy in which each of the CMS tools are employed will determine how effectively they will support and facilitate various components of each model.

Interactive Learning Dimensions Model

To help guide research in the design and evaluation of WBI in CMS, a more comprehensive and richer understanding of Web-supported interactive learning dimensions is needed. To address this need, Reeves and Reeves (1997) proposed a model that describes ten pedagogical dimensions that the Web can support (Figure 1). The authors have grounded and couched the dimensions in

Figure 1. A model of WWW interactive learning dimensions (Reeves & Reeves, 1997)

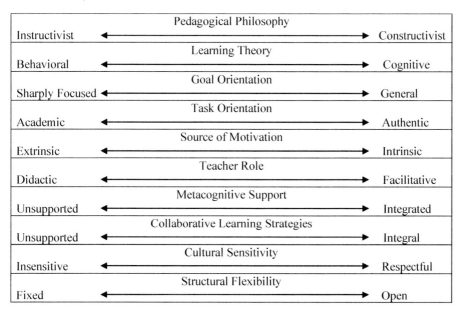

research, theory, and literature from the domains of adult learning, cognitive science, and instructional technology. In addition, the authors provide examples of the dimensions with respect to WBI.

In this model, each dimension is represented on a two-ended continuum, with contrasting values at either end. Although Reeves and Reeves (1997) acknowledge that the set of pedagogical dimensions in this model is not exhaustive, they suggest their model can serve as the foundation for constructing an instrument that can be employed in studies of the effectiveness and impact of WBI. Ultimately, the effectiveness of WBI in CMS is a function of the degree to which it supports appropriate pedagogical dimensions since these dimensions — rather than the technological aspects of the Web — influence learning most directly (Clark, 1994; Reeves & Reeves, 1997; Reeves, 2000).

The Interactive Learning Dimensions Model Supported in CMS

According to Reeves and Reeves (1997), the location of a learning environment on any individual dimension is not as important as the overall profile of the environment across all ten dimensions (Figure 2). The latter is intended to represent the overall pedagogical or instructional design and can be used for course comparison purposes.

The specific application of CMS tools determines at what points on the continuum each learning dimension is addressed. It proves challenging to map specific CMS tools to various dimensions due in part to the nature of the learning dimensions and the flexible nature of the tools capable of being adapted and utilized in a variety of ways, often even in opposite ways (i.e., supporting opposite ends of a learning dimension continuum). The choice of tools used in a CMS also directly addresses which learning dimensions can be supported and facilitated. Figure 2 provides an example of two courses using this model. The numbers 1 through 5 are provided as reference points along each learning dimension continuum. In this example, the CMS tools in Course A support a mix of instructivist and constructivist perspectives in contrast to CMS tools in Course B, which are employed strictly in a constructivist design fashion. The choice and the implementation of tools in each course can radically impact the pedagogical and instructional design of courses. The use of this model also has implications in evaluation, although to date no such reliable or validated evaluation instrument based on this model exists.

Figure 2. Comparing two courses using the interactive learning dimensions model

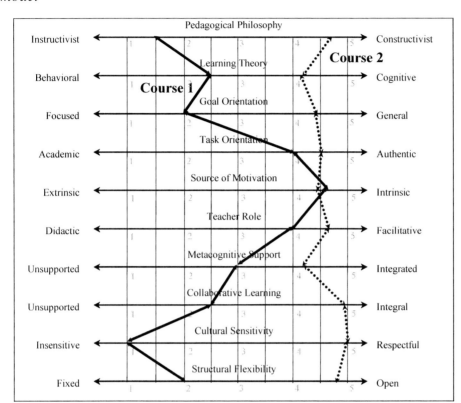

Good Teaching Principles Model

Another useful framework in this area is Chickering and Gamson's (1987) "Seven principles for good practice in undergraduate education," which is based on their review of 50 years of research on teaching and learning in higher education. Their work has been applied to the online environment both as a framework for evaluative research and for design of WBI in CMS. These seven principles are those teaching practices that 1) encourage student-faculty contact, 2) encourage cooperation among students, 3) encourage active learning, 4) give prompt feedback, 5) emphasize time on task, 6) communicate high expectations, and 7) respect diverse talents and ways of learning.

Nine years later Chickering and Ehrmann (1996), recognizing the potential for the newer technologies to support these principles, published an article describing how technologies can be leveraged to advance these seven principles. WebCT™, Inc. adopted Chickering and Gamson's seven principles as the framework for training clients on its CMS and as part of the curriculum for some of its workshops designed to teach faculty and support personnel about effective WebCT™ use. WebCT™ provides a table of CMS tools (*www.webct.com/WYW/ViewContent?contentID=2627458*) and describes how each of them could be used to support these various principles.

Graham, Cagiltay, Lim, Craner, and Duffy (2001) used Chickering and Gamson's seven principles as a framework to evaluate four online courses at a large Midwestern university. Their analysis was focused on online course materials, student and instructor discussion forum postings, and faculty interviews. The evaluators found examples of each of the seven principles in the four courses. Based on their observations and analysis of the particular principle in each course, the evaluators offered "lessons learned" and recommendations on how each principle could be best supported in an online environment. Though qualitative in nature, the four case studies provided useful insights into the evaluation team and for others exploring this model.

The Good Teaching Principles Model Supported in CMS

WebCT™ provides a table of examples of how CMS tools can be used to support these seven principles and lists the principles the various tools can

Figure 3. The discussions tool and the good teaching principles model

WebCT Tool	How the Tool Is Being Used	Good Teaching Principles the Tool Facilitates
Discussions	"I have an attendance forum where the online students are required to post a brief 'attendance' message each week. I have a public forum for each major topic we cover in the course and I require the students to post a certain number of messages and/or replies to these forums. For example, I might have a forum called 'Societal Issues and the Internet' where students can post their thoughts on legal and ethical issues, or post information about articles they have read that are related to the topic."	1. Faculty-student interaction 2. Student-student interaction 3. Rich, rapid feedback 4. Active learning 5. Respect for diverse learning

support (see *www.webct.com/WYW/ViewContent?contentID=2627458*). Figure 3 shows an example of one tool, the discussions tool, as an example of tool use and the good teaching principle it supports.

This "mapping" of CMS tools to specific principles provides a useful resource for faculty when designing instruction. By first deciding on the principles they wish to support in their CMS course, and then choosing appropriate CMS tools (that support these principles) to facilitate the relevant instructional activities and implementing them appropriately, faculty can utilize this table as a practical guide in the instructional design of their courses.

Learner Pedagogical Dimensions Model

Bonk and Cummings (1998) used the 14 learner-centered principles (LCPs) from the American Psychological Association, or APA (1997), as a framework to design and implement their Web-based undergraduate educational psychology course. Wagner and McCombs (1995) devised these 14 principles in an attempt to identify and describe what they called "learner-centered educational practice." According to the APA, the principles are "consistent with more than a century of research on teaching and learning…and…integrate research and practice in various areas of psychology, including developmental, educational, experimental, social, clinical, organizational, community and school psychology" (1997, p.1). These 14 principles are:

Cognitive and metacognitive factors:

1. Nature of the learning process.
2. Goals of the learning process.
3. Construction of knowledge.
4. Strategic thinking.
5. Thinking about thinking.
6. Context of learning.

Motivational and affective factors:

7.   Motivational and emotional influences on learning.
8.   Intrinsic motivation to learn.
9.   Effects of motivation on effort.

Developmental and social factors:

10.   Developmental influences on learning.
11.   Social influences on learning.

Individual differences factors:

12.   Individual differences in learning.
13.   Learning and diversity.
14.   Standards and assessment.

Based on their experiences teaching this Web course, as well as feedback from student formative and summative evaluations, Bonk and Cummings adapted the 14 principles and proposed 12 pedagogical recommendations. These recommendations connect WBI to the 14 LCPs and are designed to "foster student thinking skills, problem solving abilities, teamwork and social interaction and debate" within an online environment (1998, p. 82). These 12 learner-centered pedagogical recommendations include:

1.   Establish a safe environment and a sense of community.
2.   Exploit the potential of the medium for deeper student engagement.
3.   Let there be choice.
4.   Facilitate, don't dictate.
5.   Use public and private forums of feedback.
6.   Vary the forms of electronic mentoring and apprenticeship.
7.   Employ recursive assignments that build personal knowledge.

8.   Vary the forms of electronic writing, reflection, and other pedagogical activities.

9.   Use student Web explorations to enhance course content.

10.   Provide clear expectations and prompt task structuring.

11.   Embed thinking skill and portfolio assessment as an integral part of Web assignments.

12.   Look for ways to personalize the Web experience.

Bonk and Cummings provide explanations and examples of each of these recommendations in a Web-based environment.

The Learner Pedagogical Dimensions Model Supported in CMS

The tools in Figure 4, when implemented appropriately, have the potential of supporting the 12 pedagogical dimensions as described by Bonk and Cummings (1998). This is not meant to be an exhaustive list — other CMS tools may be useful to this end contingent on the instructional activity.

Figure 4. Learner pedagogical dimensions model and the supporting CMS tools

Pedagogical Recommendations	Supporting CMS Tools
Safe environment Sense of community	chat, discussions, e-mail, homepage
Deeper student engagement	assignments, audio, discussions, goals, links, video
Choice	assignments, audio, CD-ROM, discussions, glossary, goals, image database, index, links, references, video
Facilitation	discussions, e-mail, homepage, whiteboard
Public/private forums	chat, discussions, e-mail, homepage, presentations, whiteboard
Mentoring, apprenticeship	chat, discussions, e-mail
Recursive assignments	assignments, CD-ROM, discussions, links
Writing, reflection	annotations, assignments, chat, discussions, e-mail, homepage, presentations
Web explorations	discussions, homepage, links, search, whiteboard
Clear expectations Prompt tasks	assignments, discussions, glossary, goals, organize page, quiz
Portfolio assessment	assignments, discussions, CD-ROM, links
Personalization	annotations, assignments, compile, discussions, homepage, presentations, progress, resume

Qualities of Meaningful Learning Models

Jonassen (1995) identified and described seven characteristics or qualities of meaningful learning. Jonassen saw technology as a means to support these qualities through various activities that would engage the learners in meaningful conversation. He described these qualities as "interrelated, interactive, and interdependent" (p.61) and used the model in Figure 5 to convey these relationships. Figure 6 presents this same information in table format.

LeJeune and Richardson (1998) view good instruction as being grounded in educational theory regardless of the context, content, or technology used to deliver the instruction. They assert that effective WBI must be couched in traditional learning theories. Their model for WBI is based on Jonasson's seven qualities, which they refer to as learning strategies. Lejeune and Richardson describe each learning strategy's origins in theory and research, tying them each to complementary learning theories. In addition, the authors extend these strategies to the Web, employing research on Web-based instruction to discuss effective implementation. Their article offers a practical tool for those looking to adapt Jonassen's model for WBI.

Figure 5. Seven qualities of meaningful learning (Jonassen, 1995)

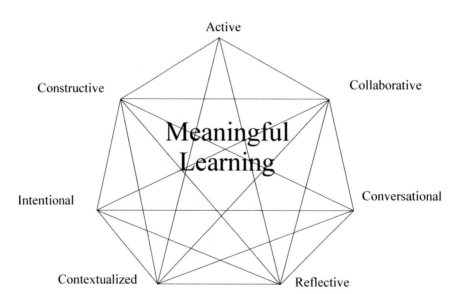

Figure 6. Description of the seven qualities of meaningful learning (Jonassen, 1995)

Qualities or Key Learning Strategies	Description
Active	Learners are engaged by the learning process in mindful processing of information, where they are responsible for the result.
Constructive	Learners accommodate new ideas into prior knowledge in order to make sense or make meaning or reconcile a discrepancy, curiosity, or puzzlement.
Collaborative	Learners work in learning and knowledge building communities, exploring each other's skills while providing a social support and modeling and observing the contribution of each member.
Intentional	Learners are actively and willfully trying to achieve a cognitive objective.
Conversational	Learning is inherently a social, dialogical process in which learners benefit most from being part of knowledge building communities both in class and outside school.
Contextualized	Learning tasks are situated in some meaningful real-world task, or are simulated through some case-based or problem-based learning environment.
Reflective	Learners articulate what they have learned and reflect on the process and decisions that were entailed by the process.

The Qualities of the Meaningful Learning Model Supported in CMS

Although there are multiple ways of supporting this model with a CMS (as with any of the other models in this chapter), the most practical approach is to provide a mapping of specific tools to model components. Figure 7 lists a

Figure 7. Six conceptual frameworks model and the supporting CMS tools

Qualities or Key Learning Strategies	Supporting CMS Tools
Active	discussions, index, mail, organize page, presentations, references, search, whiteboard
Constructive	audio, CD-ROM, image database, links, presentations, search, video
Collaborative	discussion, chat, e-mail, homepage, image database, presentations, whiteboard
Intentional	annotations, assignments, compile, goals, homepage, self-test
Contextualized	audio, CD-ROM, glossary, image database, presentations, video
Reflective	annotations, assignments, chat, compile, glossary, homepage, index, references, self-test
Conversational	discussion, chat, e-mail, homepage, image database, presentations, whiteboard

number of the tools that, when implemented effectively, can be used to support the seven qualities or key learning strategies in this meaningful learning model.

The Web-Based Course Design Model

Campbell (n.d.) offers six conceptual frameworks for the design of Web-based instructional environments (Figure 8). The frameworks are based on a constructivist perspective and employ a variety of cognitive instructional

Figure 8. Six conceptual frameworks for WBI

Framework	Key Elements	Use When...
Multiple Representations of Reality	• Learner experiences reality from another perspective • Reflective component requiring reconstruction of experience • Learner's values and experiences are legitimated	• Goal is development of different perspectives • There is an element of curiosity • Content is too complex • A reflective component is important
Authentic Tasks	• Anchored instruction • Real contexts and tasks	• Task can be related to the real world of practice • Content domains are affective or psychomotor • Cognitive apprenticeship is sought
Real-World, Case-Based Contexts	• Cognitive apprenticeship • Lateral thinking • Story-based	• Instruction is based on simulating real practice (e.g., flight simulators) • Rich repository of expert stories available • Coach or facilitator is accessible
Fostering Reflective Practices	• Access to experts/facilitators • Questioning own practice	• The process is important • Learners would benefit from conversation with others • Instruction is effectively based • Learners have access to a facilitator
Knowledge Construction	• Situated learning • Social interaction	• Learners are to arrive at a new point of view • Problem-solving is a goal • Personal knowledge base includes incidental • Knowledge on which to build already exists • There are opportunities for dialogue in groups
Collaborative Learning	• Negotiation through conversation • Interdependency, accountability to peers	• Learners will work in small groups • A product is to be created • Teaching social or communicative skills • Content is complex

strategies/learning theories. The author describes appropriate applications of the framework and provides URLs of real examples of Web-designed instruction based on these frameworks.

The Web-Based Course Design Model Supported in CMS

Figure 9 lists the six frameworks in this model, the media elements for each framework, and the various CMS tools that can be used to support them.

Transitioning from the Traditional Mode to WBI in CMS

Regardless of the model adopted, faculty generally proceed through "stages of development" from a traditional environment to the Web. This transition may be unconscious and undeliberate. Studies have indicated that the CMS tools and the CMS environment may be directly responsible in facilitating this transitionary process.

Dabbagh and Schmitt (1998) examined the pedagogical implications of redesigning instruction for Web-based delivery through a case study of an undergraduate computer science course originally designed for a traditional learning environment but later transformed to a Web-based course. Dabbagh and Schmitt concluded that the components and tools of their CMS and the attributes of the Web-based environment and tools encouraged and afforded instructional events and activities that were not possible or perceived in a traditional mode. They use three terms to describe these instructional activities: "generative development" through the posting of drafts and focused discussions, "facilitation" evidenced through asynchronous tools such as e-mail and threaded electronic discussion boards, and "inside collaboration" demonstrated through online group work supported through a variety of tools. The authors reported that the use of their CMS enabled learning strategies and instructional methods that transformed the course from an instructivist orientation to a constructivist one.

Collis (1997) refers to this transformative process as "pedagogical re-engineering." Collis recommends a "pedagogical re-engineering" approach to WBI

Figure 9. Six conceptual frameworks and the supporting CMS tools

Framework	Media Elements	Supporting CMS Tools
Multiple Representations of Reality	• Flat text • Video and audio to bring the context closer to reality • Virtual reality environments	audio, CD-ROM, image database, presentations, video
Authentic Tasks	• Interactive multimedia • Computer-based simulations and modeling • "Canned" expert lectures or advice • Conferencing	audio, CD-ROM, glossary, image database, presentations, video
Real-World, Case-Based Contexts	• Text-based or multimedia • Advice "canned" and always available, or available synchronously through chat rooms or conferencing systems or available asynchronously through CMC	audio, CD-ROM, chat, image database, presentations, video
Fostering Reflective Practices	• Note-taking facility • Creation of study guides (wizards, etc.) • Expert narrative available • Conferencing • Shared work documents • MOOs, MUDs	annotations, assignments, chat, compile, glossary, homepage, index, references, self-test
Knowledge Construction	• Real contexts in which learning takes place • Simulated work places • Video and graphical images that respond to manipulation • Optional audio • Learners must "act on" the environment (building something, starting a system, etc.) • Ways to create new products	annotations, audio, CD-ROM, chat, Homepage, image database, presentations, video
Collaborative Learning	• Tools for shared communication • Tools for collaborative work (shared screens, etc.) • Resource base (or database) of information, elements, etc.	discussion, chat, e-mail, homepage, image database, presentations, whiteboard

that capitalizes on the unique affordances of the Web to change the profile of learning activities and provide new learning opportunities focused on a more collaborative and learner-centered perspective.

Freeman and Abeygunawardena (2002) also provide evidence of this type of transformation with the transition to CMS. Their study examined how a CMS was used by instructors as a supplement to classroom instruction. Their goal was to evaluate whether the availability of Web-based tools influenced instructors' pedagogical practices in undergraduate education. The study involved 15 instructors in 19 courses with 828 undergraduate students participating. The authors employed a mixed methodology using semi-structured interviews and surveys with faculty and anonymous surveys with students. Faculty interviews revealed that:

> *Their decision to use WebCT™ and the subsequent choices they made in how to use the tools was guided not by pedagogical need but by the perception of possible gains in administrative efficiency...instructors did not intentionally adapt their pedagogical choices to the opportunities afforded by Web-based instructional tools* (p. 8).

Student responses to open-ended questions and anecdotal conversations with faculty suggested that the addition of Web-based tools was causing changes in the learning environment; instructors were discovering new ways of distributing teaching time and students in these courses were taking more responsibility for their learning.

In a similarly purposed study involving interviews, logs, and surveys of more than 730 faculty and instructional staff throughout the University of Wisconsin system using course management systems for teaching, Morgan (2003) found evidence to support that faculty often unintentionally do rethink their course instruction and their instructional context, resulting in an "accidental pedagogy." Similar studies have found that although many faculty initially choose to use CMS for reasons other than pedagogy (convenience, administrative advantages, better course organization, etc.), with continued use, some faculty change their methods of teaching and online pedagogy as a direct result of their experience in CMS (Britto, 2002; Freeman & Abeygunawardena, 2002; Morgan, 2003).

Summary of Models

Five models have been presented in this chapter for design and evaluation considerations. It is clear the sophistication and flexibility of CMS afford a myriad of instructional and learning possibilities. Research is emerging that indicates that the World Wide Web is technically capable of supporting virtually any instructional strategy and is well-suited to being utilized as a powerful cognitive tool in a variety of learning activities (Lajoie, 2000). Mounting evidence also shows that the unique attributes of the Web offer unparalleled instructional advantages and opportunities (Aggarwal, 2000). However, shaping and designing CMS to support appropriate instructional methods and strategies is often a complex task. There are no guidelines, cookbooks, or shortcuts to quickly or easily create the appropriate learning environment. The instructor needs to fully understand the inherent capabilities and limitations of CMS in order to effectively design instruction in these systems. Many contend that CMS, like other instructional tools, can be employed effectively or poorly in instruction. The power lies in instructors using CMS to create effective lessons in stimulating learning environments. As Owston states, "the key to promoting improved learning with the Web appears to lie in how effectively the medium is exploited in the teaching and learning situation" (1997, p. 29). Of course, an instructor needs to understand how to design a good learning environment in any context. Sadly, regardless of the design options available, there is evidence to suggest that faculty new to CMS do not carefully or deliberately plan or design their courses differently online — they simply attempt to replicate their traditional classroom and choose tools that align with their traditional instructional strategies (Britto, 2002; Morgan, 2003). As Bonk and Cummings put it, "perhaps the greatest challenge of the Web is to create learning activities that take advantage of the characteristics and assets of the medium, rather than duplicating activities that typify conventional classrooms" (1998, p. 84).

CMS Evaluation Instruments

In 1995, Nichols (as reported in Henke, 1997) predicted that "the potential benefit from formulating evaluation methodologies for the Web [for instructional materials] depends on whether or not the Web will become a permanent medium or a passing fad" (p. 1). A passing fad, it is not — no one would argue that use of the Web and CMS is not firmly entrenched and growing in the instructional corridors of higher education. Unfortunately, as Izat, McKinzie, Mize and McCallie (2000) conclude, there is a "dearth of research studies published that offer validated evaluation survey instruments specifically written for World Wide Web–delivered courseware" (p.2).

A literature review in 2004 demonstrated that this trend has continued with rare exceptions. Education journals and publications are replete with studies involving the use of CMS in instruction. Sadly, many of these studies tend to be non-research-oriented focusing more on practical experiences. Most of the studies that focus on the development of new CMS evaluation instruments appear to lack the rigor of appropriate design and research to give any credibility or usefulness to their instruments, making their results and findings highly suspect. Better and more rigorous research in CMS studies is urgently needed.

Scholars have described how CMS have been and can be harnessed to support a variety of pedagogical philosophies and teaching and learning styles, how to design instruction appropriately and effectively in these environments, and how CMS can be integrated into instruction in a number of ways and at a number of levels using a variety of instructional methods and strategies. However, it is still not clear how each choice and the combination of these choices impacts student learning and how these results can be evaluated. Clearly, more evaluative research of CMS is warranted. Unfortunately, evaluation models of CMS are in great demand but in short supply.

Conclusion

Despite enormous resources committed to CMS in higher education, there is a dearth of information concerning its effectiveness and impacts on how faculty members teach and what students learn. Educational institutions have invested and continue to invest heavily in CMS without a clear understanding of its influence on teaching and learning. As the use of CMS in higher education continues to grow at an incredible pace, it becomes imperative that institutions be able to evaluate their effectiveness. As more and more faculty members move into CMS, evaluation needs to be an integral component of the design and planning process.

Although there is a great deal of descriptive and anecdotal information concerning CMS in higher education, studies that provide reliable and valid information concerning faculty and student perceptions of CMS are relatively rare. One reason for this is the lack of robust, validated evaluation instruments for measuring the implementation of the pedagogical dimensions of CMS. To date, there appears to be a paucity of sound research examining the effectiveness of CMS, due in part to a lack of robust evaluation models and evaluation instruments in WBI that are necessary to aid in the design and development of effective WBI in CMS. Other factors include the relative newness of the field, the broad scope, the diversity and vagueness of WBI, and a lack of unified theoretical framework for WBI evaluation (Yu, n.d.).

As CMS continue to grow and flourish in higher education institutions, a concerted and coordinated effort must be made to nurture and cultivate ongoing research directed at exploring, testing, and eventually validating effective CMS evaluation instruments. Furthermore, the evaluation of teaching and learning in CMS must be approached from a multidisciplinary perspective because of the variety of appropriate methodological paradigms in a variety of disciplines that may be beneficial for this type of research (Spires & Estes, 2002). CMS have the potential to influence teaching and learning like no other technology. As CMS continue to improve and evolve, design and evaluation considerations must be a vital part of future developments for this potential to be realized.

References

Aggarwal, A. (Ed.). (2000). *Web-based learning and teaching technologies: Opportunities and challenges*. Hershey, PA: Idea Group Publishing.

American Psychological Association. (1997). Learner-centered psychological principles: A framework for school redesign and reform. Retrieved July 12, 2001, from *http://www.apa.org/ed/lcp.html*

Boettcher, J.V. (2003). Course management systems and learning principles: Getting to know each other. *Syllabus*. Retrieved November 25, 2003, from *http://www.syllabus.com/article.asp?id=7888*

Bonk, C.J. & Cummings, J.A. (1998). A dozen recommendations for placing the student at the center of Web-based learning. *Educational Media International, 35*(2), 82-89.

Britto, M. (2002). *An exploratory study in the development of a survey instrument to measure the pedagogical dimensions of Web-based instruction.* Unpublished doctoral dissertation. Athens, GA: University of Georgia.

Campbell, K. (n.d.). The Web: Design for active learning. University of Alberta. Retrieved on July 3, 2001, from *http://www.atl.ualberta.ca/articles/idesign/active1.cfm*

Chickering, A. W., & Ehrmann, S.C. (1996). Implementing the seven principles: Technology as lever. Retrieved June 12, 2001, from *http://www.aahe.org/Bulletin/SevenPrinciples.htm*

Chickering, A.W. & Gamson, Z.F. (1987). Seven principles for good practice in undergraduate education. *AAHE Bulletin, 39*(7), 3-7.

Clark, R.E. (1994). Media will never influence learning. *Educational Technology, Research and Development, 42*(2), 21-29.

Collis, B. (1997). Pedagogical reengineering: A pedagogical approach to enrichment and redesign with the World Wide Web. *Educational Technology Review, 8,* 11-15.

Dabbagh, N.H., & Schmitt, J. (1998). Redesigning instruction through Web-based course authoring tools. *Educational Media International, 35*(2), 106-110.

Freeman, W.E., & Abeygunawardena, H. (2002). Faculty and student reflections on using Web tools to support undergraduate classroom-based instruction across faculties. *Proceedings of the American Educational Research Association Conference 2002,* New Orleans, LA.

Friedman, T.L. (1999). Next, it's e-ducation. *The New York Times,* (pp. A25). November 17. Retrieved June 3, 2001, from *http://crab.rutgers.edu/~goertzel/e-education.htm*

Graham, C., Cagiltay, K., Lim, B., Craner, J., & Duffy, T. (2001). Seven principles of effective teaching: A practical lens for evaluating online courses. Retrieved June 18, 2001, from *http://horizon.unc.edu/TS/default.asp?show=article&id=839*

Green, K.C. (2000). The campus computing project. Retrieved June 01, 2001, from *http://www.campuscomputing.net/summaries/2000/index.html*

Henke, H. (1997). Evaluating Web-based instructional design. Retrieved on June 23, 2001, from *http://scis.nova.edu/~henkeh.story1.htm*

Izat, J.G., McKinzie, L., Mize, C.D., & McCallie, T. (2000). Evaluation of World Wide Web delivered university courseware: Creating an instrument appropriate for a new course delivery medium. *Proceedings of the Society for Information Technology & Teacher Education International Conference*, San Diego, FL.

Jonnasen, D.H. (1995). Supporting communities of learners with technology: A vision for integrating technology with learning in schools. *Educational Technology, 35*(4), 60-63.

Lajoie, S.P. (Ed.). (2000). *Computers as cognitive tools: No more walls* (Vol. 2). Mahwah, NJ: Lawrence Erlbaum Associates.

LeJeune, N., & Richardson, K. (1998). Learning theories applied to Web-based instruction. Retrieved February 19, 2001, from *http://ouray.cudenver.edu/~nflejeun/doctoralweb/Courses/EPSY6710_Learning_Theory/LearningTheories-WBI.htm*

Morgan, G. (2003). *Faculty use of course management systems.* Boulder, CO: ECAR Research Publication.

Owston, R.D. (1997). The World Wide Web: A technology to enhance teaching and learning? *Educational Researcher, 26*(2), 27-33.

Reeves, T.C. (2000). *Teaching and learning online: Opportunities and responsibilities.* Guest Speaker Series at *Pathways Colloquia,* University of Alberta, Edmonton, Alberta. Available online at *http://www.atl.ualberta.ca/pathways/reevesppt.ppt*

Reeves, T.C. & Reeves, P.M. (1997). Effective dimensions of interactive learning on the World Wide Web. In B.H. Khan (Ed.), *Web-based instruction* (pp. 59-66). Englewood Cliffs, NJ: Educational Technology Publications.

Spires, H.A. & Estes, T.H. (2002). Reading in Web-based learning environments. In C.C. Block & M. Pressley (Eds.). *Comprehension instruction: Research-based best practices* (pp.115-125). New York: Guilford Press.

Wagner, E.D. & McCombs, B.L. (1995). Learner-centered psychological principles in practice: Designs for distance education. *Educational Technology, 35*(2), 32-35.

Yu, A. (n.d.). An input-process-output structural framework for evaluating Web-based instruction. Retrieved July 25, 2002, from *http://seamonkey. ed.asu.edu/~alex/teaching/assessment/structure1.html*

Chapter VI

The CMS as Shapeshifter, Catalyst, and Engaging Learning Tool

Cyprien Lomas, The University of British Columbia, Vancouver, Canada

Ulrich Rauch, The University of British Columbia, Vancouver, Canada

Abstract

Content management systems (CMS) have been purposed for different tasks on our campuses and are in danger of becoming all things to all people. In our discussion we re-evaluate those aspects of a CMS that appear to make the greatest impact on teaching and learning. While a CMS may do duty as a vessel for containing and interacting with content, we see its greatest appeal and persuasion in its availability to all learners and teachers and its potential to transform itself according to a user's need. By separately analyzing common uses and current applications of a CMS, we identify the tools and components of a CMS that offer the most promise in the future.

Introduction

Most of us have been raised believing that the impact of technology on our lives is paramount and that more often than not, technology has changed our own "everyday practices." We may all differ in welcoming social and political manifestations of a particular technology, but overall we tend to believe that a "proper" application of technology may bring benefit to our lives.

In this chapter we analyze how Course Management Systems (CMS) used as enterprise tools that ultimately support what academic institutions are all about — teaching, learning, and research. We revisit a CMS implementation at the University of British Columbia (UBC) and critically examine instructional strategies and pedagogies that have almost organically developed in their specific course environment enabled by the use of a CMS. We identify how at each stage of development, complementary principles of deeper learning are incorporated and absorbed into the teaching and learning environment of a CMS, moving from a model of content delivery and passive reception to a model of active engagement and autonomous, self-directed learning.

At UBC, the locally grown course management system, WebCT™, has acted as a catalyst to bring new learning technologies to the fore. With the use of new technologies, a set of new challenges has emerged: students, staff, and teachers engaged in the exploration of new media to interchange ideas and engage with the construction of knowledge. Content delivery in a traditional face-to-face and top-down approach was challenged by more interactive modes of knowledge acquisition. Technology, never neutral, played a big part in changing the delivery of "knowledge."[1] However, the manner in which a collective knowledge is managed and shared has become a challenge for all those engaged in the process. Learning is an interactive process. Inside a course management system, the autonomy and control of the learner, or client, to engage actively and intervene in the process of knowledge acquisition depends very much on the technical and administrative infrastructure provided by the CMS to access information.

The Beginning: All Needs Are Equal, or One Instance of WebCT™ for All

As the site where WebCT™ was developed, UBC has had a rich set of experiences with this first-generation course management system. These experiences reflect both the evolution of the Web course tool set and the accompanying shift in faculty and instructional support staff approaches as instructors and staff adapted these tools to fit the goal of teaching more effectively. Historically, the community has had to identify and overcome numerous problems in its support of WebCT™. Many of these challenges had a common starting point: all the learning technology (LT) activities shared the characteristic that they were organized centrally, treating the needs of the university community as if it was one homogenous body. Although these central initiatives did deliver guidance and support in matters of instruction and new media, and offered resources to all instructors, it was often the early adopters (Rogers, 1993), those faculty and staff that did not hesitate to spend countless hours battling promising but unreliable learning technologies and fending off skepticism from colleagues and students, who created the first openings and opportunities to put learning technologies to use.

Next Steps: Many Instances of WebCT™ Serving Many

With the push to advance CMS on campus, and with corresponding faculty buy-in, the expectations about what LTs could actually deliver increased, but the scalability of efforts to support these expectations became a serious challenge. Since expertise about using and deploying LTs was in the hands of just a few faculty and staff who were distributed across campus, and because of a cost recovery model in which technology support and academics were posited in a business relationship, the use of LT was an expensive proposition with pockets of LT-savvy technicians widely dispersed and somewhat unco-ordinated (Long, 2001).[2] In the absence of a consolidated central support, a multitude of WebCT™ servers came online operating in many locations across campus at the same time. Considering the lack of resources, it became unaffordable for many units to run their own reliable WebCT™ server.

Full Circle: One Instance of WebCT™ Serving a Diverse Clientele

With the introduction of a campus-wide login procedure, the advantages of a large central portal became even more apparent. Providing a single location for students, staff, and faculty to access their WebCT™ courseware would achieve greater efficiency and convenience. Additionally, the integration with campus-wide databases, like the Student Information System, could offer even more value to a decentralized but collaborative e-learning environment.

In a first step towards deploying a campus-wide CMS, WebCT™ in its next permutation served as a catalyst to consolidate certain core course delivery functions into a centralized but collaborative environment, while leaving integral administrative functions to separate and specialized applications.

A New Model: Aligning the Delivery of CMS Services with the Needs of Teachers and Learners

With an increase in complexity of learning tools, continuous innovation, and, as always, limited financial resources, the sharing of information and materials between and across information systems (IS) units or clients became inevitable and necessary. As a steady flow of inspiration, new ideas, and information continually redefined the instructional support landscape, practitioners in individual support units became part of an emerging campus-wide network. The convergence of learning technologies administered and connected via the CMS is paralleled by an emerging model of a self-organizing instructional support system in a decentralized environment.

Overall, the emergence of WebCT™ as an enterprise service demonstrates how a centrally maintained information technology (IT) infrastructure may interlock with a distributed IS model. Because WebCT™ requires articulated standards but also needs to be highly customizable and to function in a distributed environment, its use has not only instigated an awareness of the importance of standards and protocols, but has also pointed out the tension between a centrally administered learning resource and the need for a flexible, local service that supports the particular mandate of the client. Users of

WebCT™ require administrative powers to realize the particular learning configuration and administrative control they desire, yet the system was not designed to allow a multitude of designers to cooperate administratively or share resources across courses.

In the same vein, users of LT on campus demand access to local expertise, without losing the benefit of accessing the accumulated LT resources. These requirements demonstrate the problems inherent in providing a central service that combines the flexibility of creating and exchanging resources without losing the ability to offer a robust service that meets the needs of a variety of users with individualized teaching and learning needs across campus.

Communicative Aspects of a CMS Environment

One of the most important outcomes of using WebCT™ as a course tool is the resulting intracampus communication and the formation of a community. Communication between individual support units initially focused on managing the expectations of clients and methods to triage breakdowns in course delivery, but soon progressed to a discussion about common interests and standards.[3] It is the communicative aspect and that functionality in a CMS that promises unhindered communication between users and seamless connectivity between associated applications that we need to pay attention to in conceptualizing a new generation of CMS.

In the discussion on the new generation course management system (NGCMS), some proponents identify the CMS as a large monolith, possibly connected and even ingesting portals, repositories, and libraries. In this view, the CMS is the one and only enterprise-wide system. We cannot help but wonder if by its sheer gravity it may affect how learning and teaching are conducted on campus. Much has been written about the intersection of learning and the use of technology[4] and the propensity of monolithic course management systems to preempt or predetermine creative engagement of students in their learning. While the business community is undecided on the benefits of an enterprise resource planning (ERP) infrastructure (Worthen, 2003), within academe the creation of academic organisational structures or ERP systems is highly problematic as the cost to harmonize all operations increases (in real financial terms as well as in terms of effective learning and teaching), whereas the return decreases on two fronts: systems become inflexible and respond slowly to required change, and students and teachers are unwilling to accommodate what they perceive as an ill-fitting tool to conduct scholarly activity. Subjugating all online learning to one course tool, and pushing it into a "straightjacket" where the pedagogical fit has been defined by the *a priori* categories and tacit pedagogical assumptions embedded in a CMS, impoverishes and constrains the potential for learning in an online environment. In these terms, CMS-supported learning may easily become a prescribed endeavour, even though the learning environment may afford some flexibility in the ways in which it permits interaction between students or allows content to be presented. Certainly, the need for pluralism, dissent, and democracy in the physical classroom, so convincingly demanded by Freire (1989), also applies for the online environment mediated through a CMS.

Some Examples

CMS use at UBC has closely mirrored the growth and changes in the technical capabilities of the product, showing both incremental and evolutionary changes. In addition to increased technical capabilities of the CMS software resulting in innovative use, a corresponding increase in sophisticated users, including students, instructors, and instructional designers, occurred as well. The examples listed below document this change and identify those components of a CMS that proved most promising to embody pedagogical value. Many of these valuable attributes tend to be closely related to the social and interactive elements provided inside the CMS.

In a pattern that is broadly observed (Morgan, 2003), our instructors tend to start using the CMS in modest ways, often beginning by putting a syllabus online. This effort is then followed by adding supplementary materials, such as including an image library and a discussion board. As instructors gain confidence through positive interaction with the CMS, they often graduate to more creative use of the system. Discussion boards, quizzes, and, in science, media libraries are often found in the courses of facile instructors. Important here is the development of a support network for users of the CMS to augment lectures. Colleagues often support and challenge one another to experiment with CMS use, resulting in rapid adoption and implementation of newly developed and shared procedures.

Biology 112

Biology 112 is a large, first-year, cell biology class. Approximately 2,000 students take the course each year and are divided into sections of 200 students. The course teaches cell biology concepts using microorganisms and makes use of the wealth of images, animations, and simulations that are either freely available or licensed with the textbook. Instructors make these materials available to students both in the class through demonstrations and after class through the CMS. The CMS has become an integral part of the course and fulfills many teacher-to-student functions within the course.

CMS use in this course is primarily to augment regular lecture material. Recent additions have been to use the CMS to showcase increasingly customized content. This usage reflects a historical approach to the use of the CMS rather than any trepidation on the part of the instructors. The instructors maintain a high comfort level with technology. In terms of material, the course is one of the largest on the campus CMS. Countless images and richer media including digitized video and flash animations are stored behind the password protection of the WebCT™ course. Where possible, these materials are either used with the permission of the publishers or created by instructors. There is very little material that has been generated by students. The course is also used as a communication medium for instructors to share essential course information with students. Standard items such as the course outline, class timetable, current calendar events, and tutorial assignments are posted on the class site. For example, the course site was used as the primary means to communicate with students during a recent labor dispute, allowing students to stay informed about the status of the impending midterm.

Once comfortable with their CMS, instructors are happy to experiment with other educational technology. Recent in-class use of personal response systems (PRS) have stimulated the use of the CMS to allow students to register their devices through setting up quizzes. However, while a discussion board exists, its use is limited to "requests for help" types of posts, most of which remain unanswered. In a couple of special cases, teaching assistants (TAs) who manage their own tutorial sections use the WebCT™ discussion board to set up small, vibrant communities of students. In one or two cases, these pockets of students start to develop their community. Students form study groups and collaborate by asking and answering one another's questions and helping out with problems. In some cases, discussions evolve and include deeper philo-sophical concepts only indirectly related to the content.

This example illustrates the use of a CMS as an essential part of a class, but not as a shared resource. The site is maintained by the instructor (and one or two TAs), and for the most part, remains a site that is visited only in times of need (such as to determine when the midterm is) or for a very specific reason. Additionally, the course is used as a device to distribute course materials, perhaps bypassing more traditional and expensive pathways. As such, it resembles a repository of both copyright-cleared and uncleared material primarily generated by professionals (instructors or instructional designers).

Chemistry 121/123

Our next example demonstrates how the CMS is used to supplement and complement a very diverse and rich set of resources. Chemistry 121/123 was recently redesigned into a sophisticated, mixed-mode course with the help of a large internal grant. The course is the laboratory component of a general first-year chemistry class and has approximately 3,000 students per year.

Students supplement their lectures with hands-on practical experience in the laboratory. Concepts taught in the lectures are revisited along with appropriate scaffolding to allow their translation into methodologies useful in the laboratory. To accommodate the limited amount of student time spent in the lab, a guided inquiry approach is employed. Students are directed to take a scientific approach to problems including basic library research followed by experimental design. Execution of the design, collection of results, and interpretation follows. Emphasis is placed on interpretation and discussion of results rather than getting the right results.

The course uses Virtual Lab from Carnegie Mellon.[5] This environment makes use of elaborate Java-based simulations. In addition, students are taught scientific principles and their application within the lab through flash modules. The course has a traditional paper lab manual which is extensively supplemented by a glossary Web site, a calendar Web site, and additional resources in a standard Web site.

Given the extensive use of online materials and other media, the CMS component of this course is quite modest. The CMS is solely used to provide two features that were difficult to duplicate with other tools: a method for elaborate quizzing and electronic discussion. Students are given equations and asked to interpret results. In an effort to encourage individual work, the quizzes have been set up with variables to provide as many different possibilities and outcomes as there are students. Each student gets a question with different parameters (and answers). These quizzes mimic the lab exercises by testing students' ability to apply concepts to experimental data and are used to assess competency prior to entering the lab. Those students unable to satisfactorily manipulate the data are directed to supplemental resources.

In addition to the quizzing, the CMS is also used to provide a discussion area. The CMS is invaluable in its role as a quiz application, but as a discussion tool it serves only a small proportion of the class, which uses it to share cursory advice on what is expected in the lab. Disgruntled students occasionally use the discussion tool as a soapbox.

Biology 200: Early Days

Biology 200 is a second-year cell biology course. The material includes an introduction to cell biology looking at subcellular particles. The course itself has 1,200 students organized into five large sections taught by different instructors. The instructors have varying levels of technical savvy; one of the instructors is technically adept and is the driving force behind much of the content on the Web site. This instructor also supports his colleagues. Through several years of determined building of the course, it has become a rich set of cell biology resources. In early incarnations of the course, the instructor linked to a multitude of resources freely available on the Web. The resources presented in the course were of high quality and were plentiful. In addition to the large number of collected resources, the instructor ensured that his own notes were also available on the Web. Finally, the instructor promoted the use of the discussion board by offering participation marks for its use. The discussion board was well used by a percentage of the class. While well used, the content of the posts often consisted of requests for "the answer," which would often be supplied by the instructor. Interaction was limited to a one-way conversation.

Biology 200: Later Days

The Biology 200 course has been evolving for several years. The course has experienced both incremental and evolutionary growth. The change in the course has coincided with the change in the students' expectations and their confidence and creativity. While the number of resources has not been reduced, they have been prioritized to allow students to pick their best path through the material. Greater connections between the class notes and the supplementary materials permit students to get greater value from the demonstration materials.

Discussion board use has evolved as well. It has been transformed by the instructor's strategy of observing the discussion rather than directly answering queries. This transformation has resulted in students answering one another's questions. In addition to simply providing answers, students often post counter questions and examples. This is a great example of students taking ownership of the questions, and ultimately, the content of the course. While in the past the discussions centered around low-level topics such as requirements for the course or simple yes/no queries, the discussions observed in this class have been much more sophisticated and have included unanswerable questions relating to the limits of knowledge as well as topics as diverse as "Why do science?" and the ethics of doing experiments. Of course, the instructor does step in when a discussion really goes off course or an incorrect statement is not corrected by the class, but this class benefits from having the instructor help out only where necessary and disappearing where not needed.

Microbiology 421

Microbiology 421 is a fourth-year experimental lab course that uses WebCT™ to model a scientific discussion by creating a mini-conference. Students conceive, propose, research, design, and ultimately carry out experiments. Results are harvested and interpreted within work groups and the resulting data are shared with the rest of the class. The class serves as an academic community and proceeds to critique the reports of its members. After several iterations of rewriting and peer review, the collected works of the class are "published" to the class journal. This journal is printed and serves as a record for future students in the class.

The CMS was adapted to support the peer review process. Through innovative use of the image database tool, the instructor and students were able to submit their results and papers to the image database and share them. In this instance, the CMS serves as the glue between groups of students and the instructors. Student use the CMS to support the communities that have built up in the class. These communities mirror traditional scientific communities in that they support scientific discussion, peer review, and sharing of results. The novel approach lies in adapting the CMS to such an extent that it almost becomes invisible, defined by the creative use of the CMS tools that permit accessing shared resources and the development of a research community.

English 111: Nonfictional Prose

In developing English 111 into a blended course, great effort has been taken to allow students and instructors to use the CMS in the manner that best suits their needs. To this end, learning tools were designed from the ground up with constant input from the instructors and TAs.[6] The tools were to be completely transparent, unobtrusive, and designed to permit the instructor or the students to work and communicate in an online environment without being technical experts or knowledgeable of the CMS.

Besides the collaborative learning space created for students, with activities and tools designed to support close cooperation, a collaborative practice was embedded in its development and delivery. What was most important from the outset was the multiplicity of perspectives provided by a heterogeneous team, a fact that had considerable bearing on the architecture and design of the course. The Web pages were designed as to be easily modified by any member of the teaching group at any time.

The full mixed-mode team met regularly once a week for about two hours. It was important to set up short feedback loops between team members, and beyond electronic communication, the team established physical centers for course production and content creation in close proximity to each other.

In the process of designing and producing the course, academic members of the team became quite knowledgeable and skilful in assessing the utility of e-learning tools, such as animations, video, audio clips, and other user-friendly course management tools, while the technical staff gained a deeper understanding of the benefits of an interactive and collaborative course design. In short, the learning process began already with the course design and was not a one-sided process funneling existing knowledge into students' heads. The CMS was necessary but not sufficient by itself. It became the docking station for applications and participants, the centre of all learning activity, without determining or structuring the interactions in a hierarchical sense. It became a template that facilitated rich interaction, shaping itself according to the strategies of the learner.

A Change in Focus

The examples above show the role of the CMS in a variety of courses that have occurred over several years at UBC. In every case the CMS fulfils an essential component despite being used in a wide variety of roles. Throughout the examples, we find an evolution of the CMS tools, their interpretation and acceptance by instructors and students', and their eventual sense of ownership.

We charted the initial role of the CMS as a repository for class materials. We found that the repository may hold materials that are too difficult to distribute in another way, such as copyrighted materials. In general, we find that while a CMS may serve many roles, ranging from a repository to providing advanced capabilities such as record keeping and quizzing, it is not until it is used in a social and interactive manner that it begins to transcend "the sum of its parts." Only then does it become a resource owned and shared by the students and teachers, and only then does it begin to fully realize its potential to support student engagement and deep learning.

Where use of a CMS provided an authoritative approach to the discipline and the content and also allowed the students to take ownership of their own explorations within the discipline, instruction and learning was most effective. For example, in the early rendition of the Biology 200 course, the course site represented the authority of the instructor; this authority was emphasized through rapid answering of questions on the discussion board in a timely manner. In later revisions of the course, the instructor's conscious decision to minimize intervention resulted in greater student input and confidence of students to identify themselves as scientists. Difficult and often unanswerable questions were raised and debated in the discussion boards. In a manner mirroring work in a classroom, complex content was placed in the hands and heads of students.

A New Paradigm: Object-Oriented Collaboration and the CMS

In the last several years, the renewed focus on blended courses has been encouraged by the availability of various new technologies, accompanied by a reflection on the benefits of active and social learning.[7] Designing and teaching team-designed blended courses requires the development and recognition of a new breed of instructors and technical staff. As alternative pedagogies emerge through the opportunities afforded by "teaching with technologies," instructors need to rethink and redevelop their approach to teaching and learning, while technical staff are confronted with the development of learning tools in close context to the subject matter and with an awareness of the pedagogical intent embedded in a particular earning practice. If we accept the premise that a collaborative and highly interactive process of course design is a desirable and effective strategy for learning, then, by implication, the very processes underlying the design of a course need to be manifest in the learning practices of students taking the course. In other words, collaboration and interactivity are fundamental principles that need to be expressed at every stage of the course. It is our challenge to harness the curiosity and motivation of students exploring the many themes that may emerge as part of academic course work.

On one hand, we needed to design the infrastructure of the course to allow easy interactivity. In the English 111 blended course, the annotation feature, discussion board, and nonlinear approach to linking information are such manifestations. On the other hand, we needed to allow students to reap the benefits of their engagement — to have students not only direct but build, through their collaborative interaction, the meanings behind a given subject matter.

Slowly, the social and collaborative aspects of education are being recognized as more important than the passive consumption of educational materials. Widely used tools such as e-mail, discussion boards, and chat rooms are examples of the increasing need and opportunity for collaborative interaction in an electronic setting.

While most students are adept at using tools that expand the classroom, applying them in extending the academic setting requires careful design and experienced coaching. As students begin to collaborate with each other, we see the cyclical development of new content through interaction, where object-oriented collaborative interactions may point toward the reuse of the interactions themselves as learning objects or content. Here, knowledge building becomes three-dimensional, across content and content-based interactions, and the result is new learning objects. Content is a resource and not an end to learning.[8]

The Shapeshifting CMS

It is most intriguing to consider the CMS as a social device, conforming and adapting to the needs of the user. As more campuses develop a wired/wireless infrastructure, a CMS may be a good tool to provide students with instant access to course content: facts, figures, and simulations. Using applications such as Silicon Chalk™ Colligo™ or others, users can discover one another, set up connections, and start to communicate in an informal manner. However, we find that these highly valuable aspects, the small-scale, simple, collaborative, "back-to-basics" type of learning environment, form only a small part of the functionality of the larger CMS. In addition, tools that provide this functionality could easily be separated from the CMS with no loss in overall appeal of a CMS. In fact, the current offering of tools is particularly prescriptive, requiring a high level of confidence on the part of the instructor to push the tools to complement the effective interactions practiced in the classroom. In the example of the first-year English mixed-mode course, many of the features of the CMS are completely hidden from the instructors and students. The limitations and restrictions imposed by the CMS have been identified, and workarounds were engineered to remove them from the design process and discussion with instructors. Additionally, students and TAs have been given new roles within the course.

Students are guided and encouraged to interact with the content wherever it best fits. Students are required to make regular contributions to pre-set discussions but are able and encouraged to start discussions about any topic. Instructors have the freedom to change content wherever and whenever they see fit. This freedom has resulted in a greater sense of ownership on the part of the instructors. In addition, instructors are able to react quickly to student needs and requests. This gives students the sense that they are part of the course and that there is an equal dialogue involving students, instructors, and content. The ability to react and respond to student and class needs is an important one. Instructors in a classroom are constantly relying on their experience, instincts, and skills to shape and reshape a class to find the best mode of instruction. An experienced teacher will use any one of a number of devices and techniques depending on the events that occur in the class.

The answer is, both, the CMS, or better, its particular modules or objects, and the network of information contributed by students, may be retrieved from a previous cohort via a knowledge base, or contributions that may by external to the specific discipline of the student audience but speaking to the subject matter, or contributions by other academic and nonacademic sources. In the end, the Web of information that becomes attached to the various learning models and objects will form and emerge as a relevant, customized and conducive learning environment.

If we were to take the notion of a disaggregated CMS, consisting of discreet objects such as a Web-based collection of tools, a conglomerate of learning objects and learning tools that in piecemeal fashion attach themselves to elements of an already existing IT infrastructure, we will probably find the sweet spot for an effective learning environment. The reconstitution of a learning environment that is neither monolithic nor an afterthought to existing ERP systems, but nimble and adaptable, is possible given the plethora of learning tools developed in a standards-compliant format. But what will hold these disaggregated tools together and make them an effective learning environment?

In an environment where facts can be instantly verified, teaching value shifts from "knowing" to processing. Much of the promise of the CMS rests in its potential to support the creation of ad hoc communities, where a given task is jointly processed. Rather than teaching facts, an emphasis can be placed on teaching inquiry within a discipline. In the classroom or beyond, communities can then spring up effortlessly, allowing the sharing of research, data, and the collection of data and collaboration between students.

In this context we predict two roles for a CMS: It streamlines processes such as data creation and presentation through its easy-to-use and intuitive interface. But more importantly it also presents itself as a collaborative tool, connecting to human and technical networks alike. In the first role, it is a workable platform or outlet for the built-up e-learning infrastructures of the past several years. In its second role, it promises new approaches to learning as it mediates social interactions and group processes and harnesses technology to pave a gateway to knowledge. Serving a community of scholars in this manner the CMS will shapeshift from software application into a truly enterprise-wide but invisible learning resource.

References

Dziuban, C.D., Hartman, J. L. & Moskal, P.D. (2004). Blended learning. *ECAR Research Bulletin,* Issue 7.

Freire, P. (1989). *Pedagogy of the oppressed.* New York: Continuum.

Gilbert, S. (2004). If it ain't broke, improve it: Thoughts on engaging education for us all. *Journal of Asynchronous Learning Networks.* Retrieved February 12, 2004, from *http://www.sloan-c.org/publications/jaln/v8n1/v8n1_gilbert.asp*

Long, P. (2001, June). *"Trends" Syllabus, 14*(11), 8, *San Jose*.

Morgan, G. (2003). *Faculty use of course management systems.* Boulder, CO: ECAR Research Publication.

Rogers, E.M. (1993). *Diffusion of innovations.* New York: Macmillan.

Scott, W. & Rauch, U. (2003). *A communication-centric model for knowledge-building using collaborative tools.* Retrieved December 16, 2004, from *http://isit.arts.ubc.ca/uli/NMC_Summer_2003/Organic%20Learning%20Objects_final%20_files/frame.htm*

The IrYdium Project at Carnegie Mellon University. Retrieved on December 16, 2004, from *http://ir.chem.cmu.edu/irproject/applets/virtuallab/*

Winner, L. (1986). *The whale and the reactor: A search for limits in an age of high technology.* Chicago: The University of Chicago Press.

Worthen, B. (2003). ERP extreme makeover. *CIO Magazine.* Retrieved December 16, 2004, from *http://www.cio.com/archive/111503/erp.html*

Endnotes

[1] Conventional approaches see technology as either subservient to values established in other social spheres, such as politics or culture, or on the other hand, constituting an autonomous cultural force overriding all traditional or competing values. Both positions were popular with philosophers of the 20th century and described by Max Weber as "the cage of rationalisation", analysed by Herbert Marcuse as creating "the one dimensional man and problematized by Jacques Ellul who contends that our social world is controlled by a culture of technology. Winner's (1986) question "Do Artifacts Have Politics?" sheds a critical light on approaches to technological determinism by critically analysing the political properties embedded in technical solutions.

[2] Long, senior strategist for the Academic Computing Enterprise at MIT, notes, "the larger the institution, the more likely the occurrence of a (centralized) Teaching Learning Technology Center. Perhaps collaboration of this sort is simply harder in larger organizations" (p. 8).

[3] Long observes, "Close communication among these groups is essential, but may not require organisational union. Coordinating these services

through a common virtual location [or conduit], can provide one-click access to these resources—leading to the...Virtual TLT Center" (2001, p. 8).

4   For a refreshing take on infusing technology with education and an understanding of education as a process that includes a vast number of participants, not only learners, see Gilbert's "If it ain't broke, improve it: Thoughts on engaging education for us all" (2004).

5   "The Virtual Laboratory ... provides an environment in which students can select from hundreds of standard chemical reagants and combine them in any way they see fit. Instructors may use this environment in a variety of settings including student homework, group projects, computer lab activities and pre- and post-lab exercises to support varied approaches to chemical education". The IrYdium Project at Carnegie Mellon University.

6   To see examples of these tools, go to *http://www.learningtools.arts.ubc.ca.*

7   For a brief but comprehensive review of blended learning, see Dziuban, Hartman, and Moskal, (2004).

8   Scott and Rauch (2003) radicalise the notion of organically growing learning objects organized around interactions. Over time interactions between learners and content become replaced by interactions between learners, where the level of engagement of each learner increases to the same extent as the level collaborative knowledge building. In their presentation model they combine ideas on object-oriented content interaction with newer, emerging models of object-oriented collaborative interaction and subsequent reuse of the interactions themselves as learning objects.

Chapter VII

Learner Engagement and Success in CMS Environments

Bob Bender, University of Missouri-Columbia, USA

Abstract

This chapter is a case study in the use of course management systems (CMS) in teaching and learning. A narrative from a faculty perspective, this study discusses how technology can be used effectively to shift the burden from teaching to student learning by paying attention to pedagogy rather than to the use of technology itself. "Shakespeare and the New Movies," a course designed to stimulate student writing about Shakespeare and films based on his plays, is used to illustrate this process.

Introduction

Will our descendants two hundred years from now, for whom we are breaking the road, remember to give us a kind word? No... they will forget (Dr. Astrov in Chekhov's *Uncle Vanya*, 1897, Act IV).

In the early 1990s, I began experimenting with the use of what then were called "new technologies" to enhance the student experience in more or less traditional classes. A more accurate statement might claim these technologies were used to enhance — and facilitate — my own innovations in teaching. For many years I'd been teaching writing-intensive courses in which students were asked to do a fair amount of in-class writing along with peer reviewing each other. Time intensive as these procedures were for students, they often involved a great deal of "extra" work for me and my course assistants, transcribing student comments and proposals so they could be distributed to everyone. Since 1995, all the courses I've conducted have been Web-based and paperless, using a variety of programs to facilitate student work. Web sites were homemade, using simple HTML; discussion was enabled through the use of LISTSERV or ListProc electronic lists. Discussion archives were accessed with a number of products, including Gopher and MHonArc. When Eudora™ allowed for formatted messages, students were encouraged to use this e-mail program to compose and submit their essays.

Whatever might be said of what I was doing, it was *not* the pedagogy that was accidental — it was the technology. I knew where I wanted to go in my teaching and found myself searching for the tools that might help me get there. Today, of course, course management systems (CMS) have combined the tools in one apparently seamless package, but the starting point for most faculty using these systems is *not* the pedagogy but the technology, often perceived as "bells and whistles."

There's no question that CMS, for faculty who use them, have done a great deal to relieve some of the more onerous management tasks, but there's little evidence to suggest these environments have done much to transform student learning. While promoters of CMS can point to ever increasing enrollments, a great many college and university faculty continue to think of instructional technology in binary terms — you use it or you don't. To complicate matters, we appear to have developed the same sort of opposition in regard to "traditional," face-to-face teaching as opposed to distance education. The evidence suggests that technologies of all sorts, including CMS, are being used more to support coursework for on-campus students, who are becoming overburdened as we attempt to use technology to shift from "instruction" to "student-centered learning."

A substantial number of students across the country have several courses each, all of which have some degree of CMS support. It is not unusual for these students to be asked to participate in electronic discussions or to take online quizzes in several, if not all, of their classes. At many institutions multiple CMS platforms are used — Blackboard™, WebCT™, as well as a number of homegrown varieties — to accommodate faculty unwillingness to change. This complicates the student "experience" with technology even further. My mission in this chapter is to show what can be done with CMS to transform the learning experience, and at the same time to suggest better ways in which it might be used.

Centering Around Students

My own experience is that technology can be used effectively to shift the burden from teaching to student learning. The first questions always should be how courses can be changed to put the student at the center, not what will the technologies do. With CMS, given the ever-expanding "featuritis," technology often takes precedence over pedagogy, offering opportunities for automation rather than inducements to focus on student learning. Thoughtful planning, however, can change old patterns. One of my key realizations has been that technology can be used to enhance student communication with each other and with faculty, and that this requires rethinking such concepts as the 50-minute class session and "seat time" as an indication of learning. Students need to have out-of-class as well as in-class experiences in the same course. Moreover, the "virtual sessions," for which students are assigned work that must be completed online, outside of class, needs to be carefully planned and sequenced to have value. This can be done without CMS, but given the ways in which most systems aggregate tools in one environment, a limited, focused use of specific tools can lead to success and greater student engagement.

A slogan for the kind of use of CMS I am suggesting might be "less is more." In late summer and early fall 1998 at the University of Missouri-Columbia, unbeknownst to me, a committee was meeting to decide on an institution-wide adoption of course management software. I agreed to teach an interdisciplinary senior seminar in a WebCT™ pilot program in the winter semester of 1999. Since I'd taught this course several times before, once using no more than a listserv, another time with a full Web site, it was an easy matter for me simply to transfer the files I'd previously created to the newly chosen WebCT™. Of course, I began to notice there were a great many more tools available than I had use for, and I had to devise ways to simplify the user interface so students wouldn't constantly be asking about program features we weren't using.

Eventually, I taught a number of different courses — the interdisciplinary studies seminar, courses in Shakespeare, early British survey, and modern drama — using WebCT™, always uploading material from Websites I had previously built myself. The tools I used were "Discussion Board, Private E-mail" within WebCT™ to facilitate returning graded essays that had been submitted electronically, and "Presentation Space," where students could upload their essays and peer review each other, and where their work remains as an archive for the various courses. I also created a number of content modules to "house" information, such as "About English 370," "Course Schedule & Session Notes," and "Assignments." Using this feature allowed me to track student access to the information I was providing. In effect, this led to students taking charge of their own work in the courses; rather than having to ask me or an assistant about an assignment, it was there online for their easy access at any time. In the same way, students were "put in charge" of seeing what their grades were by going to the grade book segment of the site and tracking how often they were sending messages to the bulletin board.

Transferring these courses to WebCT™, I learned a good deal about functionality but, more important to putting the students at the center of the learning process, I recognized the need to make a number of pedagogical shifts. The first, and only, course I created wholly within WebCT™ was "Shakespeare and the New Movies." Taught in fall 2000, this course illustrates many of the techniques I developed to transform learning. The course objectives were to examine a number of Shakespeare's plays along with recent films based on these plays in relation to what we know of Shakespeare's life, the cultural contexts of the 16th and 17th centuries as well as our own times, and the nature of film adaptation. On Tuesday evenings, students watched films based on Shakespeare's plays and engaged in face-to-face discussion as time allowed. To facilitate the online portion of the course, they were required to participate in twice-weekly online discussion "sessions," each with a set topic.

Since the course was offered for writing-intensive credit, in addition to participating in online discussion groups, students were expected to do a substantial amount of more formal writing, including three 250-word response essays on individual films, written early in the semester, and three longer essays (1,500 to 2,000 words each) spaced throughout the course. All assignments were designed to focus on the writing requirements. Preliminary discussion for one virtual session involved open-ended responses to a film. Subsequent sessions involved relating previous discussion to the requirements of the essay assignment. Other sessions required posting topic proposals and responding to the proposal of other students. Students working on similar topics could easily identify peer partners for the review of rough drafts.

While I had increasingly realized the importance of providing a clear sense of what was expected in individual essays (especially the longer ones) with this "hybrid" course in which students would have less face-to-face contact, I knew the assignments had to be as clear as possible. A typical assignment began with a context-setting statement, outlining what issues students were expected to address, suggesting they view the assignment more as a problem to be solved than a simple opportunity to provide the instructors with what "we wanted," and allowing them to create their own specific topic in response to a more general question.

Additionally, each assignment included a statement on procedures and formal considerations, indicating length requirements — in words not pages since submission is electronic — criteria for grading, and a schedule for the virtual sessions and submission of final essays, all of which are designed to keep students focused on the work at hand for a period of several weeks. In describing this course, I've said little about the CMS environment. Doubtless much of what we did in the course could have been done without CMS, but it could not have been done without computer mediation. The public display and archiving of student work — drafts, peer reviews, essays, discussion — is essential to their working together and seeing themselves at the center of the learning process.

Conclusion

It's far easier to draw some conclusions about teaching this way than to come to some broader conclusions about CMS. For this course and others, it's easy to provide a list of successful practices for those faculty still shifting to the use of technology to enhance teaching and learning:

Teaching Practices:

- Forget about trying to "cover" the material. Determine what you hope students will learn, not what you *want* to teach.

- Make sure the discussion board is there for student use and interaction, rather than everyone directing e-mail to the instructor.

- Start the semester with an "ice breaker," in which students introduce themselves to one another.

- Plan a series of meaningful, sequential activities for the "virtual" class sessions; the extra work pays off in engaging diverse learners, assessing outcomes, and eventually reusing electronic teaching materials in future semesters.

- Set deadlines and keep them to ensure work is sequential and not all done at 3:00 a.m. before the due date.

Learning practices:

- Students, in our subjective judgment, write better because they interact more with each other and are less concerned about pleasing an instructor.

- They certainly write more than in a class that meets only face to face. Discussion alone in this course amounted to an average of 29.61 messages per student for a total of more than 164,000 words — and we kept having to ask them to shorten their essays. Partly, their motivation appears to come from wanting to be heard and understood by their colleagues in ways not seen when their work is read only by the instructor.

- They enjoy the collaboration and having to read and quote from each other.

- In their course evaluations, most have praised using the course site.

But what will the next generation, those for whom, in Chekhov's prophetic words, "*we are breaking the road,*" have to say about us in the future? Course management software of some sort is here to stay, precisely because it facilitates the "management" of courses. If CMS, however, are to become an effective agent for the transformation of education, many changes are required that will transform them from course management systems into seamless learning sites. Instead of focusing on *management* issues, CMS need to focus on a new pedagogy that facilitates group interaction, allows students to control much of what they are learning, and encourages ownership. The focus will cease to be on individual courses and will drift away from faculty points of view and desires. CMS, after all, are sold as "enterprise" systems. Colleges and departments need to understand the demands this use of technology places on students and need to begin thinking in terms of the entire student experience and whole programs.

As with any new technology, it is still too early to see all the unintended effects technology will have on the entire educational enterprise. Teaching with technology is largely still an individual prerogative, despite an ever-growing demand for consistent outcomes and accountability. Getting faculty to agree on text books for the same course is difficult enough; getting them to work with curriculum specialists, course designers, programmers, and support personnel — the Open University and University of Phoenix models — will be much more difficult.

Some very obvious implications jump out at us. The individual instructor will no longer be solely in charge of her or his own courses. There most likely will be a startling reduction in the variety of courses offered, and there will be attempts at course and curriculum conformation on an institutional basis, if not a national basis, signs of which have already surfaced. Finally, there is something of Henry Ford's concern for mass production and standardization in this shift to teaching with technology. Certainly, one of the problems we are now encountering is an increased attempt on the part of CMS providers to standardize their products while at the same time maintain market differentiation. There is no crystal ball to tell us where our descendants will be in one hundred, let alone two hundred, years; and it is not clear they will want to remember those of us who broke their roads.

Chapter VIII

CMS Implementation as a Catalyst for Curricular Change

Lynne O'Brien, Duke University, USA

Amy Campbell, Duke University, USA

Samantha Earp, Duke University, USA

Abstract

In this chapter, we draw on examples from selected disciplines to highlight how implementing a course management system can encourage curricular discussions and catalyze curricular change at a university. We suggest that broad use of a CMS can both drive and support changes in teaching and curricular development. We close by providing some best practices and concrete suggestions on how to use a CMS to foster technology-enhanced curricular change.

Introduction

An art history faculty member wishes to provide students easier access to her slide collections, thereby hoping to improve the learning outcomes in her class. A biology faculty member and his 20 teaching assistants look for better methods to manage and coordinate their 40 laboratory sections, providing a more consistent experience for students across varied sections and setting standards for student feedback. A sociology graduate student instructor wishes for a way to carry rich in-class conversations beyond the two-hour discussion section he leads, deepening student learning and building a sense of community among his students. A group of nursing faculty members asks for a simple way to provide distant students access to their lecture materials, allowing them to work and take classes concurrently.

In each of these examples, the course instructors or program leaders are searching for better ways to meet the needs of their classes and programs. In many cases, new technologies offer potential for meeting these needs and improving teaching and learning. However, many colleges and universities have found that significant investments in technology have not met their expectations for bringing about these types of educational changes. Difficulty in learning to use new hardware and software has limited many faculty members' experimentation with technology in teaching, and faculty with minimal technology skills often find it difficult to envision ways technology could improve their teaching or enhance their curricula. While some more technically adept faculty have had success in creating impressive new course materials or making substantive changes in their curricula, these faculty — as well as their "low-tech" colleagues — are often dismayed at the time and effort needed for this innovation. Thus, faculty members with both low and high technical proficiency often forego technology-based curricular change.

At Duke University, as at many other institutions in the U.S. (Morgan, 2003), we have found that the adoption of a Web-based course management system has served as a practical and effective tool for integrating technology with curricular change. Our CMS is a tool available institution-wide and is used by faculty in nearly all nine of Duke's schools. By learning a few basic features of the CMS, faculty have acquired a common understanding of technology tools and their potential application in university instruction and have a common platform for more deliberate infusion of instructional technologies into their courses. Faculty at both ends of the technology skills spectrum who use the CMS have more time to focus on the teaching opportunities that technology affords (Bielema & Keel, 2003). The CMS then acts as a gateway through which faculty can be introduced to other instructional technologies. And the shared experience of using the CMS in turn fosters discussion of curricular change among groups of faculty, both within and across departments (Morgan, 2003). In this chapter, we draw on examples from selected disciplines to highlight how implementing a CMS can encourage curricular discussions and catalyze curricular change at a university. We suggest that broad use of a course management system can both drive and support changes in teaching and curricular development. We close by providing some best practices and concrete suggestions on how to use a CMS to foster technology-enhanced curricular change.

Background

Duke University is a private, four-year, doctoral-extensive institution with just over 12,000 full-time students in its nine schools. Although there are several well-known distance education programs at Duke, the vast majority of Duke classes and instruction are traditional face-to-face classroom courses.

Duke first pilot-tested Blackboard™ as a CMS in Spring of 1999 with eighteen faculty. At that time, several of Duke's professional schools, especially those with distance education programs, already had custom systems or processes for providing course Web sites. Outside of those groups with custom course Web site tools, most faculty members who wished to have a course Web site created the pages themselves or hired someone to do it for them. In fall of 1999, two groups made separate instances of Blackboard™ available to faculty: the Duke Center for Instructional Technology (CIT), which serves the entire campus, and the computing support group for Duke's largest school, Trinity College of Arts & Sciences. In spring of 2001, these two pilot systems were consolidated within the CIT, and Blackboard™ was made available to any faculty member who wished to use it. In fall of 2001, after seeing substantial growth in Blackboard™ usage, the campus moved to Blackboard™'s enterprise version and began integrating it with other university systems, adding expanded support from our central computing organization, the Office of Information Technology. By fall of 2003, faculty from eight of nine Duke schools used Blackboard™, although some faculty and programs continued to use other applications. Over 1,000 unique Blackboard™ sites were in use at Duke in spring of 2004, representing about 35 percent of courses offered at Duke, with 740 of Duke's 2,400 faculty having at least one Blackboard™ course site. These figures are consistent with national patterns of CMS use as reported in the 2003 Campus Computing Survey (Green, 2003).

Blackboard™'s Impact on Curricular Planning at Duke University

As faculty increasingly adopted Blackboard™, we noticed several trends in the use of our CMS as an instructional technology tool. First, individuals who began using Blackboard™ tended to start small, using the most basic features. But as their comfort level increased, they began to use the more sophisticated, interactive CMS features as well as other technology applications after a semester or two.

As Duke faculty explored Blackboard™'s functionality, they began to broaden their conversation about how the CMS and other basic instructional technologies affected their teaching, and what these tools could mean for their department's curriculum. As deans, chairs, and other individuals in leadership roles began using Blackboard™, they saw ways it might address curricular needs, thus using their own experiences with the CMS to promote its broader use within the program, department, or school. Through CIT-sponsored events, as well as departmental and programmatic planning efforts, faculty and administrators began to have regular conversations with individuals outside of their usual working groups about the potential uses of technology to support teaching and learning. Thus, the use of the CMS has provided a platform for exciting cross-department conversations about teaching, learning, and technology.

Effects of CMS

Use of a CMS Prepares Faculty and Academic Staff for Technology Use in Curricular Change Efforts

Although some educators have criticized CMS for modeling traditional teaching practices instead of revolutionizing education, we instead see the implementation of a CMS as a useful first step in enabling curricular change. In our experience, the relative ease of use of the integrated feature set of a CMS makes it possible for faculty to get up to speed quickly on different types of technology uses. This leads, in many cases, to rapid adoption of the CMS, whose integrated tools offer multiple functions and fit well with a variety of teaching styles.

One particularly important aspect of this process is that faculty with minimal technology skills can learn to use a CMS in a short period of time. Faculty who organize their courses around lectures and readings can post lecture slides and reading assignments in a CMS. Those who already use multiple-choice tests can use the online quizzes the CMS provides, while those who prefer essays can have students submit papers online. Faculty who teach large, multisection classes can take advantage of self-graded pre-laboratory questions and online grade postings, while instructors with small seminar classes can make better use of class time by using pre-class discussion board questions and online exchange of essays for peer review. By reaching the "low-tech" faculty member, we are able to include new voices in discussions of technology-enhanced teaching and learning.

The CMS also offers advantages to faculty who are already comfortable with technology. For example, instructors who have developed their own HTML-based Web pages in the past may find a CMS valuable for quickly updating course information. They may experiment with the interactive features of a CMS used in conjunction with a custom-crafted Web page, or they may use the CMS to create group discussion and file exchange spaces more easily than with other tools. In addition, the use of the CMS may give these faculty a point of comparison to a tool they were already using elsewhere or offer them an easier way to organize course materials and activities created with other technology tools.

Overall, the use of the CMS prepares faculty for more extensive use of technology and for pedagogical discussions about course goals and objectives. As faculty at all levels of technical proficiency begin to use the CMS, they usually begin to think critically about their teaching in a way they might not have otherwise. In trying a new tool or method to facilitate a particular pedagogical goal, they carefully evaluate all aspects of the tool. This leads them to think about not only the factors that are strictly dependent on the technology tool itself, but also on broader curricular issues. Thus the adoption of the CMS leads not only to the implementation of a teaching tool, but also to reflection on the teaching itself.

An example of this can be seen with the Duke University history department's experience with our CMS. Several years ago, only a few Duke history faculty made use of course Web pages or online activities. Those who did were seen as technical pioneers, willing to spend inordinate amounts of time learning to develop and use Web sites. When Duke's CMS was introduced, the chairman of the history department decided to take advantage of an incentive program that matched a student worker with a faculty member to build a Blackboard™ course site. After first posting a syllabus and reading materials, he began to incorporate maps and pictures along with short video segments that illustrated historical concepts. Next, he tried using the CMS discussion board to help students prepare before class and found that his expanded use of the CMS led to more active participation and better quality discussion in class.

After his own success, the history department chair encouraged several groups of faculty in his department to work with our CIT to think about revising their courses based on introducing the CMS. Those faculty not only had the opportunity to try new types of course activities individually, but some of them met as a group monthly under the aegis of CIT's Faculty Instructional Technology Fellows program to discuss pedagogical issues. They discussed methods to encourage students to come to class prepared (e.g., using pre-class discussion board activities), better organize their lecture and class materials (e.g., posting course notes and other documents), and allow student access to primary materials (e.g., uploading scans of original documents, maps, and images). They shared suggestions, provided feedback on one another's course sites, and discussed broader issues of technology's role in teaching.

In contrast to the history department, where the CMS prompted initial experimentation with technology, faculty in Duke's Nicolas School of the Environment and Earth Sciences already used a variety of software tools, and many had created their own course Web pages by the time Duke's

CMS was introduced. Many of those faculty members continued to build custom Web pages, but some also used the CMS to post class materials or collect homework assignments. Recently, the school decided to make its master's degree program in environmental leadership available to distant students. A group of faculty is working together to plan the online version of the curriculum using the CMS as well as custom Web sites and other technology tools. In this case, the CMS is part of a suite of tools supporting curricular changes driven by other educational goals.

In short, a CMS offers quick wins for novice and experienced technology users. The resulting widespread use of CMS increases faculty members' general skill and comfort level with technology and allows them to participate in informed discussions about using technology in teaching. And, by reducing the time and effort needed to use the technology, the CMS allows faculty to focus more energy on their pedagogical goals.

Widespread Use of a CMS Stimulates Changes in Pedagogy and Curriculum

In fall of 2000, Duke introduced its new Curriculum 2000 for undergraduate studies, which emphasized competency in foreign language, writing, and research; the new standards soon began to prompt curriculum changes. Because the CMS was available to all instructors for a low initial investment of training and time, program administrators could easily incorporate CMS-supported changes into their program redesign planning processes. As the use of the CMS increased, the university realized another benefit: the structure and terminology of the CMS gave faculty a common language for discussing teaching. This facilitated discussion about pedagogy among faculty, spurring further curricular changes. In this section, we offer examples of those changes.

The University Writing Program wanted to implement a program-wide assessment of student performance at the beginning and end of its curriculum. To accomplish this, the program used the CMS to coordinate a massive pre- and post-course student writing assessment. Students in each of about 80 sections of the introductory writing course used the CMS electronic drop box to submit writing samples at the beginning and end of the semester. Faculty compared the two samples to judge student improvement. The use of the CMS in this case allowed the program to achieve its evaluation goal and focus on program improvement. Such a comprehensive assessment process across an entire program would have been much more difficult to implement without the use of technology.

In the undergraduate foreign language programs, Curriculum 2000 brought a new emphasis on providing sufficient class time, activities, and resources to promote oral proficiency. However, even with the addition of an extra class period each week, students did not have time to speak frequently enough in class for instructors to evaluate their performance. And, there was no easy way for instructors to interview students individually to gauge their oral language development. By using the CMS file exchange features in conjunction with an audio recording software tool in the language labs, the language programs were able to implement regular oral language assignments, thus facilitating a key component of the redesigned curriculum.

With close to 100 sections each semester, our introductory undergraduate chemistry courses presented logistical challenges to instructors. One challenge was ensuring consistency in what is taught across course sections, given the large number of teaching assistants. Other challenges were preparing large numbers of students for each week's laboratory work and providing accurate and timely feedback to students. In addition, over the past several years, chemistry faculty have undertaken curriculum reforms to bring the topics and methods of teaching in these courses more in line with those found in the chemistry profession. The CMS contained the functionality to accomplish the program goals (e.g., online lab quizzes, electronic laboratory notebook capability), and also provided a focus for technology training for the teaching assistants. With teaching assistants being more uniformly prepared, students received a more consistent course experience across all sections. Attempting to restructure the chemistry curriculum to this degree without a CMS as a common platform would have been extremely difficult.

A final example: prior to the CMS, Duke's Clinical Research Training Program (CRTP) used custom-created and updated Web sites, as well as CD-ROMs and print materials, to distribute course content to local and distance education students. The program wanted to provide consistent and timely information to students and make it easy for program support staff to update Web sites and course materials. The CMS provided the functionality the program needed to maintain its high quality, while also expanding the number of students in the program.

CMS Helps Institutionalize Change

As other authors have pointed out, higher education institutions have nurtured individual experiments and pilot projects but have been less effective in spreading "proven" innovations and helping them take root in the campus culture (Keehn & Norris, 2003). The campus-wide adoption and use of a course management system can help to institutionalize positive changes in teaching and curricular development.

First, the CMS helps to institutionalize change by providing an easy-to-use structure for repositories of materials and resources. Instructors of individual courses can reuse course sites from one semester to the next, taking advantage of the work already done and enriching existing content with new resources. Coordinators of multiple-section courses and programs can develop standardized CMS-based sites that provide access to the same information and resources. In foreign language courses at Duke, the CMS has also been used to create program-wide resource sites for instructors and students. The instructor resource Web sites house syllabi, assignments, lesson plans, teaching tips, and resources contributed by all faculty and allow the language programs to maintain examples of innovative activities, even if their authors leave the university. This helps maintain program continuity from one semester to the next and is invaluable in acclimatizing new faculty and graduate student instructors. The student resource Web sites provide access to audiovisual, text-based, and interactive materials and showcase model student projects. These sites have helped build student awareness of language development and a sense of community among students enrolled in multiple sections and courses.

The use of the CMS has also helped to initiate a change in the way teaching is made accessible to others. Traditionally a private, mostly individual activity, teaching with the CMS becomes more visible, concrete, and public. By placing course information, readings, discussions, model activities, assessments, and student work on a CMS site, the instructor creates a tangible record of a course. This makes it easier for the faculty member to communicate the goals and content of the course to others (potential students, colleagues, faculty from other departments and institutions). This, in turn, can facilitate discussion about teaching styles, methods, and tools. It can also help programs and departments address articulation issues more productively by making it easier to describe and compare pedagogical goals and course "products" across sections and courses.

Finally, the common experience of using the CMS allows us at the CIT to replicate innovations across departments, gather information about needs more broadly, and better plan how to best address those needs. At the instructional level, innovative uses of CMS-based tools can be replicated across departments and disciplines. At Duke, this can be seen with the use of discussion boards and file exchange features. These features were initially used in only a few courses in languages and writing, but word of their utility spread quickly and they are now used widely in many disciplines at all levels of the curriculum. At the support level, the use of a common tool set makes it easier to develop the documentation and support staff expertise needed to help faculty and students use the CMS effectively. This same commonality of experience also makes it easier to identify patterns of usage and emerging technology needs across the university. For example, by looking at the kinds of information and help requests that came in regarding the use of our CMS, it became clear that there was widespread interest in the use of digital images and streamed audio and video. By helping faculty use digital media in their CMS course sites, we have acquired the experience needed to initiate a discussion among faculty, the libraries, and technology service providers on how to best organize, deliver, and support these types of course material. More broadly, assessing instructional technology usage and needs through the lens of a campus-wide tool has also given us an opportunity to address related issues such as classroom technology support, student and faculty training, and departmental IT planning.

Use of a CMS Draws Out Questions About Teaching and Curriculum

The adoption of the CMS has brought into relief questions about pedagogical issues that were seldom discussed widely before:

- *How public should teaching be?* For example, should the Web site for a course (and, thus, the teaching and learning in a course) be publicly accessible or private? Who — if anyone — should have access to a private course site besides the students and the instructor? Faculty at Duke are divided on this issue, but most would like more flexibility than our CMS provides for making different parts of a course open or closed to public view.

- *Is it reasonable to expect faculty to have a course Web site?* While this issue is not particular to the availability of a CMS, the ease of use of the CMS removes some of the obstacles to creating a course site. In some cases, faculty who have never perceived a need to use Web-based tools may feel pressured to create a CMS-based course site in response to departmental initiatives or student demand. Some faculty may prefer to deliver Web-based materials through other systems or custom-built Web pages rather than using the CMS. And others may feel that the use of the CMS could make it easier for departments and supervisors to monitor the content of their courses. While faculty at Duke are not required to use the Web in general or the CMS specifically, these are some of the concerns that have been raised. It is important to address these in ways that emphasize the CMS' utility in addressing specific pedagogical and programmatic goals while continuing to recognize the faculty's right to make decisions regarding the courses they teach.

- *Should a course be a totally unique creation of an individual instructor, or should there be consistency in course content from semester to semester, or across course sections?* When multiple faculty teach the same course, should they use a common course Web site or individual ones? Should a course site created by one instructor be available to the next instructor who teaches that course?

- *Should the university maintain an archival record of what is taught in courses?* If so, how long should course sites and their contents be available to the students who used them? Should this be determined institutionally, programmatically, or individually by instructors? If Web-based course materials should be archived, what record should be kept of non-Web materials?

- *What expectations should students have for technology use in courses?* For example, should all classes have some minimum information posted in a course Web site? How frequently should students be expected to check a course Web site for updated information?

- *How should the university assist faculty with using copyrighted materials?* Does a CMS change the locus of responsibility for meeting legal requirements of fair use? The login required by our CMS assists those who wish to restrict access to copyrighted materials, but the same login reduces the ability to make an entire course site publicly viewable.

At Duke, both faculty using the CMS and the CMS administrators are looking for guidance in developing policies around CMS use. It is not always clear what the appropriate university body is to answer these questions, nor what the process is for bringing questions to that body. Duke has many groups that advise on academic policies: an information technology advisory group, intellectual property group, the faculty senate, the deans of the university, the provost, the libraries, the university counsel, and other campus constituencies. But when different groups — and different individuals — disagree about policy issues, it is not clear how decisions are best made. One significant challenge Duke faces is developing the decision-making processes and bodies necessary for this new kind of technological system.

Best Practices Can Make It More Likely for CMS to Bring About Change

Given the rapid rate at which colleges and universities have adopted some type of CMS, it seems likely that this trend will continue. And, given the expense of supporting a CMS, it is reasonable to expect these tools to have educational value. Our experience at Duke suggests there are several factors that can make CMS not only a widely used tool, but also a force for teaching improvement and curricular change. Here are the best practices we have discovered.

Make It Easy to Experiment With Your CMS

To encourage broad use and widespread discussion of CMS, make it easy for faculty and IT staff to opt in. At Duke, we make our CMS available to all faculty in all schools without requiring any formal training. At the same time, we offer many avenues for learning to use the CMS in the way that fits their preference. Faculty who are unsure what a CMS is or could do for them can visit a well-developed sample course site, or use a Duke-created CD-ROM, which provides videos of eight Duke faculty from different schools discussing their varied uses of the CMS.[1] Instructors who want individualized help can use our office-visit program, in which a trained student worker or staff member will show the instructor how to use the features he or she is interested in. Faculty who prefer to learn on their own can take advantage of online tutorials and help materials to get started, and then use our multi-tiered help system for questions.

A course shell is automatically created for most courses, populated with student rosters and linked to the library's e-reserves. Faculty members use their existing university NetIDs to log in, and then simply turn on their course site to begin. Although we make it easy for faculty to use the CMS, Duke does not require it. Faculty maintain control of how they offer their courses and whether or not they want to use a CMS. As support for and integration of our CMS has improved, more faculty members have chosen to use it.

Give Faculty Confidence in Your CMS

The chairman of one department at Duke told us recently that he would not recommend the CMS to his colleagues until it had been in use for three years. He was unwilling to encourage faculty to spend their time on experimental software. But now that the CMS is integrated into our campus technology environment, he has asked all faculty in the department to try using it in at least one course.

Before faculty can consider CMS-supported curricular change, they need to know that the CMS is a key component of the campus technology infrastructure, so that their investment in using it is likely to pay off. Good integration with other campus tools, strong support, and long-term commitment build confidence in a CMS. After two years of experimenting with the CMS, we began to link it to other enterprise systems. The CMS is now backed up like other enterprise systems, supported through a central help desk and integrated with our campus authentication system, our student information systems, and our library e-reserves service. If Duke were to switch to a different CMS tool, we would be committed to providing a smooth transition for faculty.

Focus on Teaching Before Technology

If you want your CMS to be used for pedagogical change, focus advertising, training, and incentives on *teaching* with the technology — not just *using* the technology. Duke's CIT, the organization that introduced the CMS at Duke, decided from the beginning to use incentive grant funds to support curricular uses of technology. Unlike some schools, we do not require or offer incentives for faculty to attend CMS training. Instead, we provide grant programs and support services for various levels of teaching innovation. Faculty who develop proposals for making modest educational changes in a course using our CMS receive start-up help from a student assistant. Those who want to make more substantial educational improvements in a course can apply for our Faculty Instructional Technology Fellows program, in which they spend a year experimenting with our CMS and other software tools. These IT fellows discuss their experiences throughout the year with other faculty in the program and then serve as a resource for instructional technology planning in their departments. In return, faculty IT fellows receive a full year of consulting from an academic technology consultant, course development help from a student worker, and a salary stipend. Groups of faculty from a department or school undertaking an extensive curricular change project using the CMS and other technologies are eligible for funding and extended consulting via our Instructional Technology High Impact Grants program. In all of our incentive programs,[2] we start by asking faculty about their educational goals so we can tailor all training and consulting toward accomplishment of those goals.

Let Faculty Tell the Story

The best advocate for trying a new type of instructional technology is a faculty member who has already used it. Early in our CMS project, we began collecting faculty stories about ways they had found the CMS useful. These stories were published on Duke's CMS support Web site.[3] We selected stories representing different disciplines and teaching approaches and published them on a CD-ROM, which included an introduction by our provost and a self-paced tutorial on learning to use the CMS.

We also invite all faculty members using instructional technology to share their successes and recommendations for others at our annual spring Instructional Technology Showcase.[4] Faculty who complete the Faculty IT Fellows program also share their ideas with the next year's group of fellows and with colleagues in their departments.[5] These faculty-centered strategies not only motivate individuals to experiment with the CMS, but also provide feedback to IT staff about making the CMS more useful in the future.

Make CMS a Factor in Integrating Instructional Tools

As faculty begin to use more of the CMS' components, they may become more interested in using other types of technology, particularly those technologies integrated into the CMS. For example, many faculty who initially used the CMS later became interested in incorporating scanned images, streaming media, and interactive testing tools. These are all technologies our CIT has worked with other campus IT units to integrate with the CMS, allowing course sites to serve as a hub for class planning and pedagogical reflection.

Support the CMS Centrally and Locally

One challenge presented by growing use of a CMS is an increased need for user support. Duke has a decentralized technology support structure that relies on specialized help from school-based technology staff and infrastructure development from the central Office of Information Technology (OIT). As CMS use grew at Duke, we integrated CMS support into all levels of IT support on campus. For example, any instructor or student at the university who needs help with the CMS can call the OIT help desk, which supports a variety of other software tools as well. The CIT works closely with the help desk to resolve problems that cannot be solved in an initial phone call. In schools or departments that use our CMS extensively, CIT provides onsite training and extra assistance to their technical staff. For example, when the sociology department decided to encourage all faculty to use the CMS, CIT trained and funded a sociology graduate student to work one-on-one with faculty for two semesters and provided a CIT staff member to meet regularly with the graduate student. This mix of local and central help ensures that faculty get fast, consistent help for general and specialized use of the CMS.

Encourage Broad Participation in CMS Decision-Making

Where a single CMS is used across a university, it is especially important to include representatives from many parts of the university in planning and decision making about its use. Schools offering distance education programs with the CMS may have very different needs from ones where CMS is used as a supplement to on-campus course activities. For a CMS to be useful in supporting curricular initiatives, it has to meet the needs of all groups.

At Duke, faculty, staff, and students participate in CMS planning and monitoring in several different ways. A CMS advisory committee with faculty and staff from all nine schools reviews current issues in CMS use and offers suggestions for future development. The CIT Advisory Board, which addresses a range of instructional technology issues, also reviews CMS use and plans. The Information Technology Advisory Committee, which addresses technology planning for both administrative and academic computing, is another group that reviews current CMS use and plans.

To help with planning, CIT regularly surveys faculty and student CMS users and also conducts interviews and focus groups with non-CMS users. Summary reports of these surveys, as well as reports on CMS plans and usage, are published on CIT's Web site and distributed to campus IT planning groups. CIT staff also network with the broader academic community around CMS planning by participating in conferences, professional organizations, and ad hoc meetings.

Conclusion

In conclusion, a CMS can promote and support teaching innovation and curricular change. By giving faculty a shared set of tools that are easy to use and matched to a variety of teaching styles, a CMS provides common ground for discussing and experimenting with technology in teaching. As faculty become more confident in using technology, they also begin to have higher expectations for the CMS. Once they are comfortable using basic tools, they see ways they could use more sophisticated software for more complex teaching activities. It is not surprising that the schools that were early adopters of CMS are now pressuring commercial CMS developers to offer more open and flexible systems or are developing their own CMS, which can be customized to meet faculty needs. As CMS systems evolve over the next few years, they have the potential to become even more useful in fostering effective educational change.

References

Bielema, C. & Keel, R. (2003). Faculty use of MyGateway, WS 2003. Available at *http://www.umsl.edu/technology/mgwhelp/mgwinfo/ws03facsurvey.pdf*

Green, K.C. (2003). Tracking the digital puck into 2004. *Syllabus.* Available at *http://www.campus-technology.com/article.asp?id= 8574*

Keehn, A.K. & Norris, D. M. (2003). IT planning: Cultivating innovation and value. *Syllabus.* Available at *http://www.campus-technology. com/article.asp?id =8454*

Morgan, G. (2003). *Faculty use of course management systems.* Boulder, CO: ECAR Research Publication. Available at *http:// www.educause.edu/LibraryDetailPage/666?ID=ERS0302*

Endnotes

[1]   *http://cit.duke.edu/pdf/erroyo-report-full-updated-overview.pdf*

[2]   *http://cit.duke.edu/help/funding/funding.do*

[3]   *http://blackboard.duke.edu/about/profiles.do*

[4]   *http://cit.duke.edu/showcase/2004/*

[5]   *http://cit.duke.edu/help/funding/fellows/fellows.do*

Chapter IX

NGCMS:
Exploring and Supporting Effective Faculty Use

Youmei Liu, University of Houston, USA

Abstract

The effective faculty use of course management systems (CMS) is the key to the successful online instructional delivery. This chapter focuses on two main areas: 1) understanding CMS to innovatively adapt and customize CMS to accomplish educational objectives; and 2) understanding the process of technology adoption from the perspectives of developing effective faculty training programs for using CMS to ease the transition of incorporating technology into the process of teaching.

Introduction

CMS are becoming increasingly important as part of academic systems in institutions of higher learning (Morgan, 2003). CMS have been in use for decades, but because of the complicated process of adoption, their use is still in the stage of being tested, evaluated, and improved. The adoption of CMS is not merely a simple process of learning and using a new technology, but is, more importantly, a challenge to the mindset of the "higher education mission that has been the subject of refinement and protection for nearly a millennium" (Katz, 2003, p. 9). The focus of this chapter is on exploring the issues related to a better understanding of CMS from educational perspectives, of faculty technology adoption, and of CMS support within extended faculty development strategies.

What CMS Promise to Do and Their Limitations

CMS include features and tools for delivering content, for sharing and managing materials, for promoting both synchronous and asynchronous communication and virtual collaboration, and for assessing students' learning. Because CMS can provide functionality that meets the needs of the academic challenges in an online learning environment, "the number of faculty and students committed to a CMS is growing" (Carmean & Haefner, 2003, p. 4). For example, the University of Houston has experienced a 15 percent increase in the use of CMS each year. CMS impact and shape the way in which courses are structured and delivered and have "significantly changed the educational experience in many courses" (Carmean & Haefner, 2003, p. 4). Yet, a successful education cannot be automated by the sole incorporation of CMS into the educational process. The reality of using CMS is not as rosy as those mission statements purport. It is necessary that we understand the complexity of education and both the advantages of CMS that can be used to benefit education and the limitations that might impede education.

It is critical to consider both CMS advantages and limitations as related to the process of teaching. Advantages of CMS use are many. CMS create a secure and password-protected virtual learning environment. Cyber security has become an increasingly critical issue in online education. A secure cyber-learning space can protect educational assets as well as promote academic exchanges. Only secure learning environments can guarantee a smooth, fairly problem-free education. As instructors, you do not need to worry about the safety of your research materials or about infringements on the copyrights of your work. Students can communicate privately and access their grades conveniently and safely without exposing their private identities. CMS also integrate content delivery, course management, and student assessment. You can develop online materials for a course, and upload and update these materials easily. The internal management systems enable you to organize and manage student data, to group students into effective learning groups, to create interactive learning activities, and to integrate research resources to improve the quality of instruction. You can also create diverse assessments and self-tests. The quiz tool can automate the assessing process and provide related statistical feedback that lets you analyze your teaching and students' learning. The grade book tool allows students to track their grades, and "students enjoy this feature because they like to have a record of their accumulating grades" (Foreman, 2001, para. 7).

Another advantage of CMS is that they promote online communication. Effective communication is the key to the success of learning. Communication tools (discussion board, e-mail, chat, and whiteboard) facilitate the relationships between you and your students as well as among students themselves. Each tool has its own unique features that can suit you and students as part of different communication modes, both synchronous and asynchronous, anywhere and anytime. Hong Kong University uses communication tools to reach out to international communities to promote cross-cultural communication between western and eastern countries.

CMS are designed to support the user. They are easy to use without the need of high-level technical skills or the knowledge of programming languages. You can use CMS' built-in interactive features to design online material without any knowledge of complex programming coding. The interactive tools, such as discussion boards, e-mail, quizzes, and chat, can improve the pedagogical value of online education. These features can help you develop and enhance your instructional capabilities. CMS have a structured and common interface by default, which reduces problems related to student learning and support. Students can easily get the logging rules and the navigational system. This ease of use improves students' efficiency in using CMS. The file management systems in CMS not only store information, but also allow you to manage files for effective use. In the latest version of WebCT Vista, for example, you are able to use your course materials across sessions, as well as share and exchange resources with other faculty. Additionally, CMS have automated features that can "greatly relieve the workload and free time for course development and interaction with students" (Clark, 2000, para. 12). You can use the assessment tools to create different formats of quizzes, tests, and exercises. You can arrange quiz questions dynamically and randomly to improve the quality of assessing students' learning. Discussion groups and study groups can also be generated through the automatic features. Students can be grouped or they can group themselves to form learning communities, thereby facilitating the process of learning and promoting mutual communication.

There are equally compelling disadvantages to CMS. First, CMS are based on template-driven structures with rigid systems. These templates do not satisfy the needs of all faculty members and sometimes do not suit the nature of the course. It is not easy for beginners to customize the structure and the look of courses, so the majority of CMS courses look almost identical. Next, CMS offer very limited editing and revising features, which make the system less powerful and inconvenient to use. You have to use other applications to make even small changes, such as changing the size and format of an image. CMS also lack pedagogical instructions for the use of the tools. Neither examples nor image-based illustrations are given as part of the help instructions.

It is also hard to overlook the fact that current CMS have browser and operating system compatibility issues. Sometimes it is especially problematic for Mac users. Your content materials or quizzes might display differently across the platform and browsers. Both you and your students need to keep browser and plug-in information updated constantly. Although relatively intuitive, file exchange in CMS is time-consuming. For example, in WebCT™, there is no document-editing feature. Therefore, you must download each assignment to your computer, then grade or mark it using a word processing or marking program, and then upload the document back to the assignment dropbox for the student to retrieve. "WebCT's file exchange is mindless work at its worst: boring and repetitive, requiring intense concentration" and it is laborious and time-consuming (Foreman, 2001, para. 12). Finally, CMS offer limited customizable features for individual students. Once the course is developed using CMS' structure, students cannot rearrange the course content materials to suit their individual needs and preferences.

It benefits all users to be familiar with both the advantages and limitations of CMS. Measures can and should be taken to limit the potentially negative impact of these disadvantages. Institutions should make it easier to seek help and advice from instructional designers and technical staff and for faculty to work together to find out the best solutions to overcome these disadvantages.

Understanding the Process of Adopting Technology: CMS

Diffusion of Innovation: Communication

In a 1962 work on his diffusion theory, Rogers explores how a given innovation is presented to the members of a social system and how these members form attitudes toward the innovation. He discusses four theories of diffusion: the innovation decision process, individual innovativeness, rate of adoption, and perceived attributes. In the innovation decision process theory, the stages through which a technological innovation passes are the stages of knowledge, persuasion, decision, implementation, and confirmation. To be a technological innovator, one needs to be exposed to the technology and understand its functions. A favorable attitude toward the technology is formed through persuasion. Decision is made by committing to the technological adoption. Implementation includes utilizing the innovation and is followed by a positive outcome resulting from its use. In the individual innovativeness theory, Rogers describes different adopter categories. He states that individuals who are predisposed to being innovative will adopt an innovation earlier than those who are less predisposed. In the process of diffusion, neither innovators nor conservatives will compose the main population of the whole system. In his rate of adoption theory, Rogers discusses the pattern of diffusion, which resembles an s-shape curve. The theory of perceived attributes states that potential adopters base their adoption of innovation on five attributes that impact the rate of adoption: relative advantage, compatibility, complexity, trialability, and observability.

The applicability of Rogers' diffusion theory in instructional technology is two-fold. It helps administrators better understand the process of technology diffusion so as to develop a systematic prescriptive model of adoption and diffusion. It also provides a valuable process for instructional technologists to create effective faculty training programs and to identify existing problems. An instructional technologist who understands the innovation process and theories of innovation diffusion will be more fully prepared to work effectively with clients and potential adopters (Schiffman, 1991).

Communicate Technology to Faculty Members

The first and most important factor in Rogers' diffusion theory is communication. It is the key process to a successful adoption of technology. Research studies indicate that in institutions of higher learning, technologies are disseminated to faculty members through:

- Diverse training programs, with the option of online training sessions (instructor-led or self-paced) and online technology reference materials.

- Recommendations from instructional technology (IT) professionals (Liu, 2002): Faculty members seek advice from IT personnel for recommendations on educational technologies and ask their opinions on CMS before starting to use them.

- Influence from peers: one of the key findings in Morgan's study (2003) indicates that faculty's increased use of CMS results from the discussion of them with colleagues.

- Technology seminars and workshops: the University of Houston holds an annual COW (CampusNet Online Workshop). Faculty members from different campuses in the UH system get together to participate in a two-day workshop. In hands-on sessions, they learn to use CMS' tools and to incorporate them effectively into the courses, and they also learn different applications to prepare teaching materials. In round-table sessions, faculty members, instructional designers, and technologists discuss the issues and challenges of online education with CMS.

- Academic technology activities, such as Teach Expo, held every semester at the University of Houston: faculty members share their experiences of effective use of CMS' tools and showcase their best practices.

- Monthly CMS brown bag lunches (University of Maryland).

- Online faculty testimonials and faculty profiles (University of Delaware): Faculty members share their pedagogical tips, thoughts, and ideas in using technologies and CMS' tools in different learning environments, discuss learning experiences from both teaching and learning perspectives, and present their case studies and their most effective problem-solving methods. This is a wonderful way for faculty members to learn from each other and to improve the quality of education jointly.

- Faculty CMS list server (University of Houston): faculty members discuss CMS issues among themselves. The discussion is open to technologists and instructional designers who can offer technical solutions to CMS' problems, while faculty members can provide pedagogical advice from their experiences.

If technology-related information is conveyed effectively, then faculty members will be convinced that technology will help them meet educational challenges and solve problems. It is important that the demonstration of technology be realistic so that potential adopters feel that they will be able to try it without too much trouble and without too steep a learning curve. The most efficient way to display the positive aspects of technology is to provide samples of technology use in different subject areas as part of a diverse learning environment. Faculty will then feel confident that using technology in their own areas is both feasible and beneficial.

Another important issue relates to technologists' and instructional designers' need to communicate with faculty members in plain language, not with technical terms and jargon, or hard-to-grasp principles and rules. Principles of design should be infused into the best practices. This certainly raises the bar for support staff who should understand that technology itself is far from sufficient in supporting faculty members. Sound advice and effective practice come from a thorough understanding of faculty needs. Support should include familiarity with instructional theories and principles, educational environments, and student learning styles, as well as computer technologies and CMS.

Technology Acceptance: Attitude

Functionalist theory stresses the aspect of usefulness. Davis (1989) adds another aspect, "perceived ease of use," to form his technology acceptance model (TAM). He believes that perceived ease of use is an equally important factor that influences the attitude toward the use of technology. He established a causal relationship between attitude and behavior based on the theory of reasoned action (Ajzen & Fishbein, 1980). A positive attitude is developed when a positive input is received from perceived ease of use and perceived usefulness. Attitudes serve an instrumental function. People develop favorable attitudes toward things that they perceive as helpful or rewarding (Katz & Kahn, 1978). An attitude change occurs when the attitude no longer serves its function and when the individual feels hindered or frustrated (Katz & Kahn, 1978).

If faculty do not feel that a technology is easy to use and can help them teach, they will be unlikely to use it. By incorporating CMS into a course, faculty members not only use the tools but also evaluate them through their experiences. The results of a research study conducted at the University of Houston (Liu, 2002) indicate that attitude and behavior have a reciprocal effect on each other. Attitudes do not stop at serving behavior. The outcome of behavior can either reinforce one's attitudes or weaken them. The reciprocal relationship is illustrated in Figure 1.

Although CMS are initially easy to use, the process of adoption is not as simple as it may seem. Some faculty members quit using CMS because they find that their system is not intuitive or easy to customize (Liu, 2002). In her key findings, Morgan (2003) also shows that there is a decrease in the use of CMS because "technology is time-consuming, inflexible and difficult to use" (p. 3). In their integrated technology adoption and diffusion model, Sherry, Billig, Tavalin and Gibson (2000) describe a learning/adoption trajectory, which is a four-stage process in which "teachers evolve from learners (teacher-trainees) to adopters of educational technology, to co-learners/co-explorers with their students in the classroom, and finally, to a reaffirmation/rejection decision" (para. 9). In the fourth stage, teachers decide whether to incorporate technology into their teaching based on whether the technology is "contributing to their self-efficacy as teachers; compatible with their personal vision of learning; and worth the time and effort that they have put into mastering a new set of skills" (Sherry et al., 2000, para. 9).

Create Activities and Support Services to Reinforce Faculty-Positive Attitudes

According to Carr's work on technology diffusion (1999), "Successful adoption was highly dependent on the degree, stability and wisdom of administrative

Figure 1. The reciprocal effect of attitude and behavior

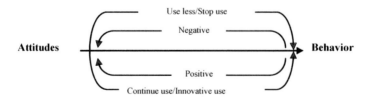

sponsorship" (para. 5). Administrators need to develop strategic plans that ensure the readiness for technology adoption and improve campus culture and environment so that educational technology development is sustained. David Brown (2003) states, "with reinforcement from a generous administrative attitude, the quality of teaching will constantly improve. Positive strokes work best, especially when they are deserved" (p. 3). Effective support services comprise collaborative teamwork from three areas: administration, technology, and academic.

Administrative support requires that leadership should develop long-term strategic plans for the adoption of technology with the involvement of stakeholders — experienced faculty, technology experts, and IT professionals. Faculty members should be provided with funding and release time to develop CMS courses and supplied with updated computer hardware and software to prepare course content materials efficiently. Most importantly, orientation and training should be held for new faculty and students to provide them with the necessary skills for mastering CMS tools. Technology should not be taken for granted. Quality of school-wide network connection and security should be guaranteed. The sophisticated features of CMS increase the demand on computer configurations and software compatibility. Computers in classrooms, labs, and libraries should be constantly checked for plug-in updates, browser compatibility, and viruses.

Technology support must involve a variety of strategies if CMS initiatives are to be successful. Customized and ongoing faculty CMS training programs should be provided in different formats (face-to-face, online, on CD, and using online streaming video) to suit faculty needs and different learning styles. The training programs should be proactive and outreaching. CMS training programs are more efficient if the training programs are reaching out to faculty instead of waiting for faculty and work better if they are localized in the departments. The University of Houston has a centralized training center for faculty members like most other institutions. UH instructional designers also hold CMS training in the individual departments. The record shows that the attendance rate is always higher if the training is in the departments. Faculty members are more interested when the training programs can address the specific problems in their own subject areas. The departmental training also fosters communication among faculty members so that they can learn from and share with one another. Online faculty training should be provided inside CMS. In workshops, faculty members learn to use CMS from the perspective of students. Through the learning process, they will have a better sense of how course design will affect student learning via their own experiences so that they can improve their own course design. Training programs should be both systematic and dynamic. CMS sequential training programs should be designed to ease faculty members into the systems without a large learning curve. Learning theories and principles should be built into the training on tool use. Since CMS are undergoing constant updating, short training sessions should be set up for faculty to keep them updated on the changes that will affect their teaching and student learning.

When fully online courses are a goal of the program, comprehensive course development services are necessary, including an effective learning environment, curriculum design, course structure, site layout, learning objects, multimedia components, academic activities, and the effective use of third-party applications in CMS. Moving a course online involves much more than just uploading material into CMS and adding a couple of tools. It needs collaboration from faculty content experts and online course design experts. Since online learning has become global, so should online support services (consulting, e-mail, Internet, phone calls, etc.). It will not be too far in the future that institutions of higher learning will collaborate on faculty support globally. It is difficult for one school to provide 24/7 support services, but if two or more schools located in different time zones come together, providing needed support will not be difficult. Timely support will facilitate both faculty and students in online education.

It is the responsibility of instructional support staff to use their expertise in introducing the most appropriate technology. The results of a study (Liu, 2002) conducted at the University of Houston also indicate that faculty are not using the best-suited technology to develop course materials in CMS. This lack of appropriateness can lead to inefficiency and frustration. Effective student support services are very important for a learner-centered environment. If students are not properly supported, it will not only affect motivation, retention, and learning, but will also backfire on faculty members' technology adoption and affect their attitudes towards using technology. When transferring to a new CMS system or when updating to a different version, technical support people need to provide diverse support services to make sure students can access and use the systems without major problems, such as by providing an online tutorial, a help desk, and face-to-face training. Counseling is necessary for new online learners who are easily discouraged with learning problems.

Academic support is the third arm of support services and provide motivation and examples for use of technology. Successful faculty adopters of technology should be rewarded and have their success recognized. This recognition will further promote the innovational use of technology. Successful testimony is the best way to persuade skeptical users. Such reinforcement will also create an institution-wide positive impact on technology adoption. Academic presentations of the best CMS-related practices set good examples for other faculty members who seek to improve the quality of their courses. Collaboration should be encouraged so that faculty members can share reusable learning objects and their online teaching and course design experiences. "The most successful faculty development programs are ones that use existing channels, value systems, and networks of trusted colleagues" (Brown, 2003, p. 13).

Learning-Style/Conceptual-Style Interaction Model: Development

Casmar and Peterson (2002) studied faculty's adoption of technology, taking into account personal behavioral patterns and looking into individual internal factors. A learning-style/conceptual-style interaction model emerged from an analysis of the data gathered from observations and interviews with faculty who were using instructional technology. Faculty members' technology adoption is a "very subjective event" because they have "opportunities and experiences that are based on their own unique context" (Casmar & Peterson, 2002, p. 1). They concluded that two factors explain most usage styles. The first factor is "the amount of flexibility versus concreteness that faculty showed in working with computer technology." The second factor is "the amount of vision versus practicality that faculty showed in using the technology to accomplish goals and objectives" (p. 2).

They classify faculty members into four learning style categories based on the learning-style/conceptual-style interaction model. *Concrete-practical* users learn new technology in a rote and premeditated fashion without applying a prior base of skills to the new learning. *Concrete-visionary* users learn in the same way as concrete-practical users, but they can make connections between technology and their subject area. *Flexible-practical* users learn new programs quickly by applying their previous computer experience, but they cannot use the program innovatively. Lastly, *flexible-visionary* users are intuitive learners and are able to learn new technological skills through "transference and through trial and error learning" (Casmar & Peterson, 2002, p.3).

Customize Training Programs to Accommodate Different Faculty Learners

According to the analysis of the conceptual model, everyone belongs to one of the four types and learns uniquely. Training programs should be designed in consideration of these learning styles and should be customized to meet faculty needs. Faculty feedback is important for further improvement of the quality of training.

Training programs should be designed from the perspectives of faculty rather than that of technology and should respect the skills that faculty bring to the training. CMS training sessions should be divided differently according to the learning levels of different faculty users. Learning should be contextual. For concrete-practical learners, training should start on a micro level. Trainers should present a specific teaching scenario, or faculty can present the issues related to course design or instructional delivery. Trainers should select the most appropriate tools to address those issues by providing examples from best practices. This tailoring will help faculty draw upon their experience and make instructional connections within their own course, and it will motivate them to learn since the acquisition of knowledge can assist them in addressing their own practical issues. If they learn to use the tools using real-world teaching examples, they will learn better and will be more likely to use the tools in their own courses. Trainers should start slowly and make sure that faculty members are comfortable with the basic skills before possibly overwhelming them with more complicated concepts.

For flexible users, the training pace can be faster and conducted on a macro level. Instead of teaching the tools one by one, training can start by providing a broader view of the course and introducing the tools as part of each step in course design. Since these types of learners are more creative, they can be exposed to more advanced concepts and can begin working with more advanced features. This depth will better engage them in learning, and they will be able to transfer the knowledge innovatively into their teaching.

One-on-one tutorials and consulting sessions should also be offered. These sessions work very well with faculty members who have difficulty coming to scheduled training classes, who have special needs, and who do not feel comfortable or psychologically secure in large class settings. This method is welcomed by faculty members since it is very quality-conscious. It caters to faculty members by addressing their individual course design and delivery issues.

It is important to infuse design principles and rules into the presentation of best practices. Design guidelines and principles are important to course design, but it is very difficult for faculty members to implement them effectively due to their lack of technical skills and unfamiliarity with CMS tools. Visualizing each principle and guideline by demonstrating the best practices will not only help faculty members understand these concepts better but, more importantly, will enable them to make visual connections to their own course designs.

The above theories and models analyze technology adoption from different perspectives and provide meaningful information necessary to understand the process of technology diffusion and to illustrate the importance of communicating technology to faculty. The development of training programs involves the whole process of understanding faculty members, analyzing their learning styles, and identifying their needs. These theories shed light on the development of effective faculty training programs for using CMS to ease the transition of incorporating technology into the process of teaching.

Conclusion

No matter how powerful they are, CMS should not by themselves drive the delivery of instruction. Faculty members are the key factors for successful technology-enhanced education. In order to take full advantage of CMS, it is imperative for us to understand CMS and how to innovatively adapt and customize CMS to accomplish educational objectives.

The successful development of faculty is the key to effective incorporation of CMS into educational systems. This success cannot be achieved without strong support from the administrative level. Effective communication, quality training programs, and full-scale support services will greatly reinforce faculty members' positive attitudes towards technology adoption.

The transformation of the classroom is promising with the further improvement of the quality of CMS, with the increased technology-based skills of faculty members, and with the theoretical and practical contributions relating to technology's effective use by educators, researchers, and practitioners. A more flexible and scalable learning environment created with the effective integration of technology will improve the quality of face-to-face, hybrid, and online education.

References

Ajzen, I. & Fishbein, M. (1980). *Understanding attitudes and predicting social behavior.* Englewood-Cliffs, NJ: Prentice-Hall.

Brown, D. (2003). *Developing faculty to use technology.* Bolton, MA: Anker Publishing Company.

Carmean, C. & Haefner, J. (2003). Next-generation course management systems. No.1, *Educause Quarterly.* Available at *http://www.educause .edu/ir/library/pdf/eqm0311.pdf*

Carr, V.H. (1999). Technology adoption and diffusion. Retrieved March 15, 2004, from *http://www.au.af.mil/au/awc/awcgate/innovation/ adoptiondiffusion.htm*

Casmar, S. & Peterson, N. (2002). Personal factors influencing faculty's adoption of computer technologies: A model framework. Retrieved October 20, 2002, from *http://coe.sdsu.edu/scasmar/site2002.pdf*

Clark. T. (2000). The constraints and possibilities of online course management software. Retrieved November 29, 2003, from *http:// www.nw99.net.au/papers/clark.html*

Davis, D. (1989). Perceived usefulness, perceived ease of use, and user acceptance of information technology. *MIS Quarterly, 9*, 319-339.

Foreman. J. (2001). Trading mules for tractors: The pros and cons of adopting a course management system. Retrieved February 17, 2004, from *http:/ /ts.mivu.org/default.asp?show=article&id=825*

Katz, D. & Kahn, R. (1978). *The social psychology of organizations* (2nd ed.). New York: John Wiley.

Katz, R. (2003). Balancing technology and tradition. *Educause Review.* Available at *http://www.educause.edu/asp/doclib/abstract.asp?ID= ERM0343*

Liu, Y. (2002). *Relevant factors in the selection of computer programs for class Web site design.* Unpublished Doctoral Dissertation, University of Houston, Houston, Texas.

Morgan, G. (2003). Faculty use of course management systems. Retrieved November 30, 2003, from *http://www.educause.edu/ir/library/pdf/ ERS0302/ekf0302.pdf*

Rogers, E.M. (1962). *Diffusion of innovations*. New York: The Free Press.

Schiffman, S.S. (1991). *Instructional technology: Past, present, and future* (2nd ed.). Englewood, CO: Libraries Unlimited.

Sherry, L., Billig, S., Tavalin, F., & Gibson, D. (2000). New insights on technology adoption in communities of learners. Paper published in *Proceedings of the AACE/SITE 2000 Conference*, San Diego, CA. Retrieved February 19, 2004, from *http://www.rmcdenver.com/webproject/SITEproc.html*

Section II

Research Implications and Creative Innovations for Future Design of CMS

Chapter X

Over the Rainbow:
Waking up in Tomorrow's OZ

Patricia McGee, The University of Texas at San Antonio, USA

Vicki Suter, iCohere, USA

Jennifer Gurrie, WebCT, USA

Abstract

Next generation course management systems must represent a convergence of the needs and perspectives of all of those who are engaged in the teaching and learning experience. To represent these points of view, we imagine one scenario in which four roles are enacted: instructional designer, traditional student, non-traditional student, and faculty member. This chapter draws on research and theory to illustrate the convergence between content-, learning-, and knowledge- management systems as well as processes managed by both *learner and instructor.*

Introduction

We might compare the current reality and future vision of course management systems (CMS) to Dorothy and her band of needy sojourners in the Wizard of Oz (Baum, 1900) who each believed that all of the solutions to their problems would be solved effortlessly, with a responsive and individually tailored wave of a wand. What the determined bunch found out, of course, was that no matter what they thought was going to work, there were plenty of detours and barriers along the way to reaching the wonderful wizard (who wasn't quite what he was promised to be). Their reality more closely resembles early 21st-century CMS with workarounds and "widgets," generic fixes, and, typically, a belief that there is no better place that the traditional classroom "home."

Thomas (1994) believes there is an interactive relationship between technological determinism[1] and organizational choice of how systems are valued and used, as well as how these systems relate to processes of change. He argues that to effect institutional or organizational change, the process of designing and implementing new technology must change. CMS are typically forced into institutions with little or no engagement of the end user (student or instructor). We contend that it is the responsibility of the end user to design the journey and be active, not just in getting on the road to Oz, but also in making sure that what is over the rainbow, stated in needs and desired outcomes, are clearly articulated so that engineers, software designers vendors, and higher-education decision makers can make informed decisions about how CMS are designed and operate.

So how do we decide what a next-generation course management system should look like and function to best support learning? The EDUCAUSE Learning Initiative (ELI), formerly known as National Learning Infrastructure Initiative (NLII), has provided us with a conceptual framework that should guide the design of functionality and the teaching and learning situated within the system. Our goal in this chapter is to relate theory to function. The CMS community of developers and users needs more than functions that serve as information communication technologies (ICT); they also require illustrations of situations that exist today but exemplify what learning in the 21st century will look like. For instance, we believe that lifelong learning cannot be restricted by or confined to a course "receptacle," and transfer of learning is more likely to occur through experiences in which learners deal with more complex content requiring them not only to relate theory to practical application, but to also make connections among courses taken over their academic experience. Next-generation CMS, however, must represent a convergence of the needs and perspectives of all of those who are engaged in the teaching and learning experience. To represent these points of view, we imagine one scenario in which four roles are enacted: instructional designer, traditional student, non-traditional student, and faculty member. As introduced in this chapter and elaborated in subsequent chapters, we attempt to illustrate the convergence between content, learning, and knowledge management systems as well as processes managed by *both* learner and instructor.

Who is Looking for the End of the Rainbow?

Teaching and learning in today's online learning environment requires consideration of roles, perspectives, and needs of many people: learner, instructor, instructional designer, and administrator. Research suggests that learning with and through technology will only be successful when learning processes, faculty development, and institutional systems are transformed (Buckley, 2002; Jamieson, Fisher, Gilding, Taylor, & Trevitt, 2000; Moore, 2002).

Learners are expected to be successful in systems for which they have little or no prior experience to prepare them. Research on the effectiveness of distance education or online learning programs shows difficulty with student-instructor communication, lack of socialization both with the instructor and other students, student engagement and interaction, innovation in teaching, and technical difficulties or support (see McGorry, 2003; Salisbury, Pearson, Miller, & Marett, 2002). Instructors must utilize pedagogy that addresses the needs of a changing population (Richards, 1997) with diverse learning needs in an environment with multiple means of connecting learners and instructors. Increasingly, instructors are required to manage resources in new ways in new contexts, with less readily accessible information about who the learner is and what he or she needs.

Instructional designers must consider how tools within a system can be supported, provide opportunities for collaboration, and give access to resources within and across systems while making sure that users are not burdened by unreasonable demands on their time. Instructional support models and templates must reflect best practices and standards. Information technology systems wrestle with issues of security, changing systems and standards, centralized support structures, and demands to provide quickly accessible tools and resources. Libraries are evolving into virtual centralized systems that support anytime, anywhere access.

Administration must find ways to balance economic realities with institutional assessment and the requisites for ensuring desired earning outcomes. Nontraditional students (who work, have families, or are the first in their family to attend college) are now the norm and need access to peers, instructors, and course materials while being provided feedback and opportunities to grow developmentally. Vendors are vigilant as they attempt to design sustainable innovations and make a profit.

The conceptual framework illustrated in the NLII's learner-centered principles ties all of these perspectives together through deeper learning and a common vocabulary. It is critical that we set priorities with *an authority of consensus*. Next-generation tools must reflect what is valuable across the curriculum and be accessible to all learners through a variety of systems. New ways of operating require new instructional strategies and designs that include support and guidance for faculty.

Part of learner-centered principles and practices means emphasizing learning how to learn and relinquishing "coverage anxiety," a phenomena prevalent in PK-12 education and increasingly in higher education. Passing the test and meeting standards should not be the end-all goals of higher education. It is critical that we develop a shared vocabulary across systems and disciplines if the institution of education can sustain truly meaningful lifelong learning through which not only skills are acquired, but also a love and desire for learning is nurtured.

Functional Requirements that Support Deeper Learning

Deeper learning requires control, feedback, interaction, collaboration, supports, and construction. The technical infrastructure that supports such functionality requires a transparent and background set of operations that do not draw attention to themselves. The following areas demand attention for next-generation CMS to fulfill the requirements of deeper learning (Cambridge, McGee, & Suter, 2003): access controls, assessment, cognitive supports and organizational tools, collaboration and communication tools, user interface, content creation and delivery, and instructional and learning design support.

Access controls relate to authentication and authorization functionality that determines how participants get into systems and what they are allowed to do once they are in. In order to support deeper learning, systems must allow the learner to have some degree of control over organization and navigational functions as well as to contribute to the content of the learning experience, be it a course, module, self-paced activity, etc.

Assessment functions should measure or document student learning and the effectiveness of learning materials to support student learning. CMS typically provided automated grading functions that can be attached to course assignments, but feedback about efficacy, appropriateness, and quality must come from the instructor. Learners needs responsive and just-in-time information to help them know more about their own learning and progress toward outcomes.

Cognitive supports and organizational tools are functions that support cognitive processes, reduce cognitive load of the learner, extend the cognitive capabilities of the learner or allow the learner to test ideas within problem-solving contexts, and provide support for organizing one's work. For example, rather than e-mail the course instructor about deadlines, assignment details, and where to locate course information, intelligent agents can quickly determine the answer, direct learners to the answer, or suggest they contact a peer or instructor.

Collaboration/communication tools are functions that support peer interaction, either in discussion or group work, including project/team management functionality.

User interface design and ease-of-use functionality of screens, particular to each type of user, also relieve cognitive load, and systems that allow customization can improve quality of interaction as well as efficiency for the user.

Content creation and delivery functions facilitate and support the sharing of resources and other content, generated or provided by faculty *and* students.

Instructional/learning design supports incorporate pedagogy, andragogy, and learner needs and preferences in course design and guide the instructional designer and faculty member to offer appropriate content for both the content and the learner.

The functions articulated here are starting points for envisioning how CMS could be used to intentionally and purposefully support learning while providing instructors the supports they need. To better illustrate how such functions could be realized, the following scenario captures one snapshot of what the future can bring.

The Scenario: A 21st-Century OZ

Imagine a university that applies theory to practice. The following scenario envisions the application of research and theory to an imaginary world where best practices shape policy, the design of instructional tools, and instructional practices.

Rainbow University opened its doors to undergraduate students in the early 1990s with a mission to design a liberal arts learning experience that drew from learning theory, prepared graduates for an ever-changing workplace and for the probability of career changes, and with the skills that are demanded by an increasingly global and technologically mediated world shaped by rapid economic, scientific, and social developments in which life-long learning is a necessity (Meyer, 2002). The founders of the institution recognized that there is no "typical" student; most work part- or full-time, have families or are caretakers, must borrow money to attend college, and want to complete a degree as quickly as possible.

In order to design a system that could meet the needs of current and future generations, Rainbow U. designed a "flexible learning" model (Taylor, 2001) in which students have access to interactive multimedia online, information communication tools (ICT) anytime, and Internet-based resources. All students receive a wireless laptop and can take advantage of the local telephone company's student discount for high-speed Internet access in their homes. The institution is moving toward an "intelligent flexible learning" model (Taylor, 2001), which builds on the fourth generation model[2] but will also allow "campus portal access to institutional processes and resources," allowing the institution to reduce its variable costs to close to zero. Flexible "semesters" have grading periods that are staggered so that students choose the period in which they want to complete a course cycle. Faculty have more flexibility in scheduling courses and find a distributed teaching model provides them more time to conduct ongoing research as they use technology tools to support the learner.

Instructional Designer

At Rainbow U., powerful learning experiences all begin with the Instructional Design Center, which consists of a team of talented individuals who are passionate about providing the learning experiences that empower students to meet their objectives. The team works virtually, of course, by leveraging the powerful workflow and collaborative design capabilities in their course management system to design the "learning spaces."

Today, Dot, an instructional designer, logs into the system as a designer to begin working on the remedial math learning environment, into which learners who do not achieve certain learning outcomes will be automatically enrolled for extra help and support. The environment consists of self-paced modules that students can complete based on the needs that the CMS has identified for them.

Dot starts in the design environment by searching the database of specific learning objectives (see Kreis, 2004) that have been created for the institution based on a comprehensive review of the curriculum and aligned with national standards. She decides to start by creating a specific learning object that will achieve a specific learning objective that has been identified as a critical need by the mathematics faculty. After selecting specific objectives that this learning space is being designed to help students meet, as well as some other parameters (i.e., target age range, instructional goal — which is remediation in this case — and level of interactivity), Dot clicks the "Find Content" control. This powerful function quickly conducts a federated search[3] across all of the content repositories[4] that Rainbow U. has linked or subscribed to, including their own, and presents her with a set of highly appropriate learning objects that are suited for the objectives and other contextual considerations she specified. As she reviews these content objects, she is also able to review associated comments from other instructional designers, instructors, and learners who have used them, to further inform her decision about which learning objects will best support the learning objectives. Any learning object in the university repository provides an optional rating system through which users provide feedback. This system has been used to identify best instructional design practices — voting is compared with learner achievement reports and frequency of use. This data helps to drive decisions not only about learning object design, but also about funding, pedagogical designs for classroom instruction, and the need for and design of embedded assessments. Dot is interested that one of the learning objects suggested to her was created and published by a student who was so enthusiastic about the connections and analogies she made as she finally understood a certain math concept, that she created short Flash™ movie to demonstrate her reasoning process so other students could benefit from it. "Wow," Dot thinks, "won't the faculty be excited to see this! Students are actually generating content for the course!"

After deciding on a core set of content and activities that she thinks will work well in this learning space, Dot then searches the center's instructional strategy database to get some ideas about how to best sequence and present the various activities and materials to learners, and what choices to offer them along the way. This database of strategies has been invaluable to her and has really helped Rainbow U. share best practices about instructional design and e-learning. The strategies are matched with supportive graphic user interface designs that provide a supportive learning framework. Because the design focuses on remediation, the system guides Dot to a graphical user interface (GUI) that is based on what students are already familiar with rather than introducing something new. Dot finally selects one of the instructional strategies that involves giving the learners an initial diagnostic assessment, followed by release of the content that is relevant to the specific concepts they are struggling with, as revealed in the assessment. She does decide to change the strategy slightly by embedding a group activity in which learners must review each other's steps for completing a problem and providing feedback. She then posts the object to a design forum and requests that a member of the forum review the object before it is published. There are many forums within the CMS collaborative work area. These are divided into special interests groups consisting of instructional designers, faculty members, and upper-level students who volunteer to serve as peer reviewers of objects. Once Dot receives feedback, she modifies the strategy and publishes it as a new object in the repository so that someone else may benefit from it.

Dot returns to the overall design of the remediation module once she has generated a specific learning object. The remediation area is organized by a visual map that illustrates for the learner the relationship between math concepts and how they relate to specific courses. In the design view, the objectives and instructional strategy have been laid out in a very visual way, basically looking like a flow chart or a map of the various paths the learners can take, and it is easy for Dot to add content and activities to each part of the map. The CMS allows her to access profiles of the target learners and their unique learning needs and preferences. Using this information, she can make sure that each module and the objects within the module provide the appropriate supports, tutorials, and media accommodations and can function in the GUI and instructional environment. She can associate glossaries, discussion areas, frequently-asked-question boards, e-mail to course instructors, or intelligent agents that can help students solve problems. She also makes sure that students with special learning needs have paths to interpret content in a pedagogically sound design.

Theory Behind the Practice

Computer-mediated communication tools are not typically designed so that new, or even experienced, users can quickly grasp the organization and functions of a system. GUI for learning systems is not always user-intuitive (Johnson, 2000), requiring well-honed technical skills and persistence by the user. Technology-centric interfaces, with little or no user adaptation or control over operations or look, create barriers for learning and interaction. Although attempts have been made to "internationalize" software (Wheeler, 2003), Kersten, Kersten, and Rakowski (2002) argue that software is culture-dependent because the programming is situated in the culture of the designer(s) and the embedded decision-making actions and rules of behaviors are also situated in culture. CMS should allow for not only language customization but also the unique needs and desires of learners, given their context and access points.

CMS are often promoted as being pedagogy-neutral with an assumption that instructional designers and faculty will put the instructional design into the system. However, pedagogy and interactions are determined by the system rather than the learner or instructional designer by virtue that they are tool-driven (i.e., chat, discussion, Web page development, e-mail, etc.). Adaptive learning research has explored the needs of a wide range of learning preferences with a focus on intelligent learning systems in which knowledge is transferred from the computer to the learner (du Boulay & Goodyear, 1992; McCalla, 1992). However, learning and pedagogy informs us that we should focus on knowledge construction rather than knowledge transmission (Derry, 1992; Jones, Greer, Mandinach, du Boulay, & Goodyear, 1992), which requires support for cognitive processes (Woolf, 1992). CMS can provide supports and guides in the form of intelligent agents that help the learner toward understanding, soliciting metacognitive reflection about what they know and understand. The system can then more authentically respond to the unique and individual needs of the learner (Laurillard, 1992).

Traditional Student

Leo is a 20-year-old student in the School of Architecture. While working at his part-time job on Sunday morning, he receives a text message on his cell phone — which he had previously designated as his preferred communication device — notifying him that a new learning module has been delivered to him, described by the next set of objectives it will help him meet. He instant messages his Web-scheduler to keep tonight open so he can spend some time reviewing the new module.

Later, when Leo arrives back home, he grabs his laptop and plunks down on the couch to check his e-mail. Here he finds an e-mail containing an update on all the activity that has taken place in his online learning environment since he last logged in. Helping Leo stay organized, the update is presented to him in a "What's New & What's Due" format that is task-oriented. This helps keep Leo focused on smaller tasks that he can complete one at a time to efficiently catch up on all the new information without getting overwhelmed. For example, instead of having to wade through all of the various discussions to find new activity of interest to him, only the threads that are both new and relevant to his learning objectives are presented to him in a digest form.

When Leo enters the learning environment, he is initially presented with another learning tool that further helps him plan out his learning activities for the night: a map that depicts a recommended learning path that has been prescribed in order to achieve the desired competencies that Leo has co-created with his e-advisor. The prescribed learning path takes into consideration all of Leo's past activity and usage data in the system and has thus built up a significant level of "intelligence" about how Leo learns best. For example, the learning path prescribes that Leo starts with a complex problem, the solution to which he must develop by actively discovering relevant resources, including research and subject matter experts, that will support the formation of the solution. Another student attempting to master the same competency might have been presented with all of the reading materials up front, some example case studies, and then an assignment to solve the problem, but that sequence doesn't match Leo's learning style as well.

The problem that Leo was presented with closely matches the personal interests that he identified in his learning profile upon entry into the program. The profile contains the higher-level learning objectives that he set with his e-advisor, along with other information such as his career aspirations, extra-curricular interests and hobbies, and past learning experiences. He can update most of this information at any time and the learning system will adapt accordingly. As Leo begins his quest to solve the problem, and thus achieve the desired learning objective, his learning map always appears in the corner of his screen with an indicator as to where he is at any given time. He can also "zoom out" on the map to see where this particular learning objective fits into his overall program objectives.

Collaboration and social interaction are important elements of one's learning experiences. As such, the learning system now automatically enrolls Leo into a virtual meeting room, where he can interact both asynchronously as well as real-time with other learners who are working toward similar objectives. In this "room," Leo can seek support from his peers, as well as share with them any relevant resources or knowledge he has discovered along his own learning path. From a student at a school across the country, he becomes aware of a subject matter expert whom he can contact to conduct an interview with in order to become familiar with this individual's very recent research.

As Leo actively seeks other online resources to help develop a solution to the problem he is working on, his learning system allows him to use a hot key (keyboard shortcut), which automatically adds the bibliographic information (metadata[5]) to his master list of learning resources. This will become, in essence, his virtual personal library of relevant information he collects along his lifelong learning journey. The metadata enables the system to automatically store the information in a categorical manner so that Leo can easily search at any time. Another helpful feature of this personal resource list is that it has the capability to proactively suggest new resources to Leo that are related to his learning objectives. He is amazed at how often the suggested resources are exactly what he was looking for.

Now, as Leo begins formulating his solution to the problem, he is able to retrace his previous path through the components of the resources that will support his solution. During his process of discovering resources, he was able to physically link concepts from one resource to another, producing sort of a problem-solving trail that both he and his instructors can see to gain insight into the process Leo undertook to get to his current point. Because the process of getting to the end result (the solution) is a significant part of assessing whether Leo has met the desired competency, the ability to review this process is incredibly valuable to Leo's instructor.

Finally, Leo posts his solution (learning outcome) on the learning map and publishes it to his official ePortfolio, where other students, instructors, and subject matter experts can view his work as well as post comments and feedback. From this external input, Leo can reflect back on his process and final product and think further about how he might incorporate some of the feedback into his future learning.

Theory to Practice

CMS provide the learner an environment in which he or she essentially experiences learning in isolation (Maroff, 2003), placing responsibilities on the learner that he or she does not experience in a traditional classroom. Time management, organization, documentation, and interaction are all different in a virtual learning environment and place different intellectual demands on the learner. In order for technology to successfully provide a learner-centered environment (Bork, 1991), it must reduce cognitive load. This is accomplished through a variety of strategies such as learner-controlled or selected navigational structures or designs (Hedberg, Harper, & Brown, 1993); multiple or combined formats of instructions and content (Mayer, 2001; Sweller, van Merriënboer, & Paas, 1998); and, chunking content into manageable bites that are accessed through a meaningful and understandable sequence (Merrill & Richards, 1983; Reigeluth & Stein, 1983).

When tasks are organized logically, providing a broad overview of the instructional scope and process, and in ways that are familiar to the learner, time management is supported. Cognitive maps can provide connections between the content stored in a system with a learner's learning path (see Bollini & Palma, 2003), particularly when CMS tools and functions are connected to course content, as well as external tools and resources for just-in-time and just-in-need learning.

Students have ownership of their learning when they produce and publicly share their work with others (Carmean, 2002) and the posting of materials in an ePortfolio creates an environment for ownership. When students know their work will be examined and possibly used by others (such as the student who generated a learning object for the remedial math repository), they are more likely to produce thoughtful and well-conceptualized work.

Nontraditional Student

Lola is in her mid-fifties and returning for an advanced degree. She has a technical background and a full-time position at a university, and is accustomed to using personal knowledge management tools, collaborative software, and productivity tools in her work. She had been exploring different doctoral programs, had even taken a couple of courses at her own university and another local college, and found the experience to be frustrating. The approach used by the faculty at each was unrelated in any way to the "learning-centered" principles they were teaching about, the materials they used were limited and obsolete (besides requiring a physical trip to campus to obtain), and the ways in which the college and university used (or more accurately, didn't use) technology were so alien to her real-world experience that she was having second thoughts about such an inefficient use of her scarce time. However, a colleague from across the country told her about Rainbow U.'s Ed.D. in educational technology, and after intensive interviews with many of the faculty, current students, and alumni, she decided that there was some hope for the relevance of higher education to her needs after all. She applied for and was accepted to the program.

Her first encounters with Rainbow U. reinforced her sense that she made a good decision. Before the semester even started, she had an account on their Knowledge, Learning, and Content Management System (KLCMS), known affectionately to users as "CLICK." She was already enrolled in the required core courses she had to take in her first year of the program and could view a complete map of each course, with the course flow laid out visually, major concepts to be covered highlighted, and learning outcomes defined, all tied to a calendar of course events for each. Even more importantly from her point of view, she could create an integrated calendar from her perspective that includes all of her classes, and export everything to the personal productivity calendar she is already using to manage the rest of her life. As an independent lifelong learner, Lola doesn't need much help getting organized as a student. But as an over-committed, busy professional, she also appreciates the intelligent agents in CLICK that remind her about upcoming deadlines and keep her time management on track. She can set the reminders to whatever interval she needs, and they pop up not only in her personal calendar, but also as separate e-mail messages — because these are the methods she chose.

CLICK also has a set of integrated virtual community functions that are not bound by a particular course, and Lola has already joined two virtual communities: a formal community set up just for her cohort, and an informal learning community of a number of people — faculty, alumnae, and external members from industry — who are interested in exploring learning objects and their impacts on teaching and learning. One of the first projects the learning object community is tackling is a research project for which a small team is applying

for federal funding. As it happens, Lola is very interested in the team's focus—
learner-created learning objects — because her university is also starting a
project and she is the team leader. Consequently, she applied and was
accepted to the workgroup. Because of the integrated nature of her program,
not only will this be work that she can leverage in her position at the university,
but as she is taking on setting up the assessment plan for the project, it will also
be her primary project for her research methods class in her doctoral program.
Because this is a community-sponsored project, the entire workgroup has been
approved to use CLICK as its Web-based collaborative environment for
managing the project, whether members are directly affiliated with the university or not. The only string attached to this use is that the group has to work with
another Rainbow U. faculty member to develop some resources within CLICK
for another class on designing learning objects. Lola can already see that
CLICK is going to help the project team work together more effectively. For
one thing, she is pretty tired of searching through all her e-mails for the latest
versions of the grant proposal, and having collaborative editing and document
version control will help eliminate that time-waster.

Lola is finding it to be a pleasure to work in one integrated environment for all
these purposes — whether asynchronous or synchronous communication,
informal collaborative work, project management, resource and information
sharing, or even knowledge creation. She has discovered that her focus and the
flow of her thinking, learning and creativity is much more continuous and
cumulative when it isn't constantly interrupted by having to switch to a new
environment and new user interface for each task or activity. Even though she
enjoys learning and using new technologies, Lola feels that her productivity is
decreased for every unique new user interface she has to navigate, and every
time she has to remember where she has stored a file or reference or resource
among multiple systems. For example, for one class, she is participating in a
dynamic, high-quality online discussion about the nature and power of "presence" in an online environment and has found it to be much more engaging than
in her previous experiences with asynchronous online discussions (usually she
is impatient with the sprawling, undisciplined character of these discussions).
She thinks that part of the improvement in the quality of the discussion (and her
experience) is that the interaction and the content aren't separated into different
silos; from inside the discussion she can immediately go to the specific area of
the document or online resource referenced in a post (and vice versa — from
a document she can link into a relevant discussion). Also, the environment
allows the discussion moderator to scaffold the discussion so that it evolves and

develops as posts build on each other (and the rubrics for quality participation were defined very clearly and are part of the scaffolding).

Another quality-enhancer for Lola is the ability to organize the discussion visually. This can be done automatically according to the scaffolding (basic assertion, new idea, challenge or different view, resource post, etc.), but the embedded collaborative visualization tool also allows Jacob, one of the other students, to "map" the discussion according to emerging themes. Lola participated in an online chat with Jacob and a few other interested students (using instant messaging and the same collaborative visualization tool, only synchronously) and found it very helpful to the organization of her own thoughts to review the visualization, contrast it with her own understanding, and contribute to the higher-level harvest of the discussion.

Finally, as someone who must plan well ahead to balance all the aspects of her busy life, Lola is already thinking about her dissertation topic. She realizes that she will likely change her topic and her research focus several times, but she also knows that the topic is likely to be oriented around the domain of learning communities in one way or another. She had been doing a great deal of reading on her own in this area and has noticed that the reading list in one of her first classes also seems to be organized around the topic of virtual communities, communities of practice, and learning communities., With all of this reading, she has a lot note-taking to do. Lola has discovered electronic note taking and e-annotation of resources, and has already organized a personal taxonomy of key words about these topics of interest for the bibliographic system integrated into CLICK. She can store her references and her notes about them in searchable format. She can foresee that this might reduce the pain of certain phases of her dissertation work and appreciates that she can already organize resources in a way that is meaningful to her, based on her own experiences and ways of thinking about things (and especially that she will not have to search back through some arbitrary organization by course). She is also excited about the personal journal that the ePortfolio system supports, so she can observe how her thinking about these topics evolves over the course of her program. As an active learning lurker in a virtual community of practice on communities of practice, she's been adding notes to her electronic journal about her reactions to the postings by experts in the field, identifying where new terms and ideas have been confusing to her and collecting in her bibliographic notes (with attribution and permission) some of the responses to private messages she has sent to posters.

Theory to Practice

Lola's story demonstrates the importance of all four environments for learning identified in the foundational work, *How People Learn* (Bransford, Brown, & Cocking, 2000): the learner-centered environment, the community-centered environment, the knowledge-centered environment, and the assessment-centered environment. Lola's experience of the Knowledge, Learning, and Content Management System (and its implementation and use at Rainbow U.) is that the course design and the use of educational technology is learner-centric, personalizing her organization of time, resources, content, and learning activities, recognizing her as an active learner with her own context and experience. While Bransford, Brown, and Cocking do not minimize the importance of facts and memory, they recognize that supporting and developing the learner's context is essential to understanding and knowledge construction. From Lola's professional experience, she recognizes the value of communities of practice and is able to transfer that experience into the educational setting, as the KLCMS integrates interaction and content into a community environment where the interaction with and feedback from experts and peers is an essential learning activity. Finally, the ePortfolio system and the support for journaling and continuous, longitudinal reflection across her academic experience will help provide many opportunities for authentic formative assessment to help Lola recognize, revise, and improve her thinking, with the assistance of faculty and her peers as they respond and give feedback.

Two additional theoretical systems are of particular relevance to Lola's story: communities of practice (Lave & Wenger, 1991; Wenger, 1998) and activity theory (Cole & Engerstrom, 1993). What is common to these theories is the suggestion that the "individual's changing role in the community or activity system enables his or her developing knowledge" (Polin & Riel, 2004, p. 19). Again, the KLCMS as described supports Lola metacognitively as she participates at the periphery of the community of scholars in the process of learning to become a scholar. This is only possible if the institution can, as Rainbow U. has, take on the role of integrating the task-based (class-oriented), the practice-based (communities of practice), and the knowledge-based (communities of inquiry)—because the KLCMS in the story does *not* limit the institution to organizing learning activities by "class." In addition, the KCLMS did support the essential "backbone of searchable database of Web objects (text, images, graphs, spreadsheets, and so on), ability to link objects together for personal use, support of collaborative or shared workspace, and ability to push information to others (through publishing, e-mail, or other broadcast methods)" necessary to knowledge management (Polin & Riel, 2004).

Instructor

Maizie has taught math foundations and algebra at Rainbow U. since it opened its doors, after teaching for four years at a large urban research institution where she struggled to publish and meet the needs of her students. The flexible learning model allows her to plan and complete research projects much more expediently since she can decide when and for how long courses will run. She works with an instructional designer to design courses that are primarily online; however, freshmen-level courses include some face-to-face meetings. Because her courses are required for most students, class size is large. Students may or may not be prepared for college math, so time and instructional design are critical issues for Maizie. As a new faculty member, she quickly recognized that more novice learners require specific and immediate feedback and support that can take an inordinate amount of time when teaching online. Over time, she found that the campus KLCMS, or CLICK, had tools that she could use to better support students while not demanding too much of her time. She and the instructional designer spent a good deal of design time prior to the beginning of the semester generating student tips that can be accessed through a database as well as through course content. These tips are revised each semester so that after about four semesters, Maizie found that there was little to change. She also uses the post-it function to give reminders, complements, or suggestions to students. The system gives her a choice about how messages are conveyed to students based on their preferences, and Maizie gets a much higher response rate when students make this choice.

Student assignments are graded automatically by the assessment engine in the KLCMS, so Maizie has more time to focus on addressing areas of problems or concerns that students may have but may not be willing to share with her. The system allows her to capture data that may indicate problems, through searching, sorting, and high-level intelligent agents that can identify patterns across different functions as revealed in student course maps. Since each student takes different paths, it is helpful to see how the paths are enacted and what implications they have for course design. From the data capture, Maizie learned that students have special interests that have not come out directly. Over time, she recognized that a community of learners would help future, current, and former students, so she established a student-led Virtual Community of Practice, or VCOP, that is outside of any one course but attached to all courses she teaches.

Since the system allows users to choose how they want to view and interact with content, Maizie has collected (and created some herself) learning objects that are stored in a repository accessible through a search function in CLICK. If students need or want to view content in another format, they only have to key the appropriate search term (embedded in the content) and use the object that is called up. Maizie can track what objects student are using, and that informs her about their needs and progress. Since faculty, staff, and students can contribute learning objects to CLICK, students can find objects on topics that Maizie might not have thought they needed to use. Maizie joined the CLICK virtual community of practice and found a research community examining many facets of learning objects. As a mathematician, she is particularly interested in how knowledge is conceptualized and presented to others, and she finds learning objects a perfect fit for her scholarship.

Maizie finds math is often perceived as dry, and students are not used to being engaged in math classes, so she has a variety of strategies for interactivity. She has a variety of discussions, some ongoing (e.g., mentoring, help), some task-specific (e.g., debates and problem solving challenges). Students also must create a learning object that is contributed to the course content and has to undergo a peer review. Students choose the topic of the object based on what the KLCMS learns about their knowledge sets in the course interactions and what resources they repeatedly use. She believes that when a student is struggling with a concept or rule, he or she can best learn by teaching others. She encourages them to create an object on a topic that is difficult to them. To help in this process, she has set up a collaborative online tutoring system with several high schools across the U.S. Her students can prototype objects and field-test them with APA course students as well as teachers. In this way they are getting feedback from expert sources and ensuring that their object accomplishes what they intend it to. This practice also helps to bridge the K–20 continuum as high school students interact with university-level content and processes. Objects are nominated for awards each semester through the peer review network. The CLICK learning object VCOP then reviews nominated objects, and winners are rated with five starts in the repository. Maizie has seen her role shift over time to coach and facilitator, as well as co-learner.

Teaching is just one part of Maizie's work. Remarkably, the flexible scheduling and CLICK are allowing her to be very productive in her scholarship. Her participation in the learning object VCOP has generated a new line of research that is garnering her recognition in her field as well as across campus. Learner-generated learning objects have been an effective strategy to examine how learners at different stages of knowledge acquisition conceptualize concepts and principles. More importantly, she has examined how experts conceptualize content and discovered what works best with different levels of prior knowledge and learning preference. By combining the scholarship of teaching and learning with research, she connects theory to practice.

Theory Behind the Practice

Maizie's story illustrates a variety of principles that ensure effective teaching in higher education. Collis and Strijker (2003) believe that student-generated learning objects can contribute to the knowledge content of a course that grows over time. Learner-generated objects that are reused and repurposed contribute authenticity to the presentation of content in that the user is the creator; who better to convey knowledge than a member of the target population? Objects can be revised by future learners, and the institution can examine how knowledge is encapsulated and evolves over time (Collis & Winnips, 2002). The idea of a contribution-pedagogy model of knowledge management shifts from the traditional transition model of knowledge transfer to a construction model (Diaz & McGee, in press). The interactive and cross-generational interactions support Laurillard's "conversational framework." Laurillard and McAndrew (2003) see this as an iterative process that requires learners to engage, act, and reflect upon what they know and how they come to learn.

Maizie's emergent scholarship of teaching and learning design reflects Boyer's (1997) scholarship of discovery, integration, application, and teaching. Maizie is learning about her discipline as she applies theory to her practice and contributing to the larger body of knowledge — not just about her discipline, but also the disciplinary pedagogy. The CLICK system affords her a seamless world in which practice, research, and theory are blended in a holistic ecosystem that supports the fertilization and development of her scholarship.

The End of the Rainbow

CMS can support a convergence between content, learning, and knowledge management as well as processes (as managed by learner and instructor). The system should not determine how instruction is designed or enacted, nor should it dictate how the learner may choose or need to learn at any given time. In the traditional classroom, learners can organize notes, switch chairs, instant message, meet with peers outside of class, create summaries and other learning supports, and practice in any manner they choose. In the traditional classroom, instructors can adjust and adapt as they perceive necessary based on the interactions and signals relayed by learners. CMS should afford both the same accommodations. In the stories provided here, content is disaggregated from the course and generated by instructional designer, learner, and instructor. Instructors learn from the learner's embodiment of content. All contribute to a shared body of knowledge that breaks down the walls of the classroom and expands the "course" to a community of learners and practitioners. In this way students acquire a status and voice that has heretofore been, for the most part, inaccessible to them. In this sense, the users become designers and custodians of their learning environment as they construct and manage the knowledge that they generate, both within formal learning experiences and those that are self-initiated and directed.

References

Baum, L. F. (1900). *The wonderful wizard of Oz*. Chicago; New York: George M. Hill.

Bolinni, L. & Palma, G. (2003). Web interface design based on cognitive maps: Generative dynamics in information architecture. Paper published in the *Proceedings of the Generative Art Conference*, Milan, Italy. Available at *http://www.generativeart.com/papersga2003/a07.htm*

Bork, A. (1991). Computers and educational systems. *Australian Educational Computing*, September, 34-37.

Boyer, E. (1997). *Scholarship reconsidered: Priorities of the professoriate*. New York: Jossey-Bass.

Bransford, J., Brown, A., & Cocking, R. (2000). *How people learn: Brain, mind, experience and school: Expanded edition*. Washington, D.C.: National Academies Press. Also available at *http://www.nap.edu/openbook/0309070368/html/3.html*

Buckley, D. (2002). In pursuit of the learning paradigm. *EDUCAUSE Review*, January/February.

Cambridge, D., McGee, P., & Suter, V. (2003). *NLII Spring Focus Session 2003 Meeting Notes.* Boulder, CO: EDUCAUSE. Available at *http://www.educause.edu/asp/doclib/abstract.asp?ID=NLI0343*

Carmean, C. (2002). Learner-centered principles. Retrieved March 11, 2004, from *http://www.educause.edu/MappingtheLearningSpace/2594*

Cole, M. & Engestrom, Y. (1993). A cultural-historical approach to distributed cognition. In G. Salomon (Ed.), *Distributed cognitions: Psychological and educational considerations*. New York: Cambridge University Press.

Collis, B. & Strijker, A. (2003). Re-useable learning objects in context. *International Journal on E-learning, 4*(2) 5-16. Retrieved October 13, 2004, from *http://dl.aace.org/14190/*

Collis, B. & Winnips, K. (2002). Two scenarios for productive learning environments in the workplace. *British Journal of Educational Technology, 33*(2), 133-148.

Derry, S. (1992). Metacognitive models of learning and instructional systems design. In M. Jones & P. Winne (Eds.), *Adaptive learning environments: Foundations and frontiers* (pp. 257-286). Berlin: Springer-Verlag.

Diaz, V. & McGee, P. (in press). Distributed learning objects: An open knowledge management model. In A. Metcalfe (Ed.). *Knowledge management and higher education: A critical analysis.* Hershey, PA: Idea Group Publishing.

du Boulay, B. & Goodyear, P. (1992). Student-system interactions. In M. Jones and P. Winne (Eds.), *Adaptive learning environments: Foundations and frontiers* (pp. 317-324). Berlin: Springer-Verlag.

Hedberg, J.G., Harper, B., & Brown, C. (1993). Reducing cognitive load in multimedia navigation. *Australian Journal of Educational Technology, 9*(2), 157-181.

Jamieson, P., Fisher, K., Gilding, T., Taylor, P., & Trevitt, A. (2000). Place and space in the design of new learning environments. *Higher Education Research and Development, 19*(2), 221-237. Available at *http://www.oecd.org/els/pdfs/EDSPEBDOCA027.pdf*

Johnson, J. (2000). *GUI bloopers: Don'ts and do's for software developers and Web designers*. San Francisco: Morgan Kaufmann.

Jones, M., Greer, J., Mandinach, E., du Boulay, B., & Goodyear, P. (1992). Synthesizing instructional and computational science. In M. Jones & P. Winne (Eds.), *Adaptive learning environments: Foundations and frontiers* (pp. 383-401). Berlin: Springer-Verlag.

Kersten, G. E., Kersten, M. A., & Rakowski, W. M.. (2002). Software and culture: Beyond the internationalization of the interface. *Journal of Global Information Management, 10*(4), 86-101. Retrieved on April 10, 2004, from *http://interneg.org/interneg/research/papers/2001/01.html*

Laurillard, D. (1992). Phenomemographic research and the design of diagnostic strategies for adaptive tutoring systems. In M. Jones & P. Winne (Eds.), *Adaptive learning environments: Foundations and frontiers* (pp. 233-248). Berlin: Springer-Verlag.

Laurillard, D. & McAndrew, P. (2003). Reusable educational software: A basis for generic e-learning tasks. In A. Littlejohn (Ed.), *Reusing online resources: A sustainable approach to e-learning.* London: Kogan Page.

Lave, J. & Wenger, E. (1991). *Situated learning: Legitimate peripheral participation.* New York: Cambridge University Press.

Maroff, G. I. (2003). *A classroom of one: How online learning is changing our schools and colleges.* New York: Palgrave Macmillan.

McCalla, G. (1992). The search for adaptability, flexibility, and individualization: Approaches to curriculum in intelligent tutoring systems. In M. Jones & P. Winne (Eds.), *Adaptive learning environments: Foundations and frontiers* (pp. 91-122). Berlin: Springer-Verlag.

McGorry S. Y. (2003). Measuring quality in online programs. *The Internet and Higher Education, 6*(2), 159-177.

Merrill, M. D. & Richards, L. (1983). Component display theory. In C. M. Reigeluth (Ed.), *Instructional design theories and models: An overview of their current status.* Hillsdale, NJ: Prentice-Hall.

Meyer, K. A. (2002). Quality in distance learning. *ASHE-ERIC Higher Education Report, 29*(4) 1-121.

Moore, M. G. (2002). A personal view: Distance education, development and the problem of culture in the information age. In V. Reddy & S. Manjulika (Eds.), *Towards virtualization: Open and distance learning* (pp. 633-640). New Delhi, India: Kogan Page.

National Learning Infrastructure Initiative (NLII). (2003). Next-generation course management systems. Tucson, Arizona. Available at *http://www.educause.edu/nlii/meetings/nlii032/*

Reigeluth, C. M. & Stein, F. S. (1983). The elaboration theory of instruction. In C. M. Reigeluth (Ed), *Instructional design theories and models: An overview of their current status.* Hillsdale, NJ: Prentice-Hall.

Polin, L. & Riel, M. (2004). Learning communities: Common ground and critical differences in designing technical environments. In S. A. Barab, R. Kling & J. Gray (Eds.), *Designing for vcirtual communities in the service of learning.* Cambridge, MA: Cambridge University Press.

Richards, T. (1997). Educating in a time of changing student demographics. *The Technology Source.* Available at *http://ts.mivu.org/default.asp?show=article&id=544*

Salisbury, W. D., Pearson, R. A., Miller, D. W., & Marett, L. K. (2002). The limits of information: A cautionary tale about the distance education environment as perceived by students. *e-Service Journal, 1*(2), 65-82.

Sweller, J., van Merriënboer, J. J. G., & Paas, F. G. W. C. (1998). Cognitive architecture and instructional design. *Educational Psychology Review, 10,* 251-296.

Taylor, J. C. (2001). Fifth generation distance education. *Higher Education Series,* 40. Retrieved March 10, 2004, from *http://www.dest.gov.au/highered/hes/hes40/hes40.pdf*

Thomas, R. (1994). *What machines can't do: Politics and technology in the industrial enterprise.* Berkeley, CA: University of California Press.

Wenger, E. (1998) Communities of practice: Learning as a social system. Systems Thinker. Retrieved December 12, 2004, from *http://www.co-i-l.com/coil/knowledge-garden/cop/lss.shtml*

Wheeler, D. A. (2003). Why open source software/free software (OSS/FS)? Look at the numbers! Retrieved January 12, 2004, from *http://www.dwheeler.com/oss_fs_why.html*

Winter, L. (1977). *Autonomous technology: Technics-out-of-control as a theme in political thought.* Cambridge, MA: MIT Press.

Woolf, B. (1992). Towards a computational model of tutoring. In M. Jones, & P. Winne (Eds.), *Adaptive learning environments: Foundations and frontiers* (pp. 209-232). Berlin: Springer-Verlag.

Endnotes

[1]   Technological determinism means that technology is a driving force for change. From this perspective, the CMS determines how teaching and learning occurs and possibly shape pedagogy. Winter (1997) believes that institutions experience a technological shift due to inattentiveness that results in acculturation.

[2]   Taylor's fourth-generation flexible learning model utilizes online and interactive multimedia with Internet-accessible resources and computer-mediated communication.

[3]   A federated search allows users to enter keywords into one search interface but searches multiple directories or repositories. Results are then sorted by a predetermined hierarchy, such as title, source, media, etc.

[4]   Content repositories are databases of learning objects that are designed to support specific objectives and which can be added as a resource or part of a course requirement.

[5]   Metadata is descriptive data that is embedded in or attached to a learning object, allowing search engines to more effectively locate digital materials.

Chapter XI

Pushing the Envelope:
Designing Authentic Learning Activities Using Course Management Systems

Nada Dabbagh, George Mason University, USA

Abstract

This chapter describes how course management systems (CMS) can be utilized to support learner-centered practices and meaningful learning in distributed or online learning environments. Specifically, the chapter provides: (1) a pedagogically-oriented classification of the features and components of CMS enabling the online course developer to comprehensively understand the pedagogical potential of a CMS; and (2) a framework that explicitly demonstrates how to design authentic learning tasks using the features and components of CMS to create course designs and distributed learning interactions that engage students in meaningful learning.

Introduction

Recent advances in Internet and Web-based technologies have redefined the boundaries and interactional pedagogies of traditional face-to-face classroom learning by stretching its scope and deepening its interconnectedness (Dabbagh & Bannan-Ritland, 2005). New learning interactions that were not perceived possible before can now be facilitated, such as the coupling of experts from around the world with novices, the instantaneous access to global resources, the opportunity to publish to a world audience, the opportunity to take virtual field trips, the opportunity to communicate with a diverse audience, and the ability to share and compare information, negotiate meaning, and co-construct knowledge. These types of learning interactions can be described as *distributed forms of interactions* because they are distributed across space, time, and various media. They are also perceived as tools or activities that promote higher-order thinking, enhance social learning skills such as communication and collaboration, and sustain motivation in distance education settings (Navarro & Shoemaker, 2000).

Distributed forms of interactions can be used to supplement face-to-face instructional activities, bringing to the forefront an important distinction between a traditional course and the notion of "distributed course events" or a "distributed course" that holds complex challenges for the course designer (Dede, 1996; Dabbagh, 2000). A distributed course can be defined as a course in which one or more of the instructional events that traditionally have occurred in the classroom are distributed to learners so that they may occur while learners are separated by either time or space from one another and the course instructor (Locatis & Weisberg, 1997). Learning can therefore occur at the same time in different places (e.g., through scheduled video conferencing events), at different times in the same place (e.g., meeting face-to-face in the classroom to attend guest lecturers), or at different times in different places (e.g., using e-mail to communicate with the instructor and with each other). Research indicates that a distributed or blended learning model, one that combines face-to-face and online interactions, has the most impact on student achievement (Dean, Stahl, Sylwester, & Peat, 2001).

Among the leading Web-based technologies utilized to facilitate the design, development, and delivery of distributed course events in schools, corporate training, and higher education contexts are CMS or learning management systems (LMS), defined in the preface of this book. According to Harasim (1999), the goal of a Web-based authoring system such as CMS or LMS is "to provide a flexible framework to support advanced pedagogies based on active learning, collaboration, multiple perspectives, and knowledge building" (p. 45). However, several researchers and practitioners have argued that CMS have limitations with regards to supporting open and flexible instructional designs that promote learner-centered practices and meaningful learning.

For example, Hedberg and Harper (1998) suggest that most course authoring tools limit the designer to the preprogrammed modules of the tool and to the underlying assumptions of highly structured instructional design models. Oliver (2001) states, "a major concern of online course management systems is that they emphasize faculty dissemination tools over student processing tools, even though the latter are more likely to promote student interaction and engagement" (p. 47). Marra and Jonassen (2001) contend that a limitation of CMS is their inability to effectively accommodate multiple and alternative forms of student knowledge representation and authentic assessment, which are fundamental principles of constructivist learning. Harvey and Lee (2001) suggest that marketing approaches of CMS vendors tend to promote the rapid and efficient deployment of online courses, "causing the relegation of teaching methods to a secondary consideration behind the technical components of the course" (p. 37). In other words, by focusing on increasing the efficiency with which institutions can develop Web-based versions of their courses, the technological convenience of CMS in facilitating this transition may take priority over sound pedagogy (Firdyiwek, 1999). In addition, Harvey and Lee (2001) suggest that the course templates and structures of CMS appear to make implementing constructivist or learner-centered practices more difficult than implementing objectivist or teacher-directed instructional practices.

Although the above critiques are credible and well supported, I argue in this chapter that the problem with pedagogical designs resulting from the use of CMS is not with their implicit teacher-centered interface or their template controlled authoring architecture, nor is it with the propensity to migrate as many existing courses as possible, in the shortest time possible, to an online delivery format. Rather, the problem is first with the tendency of early adopters of CMS to use only the most obvious and easily accessible components and features of the system whose purpose is largely to deliver content and disseminate information, and second with the lack of pedagogical advisement and support needed to ensure that distributed and online course developers and instructors are rethinking their teaching approaches and course designs based on current research on distributed and online learning. Hence, a comprehensive examination of the features and components of CMS and the mindful integration of the instructional and learning tasks afforded by these features will yield flexible and effective pedagogical designs that promote learner-centered practices and meaningful learning. The next section of this chapter provides a pedagogically oriented classification of the features and components of CMS, enabling the distributed or online course developer to comprehensively understand the pedagogical potential of CMS.

Pedagogical Features of Course Management Systems

There are several common features that are integral to all course management software (Barron & Liskawa, 2001). These include asynchronous communication, synchronous communication, online testing, home pages (for students and instructors), security features (e.g., password protection and level of usability), course design and management, student management, and student and site tracking. An alternative classification of common features proposed by the Center for Curriculum Transfer and Technology (2000) includes Web browsing, asynchronous and synchronous sharing, student tools, resources, lessons, course data, administration, help desk, and technical information. Although these categories capture the integral features of CMS, they do not provide a pedagogical classification of the specific components or tools that support such features. For example, what are the tools that support synchronous and asynchronous communication, course design and management, and online testing? What are their pedagogical functions? How are those tools used to design distributed forms of interactions?

To address these questions, a broader and more pedagogically oriented classification of the features of CMS is provided. This classification includes five categories: (1) collaborative and communication tools; (2) content creation and delivery tools; (3) administrative tools; (4) learning tools; and (5) assessment tools (Dabbagh & Bannan-Ritland, 2005). Next, each category is described and examples of specific features within each category are provided from WebCT™ (*www.webct.com*), Blackboard™ (*www.blackboard.com*), Lotus LearningSpace™ (*www.lotus.com/products/learnspace.nsf/wdocs/homepage*), and Virtual-U™ (*www.vlei.com/*). These particular CMS were selected because of the author's familiarity with their use. The proposed classification, however, applies to any CMS or LMS.

Collaborative and Communication Tools

This category or class of tools includes asynchronous communication tools, synchronous communication tools, and group tools. Asynchronous communication allows instructors and learners to "post messages, read and respond to messages, reflect on responses, revise interpretations, and modify original assumptions and perceptions" (Chamberlin, 2001, p.11). These functions are possible because of the time-delayed nature of asynchronous communication. Asynchronous communication is an inherent feature of Internet-based communications technology and has become an essential facility for online learning. CMS have incorporated asynchronous communication through components or tools such as e-mail, threaded discussion forums, and bulletin boards, enabling one-to-one, one-to-many, and many-to-many interactions. Additionally, tools such as "Student Profiles" in Lotus LearningSpace™, "Personal Info" in Blackboard™, and "Student Homepages" in WebCT™, allow students to post bios and share personal and background information and experiences prompting meaningful communication and socialization.

Synchronous communication gives participants the ability to interact in real time (as in face-to-face learning). Students and instructors log on at the same time and are virtually present together. They can discuss an issue, present on a topic (using PowerPoint®, for example), collaborate on a task or project, model or explain a procedure or a concept, and engage in brainstorming or hypotheses-generation activities. Synchronous communication is more informal and spontaneous than asynchronous communication. CMS have incorporated synchronous communication through features or tools such as virtual chat, electronic whiteboards, instant messaging, screen sharing, and audio and video conferencing.

Group tools support both asynchronous and synchronous communication to enable groups of students to work and learn as a team. CMS have the capability of generating group discussion areas and to provide groups with document sharing and editing tools to engage students in completing group assignments and tasks. Group tools can support formal (e.g., presenting the final product of collaborative work) and informal (e.g., work in progress) types of group activities. Examples of group tools include group discussion forums, virtual chat areas, file exchange tools, group posting areas, breakout sessions, and group e-mail.

Some group tools also allow learners to create their own learning communities with peers or others outside the course, in contrast to groups or teams defined by the instructor. For example, Blackboard™ has a user directory tool or feature that connects learners with all users of Blackboard™ on campus, irrespective of what course they are enrolled in. There is also a class roster tool in Blackboard™ with e-mail links so that learners can contact each other and form virtual study groups. Virtual-U™ has a synchronous tool called "Café" that allows students to socialize in an informal setting.

Content Creation and Delivery Tools

This category includes tools for instructors that enable them to deliver course content and resources, and tools for learners that enable them to contribute course content, submit assignments, and interact with course resources. For example, Blackboard™ has tools such as "Course Information" and "Course Documents" that enable instructors to post the course syllabus and documents related to course assignments. Instructors can upload documents as Microsoft Word® files, HTML files, or PDF files. The files appear as links for students to click on and download to their computer, or view as HTML files in their browser. Blackboard™ also has an external links feature that enables instructors to provide students with Web links (hypermedia links) related to the course content.

WebCT™ has tools such as "Add URLs and Pages", "Content Module", and "Manage Files" that allow instructors to organize the course content in a variety of formats ranging from a linear/sequential format, in which learners view the content much like turning through the pages of a book, to a more random or nonlinear format, in which students view the content in any order they choose. The "Content Assistant" feature in WebCT™ provides instructors with help and options on how to generate course content.

Examples of student content creation tools include a student presentation area in WebCT™, which allows students to post their assignments, reflection journals, and solutions to case studies. Student presentation areas also enable students to contribute additional course resources for exploration by peers. Students (or the instructor) create an HTML file (called the index file) that serves as a menu of hyperlinks to the documents that students upload to their designated area. WebCT™ also has an assignment feature that allows instructors to post an assignment or class activity, assign points to the activity, and list a start and end date. Students can download the activity and submit their solutions to a designated area for the instructor to grade or provide feedback. Blackboard™ has a similar feature for activities and assignments called

"Tasks." For more examples of content creation and delivery tools pertaining to the selected CMS, visit *www.prenhall.com/dabbagh/ollresources/tools-pedagogical-classification.html* (Dabbagh & Bannan-Ritland, 2005).

Administrative Tools

This category includes: (1) tools to manage students and student information, such as importing the class roster from the institution's registration system, updating or editing student info, assigning user IDs and passwords, removing users, generating presentation areas and generating an e-mail list; (2) tools to manage teaching assistants, such as adding assistants, graders, and course designers to the course and providing guest access; and (3) tools to manage group work, such as generating student groups and group work areas and presentation areas to post group work. For example, in WebCT™, instructors can generate a student presentation area by assigning one area per student or group areas. So, the student presentation tool can be considered a content creation and delivery tool from a student standpoint, and an administrative tool from an instructor standpoint. Administrative tools also include functions such as setting the duration of the course, controlling enrollment options, categorizing the course in the course catalog, and setting the course availability (access to the course).

Learning Tools

This category includes tools primarily for learners, enabling them to interact meaningfully with course content. In the process of exploring course content, working on assignments, and participating in learning activities, students are able to apply learning and organizational strategies to process the content in a meaningful way and organize their learning experience. Learning tools can be thought of as tools that enable learners to manipulate content online and create personalized experiences during the learning process in contrast to tools that allow students to post the end products of their learning in a presentation area or dropbox. The abilities to annotate text while exploring course content, take notes (online), link information, and build a personal folder of relevant material are examples of learning tools.

There are several types of learning tools embedded in CMS. These include:

- Collection tools, such as bookmarks, personal folders, and a compile feature that enables individual compilation of course materials and discussion forums for later use.

- Expository tools, such as diary or journal-type note-taking tools that are generally nonshareable, post-it or annotation-type features that can be directly associated with course materials and can be shareable, and student calendars that learners can use to organize tasks and define schedules.

- Exploratory tools, such as open-ended search tools that can scan course materials, the entire course site, or the Web, and customizable portals that students can use to explore sites for prespecified information or news.

- Scaffolding tools, such as glossary, help tools, index, and course maps or navigation maps that support learners in finding course information and navigating through course content.

For more examples of learning tools pertaining to the selected CMS, visit *www.prenhall.com/dabbagh/ollresources/tools-pedagogical-classification.html* (Dabbagh & Bannan-Ritland, 2005).

Assessment Tools

This last category includes assessment tools primarily for instructors, although the tools can engage learners in self and peer assessment activities depending on the pedagogical orientation of the course. Most course management systems integrate assessment tools that are objectivist in nature. For example, some of these tools provide the ability to create programmed quizzes or tests that are generally true/false, multiple choice, matching, ordering, or fill-in-the-blank. These forms of assessment are electronically scored and can provide instant feedback to the student. Questions can also be randomized from a pool of questions or a question bank to ensure that students are not simply memorizing the test.

Additional forms of assessment include comprehension essay-type tools in which the student submits a text-based assignment directly to the assessor via a communications component or a submission box-type feature such as the

"Digital Dropbox" tool in Blackboard™. Essay-type tests or assignments are more subjective in nature and can be used to assess higher-order learning skills. It might be possible to grade essay-type tests by an intelligent parser (a program that can search text and match or compare results against pre-established text parameters set by the instructor); however, currently CMS do not have embedded intelligent agents or parsers, and instructors must grade such assignments using traditional grading methods and provide feedback to students via a communication tool such as e-mail.

Assessment tools can also be used to develop self-assessment tests. Self-assessment tests are an example of authentic assessment allowing students to monitor their own comprehension and learning. WebCT™ has a specific self-test tool that instructors can use to construct self-assessment tests. Authentic assessment can also be implemented using content creation and delivery tools. For example, instructors can engage students in peer assessment activities by developing rubrics for assignments, posting such rubrics using a content delivery tool, and requiring students to use these rubrics to evaluate each other's work. Peer evaluations can be submitted using a communication tool or a content delivery tool such as "Student Presentation" in WebCT™. Instructors can also promote self-assessment by requiring students to submit reflection journals and create electronic portfolios to demonstrate their learning. Instructors can use the e-mail feature to provide constructive feedback on such assignments. Instructors can also generate surveys to assess individual contributions to group work and to collect student feedback about the course for formative evaluation purposes.

Assessment tools also include tracking features that allow instructors and students to track and monitor their progress. For example, WebCT™ allows instructors to track the number of times students access a course, which content pages students access, what time students accessed these pages, and for how long. WebCT™ also provides instructors with tools to track the number and time of postings per student and search discussion forums by student name, user ID, date, or discussion topic. Learners can also track their progress by checking grades periodically. Most course management systems include tools to report grades resulting in "Check Grades" or "Check Progress" tools for learners. Instructors can generate grading columns for each assignment, assign the number of points for each column, and record the points for each student after an assignment is submitted and graded. Instructors have the option of hiding, revealing, or releasing grades when appropriate. The grading columns behave like a spreadsheet, providing class averages per assignment and totals per student as well as other informative statistics. Instructors can also download grading areas as a single file and import the file into a database or spreadsheet program for further analyses.

Designing Authentic
Learning Tasks Using CMS

Authentic learning tasks are tasks that are anchored in a realistic setting and place the focus on solving a problem rather than learning a body of content. Students apply their prior knowledge and adapt it to new situations and problems, thereby extending their body of knowledge in meaningful and usable ways. In mathematics education, these learning tasks are sometimes referred to as "thought-revealing" or "model-eliciting" problems (Lesh, Hoover, Hole, Kelly, & Post, 2000). The onus is placed on the student to create a model to capture, in a meaningful way, the complexity presented in the learning task. Attributes of authentic learning tasks include: (a) embedding learning in complex, realistic, and relevant contexts; (b) providing for social negotiation and collaboration as an integral part of learning; (c) supporting multiple modes of knowledge representation; (d) providing the opportunity to examine the learning task from different perspectives using a variety of resources; (e) encouraging ownership in the learning process; (f) providing the opportunity for reflective thinking, self-evaluation, and self-monitoring; and (g) allowing competing solutions and diversity of outcomes (Driscoll, 2000; Reeves, Herrington, & Oliver, 2002). These attributes emphasize learner-centered practices and align with the five principles of deeper learning proposed by Carmean and Haefner (2002). Therefore, authentic learning tasks should be the primary consideration of online learning developers when designing distributed forms of interactions using CMS.

In order to demonstrate how the features and components of CMS can be used to support the design of authentic learning tasks, three types of learning tasks will be considered: exploratory, dialogic, and supportive. The next section describes each of these types of learning tasks and provides examples of how the pedagogically oriented classification of the features and components of CMS discussed earlier can be used to support the design of these learning tasks.

Exploratory Learning Tasks

Exploratory learning tasks are based on the theoretical construct of discovery learning or inquiry-based learning in which learners are provided with a scientific-like inquiry or authentic problem in a given content area and asked to generate hypotheses, gather relevant information using a variety of resources, and provide solutions, action plans, recommendations, and interpretations of the situations (Dabbagh & Bannan-Ritland, 2005). Examples of exploratory learning tasks include problem solving, exploration, hypothesis generation, and role playing. Problem solving emphasizes learning how to learn, rather than learning specific content. In problem-solving tasks, the process of problem solving, such as the learner's ability to form a hypothesis, find and sort information, think critically about information, ask questions, and reach a resolution or solution, becomes more important (Roblyer, Edwards, & Havriluk, 1996).

Exploration encourages "students to try out different strategies and hypotheses and observe their effects" (Collins, 1991, p. 135). In exploratory learning, there is limited instruction and guidance from an instructor and more student-generated learning through exploring and discovering information. "This puts students in control of problem solving," add Collins (p. 135). Therefore, exploration and problem solving are interdependent. Hypothesis generation supports concept acquisition by setting forth tentative hypotheses about the attributes that seem to define a concept, and then testing specific instances against these hypotheses (Bruner, Goodnow, & Austin, 1956). Hypothesis generation allows students to examine "what if" questions by predicting results, testing their predictions, and then engaging in a reasoning process to analyze what happened and why. The creation of hypotheses, therefore, is a type of formal scientific reasoning that is facilitated through scientific inquiry (Mayer, 1987).

Lastly, role playing allows learners to assume practitioner and professional roles such as scientists, physicians, historians, salespeople, and other roles, in order to act out situations that these professionals face in the real world. Learners can imagine that they are other people in different situations, and then make decisions as situations change (Heinich, Molenda, & Russell, 1993). Table 1 provides examples of how exploratory learning tasks can be promoted using CMS.

Table 1. Promoting exploratory learning tasks using CMS

Learning Task	CMS Tools Category	Example of Implementing the Learning Task Using a CMS
Problem Solving	Content Creation and Delivery Tools	Using the "Assignment" feature in Blackboard, instructors can create problem-based learning (PBL) environments in which students are charged with a complex problem to solve.
Hypothesis Generation	Content Creation and Delivery Tools	Students can link to Microworlds or develop hypotheses within problem-based environments using CD ROMs, image databases, and "Add Pages" and URL features of WebCT.
Role Playing	Collaborative and Communication Tools	Instructors can structure team debates using breakout sessions and chat features of LearningSpace to engage students in role-playing activities.
Exploration	Learning Tools	Students can explore the "Media Center" feature in LearningSpace to find resources according to individual learning style, curiosities, or learning needs.

Dialogic Learning Tasks

Dialogic learning tasks emphasize social interaction through dialogue and conversation. The idea is to assist learners in constructing new knowledge primarily through dialogue as a form of interaction. Examples of dialogic learning tasks include articulation, reflection, collaboration and social negotiation, and promoting multiple perspectives. Articulation involves "having students think about their actions and give reasons for their decisions and strategies, thus making their tacit knowledge more explicit or overt" (Wilson & Cole, 1996, p. 606). In other words, when students are provided with opportunities to articulate their knowledge or understanding of something, they are explaining to others what they know. As students articulate their knowledge to one another, they share multiple perspectives and generalize their understanding and knowledge so that it is applicable in different contexts (Collins, 1991). Hence, articulation implicitly supports multiple perspectives.

Reflection or reflective thinking involves asking students to review what they have done, analyze their performance, and compare it to that of experts and peers (Collins, 1991). Reflection and articulation are interdependent. Wilson and Cole (1996) point out that reflection is like articulation except that it is pointed backwards to previous tasks. Reflection can occur when students, for example, are asked to keep a journal about a learning experience and revisit this journal at the end of the experience to reflect on their learning process and reconstruct what they have learned, giving new meaning to the situation.

Collaboration and social negotiation involve interaction between and among two or more learners to maximize their own and each other's learning. Students are actively involved in researching the information they are tasked with learning, organizing it into a meaningful body of knowledge, explaining it to each other, presenting it to the class and their instructor, and relating it to what they know, thereby integrating it into their existing knowledge structures. As Duffy and Cunningham (1996) state:

> *In collaboration and social negotiation the goal is to share different viewpoints and ideas and to collaborate on problem-solving and knowledge building activities. Groups are formed to provide variation in classroom activity (face-to-face or virtual), share work-loads (permitting larger projects), and promote peer tutoring (p. 187).*

Promoting multiple perspectives involves presenting information in a variety of ways to encourage learners to view the knowledge base from multiple viewpoints and find their own connections and explanations (Jacobson, 1994). The goal of promoting multiple perspectives is to generate cognitive dissonance so that, firstly, learners are aware that there are multiple perspectives on an issue, which is the case in real-world situations, and, secondly, learners are engaged in exploring each perspective to seek a meaningful resolution to the issue at hand in the context of their own experiences and knowledge. Table 2 provides examples of how dialogic learning tasks can be promoted using CMS.

Table 2. Promoting dialogic learning tasks using CMS

Learning Task	CMS Tools Category	Example of Implementing the Learning Task using a CMS
Reflection	Learning Tools	Using the "My Notes" feature in WebCT, students can revisit their journals to relate new knowledge to old and to identify any unresolved questions.
Articulation	Collaborative and Communication Tools	Using the "Discussion Board" or "Virtual Classroom" features in Blackboard, students can make their tacit knowledge explicit by presenting their ideas in a structured environment.
Collaboration and Social Negotiation	Collaborative and Communication Tools	Students can use the "VGroups" feature in Virtual-U to discuss solutions to complex problems in real time with their team members. Students can initiate VU-Chat rooms in Virtual-U to confer informally.
Multiple Perspectives	Content Creation and Delivery Tools	Students showcase their projects and problem solutions in the presentation area of WebCT. Classmates can contrast their own work with the posted work of others.

Supportive Learning Tasks

Supportive learning tasks are typically enacted by the expert, coach, mentor, instructor, or embedded performance support system with the goal of modeling the desired performance, skill, or process and observing and supporting learners during their execution of a learning task (Dabbagh & Bannan-Ritland, 2005). The goal of supportive learning tasks is to provide scaffolding for students and create a resource-rich learning environment to support learner-centered practices. Examples of supportive learning tasks include modeling and explaining, coaching, and scaffolding. Modeling and explaining provide learners with an example of the desired performance by focusing on the expert's performance (Jonassen, 1999). Essentially, modeling shows how a process unfolds, while explaining involves giving reasons why it happens that way. For example, when teachers model and explain, they verbalize internal information processing and reasoning while performing the procedures involved in a task. Teachers often use think-aloud protocols to model problem-solving strategies. Similarly, experts show and tell what strategies are being used in solving problems. Modeling and explaining of internal processes is an effective way to scaffold students' performance. By experiencing a teacher or expert's cognitive processes, students are better able to adopt the expert's mode of thinking (Gorrell & Capron, 1990). Therefore, explaining the thought processes behind an action or decision is key in modeling expert performance.

Coaching means observing or monitoring student performance when completing a task, and providing guidance and help when appropriate (Wilson & Cole, 1996). The purpose of coaching is to improve learners' performance. Hence, a good coach motivates learners, monitors and analyzes their performance, provides comments and feedback, and promotes reflection and articulation on new information learned (Jonassen, 1999). When implementing coaching strategies, it is important not to stifle learner exploration and problem solving. This can easily happen when coaches or coaching systems provide too much guidance too quickly. Scaffolding involves supporting novice learners by limiting the complexities of the context and gradually removing those limits (a concept known as fading) as learners gain the knowledge, skills, and confidence to cope with the full complexity of the context (Young, 1993). Assistance to learners is provided on an as-needed basis and as their task competence increases; assistance is gradually faded to allow learners to complete the task independently (Pressley, Hogan, Wharton-McDonald, Mistretta, & Ettenberger,

Table 3. Promoting supportive learning tasks using CMS

Learning Task	CMS Tools Category	Example of Implementing the Learning Task Using a CMS
Modeling and Explaining	Collaborative and Communication Tools	Students can observe expert demonstrations with the "Whiteboard" feature of Blackboard.
Coaching	Administrative Tools	Students can consult with instructors during virtual office hours provided by the "Regular Events" component in Virtual-U.
Scaffolding	Content Creation and Delivery Tools	Instructors can provide sequenced instruction in Blackboard's "Learning Units" feature to assist students who need a more directive learning environment.

1996). Table 3 provides examples of how supportive learning tasks can be promoted using CMS.

Implications

Depending on how the features and components of CMS are used in a distributed or online course by the instructor and the learners, the pedagogical philosophy underlying the design of the course can range from a strict instructivist approach to a radical constructivist approach (Reeves & Reeves, 1997). A strict instructivist approach typically results in a Web-based or online course that has a tutorial structure in which the content is organized by the instructor and *delivered* or imparted to the students. A radical constructivist approach, on the other hand, typically results in a learner-centered pedagogy where students use Web features as tools to construct their own knowledge representations by restructuring content and creating and contributing their own resources to the course structure (Bannan & Milheim, 1997; Reeves & Reeves, 1997). The pedagogically oriented classification of the features and components of CMS discussed in this chapter and the examples demonstrating how to design authentic learning tasks are aimed at enabling the online course developer and instructor to design learner-centered or constructivist practices that engage learners in meaningful learning.

With the inclusion of learner tools in CMS, online learning environments are becoming increasingly learner-centered. Learners can create and organize information in a meaningful way, and in the process, learn how to take responsibility for their own learning. Using learner tools, assessment tools, and collaborative and communication tools, learners can reflect on their learning, self-evaluate and self-monitor their progress, and engage in continuous dialogue, becoming productively and continuously active. However, the use of CMS, or any authoring tool, could still result in an instructivist or teacher-centered approach if the potential of the tool's features is not effectively integrated into the learning design. As Tiedemann (2002) contends, "The challenge is not so much in selection and infrastructure implementation as it is in the appropriate design and use of the selected tool" (p. 9). For example, it is possible to design an online course using a CMS that is self-contained and requiring minimal instructor intervention and interaction with other learners. Practice and feedback activities can be embedded in an online course using a CMS, and learners can proceed through linearly sequenced, tutorial-like content presentations at their own pace, resulting in a program-centered or instructivist learning environment.

Therefore, if the goal is to create learner-centered practices and meaningful learning, caution must be exercised to ensure that the pedagogical potential of a CMS is comprehensively examined and its features and components are utilized as discussed in this chapter. As Clark and Lyons (1999) suggest, "The lesson that we have learned over decades of technological evolution is that each new medium provides instructional capabilities that are unique. And each medium demands a new approach to exploit its capabilities for promoting learning" (p. 52). Hence, if the pedagogical potential of CMS is examined as in this chapter, it is more likely that courses initially designed for traditional face-to-face learning environments and later transformed to a Web-based format using a CMS will undergo a *pedagogical reengineering* that is more constructivist and less instructivist in nature (Dabbagh & Schmitt, 1998).

References

Bannan, B. & Milheim, W. D. (1997). Existing Web-based instruction courses and their design. In B.H. Khan (Ed.), *Web-based instruction* (pp. 381-388). Englewood Cliffs, NJ: Educational Technology Publications.

Barron, A. E. & Liskawa, C. (2001). Software tools for online course management and delivery. In B. Khan (Ed.), *Web-based training* (pp. 303-310). Englewood Cliffs, NJ: Educational Technology Publications.

Bruner, J. S., Goodnow, J. J., & Austin, G. A. (1956). *A study of thinking.* New York: Wiley.

Carmean, C., & Haefner, J. (2002). Mind over matter: Transforming course management systems into effective learning environments. *Educause Review, 37*(6), 26-34.

Center for Curriculum Transfer and Technology. (2000). Online educational delivery applications: A Web tool for comparative analysis. Retrieved June 2002, from *http://www.edutools.info/course/*

Chamberlin, W. S. (2001). Face-to-face vs. cyberspace: Finding the middle ground. *Syllabus 15*(5), 11, 32.

Clark, R. C. & Lyons, C. (1999). Using Web-based training wisely. *Training, 36* (7), 51-56.

Collins, A. (1991). Cognitive apprenticeship and instructional technology. In L. Idol & B. F. Jones (Eds.), *Educational values and cognitive instruction: Implications for reform* (pp. 121-138). Hillsdale, NJ: Erlbaum.

Dabbagh, N. (2000). The challenges of interfacing between face-to-face and online instruction. *TechTrends for Leaders in Education and Training, 44*(6), 37-42.

Dabbagh, N. & Bannan-Ritland, B. (2005). *Online learning: Concepts, strategies, and application.* Upper Saddle River, NJ: Prentice Hall.

Dabbagh, N. & Schmitt, J. (1998). Pedagogical implications of redesigning instruction for Web-based delivery. *Educational Media International, 35*(2), 106-110.

Dean, P. J., Stahl, M. J., Sylwester, D. L. & Peat, J. A. (2001). Effectiveness of combined delivery modalities for distance learning and resident learning. *The Quarterly Review of Distance Education, 2*(3), 247-254.

Dede, C. (1996). Emerging technologies and distributed learning. *American Journal of Distance Education, 10*(2), 4-36.

Driscoll, M. (2000). *Psychology of learning for instruction* (2nd ed.). Needham Heights, MA: Allyn & Bacon.

Duffy, T. M. & Cunningham, D. J. (1996). Constructivism: Implications for the design and delivery of instruction. In D.H. Jonassen (Ed.), *Handbook of research for educational communications and technology* (pp. 170-198). New York: Simon & Schuster Macmillan.

Firdyiwek, Y. (1999). Web-based courseware tools: Where is the pedagogy? *Educational Technology, 39*(1), 29-34.

Gorrell, J. & Capron, E. (1990). Cognitive modeling and self-efficacy: Effects on preservice teachers' learning of teaching strategies. *Journal of Teacher Education, 41*(2), 15-22.

Harasim, L. (1999). A framework for online learning: The Virtual-U™. *Computer*, 44-49.

Harvey, D. M. & Lee, J. (2001). The impact of inherent instructional design in online courseware. *The Quarterly Review of Distance Education, 2*(1), 35-48.

Hedberg, J. & Harper, B. (1998). Visual metaphors and authoring. ITFORUM. Available at *http://it.coe.uga.edu/itforum/paper25/paper25.html*

Heinich, R., Molenda, M. & Russell, J. (1993). *Instructional media and the new technology of learning* (4ᵗʰ ed.). New York: Macmillan.

Jacobson, M. J. (1994). Issues in hypertext and hypermedia research: Toward a framework for linking theory-to-design. *Journal of Educational Multimedia and Hypermedia, 3*(2), 141-154.

Jonassen, D. H. (1999). Designing constructivist learning environments. In C. M. Reigeluth (Ed.), *Instructional-design theories and models: A new paradigm of instructional theory* (Volume II, (pp. 215-239). Mahwah, NJ: Lawrence Erlbaum Associates.

Lesh, R., Hoover, M., Hole, B., Kelly, A. & Post, T. (2000). Principles for developing thought-revealing activities for students and teachers. In A. E. Kelly & R. A. Lesh (Eds.), *Handbook of research design in mathematics and science education* (pp. 591-645). Mahway, NJ: Lawrence Erlbaum Associates.

Locatis, C. & Weisberg, M. (1997). Distributed learning and the Internet. *Contemporary Education, 68*(2), 100-103.

Marra, R. M. & Jonassen, D. H. (2001). Limitations of online courses for supporting constructive learning. *The Quarterly Review of Distance Education, 2*(4), 303-317.

Mayer, R. E. (1987). *Educational psychology: A cognitive approach.* Boston: Little, Brown, & Company Limited.

Navarro, P. & Shoemaker, J. (2000). In M. G. Moore & G. T. Cozine (Eds.), *Web-based communications, the Internet, and distance education.*

(pp. 1-15). University Park,. PA: The American Center for the Study of Distance Education, The Pennsylvania State University.

Oliver, K. (2001). Recommendations for student tools in online course management systems. *Journal of Computing in Higher Education, 13*(1), 47-70.

Pressley, M., Hogan, K., Wharton-McDonald, R., Mistretta, J. & Ettenberger, S. (1996). The challenges of instructional scaffolding: The challenges of instruction that supports student thinking. *Learning Disabilities Research and Practice, 11,* 138-146.

Reeves, T. C. & Reeves, P. M. (1997). Effective dimensions of interactive learning on the World Wide Web. In B.H. Khan (Ed.). *Web-based instruction* (pp. 59-66). Englewood Cliffs, NJ: Educational Technology Publications.

Reeves, T. C., Herrington, J., & Oliver, R. (2002). *Authentic activity as a model for Web-based learning.* Paper presented at the annual meeting of the American Educational Research Association, New Orleans, LA, April 1-5, 2002, session 41.06.

Roblyer, M. D., Edwards, J. & Havriluk, M. A. (1996). Learning theories and integration models (Chapter 3). *Integrating educational technology into teaching* (pp. 54-79). Upper Saddle River, NJ: Merrill, Prentice Hall.

Tiedemann, D. A. (2002). Distance learning development and delivery applications. *Educational Technology and Society, 5*(1).

Wilson, B. G. & Cole, P. (1996). Cognitive teaching models. In D. H. Jonassen (Ed.), *Handbook of research for educational communications and technology* (pp. 601-621). New York: Simon & Schuster Macmillan.

Young, M. F. (1993). Instructional design for situated learning. *Educational Technology Research and Development, 41*(1), 43-58.

Chapter XII

From Course Management to Curricular Capabilities:
A Capabilities Approach for the Next-Generation CMS

Van Weigel, Eastern University, USA

Abstract

The course management system (CMS) has become a focal point for conceptualizing the place and purpose of e-learning in higher education. Because of the architectural biases of these systems, some pedagogical approaches seem more "natural" or "feasible" while other — potentially more promising — approaches remain unexplored. This chapter begins by presenting four student-focused core capabilities that should be at the forefront of our pedagogical thinking — the development of skill sets related to critical thinking, self-confidence, peer learning, and knowledge management capabilities. Using this foundation, the author explores four basic curricular capabilities (or services) that learning systems of the future will require: 1) a discovery-based learning capability; 2) a 360-

degree out-of-the-course capability; 3) a knowledge asset capability; and 4) a teach-to-learn capability.

Introduction

The contemporary CMS is both a blessing and curse for our evolving understanding of the value of e-learning technologies within the context of higher education.

The upside of the CMS is that popular e-learning platforms like WebCT™ and Blackboard™ have provided faculty with an array of user-friendly tools for the rapid publication of course content and management. This has increased our collective knowledge base about successful online practices and the readiness, or lack thereof, of specific student populations for this mode of educational delivery. However, the downside of the CMS is that it canalizes our collective creativity by forcing e-learning technologies into the familiar classroom categories of lectures, discussions, and exams (with an occasional opportunity to chat with the professor or other students "after class"). The overall effect of these developments is that many educators and administrators are locked into a "classroom on steroids" model of e-learning that is more preoccupied with the categories of accessibility and convenience than pedagogical effectiveness and skill development.

The genetic weakness of the contemporary CMS stems from its uncritical acceptance of the traditional features of the classroom model. This, of course, is understandable, in light of the market-based desire for rapid adoption among faculty and the early association between the CMS and distance learning. The idea that e-learning was going to replace the traditional classroom with a virtual one necessitated a hierarchical, centralized architecture that placed the teacher firmly in control of core classroom interactions and content creation and management. The "classroom-plus" model of e-learning is well exemplified within the "no significant difference" literature, which used the traditional classroom as a baseline for evaluating the effectiveness of e-learning technologies. It was telling that advocates of Internet-based distance learning viewed the general conclusions of this literature as being favorable (i.e., there is no significant difference in educational outcomes between traditional classroom and online delivery systems); perhaps this view is reflective of low expectations associated with e-learning technologies or indicative of the perceived trade-off between educational quality and the convenience factor that favored these new technologies.

Toward a Capabilities Approach

One suspects that the piecemeal criticisms that have been directed at the contemporary CMS point to more foundational questions about the nature of learning and respective roles of teachers and students in this process. Toward this end, a capabilities approach to learning could provide us with a forceful and intuitive means for envisioning what the next-generation CMS might look like. In this regard, the work of the Indian economist Amartya Sen, the 1998 recipient of the Nobel Prize in Economics, is instructive.

In his path-breaking book, *Development as Freedom* (2000), Sen outlines an approach to development economics and human rights that he calls "the capabilities approach." This development framework, in Sen's thought, becomes an organizing principle for unifying the traditional aims of human rights (related primarily to the exercise of freedom) with the goals of economic development. One of the signal strengths of the capabilities approach is that poverty is understood as a capability deficit — not simply restricted to the familiar domains of need deprivation or low household income. Sen's capabilities approach not only ties together disparate strands within development studies and human rights theory, but also provides us with an understanding of poverty that is equally relevant to both the more developed and less developed regions of the world.

What would a capabilities approach for e-learning or the next-generation CMS look like? I would like to set forth a heuristic model of such a capabilities approach by presenting four learner-focused capabilities and four capabilities that could be incorporated into new and improved versions of the CMS. The learner-centered capabilities are: 1) a critical thinking capability; 2) a self-confidence capability; 3) a peer-learning capability; and 4) a knowledge management capability. The CMS curricular capabilities are: 1) a discovery-based learning capability; 2) a 360-degree out-of-the-course capability; 3) a knowledge asset capability; and 4) a teach-to-learn capability.

Learner Capabilities

A Critical Thinking Capability

If education is about anything, it is about cultivating the skill of critical thinking. This appropriately occupies first place in the hierarchy of desired educational outcomes. It also lies at the foundation of metacognitive capabilities — the learner's ability to understand and manage his or her own learning processes. In this respect, critical thinking undergirds our ability to map unfamiliar knowledge domains and to discern plausible connections with more familiar domains. It is not insignificant that multidisciplinary curricula often provide a powerful matrix for the development of critical thinking skills.

One central attribute of critical thinking is the ability to compare one's own approach to the analysis of a problem or navigating an unfamiliar knowledge domain with the way that others explore and examine a similar problem or unfamiliar knowledge domain. This comparison of cognitive performances is made possible by first grappling with a problem or stumbling around within an unfamiliar knowledge domain — either by oneself or with others — and then reflecting on how those experiences compare with the performances of others (whether these are peers with a similar level of expertise or more experienced practitioners of the knowledge domain in question). In this regard, the theory of cognitive apprenticeship, with its methodological bias in favor of the modeling and coaching roles of both professors and students, provides a rich pedagogical framework for developing critical thinking skills (Brown, Collins, & Duguid, 1989; Collins, 1991; Collins, Brown, & Newman, 1989; Jonassen, 1996; Teles, 1993). One way to achieve this development is to provide students with meaningful opportunities for collaborative research with faculty, as is advocated by the National Research Council's report, *Bio 2010: Transforming Undergraduate Education for Future Biologists* (2003). We also have a longstanding and robust tradition from the U.S. Army that tries to achieve a similar critical perspective, called the "after action review," which requires participants to "pin their stripes on the door" in assessing what went right and what went wrong in a particular military action. This tradition has been respected even in the midst of heated battle (Collison & Parcell, 2001, pp. 75-86; Dixon, 2000, pp. 37-46).

One of the great failures of contemporary higher education is the paucity of opportunities — particularly among undergraduates — for problem-based learning and the exploration of new knowledge domains. The surface-learning approach that characterizes much of undergraduate education places more emphasis on information acquisition and retrieval than developing the skills associated with the art of thinking. Moreover, there is a developing body of literature within the neurosciences that suggests that learning takes place by reflectively acting upon the material and thereby making it one's own (Bransford, Brown, & Cocking, 1999; Zull, 2002). It is not clear that there is any real long-term value associated with stuffing facts and figures into one's head and demonstrating one's short-term competency on an exam, except perhaps related to developing the skill of test taking or gaining a cursory (and usually short-term) understanding of a discipline's vocabulary, history, and methodologies.

A Self-Confidence Capability

Self-confidence, next to critical thinking, is likely one of the most valuable outcomes of education — not only as a predictor for success in terms of one's career and professional development, but also in terms of one's overall readiness to take on new learning experiences. Self-confidence is nourished by the experience of challenge (whether this is physical, intellectual, or social), and, most importantly, by the ability to process failure constructively. It is not insignificant that one of the great stories of leadership in the 20th century, which has received considerable public attention within the past few years, has been a story of failure: the Antarctic expedition of Sir Ernest Shackleton (Morrell & Capparell, 2001).

Perhaps the most striking deficit of both the contemporary, face-to-face classroom and online learning is the absence of meaningful challenge. It has sometimes been said that curriculum developers would be out of work in a week if they applied their trade to the video game business. What is the challenge of a video game if you can reach level ten in the first couple of tries — or if there are no levels of difficulty to begin with? The experience of failure, even if it is safe and simulated, is an integral facet of the learning process (Shank, 2002, pp. 61-71). The proverbial $64,000 question, though, is how do you provide a meaningful and reflective environment for failure that also does not discourage learners? There are no easy answers here, but one thing is for certain: our current exam-centric definitions of success and failure allow for little in the way of a learning payoff associated with the experience of failure. Similarly, within the context of online learning, failure has been treated more as a navigational aid for directing the student to additional tutorials than as a meaningful object of learning.

One promising approach in the development of self-confidence skills is to encourage students to grapple with complex and ill-defined problems in the context of collaborative "think tank" groups. The attitude that should imbue these groups is not that of a traditional division of labor, but rather a perspective that views the group as an essential resource for analyzing problems and presenting solutions. Such a framework might also involve building in a scaffolding provision for outside consultants or experts (e.g., teaching assistants, industry professionals, more experienced student colleagues) as a resource for the group. In addition, one could require such think tank groups to develop a "failure narrative" of sorts, which details all of the unproductive approaches and dead ends that the group encountered along the way.

A Peer-Learning Capability

Among the more significant insights that have emerged from historical and ethnographic research on the traditional apprenticeship model (Lave & Wenger, 1993; Rogoff, 1990; Wenger, 1998) has been an appreciation of the neglected yet important role of apprentice-to-apprentice learning in contrast to the more prominent master-to-apprentice interactions. This insight on the apprenticeship model, underscoring the importance of peer learning, has received powerful and eloquent expression in the more recent "communities of practice" literature within the corporate realm (Wenger, McDermott, & Snyder, 2002; Wenger & Snyder, 2000).

There is, of course, some peer-learning component built into traditional curricula in higher education, largely taking the form of discussion or study groups in undergraduate contexts. Yet, the focus of these discussion or study groups is usually centered on digesting the material conveyed in a lecture or achieving a division of labor in preparing for an exam. The notion that the student sitting next to you might be a relevant and important source of knowledge — based upon his or her experience, aptitudes, and interests — is largely unexplored in most educational curricula (outside of the rarified environment of PhD programs). Given the importance of peer learning for a student's eventual success in the workplace, which often depends on strong networking skills and the ability to mine tacit knowledge stores, one would think that developing a peer-learning capability should be a chief goal of any 21st century curriculum.

The evidence from workplace-related experience in peer learning, such as British Petroleum's "peer assist" initiative, suggests that a critical prerequisite for peer learning is encouraging people to drop their inhibitions in asking for help and to raise their overall awareness of the value of tacit information resources (through skill inventories and the formation of virtual communities). Two mechanisms that BP has used in reinforcing the value of peer learning include the use of "after action" reviews (both during the execution of a project and at its conclusion) and involving employees in the development of knowledge assets that have clearly defined "customers" and are adopted and updated by a relevant community of practice (Collison & Parcell, 2001). One prime area of application for the BP model in higher educational curricula would be the use of longitudinal, multigenerational research projects (involving the participation of successive "generations" of students) or one-time interdisciplinary research projects that have a clearly identified client (e.g., a community group, nonprofit organization, corporation, governmental agency).

A Knowledge Management Capability

The skills required by knowledge-based economies are not absorption and recall, but discovery and discernment. If higher education is about preparing students to assume positions of leadership and responsibility in the workplace, it must also be about helping students explore new frontiers of knowing and critically discerning the significance of "new" knowledge to "old" knowledge, mapping connections between more familiar knowledge domains to those that are less familiar. In sum, a 21st-century education should prepare students to be knowledge creators — not simply receptacles of existing knowledge.

There is a common misconception that knowledge changes so rapidly in the Information Age that it quickly becomes obsolete. This attitude reflects a fundamental confusion between knowledge and data or information (Stewart, 1997). Data or information change rapidly and have a very brief half-life; knowledge is a much durable entity because it is rooted in both associational and critical judgment. Knowledge is more like a skill that is sharpened over time — not a textbook to be digested or something archived in a database.

Knowledge management (KM) theorists frequently draw distinctions among the terms *data, information, knowledge, and wisdom*. Data are simply raw, undigested facts. They often have an exceedingly small window of relevance. Information is data placed within a meaningful context. Because information is data-centric by nature, it also has a brief half-life. Knowledge differs from data or information in that it requires skills of interpretation and judgment. Facts (i.e., data) and facts in context (i.e., information) become useful to us when they are interpreted and placed under the lens of human knowing; wisdom, which is rooted in knowledge, is the most durable of all.

While one can make a compelling case that all varieties of data and information must be interpreted in order to be sensible, this is particularly true with knowledge. Knowledge requires some exercise of judgment — either of an associational or critical nature. Associational judgments are based upon perceiving patterns, correspondences, commonalties, and dissimilarities that enable information mapping and support inferential reasoning. Critical judgments evaluate information from the standpoint of higher-order perspectives or templates, such as the principles of logic or aesthetic and moral values. Both associational and critical judgments are shaped by new information — sometimes requiring radical realignments in human judgment. However, knowledge is typically built upon a durable platform of associational and critical skills that are relatively stable in relation to wholesale changes in information landscapes.

Wisdom might be described as the most durable variety of human knowledge, having qualities that appear almost timeless in character. Aristotle et al., in *The Nicomachean Ethics*, called wisdom "the most precise and perfect form of knowledge" (1998). Wisdom is more easily apprehended than defined; those who encounter it understand its value and immediately accord it with respect. One might also say that knowledge tells us "how," but wisdom tells us "why" (Pelikan, 1992, p. 35). The capability that enables people to "deliberate well" — what Aristotle called "practical wisdom" — is strongly tied to the attribute of discernment. The ability to filter the important from the insignificant, to perceive worth among the ordinary, and to hear a voice of authenticity above the din of background noise — these are qualities that exemplify discernment. The same holds true for wisdom.

If higher education is about anything, it must be about the furtherance of knowledge and wisdom, and this requires going beyond the limitations of what Michael Polyani (1966) calls "explicit knowledge" — knowledge that can be readily codified and shared with others — and venturing into the realm of "tacit knowledge," or knowledge that is inherently bound to the experiences, skills, and judgment of a person. Explicit knowledge can be organized in a database or set forth in a document; tacit knowledge must be teased out in the exercise of skills, problem solving, or judgments of an associational or critical nature. Tacit knowledge is mined through conversation, not computers; it is inherently "messy," requiring dialogue, observation, or storytelling to be shared with others (Davenport & Prusak, 1998, pp. 81ff.). It is not insignificant that when the World Bank undertook a major KM initiative, it began by setting up help desks and discussion groups that focused on sharing best practices, instead attempting to catalog them in a large database (O'Dell & Grayson, 1998). Moreover, tacit knowledge, because it integrates experience with judgment, has the capability to generate new knowledge.

CMS Capabilities

What sort of CMS could facilitate the development of student capabilities in critical thinking, self-confidence, peer learning, and knowledge management? While no CMS — this generation or the next — can assure the successful development of these student capabilities, given the importance of sound curricular design and faculty engagement for learning, one could point to four attributes of a next-generation CMS that would facilitate this student development: 1) a discovery-based learning capability; 2) a 360-degree out-of-the-course capability; 3) a knowledge asset capability; and 4) a teach-to-learn capability.

A Discovery-Based Learning Capability

One of the great weaknesses of the contemporary CMS is its facile acceptance of behaviorist approaches to learning, which emphasize parceling up knowledge or skills into bite-sized chunks that can be easily digested (Fosnot, 1996; Walker & Lambert, 1995). Assessment mechanisms, like quizzes and exams, are designed to determine whether the student has mastered (at least in the short term) these discrete bits of knowledge before moving on to the next topic; it is up to the student, at some undefined point in the future, to put the pieces together. Learning, from this perspective, becomes analogous to moving along a well-trod and clearly marked road; and the main challenge, from a pedagogical standpoint, is to keep students moving down the road on schedule.

Unfortunately, educational technologies have largely served to reinforce the behaviorist bias in higher education. The ubiquitous PowerPoint presentation reduces knowledge to bullet-sized information parcels and adds legitimacy to the misplaced professorial concern with "covering the material" (instead of ensuring that students have some in-depth exposure to disciplinary content and methodologies). Similarly, many of the helpful aspects of computer-based instruction, such as the use of self-administered quizzes as a navigational aid in guiding students to supplemental tutorials, have an underlying bias in favor of behaviorist pedagogical approaches.

There are certainly contexts in which a behaviorist approach may make considerable sense — particular in the arena of corporate training or introductory survey courses within lower-division undergraduate curricula. However, the weaknesses of the behavioral approach become painfully apparent when it comes to developing higher-order skills in critical thinking that require grappling with ill-defined problems (Huba & Freed, 2000) and exploring unfamiliar knowledge domains. This requires a discovery-based approach to learning that will be more at home within a constructivist orientation to learning.

Discovery, in the sense that I am using it here, could include coming upon a new disciplinary insight, mapping an unfamiliar knowledge landscape, playfully making connections between different knowledge domains, or "inventing" new conceptual or methodological frameworks. Even if this process of discovery brings forth nothing that is truly novel (which will generally be the case), the payoff is that students have firsthand exposure to the adventure of learning. And this exposure cannot help but strengthen skill sets related to critical thinking, self-confidence, peer-learning, and knowledge management.

From the standpoint of the next-generation CMS, a capability in discovery-based learning could manifest itself in three respects. First, the CMS should present a rich feature set for student-to-student collaboration that facilitates the creation of "storyboards" or "solution narratives" that document the group's approach to problem solving. Second, the CMS should provide a built-in learning log component that aids students in evaluating their own performances as learners (thereby strengthening their metacognitive capabilities). Third, the CMS should be flexible enough to incorporate interdisciplinary and intercultural "border experiences" in learning that invite fresh perspectives on how knowledge in one domain relates to other domains or on the larger social-cultural implications of disciplinary knowledge.

A 360-degree Out-of-the-Course Capability

A second, next-generation CMS capability might be termed a 360-degree out-of-the-course capability. One of the key insights that has emerged from research on learning is the importance of "conditionalized knowledge" (or knowledge that specifies the contexts in which it is useful) as a core competence (Bransford, Brown & Cocking, 1999, p. 31). Knowledge that is not conditionalized — even though it may be present and highly relevant — remains "inert" (Whitehead, 1929). Both problem-based learning and interdisciplinary studies are key educational strategies that facilitate the development of conditionalized knowledge.

One of the significant liabilities of several popular CMS packages is their constitutional preoccupation with the "course" as a standard unit of measure. Everything is processed through the pre-established boundaries of the course, and this leads to the further segmentation of knowledge. There is no technical reason why this course-centric bias must hold sway. For example, one could envision CMS packages that are constructed with both course-centered and interdisciplinary (or multicourse) modules. The multicourse modules would be appropriately evaluated as works in progress until they are completed in some capstone-like, integrative course. A simpler way of expressing the same thought would be to build to a portfolio capability within the CMS.

A 360-degree CMS could also offer some exciting possibilities in terms of the incorporation of community educators (e.g., business professionals, nonprofit leaders, accomplished alumni) whose experience and perspectives can provide breadth and depth to the undergraduate learning experience. The educational services provided by such community educators could range from serving as a respondent for an online seminar or as an evaluator for a portfolio project to more substantial, team-teaching responsibilities as co-faculty members. Given the increasing numbers of retired professionals in the United States, such an avenue for continuing service is a particularly important faculty resource for colleges and universities.

Another positive feature of a 360-degree CMS is that it could facilitate the development of team-teaching cultures without significant downsides of traditional team teaching. By any measure, team-teaching, if done correctly, is a time-intensive enterprise. Unless instructors develop a close working relationship, the benefits associated with a division of labor in teaching and grading are outweighed by the logistics of planning the course and coordinating teaching roles. By incorporating interdisciplinary or multicourse modules within the CMS, some of the educational benefits of team-teaching can be captured within a traditional teaching environment.

A Knowledge Asset Capability

The ability to create, modify and maintain knowledge assets is a core function of any community of practice. Perhaps one of the most dramatic examples of this is Wikipedia,[1] an online encyclopedia that allows Web visitors to modify or add content — the resulting modifiable page is called a "wiki." Other examples include the Best Practice Replication program at the Ford Motor Company (Dixon, 2000), in which "focal points" (i.e., production engineers) evaluate and adapt best practices from other Ford plants and some fascinating recent experiments in developing internal markets that trade in information and ideas (Malone, 2004).

Providing students with the experience of creating knowledge assets that others will find useful not only provides a powerful impetus for study and research, but also encourages the development of important workplace skills (e.g., working collaboratively in virtual teams, providing critical yet tactful feedback, discerning the relevance of information) that will become increasingly important in knowledge-based economies. Ideally, these knowledge assets could be built within an "intergenerational" framework (i.e., the work of one class could become the starting point of another). In addition, if there was a specific customer in mind for the knowledge asset (e.g., a nonprofit organization or corporation), this would appropriately raise expectations concerning the overall quality and relevance of the knowledge asset.

One avenue for incorporating a creation capability for knowledge assets in the next-generation CMS would be to construct a wiki facility within the CMS package. Another possibility would be to extend the notion of student home pages into more robust Web sites. For example, one of the more promising applications of the knowledge room concept that I developed for *Deep Learning for a Digital Age* (Weigel, 2002) is the portfolio gallery, which gives students the opportunity to develop a peer-reviewed Web site on a topic of their choice.[2] This particular knowledge-room model makes it relatively easy to convert a standard research paper assignment into a Web-based presentation that can be reviewed by other students through e-mailing evaluations directly into the site.

A Teach-to-Learn Capability

A final, next-generation CMS capability might be termed a teach-to-learn capability. This approach emphasizes the importance of empowering students as educators and uses the lecture as a tool for individual learning and critical dialogue, in contrast to its traditional use as a professor-to-student medium for conveying information.

As James Zull argues in *The Art of Changing the Brain* (2002), authentic learning requires a profound interaction with content; sitting within earshot of a mind dump and dutifully taking notes does not qualify. Yet, while lectures may be poorly suited to the task of learning, this is not true for the person giving the lecture. Most of us can affirm without reservation the truth that you really don't know something until you have had the chance to teach it.

The practice of teaching emphasizes four activities that extend our mastery of knowledge domain: 1) the organization of content; 2) the articulation of content; 3) reflection on that content through questions and digressions; and 4) the reorganization of the content to make it more accessible and relevant. It is not unlike the process used by students who prepare for tests by reorganizing and rewriting their lecture notes, except that teaching is a whole lot more satisfying. Indeed, one of the prime sources of satisfaction in teaching is the sense that one is doing something useful to help others and participating in an interactive process of knowledge building and empowerment.

There are several interesting technological and pedagogical dimensions associated with implementing the teach-to-learn concept, ranging from the use of peer-to-peer software for creating "massively parallel" virtual classrooms to the thoroughgoing use of assessment rubrics.[3] One of the interesting aspects of the teach-to-learn model is the ability to utilize skill inventories and form internal consulting groups as a scaffolding mechanism for more difficult assignments. In terms of the next-generation CMS, a critical prerequisite of the teach-to-learn model is the need of high-quality and easily implemented synchronous presentation software that avoids a teacher-centered bias. Some current examples of existing software include Macromedia's Breeze® or the use of Groove® in connection with Skype™ (or another high-quality voice-over-IP tool).

Concluding Remarks

This chapter presents a heuristic outline of a capabilities approach for the next-generation CMS, focusing on both learner and CMS capabilities. The common thread that runs through this discussion is the importance of thinking through the more profound pedagogical implications of the CMS for student learning — not being content with the traditionally cited gains in administrative efficiency and end-user accessibility.

Can any single CMS package — in this generation or the next — embody these capabilities? Probably not. It is more realistic, at least in the near term, to speak of CMS "solutions" that involve the integration of two or three "off-the-shelf" applications (e.g., one for content publication and grade book management, another for small group collaboration and presence awareness, and perhaps a third for high-quality synchronous presentations). The key is to craft solutions that are elegantly simple and do not impose a substantial tax on professorial time.

Looking ahead, with the future development of fiber optic networks, digital paper, near-flawless voice recognition, holographic imaging, and virtual reality technologies, the potential for implementing discovery-based learning within a 360-degree environment and constructing knowledge assets through a teach-to-learn pedagogy will grow by several orders of magnitude. It is time to eschew the minimalist pedagogical vision of the CMS and to envision a more promising future.

References

Aristotle, Ross, D., Ross, W. D., Ackrill, J. L., & Urmson, J. O. (1998). *The Nicomachean ethics*. Oxford, UK: Oxford University Press.

Bransford, J. D., Brown, A. L. & Cocking, R. R. (Eds.). (1999). *How people learn: Brain, mind, experience, and school.* Washington, D.C.: National Academy Press.

Brown, J. S., Collins, A. & Duguid, P. (1989). Situation cognition and the culture of learning. *Educational Researcher, 18*(1), 32-42.

Collins, A. (1991). Cognitive apprenticeship and instructional technology. In L. Idol & B. F. Jones (Eds.), *Educational values and cognitive instruction: Implications for reform*. Hillsdale, NJ: Lawrence Erlbaum Associates.

Collins, A., Brown, J. S. & Newman, S. E. (1989). Cognitive apprenticeship: Teaching the crafts of reading, writing, and mathematics. In L. B. Resnick (Ed.), *Knowing, learning, and instruction: Essays in honor of Robert Glaser*. Hillsdale, NJ: Lawrence Erlbaum Associates.

Collison, C. & Parcell, G. (2001). *Learning to fly: Practical lessons from one of the world's leading knowledge companies*. Milford, CT: Capstone Publishing.

Davenport, T. H. & Prusak, L. (1998). *Working knowledge: How organizations manage what they know*. Boston: Harvard Business School Press.

Dixon, N. M. (2000). *Common knowledge: How companies thrive by sharing what they know*. Boston: Harvard Business School Press.

Fosnot, C. T. (Ed.). (1996). *Constructivism: Theory, perspectives, and practice*. New York: Teachers College Press.

Huba, M. E. & Freed, E. (2000). *Learner-centered assessment on college campuses: Shifting the focus from teaching to learning*. Boston: Allyn and Bacon.

Jonassen, D. H. (1996). *Computers in the classroom: Mindtools for critical thinking*. Englewood Cliffs, NJ: Prentice-Hall.

Lave, J. & Wenger, E. (1993). *Situated learning: Legitimate peripheal participation*. New York: Cambridge University Press.

Malone, T. W. (2004). Bringing the market inside. *Harvard Business Review*, (April), 107-114.

Morrell, M. & Capparell, S. (2001). *Shackleton's way: Leadership lessons from the great Antarctic explorer*. New York: Viking.

National Research Council. (2003). *Bio 2010: Transforming undergraduate education for future biologists*. Washington, D.C.: National Academy Press.

O'Dell, C. & Grayson, Jr., C. J. (1998). *If only we knew what we know: The transfer of internal knowledge and best practice*. New York: The Free Press.

Pelikan, J. (1992). *The idea of the university: A reexamination*. New Haven: Yale University Press.

Polanyi, M. (1966). *The tacit dimension*. New York: Doubleday and Company.

Rogoff, B. (1990). *Apprenticeship in thinking: Cognitive development in social context*. New York: Oxford University Press.

Sen, A. (2000). *Development as freedom*. New York: Anchor Press.

Shank, R. C. (2002). *Designing world-class e-learning*. New York: McGraw-Hill.

Stewart, T.A. (1997). *Intellectual capital*. New York: Currency.

Teles, L. (1993). Cognitive apprenticeship on global networks. In L. M. Harasim (Ed.), *Global networks: Computers and international communication*. Cambridge, MA: MIT Press.

Walker, D. & Lambert, L. (1995). Learning and leading theory: A century in the making. In L. Lambert, et al. (Eds.), *The constructivist leader*. New York: Teachers College Press.

Weigel, Van B. (2002). *Deep learning for a digital age: Technology's untapped potential to enrich higher education*. San Francisco: Jossey-Bass.

Wenger, E. (1998). *Communities of practice: Learning, meaning, and identity*. Cambridge: Cambridge University Press.

Wenger, E., McDermott, R. & Synder, W. (2002). *Cultivating communities of practice*. Boston: Harvard Business School Press.

Wenger, E. & Snyder, W. (2000). Communities of practice: The organizational frontier. *Harvard Business Review*, (January-February), 139-145.

Whitehead, A. N. (1929). *The aims of education*. New York: MacMillan.

Zull, J. E. (2002). *The art of changing the brain*. Sterling, VA: Stylus Publishing.

Endnotes

[1]   *www.wikipedia.org*

[2]   See *www.knowledgeroom.info*

[3]   See *www.teach2learn.info*

Chapter XIII

The Missing Link to Enhanced Course Management Systems:
Adopting Learning Content Management Systems in the Educational Sphere

Steven Shaw, Concordia University, Montreal, Canada

Vivek Venkatesh, Concordia University, Montreal, Canada

Abstract

The capabilities of the current generation of course management systems (CMS) are limited; even market-leading platforms are arguably inadequate for the needs of learners, instructors, and educational administrators. This chapter reviews the shortcomings of CMS and identifies problems associated with content capture, content re-use, search and retrieval, document management, IP management, connectivity, support for open standards, and support for learning strategies. We argue that the future lies in the adoption and adaptation of existing learning content management systems (LCMS). LCMS have evolved primarily in the corporate market and are rapidly developing into highly flexible applications that can implement a wide variety of learning and knowledge management strategies.

Introduction

CMS have been described as the next "killer app" for higher education computing (Machavec, 2001). Adoption is widespread, both for online course delivery and for hybrid solutions that supplement live class experience with online materials and activities. In the early years of the new millennium, proponents have argued that the capabilities of CMS, particularly the tools they provide to support communication and collaboration, lend themselves to the implementation of pedagogical designs that promote student engagement, increase motivation, provide participation in authentic learning tasks, and offer more contextualized learning. These designs are believed to facilitate more meaningful, deeper learning. Critics have countered that CMS are too inflexible and that the default templates and settings that come with the systems, out of the box, are limiting. Innovative instructional design and presentation strategies can be realised, but these tasks require significant technical knowledge and instructional skill and experience. Overall, detractors argue, CMS have the effect of reducing instruction to a simplistic standard model that is potentially less effective than the classroom practices they displace, and on which they are based.

The argument is not necessarily that goals such as deeper learning cannot be achieved with technology-based delivery, but rather that the current 21st-century CMS platforms are not sufficiently mature, not flexible and usable enough, to promote these goals. A very large literature on technology integration in higher education also points to factors that exacerbate the situation: for a large proportion of higher education institutions, success of technology like CMS is restricted by the presence, still, of "primary barriers." These include lack of planning, lack of technical and instructional design training or support, lack of access, lack of incentives and sufficient release time, lack of appropriate intellectual property agreements (Aaron, Dicks, Ives & Montgomery, in press; Bates & Poole, 2003; Howell, Saba, Lindsay, & Williams, 2004).

Therefore, advocates point to the potential — the match between current educational reforms and instructional theory and CMS capabilities — and, on a case-by-case basis, examples of best practices and designs that might be more widely implemented (e.g., Carmean & Haefner, 2002; De Bourgh, 2002). Critics argue that the net effect of diffusion of CMS technology, to date, is not entirely positive. There are too many instances of courses that have been converted to Web-based delivery without any of the necessary modifications of instructional components such as activities and assessments. Given the barriers mentioned above and the limitations of the current technology, this is not surprising. As a result, the skeptics see educational practice being driven by technology, and limited by it, rather than being leveraged through technology.

It is probably safe to say that both advocates and critics are right. The technology offers enormous potential while, at the same time, abuses abound. The technology is not going to go away, however. Two things need to happen to improve matters. One, institutions need to manage technology integration better, in all its various dimensions. Two, the technology needs to be improved to the point where it has the functionality necessary to meet the real needs of instructors, instructional designers, developers, education managers, systems administrators, and, of course, students.

In this chapter we focus on the capabilities of the current, early 21st-century generation of CMS. A number of limitations will be identified, and an argument will be made that, in fact, many of these limitations are already surmounted. Solutions are to be found in the best-of-breed examples in another category of platform, LCMS. LCMS are enjoying increasing popularity with both private sector corporations and public sector organizations outside of the realm of education. Essentially, we will build a case that the future of CMS is already here, in the form of technology that unfortunately has very low recognition and adoption rates within the field of education. We conclude with a case that exemplifies what we believe to be a response to the call for more robust cognitive tools that support deeper learning: topic map search and retrieval technologies.

Current Course Management Systems

Let's begin by characterizing the current, state-of-the-art CMS in 2005. A typical CMS will offer the following features and functionality:

- A class list and associated grade book.

- A space for course outlines, assignments, and content pages.

- An authoring facility to produce, upload, and content pages.

- Communication facilities including all or some of the following: e-mail, threaded discussion in conferences, notifications, synchronous messaging, or chat.

- Some capability to access external links.

- A quiz generator to produce assessments and a tool to manage assessments (including, possibly, some form of secure testing with authentication, a database for storing and randomizing test items, and a reporting mechanism).

- Capability to display various file formats such as Flash® files and documents in PDF® format.

- Simple document or content management functionality — typically in the form of organization under different folders.

- Administrative tools (to, for example, generate reports, assign privileges, sort class lists, or create conferences and folders).

Some systems will offer features such as these via a portal that can be modified and customized to meet the particular needs of the institution using the CMS. The portal may provide additional functionality, such as some e-business processes.

Learning Content Management Systems

The platforms we contrast with CMS, LCMS, are a fairly recent innovation. The term LCMS was only coined in early 2000. Since its inception, there has been rapid growth of the LCMS industry, and significant evolution in the capabilities of the systems. LCMS are true content management systems. Their defining features are:

- Structure and content are separated, allowing content to be shared or reused across courses and for different variants of a single course to be produced easily.

- Content is maintained in a back-end repository or database, using an object paradigm. Content is stored at a fairly granular level, under a taxonomy and metadata scheme. The metadata describes different aspects of the content and enables strategies to manage the lifecycle of content (version control and expiration dates, for example) to find relevant content (either by developers or end-users) and to control access and manage copyright.
- There are a variety of functions and object types that are specific to instructional development — for example, presentation tools such as a scenario object, different types of assessment items, and interactive tasks and feedback mechanisms.

LCMS are not to be confused with the larger enterprise-level commercial content management systems, such as Documentum™ though they have many points in common. The differences lie primarily in the built-in support for instructional development offered in LCMS, which is absent in enterprise content management, and in the relative simplicity of use and implementation of LCMS as compared with enterprise content management platforms. Regarding the latter point, content management systems are built on XML[1] and related standards from organizations such as the International Organization for Standardization (ISO) and the World Wide Web Consortium (W3C). Implementation is complex and requires the development of document type definitions, document schemas and style sheets (DTDs, XSLs, CSLs, DSSSLs), and strict adherence to these on an on-going basis. Development and maintenance of these building blocks is highly technical and labour intensive.

LCMS typically are not based on XML, though they may offer XML import and export options to support interoperability or communicate with other applications. With sophisticated XML capabilities, enterprise content management systems may be truly single-source, able to publish a variety of documents with content tailored to specific audiences and to different forms of output (Web, print, PDA). LCMS are not single-source publishing systems in this strict sense. They can vary content and its presentation based on user profiles, but typically they are not yet designed out of the box to produce output to different media.

LCMS are somewhat simpler in conception and function compared with content management systems. However, the cost of acquiring and implementing an LCMS is a fraction of the cost of putting an enterprise content management system in place. Industry reports in early 2004 place an implementation of LCMS for 5,000 to 10,000 users at around $200,000. A processor-based licence for one leading product is about $60,000 (this allows a one-processor server to run the application) and could serve that many users. In contrast, an enterprise system usually costs upwards of seven figures to establish.

Conceptually, CMS are organized around the notion of the course — developing, distributing, and managing a course. LCMS are oriented to content. They are used to develop, distribute, and manage content. The focus on content, and the object paradigm, allows for a wide variety of strategies other than just traditional course delivery: just-in-time learning, performance support, and others we will touch on later in this chapter.

Limitations of CMS

The problems that surface when one gets close to the application of CMS are several, and they are significant. They relate to the three basic components of content management — the processes associated with capturing, distributing, and managing content. Fundamentally, the difficulties arise because the paradigm under which CMS have developed is, as the name suggests, course rather than content-oriented. Some additional problems are a result of the "stand-alone" nature of CMS, and their lack of accommodation to any open standards.

Content Capture

The first difficulty concerns "content capture," meaning the creation, conversion, or importation of content. CMS' authoring tools are easy to use but heavily oriented towards template-based development. Out of the box, there are default settings for navigation bars, a basic interface, and templates to populate with content. While easy to use, they offer limited options. Many instructors basically cut and paste existing course notes, assignments, and reference lists into the templates provided. Any attempt at real innovation is likely to require some technical savvy — at the low end, enough to modify default settings, and at the high end, sufficient to exploit the advanced capabilities of HTML, Flash™ Java™ or JavaScript™.

In best practice, CMS-based courses generally exploit the computer-mediated communications (CMC) capabilities of the platforms, rather than provide very sophisticated presentation strategies. But it is not clear that this is always in accordance with current constructivist principles of learning, as opposed merely to a capitulation to the challenges of creating rich, interactive content, or simply a case of being technology-driven (Romizowksi & Mason, 2003).

Content Conversion

If creating rich content within a CMS can be difficult, content conversion is perhaps even more problematic. A case study of an "integration" project at a small university in New York is illustrative (Roberts, 2003). The goal of the project was to integrate TILT, the open-source Texas Information Literacy Tutorial, with Blackboard™ the industry-leading CMS (with about 40 percent of the market). The project is reported to have taken three months of intensive effort to complete. TILT pages were customized *first*, and then uploaded into a Blackboard™ course document. The TILT quiz was manually recreated as a Blackboard™ assessment. Flash was used to preserve the flow of the TILT tutorial within the CMS, and JavaScript was employed to control windows. This is hardly an integration project. It is really a very labour-intensive conversion project that required advanced technical know-how.

Contrast this scenario regarding content creation and conversion with the capabilities of learning content management systems (LCMS). Current-generation LCMS (in early 2004) adhere to a number of industry open standards, notably SCORM, the shareable content object reference model, from the United States Department of Defense's Advanced Distributed Learning Initiative, or ADL (*www.ADLNet.org*). Standards-compliant LCMS can readily exchange content. So, integrating content from one system into another is, best-case scenario, relatively straightforward. In addition, LCMS generally come complete with a variety of tools to convert or "ingest" different types of content, such as HTML-based content, PowerPoint® slides or MS Word® documents. These utilities can use structural queues within the native documents (for example, levels of headings in a Word document) to resolve them into suitable candidates for objects. Having these types of conversion utilities obviously makes it easier to share and re-use content across face-to-face and online versions of courses, to the extent this is appropriate.

The ability of LCMS to re-use content generated from other standards-compliant systems and to integrate these other types of content just mentioned is very powerful (Chapman & Hall, 2002). At international "plugfests," LCMS vendors compete to win recognition for their systems by demonstrating how quickly and effectively they can integrate or convert content. Large corporations are not dissuaded from switching LCMS by any attendant content conversion costs, let alone challenged by individual course conversion projects.

Interoperability has always been a key factor in LCMS adoption; increasingly it is becoming a point of major concern for institutions in higher education contemplating acquisition of CMS.

Content Sharing, Content Re-Use

The object paradigm underlying content management in LCMS, the separation of content and structure, the adherence to open standards, and the ability to locate content for re-use via taxonomies and metadata, are all factors that support and promote sharing and leveraging content. Let us take a concrete example. At a Canadian university, a project was initiated some years ago to replace a large number of introductory statistics courses that existed across the social and behavioural science departments with a single service course. Granted, the basic concepts were the same across these courses. Nonetheless, the project was not successful. Faculty representatives from different departments argued cogently that students needed to see and experience concepts applied within their own fields if these concepts are to be translated into useful, usable knowledge. Moreover, the norms associated with different practices in statistical analyses, and the preferred methods, vary somewhat from field to field. Learning how to select and apply statistical analyses appropriately is, in part, a process of enculturation within a specific discipline or field of practice. Furthermore, it is often considered preferable to combine the teaching of statistics with an introduction to research design. Again, approaches to design vary across disciplines, and the kind of question addressed with the very same statistical tools varies considerably. Apart from the issue of motivation, in a subject area already fraught with problems in this regard, the knowledge needs to be situated appropriately if it is to be retained and transfer successfully across contexts.

In this same Canadian university, a pilot project is currently being organized to develop an online course to serve or supplement all courses on basic statistics across the arts and sciences faculties. This time, the proposal is to build the course within an LCMS. A large proportion of this course will be standard content, seen by all. However, a certain proportion will vary, depending on the student's discipline or field of study, and even her particular preferences. There will be only one course structure, but the structure will be populated with somewhat different content, depending on the profile of the student accessing the course. Different examples and different scenarios can be used to illustrate principles and concepts, depending on academic needs and interests, thus allowing the content to be displayed in an appropriate context. This scenario is only plausible using an LCMS.

This type of approach has been relatively common in the corporate world based on LCMS technology, though virtually unheard of in the sphere of higher education. For example, a large telecommunication firm needed to develop a course on practices concerning its performance management system. Two distinct audiences needed to be served: management and unionized employees. Some of the responsibilities, processes, and messages required were different for these two populations. In the past, a single generic course would likely have been developed — a one-size-fits-all approach that serves no audience very well. Or, in a less likely scenario, two separate courses would have been mandated, at considerable expense. Using an LCMS, a single course structure was created. About 80 percent of the content populating that structure was common across the two audiences, drawn from the same objects in the repository. The remaining content was different for each audience, tailored to its specific situations and needs.

This example of shared content illustrates how LCMS technology enables the creation of customized versions of courses tailored to different audiences in a very cost-effective way. In corporate training environments, the result is increased approval ratings and increased transfer of knowledge to the workplace, given that learning is properly situated or contextualized. The same features also support other forms of localization. For example, courses could be adapted to delivery in different regions. One of the emerging challenges of online learning in higher education is how to respond to cultural differences in the context of an increasingly globalized context for delivery. Localization might include different content, but also different languages and perhaps even different interfaces. In global organizations, LCMS are already used to vary content in terms of examples, terminology, and expression, as well as to reflect local norms, practices, procedures, and policies. Through the use of global templates, courses can also easily be masked with different look-and-feel interfaces to respect any local standards.

Linguistic translation is a significant part of localization. With an LCMS, translation costs are reduced through translation facilities, which again exploit the separation of content and structure. Basically, the text objects are exported from a first-language version of a course, then translation is carried out in a spreadsheet-like environment, and the translated objects are re-imported into the production environment to automatically populate a new course. With this approach, the cost of multiple language development becomes primarily the cost of translation, rather than additional production. In commercial terms, the cost of a second-language version of a course is typically 40-to-60 percent the cost of the first-language version, and sometimes as high as 80 percent depending on how complex the course and how it was produced. Using an LCMS with a good translation facility, the cost of producing a second version of a course in another language is more likely around 20 percent of the cost of producing the original, with most of that figure comprising translation costs.

Of course, the sharing and re-use of content also simplifies content maintenance and reduces associated costs. As a simple example, if a policy concerning examinations is repeated across 100 courses, it requires only one change to the source within the repository to update that policy across the 100 courses where it appears. This is the restricted meaning, and one of the important benefits, of single source content management.

Distributed Content

One of the hottest ideas to emerge in the early 21st century in the field of content management is distributed content. This term really has two meanings. First, it refers to the distributed content creation capabilities currently incorporated within learning content and Web content management systems. Many such systems allow the content creation process to be decentralized — those involved in the process are linked through workflow management tools. However, the content being created or acted upon is stored in a central repository.

This is a significant feature of some LCMS that is absent from CMS and also from conventional desktop authoring systems. Course creation in organizational settings often involves experts from different fields and specializations. The development team might comprise a variety of subject matter experts, graphic designers, pedagogical experts, project managers, and (if you are using a participative design methodology) end users. In the academic context, course development has traditionally been overwhelmingly an individual faculty responsibility. However, since the late 1990s there has been an increase in the practice of team-based course development in higher education, involving the cooperation of multiple instructors and subject specialists (Drew & Vaughan, 2002; Toohey, 1999), and in research concerning this phenomenon as an innovation. LCMS respond to these developments; they provide the necessary functionality to work collaboratively, in an efficient way, and with proper safeguards for the integrity of the content.

An LCMS may include full support for a distributed publishing process: version control tools, check-in/check-out, workflow and task assignment and management tools, project tracking and reporting tools, annotation capability for reviews, and built-in storyboard facilities. With such tools, even a geographically dispersed team can work productively in a collaborative fashion. Some LCMS are browser-based. The availability of content within the browser further facilitates and simplifies the entire process, since any individual can view or interact with content, at any time, provided he or she has been assigned the appropriate rights. Overall, by using an LCMS, the complete cycle of development, review, revision, and approval can be streamlined, while simultaneously allowing for more input from different sources (generating better content) and improved quality assurance.

Another sense of distributed content is associated with the terms "distributed content model." An extreme version of this model proposes that content may be integrated from centralized servers within an organization, from servers across organizations, and even from individual desktops via a peer-to-peer networking architecture. Despite optimistic predictions from industry analysts (e.g., Gartner Group, 2001), this remains largely a pipe dream from any commercial standpoint.

However, a variant of the distributed content model, restricted to drawing on any number of centralized repositories, has been implemented in the new millennium in the content management world, and at least one LCMS currently supports this approach. This version of the "distributed content model" can be defined, briefly, as follows. Content is distributed across a number of different learning content management environments that have their own repositories, each with its own metadata scheme. Using parent-child relationships, these environments are able to share, manipulate, and coordinate content, while controlling its integrity. For example, Environment A may be able to access certain content in Environment B. Users of Environment A would then be able to sequence content from Environment B along with their own content retrieved from Environment A, and present the results of this aggregation through their own interfaces. However, they would not be able to modify the content from Environment B. In a sophisticated strategy, usage of copyrighted content from outside the native environment could also be tracked via metadata, and then reported for purposes of establishing royalty payments. While this scheme was developed primarily to address specific challenges facing training in the aviation industry, it is not hard to see how it could support inter- or intra-organizational content sharing within institutions of higher education.

It is worth remarking here that there has been a great deal of interest, research, and development concerning the learning object, or LO (Spohrer, Sumner & Shum, 1998; Wagner, 2002; Wiley, 2002), and LO repositories (Richards, McGreal, Hatala & Friesen, 2002) in the field of higher education. But these initiatives have garnered only limited success. There are many reasons for this: the appropriate schemes to motivate participation have not been implemented; it is hard to find content through searching repositories; the quality of objects is not uniformly good; and, overall, the technology that has been built is not that functional. Ironically, many organizations outside higher education are, effectively, using LO repositories through their exploitation of LCMS. The innovation of a distributed content model, as described above, promises to offer the basis for a useful and usable distributed LO repository, complete with powerful mechanisms to control and document usage and maintain the integrity of copyrighted material.

However, some challenges still remain. One important issue concerns the problem that arises when the organization that is fulfilling the role of content aggregator in this scheme is confronted with one or more modular repositories, each governed by its own specific taxonomy and metadata scheme. Retrieving the right content could easily be problematic for the aggregator, given the potential diversity of content to be searched and the corresponding complexity and diversity of the metadata schemes (reflecting different professional and disciplinary viewpoints) that may be encountered. One possible solution is provided by topic maps, a categorization and retrieval technology that allows for the development of different user-centred views of content (see the end of this chapter for an example of how topic maps can work in an LCMS).

An alternative solution is to agree on standards for subjective metadata — or metadata that defines the sense or semantics of the object with which it is associated — so that, in effect, the user is always confronted with metadata that is familiar. The history of content management to date is, however, replete with stories concerning the difficulties encountered in trying to get any body of people, let alone groups of individuals across different disciplines, to agree on a restricted vocabulary for indexing content. The bottom line is that in order to be useful to people from a specific discipline, the structure and metadata of a repository must reflect the way users in that discipline think and organize their knowledge.

Connectivity

One of the major complaints with CMS is that the products with the most market penetration do not conform to any open standards. This lack of standards has several drawbacks. To begin with, there is a very high cost associated with switching platforms. If a product no longer serves the institution's needs, or if the vendor fails and the product is no longer developed or supported, the migration of existing content to a new platform will be difficult in the absence of any industry-wide standards for interoperability. Thus, once a platform has been selected, the institution is pretty well locked-in with this product.

Perhaps even more serious is the circumstance that CMS cannot readily be integrated with other applications. There are many examples of institutions that have rejected or abandoned commercial CMS for this very reason. A well-funded, technology-enriched private institution in Mexico dropped WebCT™ in 2003, and is building its own CMS system because the institution could not integrate WebCT™ with systems that register students and schedule faculty. Many institutions (our own included) have created their own in-house site-generator tools or CMS because commercial CMS cannot be highly customized to their own specific needs, or because they are too costly.

In addition to objections from administrators who may wish to integrate CMS with other "business" applications or ERP-type systems, there has also been criticism from library and information services people. Machavec (2001) argues it is desirable that CMS be capable of being integrated with library systems, including databases, online journals, catalogues, digital e-reserves (which post reserve material for courses and manage related copyright), e-mail reference services, and online reference chats. Without this possibility there is a danger, he argues, that "for-profit digital commercial library services will market themselves as the answer for courseware packages" (p. 2), leading inevitably to a narrowing of the scope of information accessed by students.

There is an identifiable movement promoting open standards and even development of open-source CMS (Foster, 2004; Machavec, 2001; Olsen, 2004; Unsworth, 2003). The Sakai Project[2] to create an open-source CMS is based at Indiana University, Massachusetts Institute of Technology, Stanford, and the

University of Michigan at Ann Arbor, and is partially funded by the W. Mellon Foundation. The CMS is intended to be accessed via uPortal, another open-source system. Like many such projects, progress is slower than anticipated. It is not clear either how many institutions would adopt an open-source solution, given the additional internal development and support that would be required to implement the system successfully and develop it over time to meet evolving requirements, both technical and functional. Currently, in 2004, it is reported that about 80 percent of those institutions that are adopting CMS are committed to a commercial product.

Since Blackboard™ and WebCT™ essentially own the CMS market in higher education in 2004, there is not that much pressure to bring to bear on them to adopt open standards. Blackboard™ has announced it will move in this direction, but at present it is not clear what urgency attends this commitment. The situation in the commercial e-learning space is quite different. LCMS systems almost universally respect open standards. Competition is stiff, and noncompliance pretty much rules out sales. LCMS vendors are also more accustomed to meeting requirements of customers for custom features and for integrating their products, to varying degrees, with learning management systems (LMS), human resource (HR) and enterprise resource planning (ERP) systems, and various business applications.

In the world of higher education, institutions are caught on the horns of a dilemma right now. They can continue to support the most successful CMS products, in which case the evolution to open standards will be quite slow. Or, they can wait for the availability of a fully functional open-source solution, as per the Sakai initiative. But in this case, internal IT services will have their work cut out for them to implement and support systems, the development and evolution of CMS will be less focused, and the costs will be largely internal, rather than spread across a commercial customer base.

One way out of this dilemma is to investigate what is offered in the way of LCMS where open standards flourish. There are two factors that may impede this, apart from lack of education and awareness about LCMS. The first is perceived cost. To be sure, LCMS are not inexpensive, but a careful analysis of total cost of ownership in any given setting would likely be interesting. LCMS are often licensed on a per-seat basis, reflecting the same business model that is also dominant in the CMS market. However, alternative models also exist, including licensing based on the number of processors running the application. In this case, there is a one-time cost for acquisition and an ongoing maintenance fee (somewhere around 20 percent of the licenses) to cover support and upgrades. With a large student base, this alternative might be attractive in the long run, compared with annual per-seat licensing arrangements. At any rate, the model is certainly more scalable and can be matched more closely to levels of actual usage.

Integrated Learning Environments

The lack of support for open standards, the difficulties associated with connecting CMS with other applications, limited content management capability, and the lack of openness to customizing products from their vendors make CMS a poor choice for creating an integrated learning environment, as compared with LCMS. LCMS offer the potential for a whole range of strategies to simplify the creation and management of course content and the power to implement a wider range of mechanisms in support of contextualized, rich, meaningful learning.

LCMS can be used to deliver courses customized to different audiences according to discipline or interest. The profile information that is used to determine which content is delivered to the student can be captured from other systems and could include other performance data, as well as registration information. For example, this information might include known performance gaps in other areas of the curriculum, or known second language capability in the case of a second-language learner. LCMS are also typically fully Section 508-compliant (Agricultural and Transportation Barriers Compliance Board [ATBC], 2000; Centre For IT Accommodation [CITA], 1998; World Wide Web Consortium [W3C], 1999), so accessibility is not an issue.

Apart from delivering courses, an LCMS could afford the basis for a sophisticated learning environment incorporating the following components:

- *Just-in-time learning*: Students can use powerful search techniques exploiting the metadata and taxonomy implemented with an LCMS to access smaller chunks of instruction via a portal. This might be useful to support project-based or problem-based learning, in particular.

- *An integrated information environment*: Metadata schemes can be used to access a wide variety of reference resources managed within one integrated system.

- *Student input*: Some of the resources managed within an LCMS could be built from student input, using appropriate interfaces and templates. These might include FAQs, student projects and related lessons learned, a corpus of annotated texts (say, for corpus-based learning strategies in ESL or composition), worked examples of problem solutions (in science or mathematics), or case solutions (in engineering, business, or medicine). An LCMS could be used to develop an electronic memory, for example, of design practice within a project-based engineering design course. Some LCMS also feature advanced knowledge-sharing features. For example, in one system, any user can propose to share useful resources related to content he or she is studying. A resource might be a book, a journal article, a URL, an experience, etc. The recommendation is routed automatically to a predefined expert in the subject and, if approved, is published to the repository and becomes searchable through a portal. In an academic setting, student contributions could be tracked through metadata and reported and evaluated for course credit or other forms of recognition.

- *Prescriptive learning strategies*: Students can self-test on a variety of objectives within the LCMS, then have the LCMS link them to resources and instruction related to their reported weaknesses.

- *Online testing*: Some LCMS have very sophisticated testing and test development and management tools. Currently, the only feature missing from the most capable systems is secure testing with authentication, but this feature is sure to emerge in the near future.

- *Support for collaborative course development teams*: Instructional designers, subject matter experts, administrators, and even end users, among others, can participate collaboratively in the creation of courses through workflow management tools available in LCMS.

- *Support for rich, highly interactive content*: LCMS offer all the tools to build content with simulations, exercises, embedded quizzes, cases, or scenarios. In many cases, these tools are special object types that can be used to develop engaging content without necessarily using any plug-ins. This is also a benefit in environments that are very variable in terms of IT infrastructure, or that have low bandwidth.

- *Document management*: an LCMS with document management features could be used to manage all course-related content for both online or face-to-face versions. This could promote re-use and sharing of content across faculty. More generally, an LCMS provides a platform for implementation of a fully functional learning object repository, where faculty from within an individual institution or across partnering institutions could find material for online or classroom courses. Any intellectual property regime an institution might negotiate with faculty also could be managed within such a system.

Future Developments

Given the picture painted above, it seems clear that LCMS in their current incarnation (as of 2005) offer significant potential for implementing superior strategies for course design, support and delivery, as compared with current-generation CMS. In the future, we expect the gap between LCMS and CMS only to widen further. Driven by corporate demand, and with significant investment in research and development within the industry, LCMS are evolving quickly in response to market needs. Current trends include progress in single source publishing (output content to Web, print, PDA, cell phone), translation management, collaboration tools, workflow management, taxonomy management, and categorization, search, and retrieval of content.

The following section provides one instance of how this kind of development looks. This example presents on-going research and development in the area of search and retrieval tools and technology, arguably a key component for any kind of integrated approach to developing, maintaining, and accessing online learning resources — resources that might include course material, the contents of digital libraries and repositories (with text or media), and external Web-based content. In 2003 and 2004, a significant project was undertaken by researchers from Concordia University, Kontentsu Corporation (a content management firm), and Eedo Knowledgeware (a leading learning content management systems firm) to assess and develop topic map technology, in response to well-known problems concerning content management and content access online. The project was funded by Industry Canada under the Canarie Grants Program. What follows is a brief account of topic maps, their benefits, and the role they could play within a CMS that might be developed based on adoption of LCMS functionality.

While next-generation LCMS will include a number of powerful features, not least of which will be greatly enhanced search and retrieval capabilities —

based on topic maps or other approaches, such as implementation of thesauri (Mack, Ravin, & Byrd, 2001)—no comparable initiatives are apparent in the domain of CMS platform development.

An Illustration: Topic Mapping

Topic maps (ISO, 1999, 2002) separate the interrelated topics in a given body of knowledge from the actual resources that describe these topics. They provide context-based searches that can match context-specific search criteria entered by the user (Pepper, 2002). As a search-and-retrieval technology, topic maps provide a method to code content in terms of topics, the relationships among these topics, and any additional informational resources associated with the target subject matter (Rath, 2000). This coding allows for greater flexibility in searching because the user not only gains access to information directly associated with a topic but also gets information regarding related topics. Results are returned not by keyword "hits" but rather by the concepts or ideas present in a corpus. A search will return fewer, more relevant "hits" matching the key word with the appropriate semantic context (Rath, 2000). Given their capability, topic maps can support learning within a CMS in that content across functions can be integrated through search functionality triggered by a learner's query. Topic maps can help to provide the learner with a uniquely individualized tool that customizes how content is accessed and, potentially, organized.

Pepper (2002) refers to the elements of a topic map using the acronym TAO: Topics, Associations, and Occurrences. Let us consider a simple example of a topic map created to describe the body of knowledge related to e-learning. *Topics* pertinent to the subject matter of e-learning could include, for example, software platforms, learning management systems, learning content management systems, learning objects, industry standards, and interoperability, among others. *Associations* draw out the relationships between topics. For example, consider the following statement in which the underlined portion details an association linking the topic "SCORM" to the topic "metadata schemes": "SCORM is used in evaluating metadata schemes." *Occurrences* point the user to resources that provide information about the topics themselves. An occurrence dedicated to the topic "metadata schemes" could be a pointer to a uniform resource locator for an online article comparing the various metadata standards used in the industry. Topic maps also allow multiple naming conventions, which allow topics to be described in a variety of languages or by different titles according to user preference. Topic maps permit the assignment of metadata to information resources, similar to resources that possess XML tagging. Topics within a topic map also can be assigned a scope within which they are considered valid, thereby avoiding problems arising from the use of a topic in multiple contexts.

Arguably, the quality of the search results obtained through using a topic map depends largely on the topic map developer's ability to extract stakeholders' representations of the domain of knowledge being mapped. Proponents of the cognitive information processing (CIP) theory, proposed by Waugh and Norman (1965) and Atkinson and Shiffrin (1968), have explored the role of representations of ill-structured problems (Reitman, 1965) in various contexts (Voss, 1998; Voss & Post, 1988). Research has also shown that differences in problem solving ability between novices and experts can be partially attributed to their different problem representations (e.g., Voss et al., 1998; Torney-Purta, 1992). Taking this research into account, our development of topic maps is grounded in one or more expert's cognitive representations of the domain, and an analysis of the tasks to be performed by end-users who will be navigating the domain using the topic map. Following from our leanings towards a theory of CIP, our current research bases the construction of a topic map for a given domain on a set of validated taxonomies or ontologies that emerge from an expert's view of that domain, including its topics, associations, and occurrences.

Taxonomies, as a classification scheme or hierarchy of terms for cataloguing content, can form the basis of a system for managing large, complex collections of information. While taxonomies and ontologies are terms that are used interchangeably, ontologies tend to include instantiations, constraints, and an extra element of theory — a notion that the structure actually describes reality, not just a method of organizing data (Kabel, de Hoog, Wielinga, & Anjewierden, 2004). As such, ontologies perhaps come closer to mental models of intellectual content. McGuiness (2001) contends that ontologies must exhibit certain required properties, namely, a finite controlled vocabulary, unambiguous interpretations of classes and term relationships, as well as strict hierarchical subclass relationships. In addition, they may possess typical nonmandatory properties, such as value restriction and specifications of arbitrary logical relationships between terms. Generally, these properties permit the construction of complex knowledge structures, which give ontologies a significant advantage over other forms of organization.

In order to develop a topic map for a given domain of knowledge, the content of the domain needs to be categorized in terms of topics, associations, and occurrences. In our own work, we have manually created an ontology to classify the information found in a body of articles stored in a digital repository. The resultant topic map, when validated by experts, provided a representation of the information in the articles. The process of creating the ontology included: a) illuminating the possible terms or topics, as well as any subtopics that aided in information classification; b) describing the relationships or associations that existed between the topics and subtopics uncovered; and c) explicitly linking each of the emerging topics to a particular point in one or more articles, thereby creating occurrences, or instances of topics in the topic map.

A topic map for a given domain, once completed and validated by experts, provides learners with an observable, inspectable map or model of the domain. The map itself is a significant learning resource, supporting the learner's acquisition of ideas about the organization of the domain, the relationships among concepts, and the utility of the information within the domain, as well as related terminology. The content of courses that are offered through a CMS can be represented using a topic map.

Users browsing a topic map can view resources associated with concepts that have certain semantic relationships. Unlike conventional searches (e.g., boolean search of key words or descriptors), a topic map user can traverse a web of relationships, much as one might browse the shelves of a physical library where books with related content are stored under different, but proximal, classifications. Thus, users can encounter relevant information they would not find using full-text search or keyword search strategies. Topic maps, when adopted in the context of a CMS, can thereby afford the possibilities of contextualized, discovery-based learning experiences for learners.

Topic maps offer a solution to the problem of different terms or even languages used to describe the same concept. In the worlds of content management and information science, the difficulties associated with attempts to constrain users to describe content with a fixed and limited set of terms, and to apply these terms consistently and reliably, are well known. With topic map technology, users or user groups are free to introduce and share their preferred terminology and labels for a particular topic. With appropriately designed topic map development tools, learners who are accessing courses in a CMS can potentially generate and use their own topic maps to help them navigate the information contained in the courses. The conjoining facility offered in topic maps allows learners to view the same set of content through multiple perspectives. For example, students enrolled in a course might compare their own topic maps to those of the instructor(s) and use the differences seen between the two maps as a reference point for creating and applying new knowledge.

Topic maps are extensible. With traditional approaches, new insights into how content should be classified require that new metadata fields be defined and populated, or new key words be agreed upon and applied. These efforts are typically not feasible or extremely expensive, from a database recompilation standpoint. Though there is a large body of research on automation of indexing and extraction of key words, as with other technologies such as machine translation and natural language processing (where more work has been done to date), these approaches are limited in their success. Topic maps offer sophisticated means for developing indices that do not necessarily require that each resource be manually indexed, since the topic map operates in part at a level or levels of abstraction above regular metadata. This ease in updating and extending the relations seen in topic maps, without having to meddle with the information resources themselves, simplifies administration of courses in a CMS. When course material is updated in a CMS powered by topic maps, existing topics and associations can be edited while new topics can also be added readily to the existing ontological structure.

Customized topic maps provide different user-centred views of large digital libraries or repositories, allowing them to be accessed readily by different disciplines. This customization increases the value and utility of repositories or digital collections and has obvious implications for interdisciplinary work. As mentioned earlier, topic maps can be compared, and they can also be conjoined to create wider or more comprehensive views of content.

Conclusion

Given the capabilities described above, and the considerations around costs and licensing, it is surprising that LCMS have made little inroads in higher education. The answer may lay partly with the market focus of LCMS companies, partly with the perception within the academic world that these are "corporate" applications, partly with misconceptions concerning the cost and complexity of LCMS (confusing them with their bigger siblings, the enterprise content management systems), and partly with the limitations that were apparent in earlier versions of LCMS. On the last point, it has to be acknowledged that only a short time ago, in early 2001 and 2002, LCMS typically suffered from usability problems and were limited functionally in terms of what could be produced by the constraints imposed by early versions of standards such as SCORM. The evolution of LCMS systems into highly usable, powerful, and flexible applications has been very rapid, however, and the current generation of industry-leading products bears little resemblance to systems that were considered advanced four to five years ago.

The one remaining differentiator of CMS from LCMS may be the support within CMS for collaboration in the sense of integrated bulletin boards, conferences, instant messaging, chat, and other threaded discussion. But this gap is being closed also, as LCMS increasingly take on more general knowledge management and collaboration features. In the short term, the gap is also addressed by third-party tools that can be integrated into any system. Some LCMS also currently ship with licenses for a separate virtual meeting or virtual classroom tool, similar to WebX™ or Symposium™. Popular third-party, computer-mediated conferencing systems such as FirstClass™ may also ship with development tools and libraries that would allow for their integration with an LCMS.

Overall, the time has come to evaluate or reevaluate the contribution LCMS could make to education. One key to this process is the careful specification of needs, and the analysis of desired learning models, strategies, and resources. Only against the backdrop of such analyses can the case for LCMS be reasonably assessed, and without such analyses, the procurement of an LCMS will not advance learning in any significant way. We come back, full circle, to the comments at the outset of this chapter to the effect that careful technology planning and integration are crucial but largely missing from our institutions.

Acknowledgments

The authors acknowledge the assistance of Dennis Dicks, Gretchen Lowerison, and Dai Zhang of Concordia University in the preparation of portions of this chapter.

References

Aaron, M., Dicks, D. J., Ives, C., & Montgomery, B. (in press). Planning for integrating teaching technologies. *Canadian Journal of Learning and Technology, 30*(2).

Agricultural and Transportation Barriers Compliance Board (2000). Section 508 electronic and information technology accessibility standards. Retrieved August 31, 2004, from *http://cita.rehab.uiuc.edu/presentations/2002-04-22-IVC/sect508/sect508-web.html*

Atkinson, R. C. & Shiffrin, R. M. (1968). Human memory: A proposed system and its control processes. In K. W. Spence & J. T. Spence (Eds.), *The psychology of learning and motivation: Advances in research and theory* (Vol. 2, pp. 90-197). New York: Academic Press.

Bates, A. W. & Poole, G. (2003). *Effective teaching with technology in higher education: Foundations for success.* San Francisco: John Wiley & Sons.

Carmean, C. & Haefner, J. (2002). Mind over matter: Transforming course management systems into effective learning environments. *Educause Review, 37*(6), 27-34.

Centre for IT Accommodation (1998). Section 508 of the Rehabilitation Act (29 U.S.C. 794d), as amended by the Workforce Investment Act of 1998 (P.L. 105-220). Retrieved August 26, 2004, from *http://www.section508 .gov/index.cfm?FuseAction=Content&ID=14*

Chapman, B. & Hall B. (2002). *Learning content management systems: Comparative analysis of systems used to construct, organize and re-use learning objects.* Sunnyvale, CA: Brandon Hall.

De Bourgh, G. A. (2002). Simple elegance: Course management systems as pedagogical infrastructure to enhance science learning. *The Technology Source.* Retrieved April 30, 2004, from *http://ts.mivu.org/default.asp? show=article&id=925*

Drew, L. & Vaughan, S. (2002). The course team as the focus for contextualized professional learning. *Innovations in Education and Teaching International, 39*(3), 183-195.

Foster, A. L. (2004). Four universities join to create open-source software for professors to manage courses. *The Chronicle of Higher Education, 50*(21), 28.

Gartner Group. (2001). The emergence of distributed content management and peer-to-peer content networks. Retrieved April 30, 2004, at *http://marketplacena.gartner.com/010022501oth-NextPage.PDF*

Howell, S., Saba, F., Lindsay, N., & Williams, P. (2004). Seven strategies for enabling faculty success in higher education. *Internet and Higher Education, 7,* 33-49.

International Standards Organization (ISO). (1999). ISO/IEC 13250 — Topic maps. PDF document retrieved December 17, 2003, from *http://www. y12.doe.gov/sgml/sc34/document/0129.pdf*

(ISO). (2002). ISO/IEC 13250 — Topic maps. PDF document retrieved December 17, 2003, from *http://www.y12.doe.gov/sgml/sc34/document/0322_files/iso13250-2nd-ed-v2.pdf*

Kabel, S., de Hoog, R., Wielinga, R. S., & Anjewierden, A. (2004). The added value of task, ontology-based markup for information retrieval. *Journal of the American Society for Information Science and Technology, 55*(4), 348-382.

Machavec, G. S. (2001). Course management software: Where is the library? *Information Intelligence Online Libraries and Microcomputers, 19*(10), 1-2.

Mack, R., Ravin, Y. & Byrd, R. J. (2001). Knowledge portals and the emerging digital knowledge workplace. *IBM Systems Journal, 40*(4), 925-955.

McGuinness, D. L. (2001). Ontologies come of age. In D. Dieter Fensel, J. Hendler, H. Lieberman & W. Wahlster (Eds.), *The Semantic Web: Why, What, and How.* Cambridge, MA: MIT Press. Retrieved March 15, 2004, from *http://www.ksl.stanford.edu/people/dlm/papers/ontologies-come-of-age-mit-press-(with-citation).htm*

Olsen, F. (2004). Course management: Colleges push for an open approach. *The Chronicle of Higher Education, 50*(21), 10.

Pepper, S. (2002). *The TAO of topic maps.* Retrieved September 15, 2003, from *http://www.ontopia.net/topicmaps/materials/tao.html*

Rath, H. H. (2000). Topic maps: Templates, topology, and type hierarchies. *Markup Languages: Theory & Practice, 2*(1), 45-64.

Reitman, W. (1965). *Cognition and thought.* New York: John Wiley.

Richards, G., McGreal, R., Hatala, M. & Friesen, N. (2002). The evolution of learning object repositories: Portals for online objects for learning. *Journal of Distance Education, 17*(3), 67-79.

Roberts, G. (2003). The yin and yang of integrating TILT with Blackboard™. *Computers in Libraries 23*(8), 54-56.

Romiszowski, A., & Mason, R. (2003). Computer mediated communication. In D. H. Jonassen (Ed.), *Handbook of research for educational communications and technology*. New York: Macmillan.

Spohrer, J., Sumner, T., & Shum, S. B. (1998). Educational authoring tools and the educational object economy: Introduction to this special issue from the East/West Group. *Journal of Interactive Media in Education*. Retrieved April 30, 2004, from *http://www-jime.open.ac.uk/98/10/spohrer-98-10-paper.html*

Toohey, S. (1999). *Designing courses for higher education*. London: SRHE and Open University Press.

Torney-Purta, J. (1992). Cognitive representations of the political system in adolescents: The continuum from pre-novice to expert. In H. Haste & J. Torney-Purta (Eds.), *The development of political understanding: A new perspective* (pp. 11-25). San Francisco: Josey-Bass.

Unsworth, J. M. (2003). The next wave: Liberation technology. *The Chronicle of Higher Education, 50*(21), 16-20.

Voss, J.F. (1998). On the representation of problems: An information-processing approach to foreign policy decision making. In D. A. Sylvan and J. F. Voss (Eds.), *Problem representation in foreign policy decision making* (pp. 8-26). Cambridge, UK: Cambridge University Press.

Voss, J. F. & Post, T. A. (1988). On the solving of ill-structured problems. In M. T. H. Chi, R. Glaser & M .J. Farr (Eds.), *The nature of expertise* (pp. 261-285). Hillsdale, NJ: Lawrence Erlbaum.

Voss, J. F., Wiley, J., Kennet, J., Schooler, T. E., & Silfies, L. N. (1998). Representations of the Gulf crisis as derived from the U. S. Senate debate. In D. A. Sylvan & J. F. Voss (Eds.), *Problem representation in foreign policy decision making* (pp. 279-302). Cambridge, UK: Cambridge University Press.

Wagner, E. D. (2002). The new frontier of learning object design. *The eLearning Developer's Journal,* June 18. Retrieved July 1, 2002, from *http://www.elearningguild.com*

Waugh, N. C. & Norman, T. A. (1965). Primary memory. *Psychological Review, 72*, 89-104.

Wiley, D. A., (Ed.). (2002). The instructional use of learning objects. Agency for Instructional Technology/Association for Educational Communications and Technology (AIC/AECT). Retrieved August 31, 2004, from *http://www.reusability.org/read/*

World Wide Web Consortium (W3C). (1999). Web content accessibility guidelines 1.0. Retrieved August 31, 2004, from *http://www.w3.org/TR/1999/WAI-WEBCONTENT-19990505/*

Endnotes

[1] Extensible Markup Language, a specification developed by W3C. This programming language allows developers to create their own tags for specific information.

[2] *www.sakaiproject.org*

Chapter XIV

Virtual Classroom Facilities Imbedded in a Course Management System

Jesko Kaltenbaek, Freie University of Berlin, Germany

Abstract

A basic condition for efficient computer-supported cooperative learning in higher education is the direct support of computer-mediated communication and computer-supported cooperative work. In this chapter, it will be reasoned why a combination of these features in one system is essential for well-functioning learning management systems (LMS). In addition to theoretical considerations about the link between learning objects, cognition, motivation, social processes, and practice, different e-learning and blended learning projects at the Freie University of Berlin are outlined. Finally, desirable cooperation and collaboration tools for an LMS are presented and related to psychological learning theories.

Introduction

In order for higher education to have efficient computer-supported cooperative learning (CSCL) the direct support of computer-mediated communication (CMC) and computer-supported cooperative work (CSCW) is required. The combination of these features in one system is a move for LMS[1] into a next stage of maturity, which has been triggered by the need to associate learning objects, presentation, cognition, emotion, motivation, communication, cooperation, and practice. LMS must accommodate the variety of distributed learning formats (i.e., online, blended, hybrid, etc.) as well as the variety of learning activities that should be enacted and supported by collaborative and cooperative functions grounded in psychological learning theories.

In Germany, the idea of virtual (online) and blended learning, as well as the concept of virtual universities, is increasingly discussed in the literature and at conferences, congresses, and fairs (see Albrecht, 2003; Bett & Wedekind, 2003, Dohmann & Michel, 2003; Kandzia & Ottmann, 2003, Kerres, Kalz, Stratmann & Witt, 2004; Kerres & Voß, 2003; Rinn & Meister, 2004; Schulmeister, 2003; Uhl, 2003). Such initiatives have raised the following questions that must be dealt with: What are the benefits of computer-supported learning? How is it possible to achieve economic, motivational, and didactical quality in blended learning and e-learning courses? Which supportive structures are essential in looking at the relationship between learning objects, emotions, motivation, CMC, CSCW, and CSCL?

Conceptual Background

To approach answers to these questions, let us start with an illustration of the basic concept of "e-learning." E-Learning can be defined as:

- Computer-supported.
- Acquiring or accommodating and assimilating information or procedures (e.g., data, facts, algorithms, heuristics).
- Utilizing different forms of presentation (e.g., text, hypertext, drawings, pictures, animations, videos, speech, sounds, music).

- Leading to a change in behavior, knowledge, cognition, attitudes, feelings, motivation, or abilities.

- Tested by or presented in front of another person, a group, or representatives of a special institution (e.g., audience, school, university) or used in practice.

The main benefits of e-learning are rapid information exchange, easy connection of learners with educational resources, and vast multimedia possibilities. There are some subjects and issues that can be presented superbly in a pure e-learning program, but in many cases they should be integrated in social learning scenarios (traditional or media-mediated). But there are many combinations of e-learning with traditional classroom learning, books, and practice as well (so-called "blended learning scenarios;" see Rossett, Douglis, & Frazee, 2003).

Theoretical education in universities is carried out mostly over books and scripts, lectures, and seminars. Various ways of computer-supported and computer-supplemented learning, as well as different tools and media, can be used in both traditional, blended, and virtual learning environments. Figure 1 shows a classification of assigned electronic tools divided into a time dimension (asynchronous and isochronous) and a social setting dimension (single learner/auditory, one group, many groups). Different character sizes and font styles symbolize the estimated average frequency of use of diverse media for training and learning in universities.

Many of these tools are rarely used in higher education. But some of them have gained important significance. Almost all of them can be integrated into an LMS. If you add an interlinked CMS, you can get an LCMS with elements easy to reuse. These tools have the potential to support learning in ways that are difficult to achieve in the traditional classroom, but which can become commonplace in the blending or virtual classroom.

E-Learning at the Freie University of Berlin

With 42,000 students in almost 90 different programs of study — 4,000 graduates and 1,000 doctoral candidates each year — the Freie University of Berlin (FU-Berlin) is one of the largest universities in Germany. In the last three years, the FU-Berlin has realized almost 100 e-learning and blended learning programs and projects respectively, but they are very different: some are low budget productions realized by one or two persons, others have been designed

Figure 1. Estimated average frequency of use of different media and tools

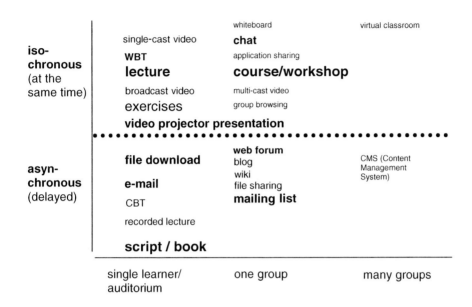

by more than ten people. Faculty members use e-Chalk™ as a course design tool. e-Chalk™ is an authoring tool that allows lecturers to write on an electronic board. It seamlessly integrates pictures and interactive programs from the Web. All actions are stored in a very small file and can be viewed with a Java™ player or printed out in PDF format.

Some have been or will be brought to market, some are only accessible for the students of one course, and others are free for anyone. A variety of special programs and projects have also been developed. Almost all of these programs are presented in German language only. However, in the internationalization and globalization programs, a translation in English is planned for many courses.

A special working group of experts from different faculties of the FU-Berlin compiled a catalog of criteria that was used to document the necessary functions and to evaluate existing LMS present on the market (see Table 1, LMS Selection Criteria). After more than three years of evaluation, the LMS Blackboard™ became the central learning platform for the entire FU-Berlin because the working group believed that Blackboard best complies with the criteria requirements. The CMS of Blackboard will soon be integrated.

Table 1. LMS selection criteria

LMS Functions	Features	LMS	Features
1. Authoring capabilities	• Production with a WYSIWYG editor • Joint authoring • E-learning standards (AICC, SCORM, IMS, LOM, etc.) • Support of rich media (mime-types) • Import and export capabilities • Separation of contents and layout (templates) • Assignments of rights • Version control • Content repository and integrity check • Indexation • Glossary • Bibliography	5. Assessment exercises	• Tests forms (multiple choice, multiple answer, etc.) • Feedback possibilities • Surveys/statistics • User tracking • Report/presentation • Import and export
		6. Personal domain/desktop	• Adaptive user interface • Annotations • Bookmarks • Notifications • Time schedule • Address database • Homepage
2. Content presentation	• Adaptable templates • Preview function • Navigation possibilities • Site map • Offline usage	7. Groups and rights	• User-defined • Multilingualism • Adaptability • Protected areas
3. Search functions	• In content • In cooperation and collaboration tools • In documents • Members	8. Administration	• System requirements • Course export • Openness (application programming interface, etc.) • Backup/recovery
4. Support and tutoring	• Calendar • Announcements • Help functions • Email support • Cooperation and collaboration tools	9. Costs and development	• License restrictions • Situation of the developer • Reference installations

By concentrating on one central system, more acceptance, higher utilization, and commitment by faculties, lecturers, and students was expected. Furthermore, the use of a centrally located set of templates supports a common layout and common standards for ease of use by students and faculty. In comparison with many single installations and small licenses, a central learning platform offers advantages in costs and efficiency. Nonetheless, several departments and faculties at the FU-Berlin decided to use their own systems. Very good experiences have been made with the open source systems Stud.IP,[2] ILIAS,[3] Plone,[4] dotLRN,[5] and Moodle.[6] Additionally, there is some use of single-cast, multi-cast, and broadcast video in various video labs at the FU-Berlin, although there are few pure online offers.

Although the FU-Berlin desires to maintain mainly face-to-face courses, several benefits of computer-supported courses are seen in the direct use of an LCMS in face-to-face courses and their preparation and reinforcement including:

- Animations, simulations, videos, and pictures that help to visualize specific concepts, providing a way to see content in multiple formats.

- Additional online material (e.g., co-authored by several lecturers and skilled students) to help extend and consolidate contents of face-to-face courses and increase application and transfer of learning.

- Multimedia tutorials that introduce students to new material or help them to review and test their knowledge.

- Simulations and explorative and experimental environments that offer self-regulated learning possibilities.

- The ability to search the entire course content and present it in a sorted way, allowing the learner to make sense of content in his or her own way.

- Calendar and announcement functions that allow up-to-date information as it is needed.

- Online tutors that can be accessed beyond the seminar terms, providing opportunities for learning supports when needed.

- Online discussion and group work that offer a vast amount of possibilities for collaboration, negotiation of meaning, mentoring, scaffolding, etc.

- Computer-supported tests and examinations to expand learning possibilities and allow learners to know their progress (or lack of) instantly.

- Hyperlinks to integrate courses from other lecturers and other academic disciplines, helping learners access content across their programs of study as well as make connections across courses.

These features support deeper thinking by providing ways of communicating, interacting, and organizing information in a virtual space that the learner and instructor can have access to at any time, extending what happens in the traditional classroom while recording the virtual activities.

Practical Example: "Learn2teach Psychological and Didactical Basics of E-Learning"

The course entitled "Learn2teach Psychological and Didactical Basics of E-Learning" was designed for master's degree-seeking students interested in media psychology. In this course, they become acquainted with different didactical instruction strategies, which help them to evaluate and conceive ambitious and adequate online and off-line learning offers. The theoretical framework for the course was the pedagogical constructivism postulating the inseparability of the process of knowledge acquisition with the process of application of knowledge (see Hoops, 1998; Jonassen, Howland, Moore, & Marra, 2003; Reinmann-Rothmeier & Mandl, 2001) while analyzing authentic problems. The "learn2teach" course covered 12 modules. The e-learning parts of the course were embedded in a blended learning scenario. In this way, a sociodynamic basis for relations between the participants was secured. This relationship is based on the assumption that face-to-face contact is more familiar to students than computer-mediated social contact and, therefore, provides more chances to form learning communities. However, computer-mediated contact brings about another quality of acquaintance and communication (see Bente, Krämer, & Petersen, 2002).

Problem-based learning (PBL) was realized in the course group work. Four small groups discussed given problems and developed solutions in teamwork.

Figure 2. The relations of learning objects, presentation, emotions, motivation, CMC, CSCW, CSCL, and practice

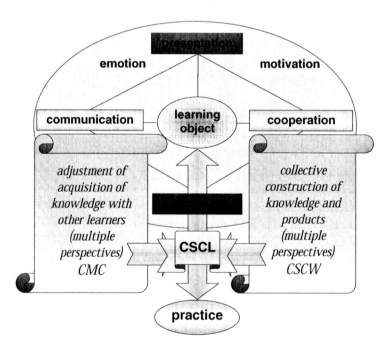

To achieve efficient computer-supported cooperative learning (CSCL), we used the direct support of computer-mediated communication (CMC) and computer-supported cooperative work (CSCW). Given this example, which supportive structures are essential in looking at the relationship between learning objects, emotions, motivation, CMC, CSCW, and CSCL? The answer can be illustrated in Figure 2.

When this model was brought together with PBL, a learning object (information) was presented in the context of a complex problem, which aims to evoke emotions and motivate the learner to solve the problem. Each of the four groups was guided by different group tutors (junior tutors). The junior tutors were normal students like the other group members, but they were jointly responsible for the completion of every task, for helping with problems, and for motivational needs (see Salmon, 2003). The junior tutors had the possibility to address a master tutor with specific problems. Master tutors were also class members, but they had greater expertise and more knowledge about the other three groups. The solutions developed by each group were compared with those of the others and examined by the participants and by the lecturer as the expert.

Apart from a continuous formative evaluation (realized over a separate forum, in which the participants had the possibility for questions, criticism, and improvement suggestions), summative evaluations were collected in the middle of the semester and in the last lecture week. From this date, a course evaluation was conducted. Altogether, the course functioned very well, but students had mixed feelings about the virtual learning experiences. On one hand, the participants felt they had more opportunity to interact with other participants in the face-to-face contact. On the other hand, they also perceived that the electronically delivered modules provided more opportunities for "greater depth of learning" and for individual participation. Over 50 percent of the participants wanted more courses in which the entire learning content is presented online, connected with classical face-to-face support (95 percent) and tutorial guidance (100 percent). The participants wanted more self-tests (multiple choice) as well as improved and more interactive communication and cooperation tools.

Our practical experience showed the following shortcoming: Blackboard (Vers. 6.0) offers insufficient features for many group processes. This limitation requires the use of more sophisticated virtual classroom applications. A virtual classroom allows the realization of a great variety of computer-mediated group work.

Nevertheless, the LMS can serve as an effective "cognitive tool"[7] (Jonassen & Carr, 1999) that offers several possibilities for active interactions with learning objects (Wiley, 2004). Although training students in Blackboard was a great effort (none of them had worked with this LMS before), the learning environment was finally used well for organizing and representing knowledge.

Virtual Classroom Functions

The technical and didactical functionalities of most of the present LMS and LCMS (embedded or integrated by application programming interfaces) are insufficient for many desirable didactical methods. Let us glance at possibilities of computer-supported information exchange and cooperation. There are different forms of CMC; e-mail and mailing lists are very old and simple forms. Newsgroups and Web forums offer collections of statements, information, experiences, and emotions of different contributors. Compared with these asynchronous features, the synchronous ones, such as IRC chat, Web chat, real-time chat, single-cast and multi-cast video, group browsing, whiteboarding, desktop, and application sharing, have their weaknesses and strengths (for experiences with other tools, see Teles, 2002). Virtual classroom systems (VCS) integrate some or all of these synchronous features.

Many functions valuable to teaching (whiteboard, desktop publishing, wiki, etc.) are not supported by present learning platforms, which is why many didactical forms of teaching and learning are impossible or very limited (Kuriloff, 2001). To be able to transfer didactical methods in an e-learning context, either sophisticated, blended learning scenarios or virtual classroom facilities directly imbedded in a course management system are required. With the functions specified above, it is possible to realize different behaviourist, cognitive, and constructivist principles in the computer-supported social environments (Table 2).

By using social learning tools, learning objects can be discussed in a net-based social exchange between individual learners, individual groups, and learners and lecturers. Particularly in virtual environments, every participant is able to annotate and enrich learning objects with their own (practical) experiences. Learning objects can be changed discursively ("peer review," see DeBourgh, 2002; Brown, 2000) and interlinked.

Table 2. Principles of learning theories and a selection of corresponding VCS features

Learning Theory	Principle	VCS feature
Behaviorism	• Reinforcement	• Feedback and marking functions
	• Direct feedback	• Raising hand, rating functions
	• Punishment	• Gagging, ignoring a participant
Cognitivism	• Organizing	• Searching and sorting functions
	• Storing	• Copying and pasting, recording
	• Personalizing, retrieving	• Personal depository, marking functions, bookmarks
	• Concept mapping, brain storming	• Particularly adequate: whiteboard, wiki
	• Different types of learners	• Importing of different media formats
Constructivism	• Create	• Creating new threads, rooms, pictures, Web pages, and online learning material
	• Construct, learner centeredness	• Selecting adequate learning environments and connecting different learning objects and work results
	• Communication, multiple perspectives, social learning	• Accessing all VCS features for social interchange (many more possibilities as telephone or e-mail)
	• Cooperation and collaboration	• Asking for and receiving answers, raising hand, working together on a document or a model
Social Learning Theory	• Modeling, vicarious learning	• e.g., in a video chat
	• Reciprocal determinism	• VCS features offer a closer relation to the social learning environment
	• Peer instruction	• Opening new public or private rooms, windows, whiteboards, and pages
Adult Learning Theory	• Independent learning	• Being flexible in the choice of learning place and learning environment

How can the "learn2teach" course be supported by the VCS features mentioned in the tables above? Let us take application sharing as an example. In one scenario, the lecturer or the master tutor gives the assignment to create a PowerPoint® presentation as a team. All students can contribute to the realization of the presentation at the same time. They neither have to meet in one place, nor have to mail their own drafts to other team members in sequence. In another scenario using group browsing and chat, all group members deal with one learning unit simultaneously. Students and lecturers can ask questions about specific learning objects and exchange answers, respectively. Collected questions and answers as well as personal notes are saved in the LMS connected with the VCS. This computer-supported cooperative learning can take place beyond course and university boundaries, making it possible to achieve economic, motivational, and didactical quality in blended learning and e-learning courses.

Oftentimes instructors attempt to achieve different functions with a plethora of independent tools. However, this abundance leads to an increasing number of technical difficulties. Additionally, the navigation and time effort of the participants are substantially enlarged. A high usability and a reasonable data exchange between the tools can be realized under a common surface only (Wolf, 2001). Then it also becomes possible to link directly to certain sections in logged chats, forums, whiteboard graphics, and wikis. Although some may argue that the technical conditions are present now and only the appropriate didactical models would be missing, many projects and the participants must cope with technical problems.

Conclusion

A good deal of manpower and money are invested into the development of computer-supported offers. The efficiency of the large effort to enrich courses in universities with computer-based elements is frequently challenged by critics. Nevertheless, in starting new e-learning projects, efficiency considerations are often outshone by personal motivation ("my project," "my dissertation"), philosophical ("the utmost possible"), sociological, psychological, political (it is en vogue in many universities to implement e-learning projects), and economical (long-term cost savings, attractiveness for foreign studying and lecturers) considerations. To carry out a great return of investment, it is important that the features mentioned above are didactically and technically linked with the other tools of an LMS. The implementation of powerful asynchronous and synchronous tools in a learning process also offers high potential for saving time. The combination of these features in one system will be a move for LMS and LCMS into the next stage of maturity and the ability to sustain computer-supported cooperative learning and work.

Technical features definitely play an important role in efficient learning; however, personal and social characteristics of students and lecturers, as well as the general situation at the universities, must not be underestimated, as "using technology is not enough" (cf., Blakeley, 2003; Chickering & Ehrmann, 1996; LeLoup & Ponterio, 2003).

References

Albrecht, R. (2003). *E-Learning in Hochschulen: Die Implementierung von E-Learning an Präsenzhochschulen aus hochschuldidaktischer Perspektive.* Berlin: dissertation.de.

Bente, G., Krämer, N. & Petersen, A. (Eds.). (2002). *Virtuelle Realitäten.* Göttingen: Hogrefe.

Bett, K. & Wedekind, J. (2003). *Lernplattformen in der Praxis.* Münster: Waxmann.

Blakeley, J. (2003). Flexible learning leaders 2002: Final report. (An initiative within the Australian Flexible Learning Framework for the National Vocational Education and Training System 2000-2004). Retrieved April 26, 2004, from *http://www.flexiblelearning.net.au/leaders/fl_leaders/fll02/finalreport/final_blakeley.pdf*

Brown, J. S. (2000). Growing up digital: How the Web changes work, education, and the ways people learn. *Change,* March/April, 11-20. Retrieved April 15, 2004, from *http://www.aahe.org/change/digital.pdf*

Chickering, A. W. & Ehrmann, S. C. (1996). Implementing the seven principles: Technology as lever. *AAHE Bulletin,* October, 3-6. Available from *http://www.tltgroup.org/programs/seven.html*

DeBourgh, G. A. (2002). Simple elegance: Course management systems as pedagogical infrastructure to enhance science learning. *Technology Source,* May/June. Retrieved April 24, 2004, from *http://ts.mivu.org/default.asp?show=article&id=925*

Dohmann, D. & Michel, L. P. (2003). *Marktpotenziale und Geschäftsmodelle für e-learning-Angebote deutscher Hochschulen.* Bielefeld: Bertelsmann Verlag.

Hoops, W. (1998). Konstruktivismus: Ein neues Paradigma für didaktisches Design?. *Unterrichtswissenschaft, 26*(3), 229-253.

Jonassen, D. H. & Carr, C. S. (1999). Mindtools: Affording multiple knowledge representations for learning. In S. P. Lajoie (Ed.), *Computers as cognitive tools II — No more walls: Theory change, paradigm shifts and their influence on the use of computers for instructional purposes* (pp. 165-196). Mahwah, NJ: Lawrence Erlbaum Associates.

Jonassen, D. H., Howland, J., Moore, J., & Marra, R. M. (2003). *Learning to solve problems with technology: A constructivist perspective* (2nd Ed.) Columbus, OH: Merrill/Prentice-Hall.

Kandzia, P. & Ottmann, T. (2003). *E-Learning für die Hochschule: Erfolgreiche Ansätze für ein flexibleres Studium.* Münster: Waxmann.

Kerres, M., Kalz, M., Stratmann, J. & de Witt, C. (Eds.). (2004). *Didaktik der Notebook-Universität.* Münster: Waxmann.

Kerres, M. & Voß, B. (Eds.). (2003). *Digitaler Campus: Vom Medienprojekt zum nachhaltigen Medieneinsatz in der Hochschule.* Münster: Waxmann.

Kuriloff, P. (2001). One size will not fit all. *Technology Source,* July/August. Retrieved April 24, 2004, from *http://ts.mivu.org/default.asp?show=article&id=899*

LeLoup, J. W. & Ponterio, R. (2003). Second language acquisition and technology: A review of the research. Retrieved February 5, 2004, from *http://www.cal.org/resources/digest/0311leloup.html*

Reinmann-Rothmeier, G. & Mandl, H. (2001). *Virtuelle Seminare in Hochschule und Weiterbildung.* Göttingen: Huber.

Rinn, U. & Meister, D. M. (2004). *Didaktik und Neue Medien: Konzepte und Anwendungen in der Hochschule.* Münster: Waxmann.

Rossett, A., Douglis, F. & Frazee, R. V. (2003). Strategies for building blended learning. Retrieved February 1, 2004, from *http://www.learning circuits.org/2003/jul2003/rossett.htm*

Salmon, G. (2003). *E-moderating: The key to teaching and learning online.* London: Kogan Page.

Salomon, G. (1993). On the nature of pedagogic computer tools: The case of the writing partner. In S. P. Lajoie & S. J. Derry (Eds.), *Computers as cognitive tools* (pp. 289-317). Hillsdale, NJ: Lawrence Erlbaum.

Schulmeister, R. (2003). *Lernplattformen für das virtuelle Lernen: Evaluation und Didaktik.* Oldenbourg.

Teles, L. (2002). The use of Web instructional tools by online instructors. *Technology Source,* May/June. Retrieved February 2, 2004, from *http://ts.mivu.org/default.asp?show=article&id=966*

Uhl, V. (2003). *Virtuelle Hochschulen auf dem Bildungsmarkt: Strategische Positionierung unter Berücksichtigung der Situation in Deutschland, Österreich und England.* Wiesbaden: Deutscher Universitäts-Verlag.

Wiley, D. A. (2004). Connecting learning objects to instructional design theory: A definition, a metaphor, and a taxonomy. In D. A. Wiley (Ed.), *The instructional use of learning objects* (online version). Retrieved on May 2, 2004, from *http://www.reusability.org/read/chapters/wiley.doc*

Wolf, K. D. (2001). Internet-based learning communities: Moving from patchwork environments to ubiquitous learning infrastructures. In S. Dijkstra, D. H. Jonassen & D. Sembill (Eds.), *Multimedia learning: Results and perspectives* (pp. 189-223). Frankfurt a. M.: Peter Lang.

Endnotes

[1]   The terms learning management system (LMS) and course management system are used synonymously in this article.

[2]   *www.studip.de*

[3]   *www.ilias.de/ios/index-e.html*

[4]   *http://plone.org*

[5]   *http://dotlrn.org/*

[6]   *http://moodle.org/*

[7]   "Cognitive tools are *tools* inasmuch as their operation depends on learners' operations; they are *cognitive* inasmuch as they serve to aid students in their own constructive thinking, enabling them to engage in cognitive operations they would not have been capable of otherwise" (Salomon, 1993, p. 180).

Chapter XV

The Use of Database-Driven Web Pages to Increase the Functionality of Current Online Learning Technology

Richard Caladine, University of Wollongong, Australia

Abstract

Online learning and course management systems are central to learning universities and colleges, and a model that blends face-to-face learning with distance education can combine benefits of the rich human learning relationships with the benefits of flexibility of where and when students learn. A large number of universities and colleges are adopting a blended model of learning. In the past, online interactions between learners generally have taken the form of text-based discussion forums, and while these have been used with great success in many courses, there are other interactions that have been difficult or impossible to undertake online. Database-driven Web sites were developed to make these interactions possible. Database-driven Web pages or collaborative, user-produced, Internet documents (CUPIDs) represent an innovation in online learning that allows learners to add, remove and edit the content of a Web page and/or upload files. As the data are input via Web forms, no programming skills are required. The data from the forms are processed by the database and the Web page is then rebuilt by the database. In this way, the database constructs or "drives" the Web page. CUPIDs have been used to facilitate a range of online interactions between learners in subjects at the University of Wollongong. The subjects all employ a model that blends face-to-face and online components. As well, learners may be distributed geographically between the five campuses of the university. The examples are: a Collaborative Online Glossary (COG); a Collaborative Online Reporting (COR); an Online Student Collected and Annotated Resources (OSCAR); as well as, a Collaborative Online Movie Review (COMR). By fostering new types of online interactions, CUPIDs provide greater functionality to online collaboration and open the door to a host of activities that are new to collaboration, online or otherwise and hence have a place in online learning of the future.

Introduction

Many universities and colleges have adopted online learning as a way to increase the effectiveness and efficiency of the courses they offer. A fewer number of institutions offer courses that are fully online and hence truly "distance education," as defined by Keegan as the "separation of teacher and student" (1986, p. 43). However the majority of institutions have adopted a blended approach to online learning in which courses have an online component as well as a face-to-face one. A blended learning approach tends to evolve through discrete stages as courses are slowly transformed from traditional classroom activities to virtual ones. The migration from the physical classroom to the virtual one, however, requires that instructional designers, instructors, and CMS managers consciously and intentionally design activities and functions that support the types of interactions that we know support deeper learning.

Since 1999, the University of Wollongong, like many others, has used a course management system (CMS). Early on it was recognized that one of the online learning functions that needed to be improved was group work, and it was believed that an online system that fostered cooperation, collaboration, and social and active learning would provide opportunities for deeper learning. In response to this need, a project modelled after Computer Supported Collaborative Learning (CSCL), was initiated and called CUPID: Collaborative, User-Produced, Internet Documents.

Background

At first, online learning at Wollongong was confined to the use of computer-mediated communications (CMCs) using e-mail and e-mail lists. These were used for interactions between learners and interactions between learners and facilitators of learning. CMCs allowed discussion to continue outside of the classroom by introducing flexibility in where and when interaction took place. In the mid-1990s, Web pages were introduced as a means of providing course materials, in graphics and text, to learners. These provided learners with materials they could interact with at times and places that were convenient. Late in that decade, the University of Wollongong purchased a licence for a course management system (CMS) that not only brought the functions of CMCs and Web pages together, but also provided further functionality, such as progress and assessment tracking, quizzes, and online multimedia. At this time the use of online learning increased dramatically, and the introduction of the course management system marked a watershed between the early adoption of online learning and its use by the majority. Since then, online learning components have been added to most subjects at the University of Wollongong.

Learning Activities Model

While the management functions of the CMS are helpful and add value to the online learning experience, there are limits to the kinds of activities that can be undertaken online. The learning activities supported can be classified by the learning activities model (LAM) as shown in Figure 1 (Caladine, 2003).

Examples of activities for each category are shown in Table 1. Note that learners directly control the activities in the category Intra-Action (IA).

Figure 1. Learning activities model

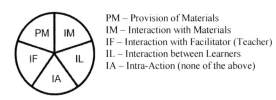

PM – Provision of Materials
IM – Interaction with Materials
IF – Interaction with Facilitator (Teacher)
IL – Interaction between Learners
IA – Intra-Action (none of the above)

Table 1. Some examples of learning activities as categorised by the learning activities model

Category	Face-to-Face Learning Examples	Online Learning Examples
PM	Books, notes, handouts, media	Web pages, images, software, plug-ins, applets
IM	Reading, etc.	Reading, simulation, animation, forms
IF	Consultation, Q and A, etc.	E-mail, list servers, message boards, instant messaging, VOIP
IL	Class discussion, etc.	E-mail and list servers, chats, discussion boards
IA	Learner-controlled activities such as informal reflection, relation of new to existing knowledge	Learner-controlled activities such as informal reflection, relation of new to existing knowledge

The Problem

While the model of online learning described in Table 1 has provided learners with efficient and effective learning experiences for the past few years, some learning needs were still not being met. Online learning as described provides limited opportunities for some of the social or collaborative aspects of learning that lead to deeper learning. For example, a need existed to facilitate online teamwork in which groups of learners produced materials.

The University of Wollongong has developed a number of graduate attributes that are the qualities the University expects all its graduates to develop while they are completing their studies. One of these is "a capacity for, and understanding of, teamwork" (University of Wollongong, 2004).

As the university has a number of campuses, and approximately 60 percent of learners undertake the online component of their learning from home, there is a need to provide opportunities for teamwork to learners who are geographically dispersed. One of the common teamwork tasks is the creation of group reports. In the past, some attempts at online group reporting have been less than satisfactory due to the time and lack of synergy inherent in the serial process of successive group members adding their contributions to the report as it is circulated through each member of the group.

To meet these needs and enhance the experiences of online learners, the University of Wollongong decided to investigate and test Web pages that were created, or driven by, databases. The project was called CUPID: Collaborative, User-Produced, Internet Documents.

The Functionality of
Database-Driven Web Sites

Database-driven Web sites, or CUPIDs, represent an innovation in online learning that allows users to add, remove, and edit the content of a Web page and upload files. As the data are input via Web forms, no programming skills are required. Once the data are input, they are processed by the database, which then rebuilds the Web page. In this way the database constructs or "drives" the Web site. Once material has been added to the page it may be edited, by users with the appropriate permission, by selecting a link to an edit

Figure 2. Schematic of a database-driven Web site or Collaborative, User-Produced, Internet Document (CUPID)

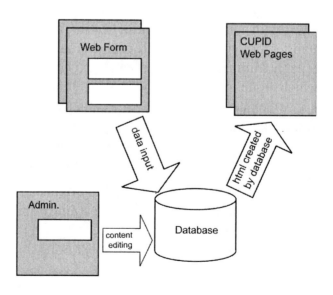

function from the page. Reloading the page then adds the new and changed material to the displayed page, thus generating the latest iteration of a collaboratively produced Web page. An administration page, generally controlled by the subject coordinator, allows control of the content and layout (Figure 2).

CUPIDs were developed in-house and use MySQL® and Oracle® database software. Scripts in the Python language provide the communications between the databases and the Web pages. The technology is functionally similar to that used by Wiki, which is "a specific type of hypertext document collection or the collaborative software used to create it" (Free Software Foundation, 2004, para.1). CUPIDs were developed using Python and databases to allow for templates or applications for specific uses, which are discussed later.

Database-driven Web sites, or CUPIDs, represent a new functionality for Web pages and online learning. Among the benefits of this functionality are:

- The visibility of work in progress to all. Permissions can be assigned to allow learners "read" or "read and write" capabilities so that members of a group can continuously monitor the development of the report or project output.

- The elimination of the serial nature of collaborative writing not only expedites the process but sponsors greater synergies as all members have multiple opportunities for input.

- If desired, materials from last year's learners may be made available to this year's learners.

For a CUPID to be beneficial to online learning, an application of the functionality, or template, needs to be developed. CUPIDs can be developed for a number of applications in which users create content in a collaborative fashion. To date at the University of Wollongong, CUPIDs have been developed for the following applications:

- Collaborative online glossary (COG).
- Collaborative online reporting (COR).
- Online student-collected and annotated resources (OSCAR).
- Collaborative online movie review (COMR).

It is anticipated that as more CUPIDs are used in online learning, more templates will be developed and envisaged future directions of CUPIDs are discussed at the end of this chapter.

Collaborative Online Glossary

The collaborative online glossary (COG) has been used by learners to develop a glossary of terms that are relevant to the subject. As the COG allows multiple entries for each definition, a discussion focused on a specific term can be generated within the glossary.

To begin the process of adding a new term to a collaborative online glossary, learners click on the button labelled "add a new term," which opens a Web form with fields for the term, the learner's name, and the definition. At this stage the user chooses to add a definition or to leave that field of the form blank. If the field is left blank, the term and the learner's name are added to the left-hand column of the glossary (Figure 3) indicating that the term has been reserved for future definition. In some cases, a time limit is placed on terms in this column.

Figure 3. Collaborative online glossary (note: learners' names have been removed)

Figure 4. Collaborative online glossary (note: learners' names have been removed)

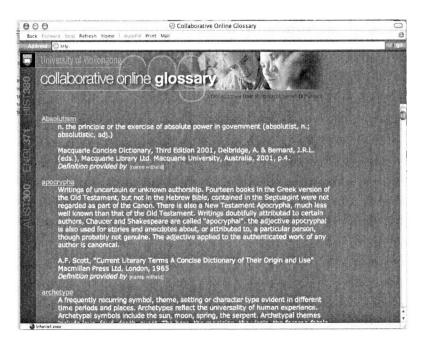

When an appropriate definition has been found, the learner who has reserved the term can add it by clicking on the term in the left-hand column. When the definition has been added, along with the appropriate attribution, the term appears in the right-hand column. Clicking on a term in this column opens the glossary to that term (see Figure 4). If learners discover another useful definition for a word that has already been defined, they can click on the word and add the new definition with an annotation. In this way, learners can build a discussion focussed on the term. It is possible to locate a link to a threaded discussion at the end of a definition if sufficient discussion was generated. The teacher also has access to an administration page, which allows quality control of student input. As definitions require attribution, the glossary can develop into reliable source material.

The COG has provided several clear benefits to teaching and learning. For example, in one course prior to using a COG, the teacher would devote one lecture to defining terms. Now that learners are responsible for this task, they have a greater sense of ownership of the resulting glossary and, hence, are more motivated to elicit nuances of meaning. Learners are also electing to define terms that the teacher had assumed they already knew. Further, as the glossary is publicly available on the Internet, learners are motivated to produce material of higher quality. Another benefit to teaching and learning provided by the COG (and all CUPIDs) arises from the flexibility of where and when learners can add material. COGs have also been used successfully when learners are geographically dispersed. COGs can provide opportunities for deeper learning as learners gain a sense of ownership of the glossary as they build it.

Collaborative Online Reporting

The process of collaborative online reporting, or COR, can support deep learning as students connect concepts researched by themselves with those of their peers. For "deep learning," Alexander (2004) states that, "students should be able to apply and generalise what they have learned. In practical terms, this means that students have to manipulate concepts they are learning, turn them inside out, and look at their connections to other concepts" (para. 2).

Students connect their contributions and concepts with those of their peers and manipulate them in the virtual group workspace of the COR system, thus providing opportunities for deep learning.

The COR system was developed to help generate team reports when learners are geographically dispersed and need flexibility of time and place. The COR allows each group member to enter his or her contribution to the report via a Web form. When all contributions have been received, they are combined into an editable Web page where the report is edited. Here, the introduction, conclusion, links, and bridging paragraphs are inserted. As the report is hosted on a Web page, these tasks can happen at the same time, in a parallel fashion, hence expediting the reporting process and creating greater opportunities for interaction between team members. In the past, the writing of group reports from geographically dispersed learners was hindered by the serial nature of communications. Typically, one learner would start with his or her contribution and then forward it, usually by e-mail, to the next member of the group and so on. While this method of group report writing had some success, it was difficult to develop a synergy derived by the presence, real or virtual, of all the group members at one time.

To initiate the process of group report, writing topics are placed on the Web site by the lecturer. Through negotiation, the group selects and claims one of the topics. The group then divides the topic into sections for individual contributions. Group members prepare their contributions to the report and paste them, with the contributor's name, to the individual contribution page (Figure 5).

At a predetermined date and time, or when all members of the group have posted their contributions, the group decides to click the group report link. This marks the transition from individual contributions to the group report. At this

Figure 5. Collaborative online reporting: individual contribution.

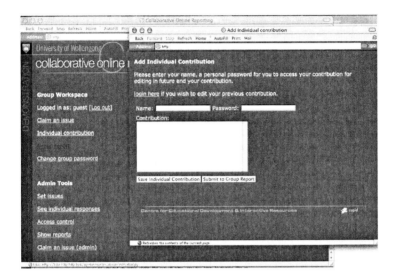

Figure 6. Collaborative online report (COR): the editable group report page and the draft report

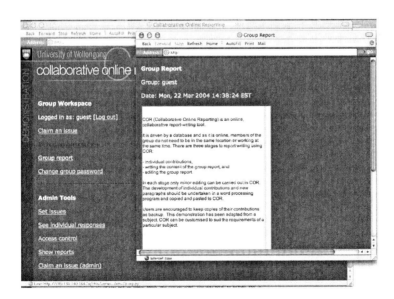

stage, a copy of the individual contributions is saved to the database for future reference. The individual contributions are now displayed together as a draft group report (Figure 6).

The group report is then ready to be edited into a cohesive whole. Through negotiation within the group, each member is assigned a task to complete the report. Tasks may include, but are not limited to, writing the introduction, writing the conclusion, writing linking paragraphs, editing for stylistic cohesion, and editing for grammar, and spelling. When the group decides that the report is complete the Publish button is pressed. This sends a copy of the finished report to the lecturer for assessment and links a copy of it from the subject homepage.

Currently, the collaborative online reporting tool has been used in two subjects at the University of Wollongong. In both cases the tool has successfully provided a way for learners to maintain the benefits of flexibility of time and place that are inherent in online learning while making possible a synergy that hitherto was only possible in a face-to-face gathering. In one of the cases, the COR was bundled with an upload facility so that learners could include images in their reports.

Online Student-Collected and Annotated Resources (OSCAR)

An OSCAR is a metasite of annotated links that are organised into categories. To date, OSCARs have been used by teachers to organise the online resources they use in their teaching and by learners to collect links to online resources that are pertinent to the area of study. The annotation required for each link in an OSCAR not only adds value to the metasite, but can also be used to help learners develop skills of analysis of online resources. The purpose of the annotation is to provide users with a brief review of the linked site and to help them determine if it will meet their needs. The process of writing a meaningful annotation requires students to create an argument for (or against) the resource they are reviewing. This argument is then presented to their peers on the OSCAR Web pages.

Data are input to the OSCAR from a Web form or upload page (Figure 7). Users are required to select the category in which the annotated link will be displayed and to enter:

Figure 7. Online student-collected and annotated resources (OSCAR): upload page (demonstration OSCAR)

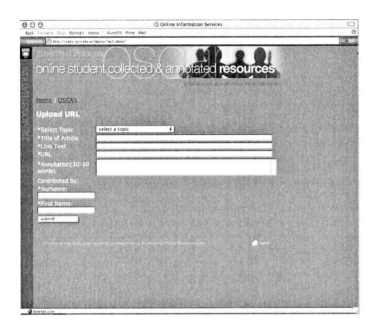

Figure 8. An OSCAR category page from the NCODE Flexible Learning Web site

- The URL.
- The text of the link.
- The annotation.
- The name of the author of the annotation.

The input information is then added to the appropriate page of the OSCAR by the database and displayed when the page is refreshed. An example of an OSCAR category page is shown in Figure 8. The OSCAR database is a unique tool for collection and categorisation of Internet resources and can be used as a tool for teaching informational retrieval and evaluation skills. Like other CUPIDs, if the information added in previous years is retained, learners in subsequent years can add to and comment on it. Thus, peer critiques of original annotations can be hosted.

Collaborative Online Movie Reviews (COMR)

The COMR was developed for a specific subject (Australian Screen Studies) in which learners were required to review eight movies as part of their assessment. As learners were distributed among five campuses (up to a five-hour drive apart), COMR provided a means by which all learners could read and interact with all reviews. As with the collaborative online glossary, COMR permitted multiple reviews of the same movie, thus providing the facility for subsequent reviews that refer to earlier ones and, hence, supporting learning by peer critique. Subsequent reviews appear directly below and often refer to earlier reviews of the same movie. In this way it is possible to structure online discussion around a focus, such as the movie under review or the term defined in the glossary.

To use the COMR, learners are instructed to first check the list of films. If the film they wish to review is not listed, they add a review link and follow the instructions. If it is already there, they select the film title and follow the prompts either to edit technical details or to add a new review. Learners are instructed that reviews should be between 200 and 300 words. The instructions also state that if you are posting the first review, it will be of a descriptive nature. However, if the review is a subsequent one, the review needs to further the discussion. That is, something new needs to be said. Examples of new comments may be:

- Whether you agree with previous reviewers, or not.
- Whether a particular scene should be highlighted and why.
- Focus on other aspects such as actors, cinematography, or location.

Learners are also asked to rate the film according to two criteria: Did you enjoy it? Did you find it useful for research and criticism purposes? The ratings are displayed using a system of stars.

Collaborative online movie review entries are retained so that learners will be able to read reviews written from earlier years, and as multiple reviews of the same film are permitted, this year's learners are able to build on the reviews from previous years. This process can be likened to a threaded discussion with comments by learners from previous years. Other benefits of the COMR stem from indefinitely displaying the work, which has motivated learners to increase the quality of the work submitted.

Looking Toward the Future

The potential of CUPIDs for future online learning is significant, as the trials at University of Wollongong have indicated that they can facilitate interactions between students that lead to deep learning in a virtual environment. They make possible asynchronous interactions, learning activities that are flexible in terms of time and place, and facilitation of learner-created production resources. These benefits can be increased when the Web site is maintained across several offerings of the same subject. When this occurs, this year's learners can interact with the materials developed by learners from previous years. When learners are aware that the materials they develop are to be displayed on a public Web site that not only their classmates will access but also learners in years to come, they are encouraged to increase the quality of the work they submit.

A number of developments are planned for the future of CUPIDs. New templates are under construction for a collaborative annotated bibliography and other custom-built reporting tools that include survey data. The uploading of files to CUPIDs poses challenges in the areas of security and permission allocations. A custom-built CUPID has been developed and piloted that allows students to upload files. It is believed that this facility will be commonplace in CUPIDs of the future.

A further development is the convergence of CUPIDs with other communications tools. For example, while the collaborative online reporting tool was successful, it will be merged with an audioconference tool in some future versions so that learners may have the option to hold an online discussion as part of the reporting process. This functionality will provide another communication channel for students but will reduce the flexibility of where and when students interact with the learning materials.

The functionality afforded by CUPIDs to online collaboration can open the door to a host of activities that are new to collaboration, online or otherwise. Thus, they occupy a vital place in online learning of the future. CUPIDs can support deeper learning through the provision of opportunities for learning in a social context in which individuals have clear responsibilities for the work of the group, engage with concepts through their own learning, and connect them to concepts presented by peers — all with the convenience of flexibility of time and place.

References

Alexander, G. (2004). Why online collaborative learning? The Open University. Retrieved on June 9, 2004, from *http://sustainability.open.ac.uk/gary/pages/oclearn.htm*

Caladine, R. (2003). *New theoretical frameworks of learning activities, learning technologies and a new method of technology selection.* PhD Thesis, University of Wollongong.

Free Software Foundation. (2004). WikiPedia: The free encyclopedia. Retrieved June 9, 2004, from *http://en.wikipedia.org/wiki/Wikipedia:About*

Keegan, D. (1986). *The foundations of distance education.* London: Croom Helm.

University of Wollongong. (2004). Attributes of a Wollongong graduate. Retrieved March 19, 2004, from *http://www.uow.edu.au/about/teaching/attributes/*

Chapter XVI

CMS Portfolios for Learning and Evaluation

Jon Lanestedt, University of Oslo, Norway

Mona Stokke, University of Oslo, Norway

Abstract

In the chapter we discuss how higher education can support learning and evaluation by use of portfolios as an integrated functionality in course management systems (CMS). A theoretical rationale for a portfolio approach in support of deeper learning is provided by a brief outline of relevant aspects of constructivist theory of learning and its process-oriented focus on formative evaluation in a group context, as opposed to the traditional emphasis on summative evaluation in terms of final exams. The use of portfolios as a method to realize such a focus is explained, along with visualisations of an instantiation of the associated CMS functionality.

Introduction

All too often, CMS are used as a mere channel for dissemination of information and assignments, testing, and broadcasting of messages from teacher to students. We suggest that this fact is not solely due to shortages in the functionality embedded in the technological artifacts but also, and perhaps even more so, to institutional issues of digital literacy and pedagogical competence among the users of those artifacts, structural organization of course offerings, and aspects of traditional academic work practices and culture. Even so, it is worthwhile to strive for CMS technology that better supports innovative educational practices and constitutes a scaffolding digital environment where these practices can actually take place.

In keeping with this aim, we discuss in this chapter how higher education can support learning and evaluation by use of portfolios as an integrated functionality in course management systems. We provide a theoretical rationale for a portfolio approach in support of deeper learning — an approach in the forefront of current Scandinavian and international educational debate — by briefly outlining relevant aspects of constructivist theory of learning and its process-oriented focus on formative evaluation (e.g., peer review and systematic feedback) in a group context, as opposed to the traditional emphasis on evaluation in terms of final exams, or summative evaluation. The use of portfolios as a method to realize such a focus is explained, and we show how functionality supporting it may be instantiated in a particular CMS — in this case the Norwegian system Classfronter™.

This chapter draws on work carried out by the University of Oslo (UO) Educational Technology Group and experiences made at UO with CMS portfolios for learning and evaluation. Our context is the national, so-called quality reform (Nyborg, 2002) of Norwegian higher education introduced in fall 2003, and influenced by a constructivist perspective on learning.[1] The challenge facing UO (32,000 students and 5,000 faculty and staff) in the beginning of the 21st century is to create a supportive, constructivist-oriented learning environment that facilitates students developing knowledge in dialogue within the collective of co-students and tutors, and to integrate in such an environment a well-designed digital infrastructure for learning with groupware and digital learning resources. The Classfronter™ CMS is one part of this scheme.

Theory: Portfolios for Learning and Evaluation

The aforementioned reform emphasizes the use of alternative evaluation methods in addition to traditional final exams. The reason is threefold. Firstly, by reducing the focus on final exams and increasing frequent and continuing evaluation, the student receives more relevant input to her learning loop; the student becomes aware of her own implicit learning strategies and is enabled to refine them into explicit strategies (metalearning). Secondly, it contributes to a more evenly distributed workload throughout the semester. And thirdly, it expresses a constructivist approach towards learning on which the reform is founded.

Constructivist Approaches to Learning and Evaluation

In this section we establish a framework for the rest of the chapter by summarizing some of the theoretical work on constructivist approaches to learning and the role of evaluation in that context. We want to focus on the building (i.e., constructing) that occurs in people's minds when they learn, and the function that informed response, such as peer review, teacher comments, etc., have with regard to learning and metalearning.

Research Traditions

Historically, two paradigms have dominated research in learning, based on behaviorist and cognitivist assumptions and theory, respectively (Säljö, 1999). According to the former tradition, learning equals submitting to sense impressions from the surrounding environment, with observable changes in behavior as the result. Knowledge is regarded as objectively given, independent of and external to individual humans. When structured in appropriately formatted chunks, knowledge may be transmitted from one human subject to the other. The implication these assumptions have for teaching and the use of technology is a strongly directed, sequential training of skills within a predefined body of educational materials. Hence, teaching is conceptualized as instruction (Ludvigsen, 1999).

Cognitivist research, on the other hand, emphasizes mental representations, strategies for problem solving, and the process of building and organizing knowledge structures. As opposed to the behaviorist approach, cognitivism regards knowledge as a highly relative and personal entity that is created and manifested in the learner through her encounter with relevant materials and active engagement in problem solving. The implication for teaching and use of technology is to provide an explorative environment in which themes and concepts may be investigated by the individual learner.

With respect to cognitivism, current constructivist theory proceeds by emphasizing that learning is no context-free, mechanical process, but rather a situated process colored by people and tools involved in the learning situation. Hence, knowledge does not belong to the individual alone, but also, or mainly, to the social group in which practices it is embedded (Wenger, 1998). Learning is a social process that takes place first through collaborative participation in a community of practice. The implication for teaching and use of technology within the constructivist tradition is to facilitate comprehensive information access and availability, facilitate the exploration of open problems, and to facilitate both the individual and collective construction of knowledge. According to this position, teaching should support the students' selecting, processing, and assessing both of subject-relevant materials and of their own work in a collaborative atmosphere and environment. The approach advocated by the computer-supported cooperative learning (CSCL) community is rooted in a pedagogy in which guidance and informed response from peer students, in addition to that from teachers and other mentors, is considered crucial and instrumental to learning (see Koschmann, 1996). The student's potential for learning is furthered when working in concert with more mature and competent colleagues (Vygotsky, 1978). Evaluation and learning become tightly connected in two ways. First, the requirement for various forms of documentation forces students to express their thinking explicitly and visually through textual and other semiotic codes, acts which foster critical reflection and learning in students as the process of production necessarily includes the evaluation of their own thinking (metalearning). Second, by making students collaborate with their co-learners and systematically exchange analytical commentary and constructive suggestions on each other's work, learning and evaluation become integrated activities. In this context, the role of the teacher is more that of a mentor and facilitator, even that of a co-learner, than that of an instructor.

All education rests on a foundation of basic assumptions about the nature of knowledge and about how to organize teaching and learning in order for these

Figure 1. Alternative assumptions of teaching and learning, and by implication, of the role of technology (based on Ludvigsen, 1999, p. 68)

Traditional Education	Learning Communities
• Teacher-controlled instruction • Correct answer oriented • Individual work • Evaluation as testing and reproduction of knowledge • Technology for drilling and skill practicing	• Problem- and activity-oriented teaching • Reasoning with concepts and knowledge • Systematic work in groups • Evaluation as peer review of and reflection on portfolio contents, as well as presentation of projects and portfolio contents • Technology for access to and processing of information transformed into knowledge by reflection in learning activities

activities to be productive (Säljö, 1999) (Figure 1). The quality reform is just one example of how such a set of assumptions gives rise to priorities, expresses values, and places particular practices and tools on the agenda.

Surface Learning and Deep Learning

Relevant to the strong relation between the student's experience of the teaching situation and the nature of the learning that is taking place are the concepts of surface learning and deep learning (Ramsden, 1988).

Surface learning has little to do with true learning and is, to a large degree, plain imitation. The student learns to master techniques related to the discipline and memorize information about its subject matter. However, her understanding does not undergo any substantial change. Furthermore, the knowledge acquired has limited personal relevance to her as learning materials and themes seem to have no connection with the actual world outside the specific learning situation.

As opposed to surface learning, the concept of deep learning refers to learning in which the commitment is strong and the student is actively engaged in the learning materials through the pursuit of resolving research questions in authentic contexts. The student presents a desire to understand the object of her efforts and relates the issues to her personal experiences and situations important to her. She tries to identify overall messages, principles, and conclusions rather than memorizing details and fragments.

Figure 2. Reasoning with concepts and knowledge; deep learning and surface learning (from Ramsden, 1988, p.19)

Strategy for Surface Learning	Strategy for Deep Learning
• Focuses on the signs, e.g., words and sentences, without reasoning about possible applications • Focuses on parts of the task as isolated phenomena • Memorizes information for later testing, with limited ability to discover connections • Connects facts and concepts without any reflection as to why and how • Does not separate rules from examples • Treats the task as something imposed from the outside world • Outer focus: oriented towards exams and tests with no regard to real-world relevance	• Focuses on author's reasoning, argumentation, and the relevant concepts • Relates previous knowledge to new knowledge • Relates knowledge from various domains to each other • Relates theoretic conceptions to everyday experiences • Relates material and arguments and is able to differ among them • Organizes and structures content in coherent wholes • Inner focus: discovers and tries to understand the real world

The quality of the student's learning is influenced by the orientation toward surface learning or deep learning (Figure 2). Deep learning is associated with higher rewards in the shape of better results and grades but, most importantly, with engagement, challenge, progress, and enjoyment (Ramsden, 1988).

Formative and Summative Evaluation

There is a relationship between the methods of teaching and evaluation and the learning strategies that are promoted. Particular teaching and evaluation forms foster surface learning whereas others promote deep learning. Evaluation may serve two complementary functions. In one context, the aim is prospective, or formative — to improve, to understand strengths and positive tendencies in order to amplify them or to identify weaknesses to remedy. The other context is retrospective, or summative — to assess concrete achievement, often as part of a process of formal acknowledgment or certification.

Empirically, traditional final exams (summative evaluation), which are not preceded by continuous follow-up and collaboration earlier in the semester (formative evaluation), foster surface learning rather than deep learning (Ramsden, 1988). The learning outcome of this form of final evaluation is limited. Such a model makes the students reproduce curriculum materials at the exam and the focus is on memory and retrieval, whereas evaluation of the reflective use of subject knowledge is less emphasized. Historically, focus has implicitly or explicitly been on summative evaluation and less effort has been invested in addressing the learning process and its formative aspect. The rationale behind introducing portfolio evaluation is to encourage deep learning at the expense of surface learning (ibid.).

As stated above, the use of portfolios is regarded not solely in terms of control and formal certification, but also of individual and collective cognitive development and learning. It is, however, important to stress that the use of portfolios as part of an evaluation methodology may, and should be, used both formatively and summatively, the difference being the actual use of the information under consideration and in which phase of the learning process the evaluation takes place. Portfolios may be used both as part of the formative feedback throughout the learning process and as a support for the summative control and certification procedure at its final stage. Portfolio tools should be designed to make as intuitive as possible which is the current stage and which is the precise role of the evaluation at that stage.

About Portfolios in Learning and Evaluation

According to Dysthe and Engelsen (2003) there are basically three types of portfolios. Each refers to a distinct target group. In a constructivist perspective, the addressee of portfolio contents is not only the teacher, but also the co-students. This presupposes a high degree of openness with respect to both technical functionality and group climate, an issue to which we will return.

- *Learning portfolios.* Learning portfolios are students' work tools throughout the study period and are not subject to final evaluation. The student herself and her peers (including, of course, the teacher) are the target group. The use of the learning portfolios is informal and free, and students use them to organize, document, and disseminate work of their own choosing as well as a basis for reflection and discussion of this work. The aim of learning portfolios is to be a support for formative evaluation.

- *Assessment portfolios.* Assessment portfolios are used in a final, summative evaluation by the teacher or committee. Their contents are a selection of student work documentation, typically copied out of the learning portfolio. The selection is made by the student, or by a mutual agreement between student and teacher.

- *Showcase portfolios*. Showcase portfolios may contain a selection of documentation from the assessment portfolio. The aim is to demonstrate competence for future employers, to support grant applications, and the like. Competency portfolios are not a part of the learning and evaluation scheme.

In the present context, our attention is directed at the two first categories of portfolios as we are addressing tools and environments relevant to formative and summative evaluation.

In the Norwegian educational tradition, the main focus of many course programs has been on the individual student's work with texts and on few but large assignments in the course of the program. In order to foster continuous learning throughout the entire study period, stringent requirements on production and documentation are being introduced (Otnes, 2003). The portfolio is a tool for formative evaluation, in which the process of learning and work in progress are at the centre of attention. It is important to point out that both types of portfolio — at least in their digital implementation — may include documentation of all media types and genres, such as recordings, drawings, visual media, software, and such texts as discussion threads and essays.

Evaluation Method and Work Practice Combined

Commonly referred to as a process encompassing the three phases of collection, selection, and reflection, sometimes with patterns of iteration, the introduction of portfolio evaluation implies both a certain type of work practice as well as a method for evaluation (Wittek, 2003). The latter allocates an active role to the student by requiring that she produces and collects documentation on her efforts, progress, and results. The student selects which works are to be presented for final evaluation, accompanied by reflection notes commenting on the learning process and explaining the argument for selection made. As a work practice, portfolio evaluation strongly governs the way teaching is carried out. The student's role is extended by the more active role she is forced to take, with a substantial degree of initiative, questioning, commenting, and dialogue participation.

According to Wittek (2002), an ideal version of portfolio evaluation includes the following elements:

- Students have an active role in collecting the evidence documenting their own efforts, progress, and results throughout the entire period of learning.

- Students play an active role in the evaluation of their own work.

- Mutual student guidance and peer evaluation play important roles in the learning process.

- Emphasis is on student reflection on the subject matter and learning process.

- Teacher and co-student response enters a learning loop, wherein students draw on this response in the ongoing learning process.

- A selection of the collected evidence is presented for evaluation, along with documentation of and reflection on both the learning and the selection processes.

In order to support learning and, or indeed as, evaluation, as we have previously pointed out, there is a need for a high degree of openness. The least open approach is one in which only the student herself and the teacher have access to the learning portfolio. Alternatively, selected co-students have mutual access to each other's learning portfolios in particular periods and cases. Finally, on the opposite end of the spectrum, all students may have free access to all learning portfolios within the course. By granting access to co-students, learning is facilitated because it is by means of collaboration, collective peer-review, and documentation — provided a clear dramaturgy on the part of the tutor — that much of the formative evaluation happens and learning takes place.

The Learning Environment

As just mentioned, all educational arrangements will be based on assumptions concerning learning and knowledge. The wish to use portfolios in the formative phase and in final assessment is founded on assumptions about how learning takes place and how teaching may be organized to support learning. Use of portfolios for formative evaluation rests on the idea that multiple people's perspectives are needed and desired in the development of knowledge, understanding, and insight. By inviting others to present criticism of his work, the student develops a voice of his own as well as ownership to works, positions, and statements. It also promotes metalearning — that is, the student's knowledge about his own production of knowledge. The students are expected to discuss what they do, how they do it, and how their understanding and reflection has developed, as well as documenting it all in the assessment portfolio.

The visual appearance of the portfolio icon in digital environments may seem to indicate a storage structure (Otnes, 2003). Portfolios are more than that. They are tools for learning as well as loci where learning is to be documented and stored. To make portfolios more than a storage facility for student works, it is necessary to communicate the philosophy, attitudes, roles, assumptions, and practices that constitute portfolios as learning tools, and make sure that these fundamental premises are internalized by the group and regarded as essential for collaboration in a fellowship of learners. To build a common understanding of portfolios as more than storage boxes and to foster success in their use, students and teachers alike must develop a common view in which the contribution and receipt of comments and criticism is a welcome endeavor considered part of an active, reflective approach to the learning process. It is necessary to develop the learning culture along with the introduction of technology. A mutual confidence and trust must be established for students to share work with others, and the atmosphere must be supportive and open for honest and straightforward comments and criticism to work within the group. Students and teachers must become familiar with the modern learning community and with the values and norms that govern the interplay between the actors involved. Learning can no longer be considered the individual's private and isolated concern, but a social practice in which the students share a commitment to their common growth.

Technology: CMS Portfolios for Learning and Evaluation

Workflow Overview of Classfronter™ Portfolio Implementation

The Classfronter™ CMS groupware, which includes virtual rooms where the actual teaching and learning activities take place, is currently used at UO almost exclusively in a blended learning mode in which face-to-face and virtual activities mutually support each other. Portfolio tools make part of each room's tool set and are, thus, a property of the room. The general structure of the workflow when using Classfronter™ portfolios for learning and evaluation is as follows (Figure 3).

This procedure mirrors the collection, selection, and reflection scheme of portfolio learning and its evaluation methodology, as mentioned previously. In the phase of learning portfolio use, there is an iterative cycle of collection (versions) and reflection on the basis of peer review or other forms of criticism.

Documents are produced, discussed, and collected in the learning portfolios. In order to select works for final assessment, the work view tool is used by the student herself and the tutor to get an overview of her entire production. Contents in the learning portfolio are identified and listed along with their associated attributes, and so are documents produced by the student and identified in other locations in the room, such as contributions in portfolio-external discussions, links to materials, etc. Documents are transferred from the work view to the final assessment portfolio along with a reflection note discussing the learning process and the criteria for selection of documents for final assessment. The whole of the assessment portfolio is evaluated by the committee. Contents from the assessment portfolio may be copied into a personal, course-independent archive portfolio, which is not discussed in this chapter.

Figure 3. Workflow when using Classfronter™ portfolios for evaluation and learning

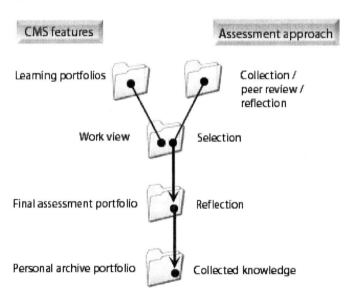

Learning Portfolios to Support Formative Evaluation

A student produces a document or other form of documentation in her learning portfolio. The portfolio is allocated the necessary read and write privileges so that a selection or all of the room's members (co-students and tutor) have one or both privileges. The learning portfolios may be of several kinds (only two kinds are hinted at in Figure 5, but there are more) and support both a many-to-many approach and a one-on-one approach, with or without functionality to handle deadlines, after which the portfolio is temporarily locked for further changes.

The fellow students and tutor then produce criticism of the student's work according to some predefined, commonly agreed-upon standards, scheme, and timeline, and following a (semi)formal invitation (several peer review techniques are discussed in Mason, 2003). Documents located in learning portfolios have various functionality depending on the types of document. Classfronter™-"foreign" documents (Microsoft Office®, etc.) imported into Classfronter™ learning portfolios may be opened, comments may be written into the running text or by using the Word comment function, and the documents may be saved while maintaining the original ownership of the file.[2] Classfronter™-"domestic" documents produced by Classfronter™'s own editor for collaborative writing may be edited by several people, a functionality that also permits commenting within the document proper. Criticism may also be supplied by means of the asynchronous discussion forum, which may be initiated and maintained inside the portfolio. The process may be iterative as the student responds to input from her peers, and several revised versions of the document are produced and commented on. If a discussion forum is used, discussion threads develop. The process may take time as the document is refined, or it may be quick as drafts are short-lived in a process-oriented approach to writing.

In Figure 4, we see our example learning community consisting of seven students, all of whose learning portfolios are located at the left of the room. One student, Rino, has produced a draft document on the "cultivation" of information infrastructures.[3] In the main application window (below "Title") is the list of current contents in Rino's learning portfolio. Now Rino has opened the discussion tool (at the front), started a discussion, and invited his peers to comment on his document. In particular, he needs their views on the theoretical perspective he has applied. Teacher Mona has opened Rino's draft (behind the discussion tool) and is writing her comments inside the document using the Microsoft Word® comment function while concurrently performing a dialogue

Figure 4. The evaluation process by use of discussion threads and direct comments in the document, carried out by the tutor and a co-student on Rino's draft document

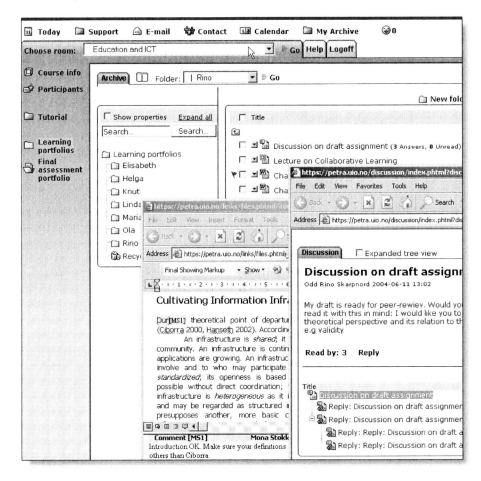

with Rino. Rino may eventually react on Mona's comments on form and content and revise his draft, or he may argue against her. The present example is just one of several options the peer review process may take. Combinations or alternatives of directly commenting in documents and using discussion tools may be used. The process Rino is involved in here may go on in several iterations, depending on the predefined procedure agreed on by all members of the learning community. With other rules, it may be the tutor who invites students to take turns in the role as opponents according to a fixed term schedule and according to predefined properties to critique (rhetoric, argument, use of sources, and so forth).

Assessment Portfolio to Support Summative Evaluation

When the end of the semester is approaching, Rino, either on his own or advised by his tutor, is to select the works he wants to present for final evaluation. Some of the rationale for this procedure is to make Rino reflect on why certain works are more worthy of credit than others and the role they played in the group discussions, and, hence, to have Rino review his own learning process. Figure 5 shows both the work view tool and the final assessment tool. On the back of the screen, the work view tool displays the part of Rino's production (these are links to the actual documents) that has not been transferred to the final assessment portfolio, including both documents and discussion messages. The

Figure 5. By use of the work view, an overview of Rino's total production is displayed, and works are selected and transferred to the final assessment portfolio

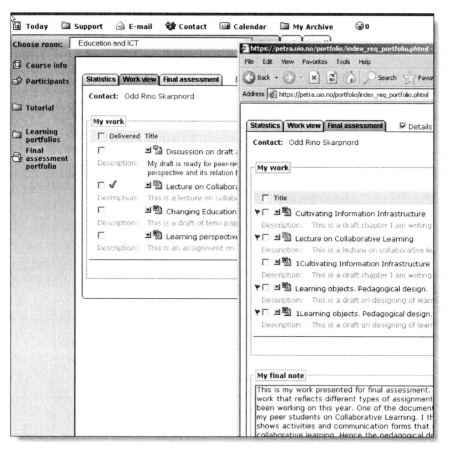

works transferred to the final assessment tool are visible in its list of documents. Rino is now in the process of developing a text on the selection criteria and his reflections on the learning experience. More often this will be a lengthier document written outside or somewhere else in Classfronter™ and imported or copied into the assessment portfolio.

The assessment committee can now assess Rino's work throughout the semester in terms of Rino's own reflections on his own learning, on the process, and on the collaborative experience, and evaluate his learning in light of the results which he has himself selected to exemplify his resulting abilities and competence.

Future Work

On the Emergent Character of Solutions and Practices

When technology is created and introduced with the aim to support particular practices, one enters a nondeterministic realm, indeed. At its introduction, the technological artifact and its associated potential use are envisioned to join with, add to, and partly reconfigure a heterogeneous, infrastructural installed base of preexisting technology, culture, communities of practice, traditions, and organization. However, there is no guarantee that the new artifact will become included in established structures and practices. A successful innovation — and the introduction in a traditional university of portfolio methodology supported by CMS groupware technology is indeed an innovation — depends on the successful enrollment over time of human and nonhuman actors (people, rules, money, organization, objects, etc.) and the eventual alignment of a comprehensive network of such actors (Latour, 1987).

On one hand, technological artifacts are constructed to align with their environment by means of, as it were, creating their own users and associated behavior patterns. According to Akrich (1994),

> *when technologists define the characteristics of their objects, they necessarily make hypotheses about the entities that make up the world into which the object is to be inserted. Designers thus define actors with specific tastes, competences, motives, aspirations,*

political prejudices, and the rest, and they assume that morality, technology, science, and economy will evolve in particular ways. A large part of the work of innovators is that of "inscribing" this vision of (or prediction about) the world in the technical content of the new object. I will call the end product of this work a "script"... (p. 208).

On the other hand, a number of factors make empirical users counter, modify, or bypass those scripts, or ignore them altogether. The actual use of the technology in question frequently comes to represent a "drift" (Ciborra & Hanseth, 2000) and deviate with respect to the practices that the technology was introduced to promote in the first place. Ciborra and Hanseth note,

alignment is a long, tortuous, and fragile process whereby multiple actors and resources try to influence each other to constitute a new socio-technical order. A number of forces, feedbacks, and self-reinforcing actions are at play. It is hard to predict an outcome: an aligned infrastructure is a rare event... (p. 5).

From the point of view of a technological artifact as a medium — of which CMS portfolios are an example — the success of its use depends on both the characteristics of the medium itself, as well as the competence in the community of users. As Eco explains, every communicative medium is dependent on semiotic codes shared with the user, or what he refers to as the "model reader" (Eco, 1979) that every media artifact postulates as part of its communicative strategy. There is a wide range of issues involved, such as shared communicative competence, shared understanding of conventions of genre, and shared cultural and ethical values, all of which may need time to develop along with new tools.

These points are made to stress the emergent character of the solutions and practices at hand. Much work remains to be done, and most of this work has to align cultural, organizational, and human issues and actors, rather than solely technical ones.

Issues to Address Further

It follows from the above that much effort in institutions of higher education has to be invested in building user competence, pedagogy, culture, and promoting institutional change. At UO, we currently address a number of these efforts. First, the current understanding of technology and its potential has to be developed among faculty. This relates both to general ICT fluency and to the application of digital media to support teaching and learning more specifically. Second, the perspectives on teaching, learning, and knowledge have to be developed. Traditional educational routines have to be redefined according to more relevant pedagogical thinking. This constitutes a most challenging effort, as the transition from linear, lecture-oriented teaching to more open models, such as case-based learning, problem-based learning, and others, radically increases student involvement and empowerment and allocates new roles to faculty. As part of this scheme, it is crucial to develop the understanding of the important role of continuous evaluation, based on a focus on the learning process as much as on the final assessment. Third, the students, too, need to develop their views and expectations in relation to teaching and learning as well as their own roles in the learning endeavor. They need to change from a relatively passive role as addressees of lectures to an active, responsible role as producers of knowledge engaged in inquiry, deep learning, and metalearning, involved in continuous evaluation of their own work and that of their peers.

Furthermore, students and teachers alike must develop a positive attitude to the idea that sharing and collaboration are fruitful and constructive activities. They must challenge their current views about what learning is and can be and internalize the fact that collaboration is built on openness and confidence. Students have to regard themselves as responsible participants in a learning community. Finally, all these issues have to be formalized in the institution's mission statements, policy documents, and curricula. Pedagogical goals have to enter planning documents and so must the use of educational technology, including portfolio learning and evaluation.

In sum, the tools for portfolio learning and evaluation are already integrated as parts of our CMS. They certainly need to be refined, but even more important now is institutional change. Many faculty and students currently exploit ICT in limited ways. Web-based ICT — CMS included — is widely seen as a channel for dissemination of information, for testing, and for one-to-many communication from teacher to students. Also, many users have not yet become sufficiently fluent as to extend its use in more advanced and pedagogically sophisticated manners. Thus, in a UO context, the Educational Technology Group has a mission and an important role to play along with other actors at the institution. However, some UO communities do develop innovative teaching with CMS, and we have to make their practices and methods visible for the rest of the institution.

UO has developed a five-year strategic plan geared at providing the reform with appropriate ICT support. A component in this strategy is the yearly allocation of project funding to department-level activities with the aim to develop constructivist, ICT-supported course offerings and practices that implement the reform's explicit aims of an increased level of student-active learning, evaluation forms that support learning, and closer student follow-up. "Money talks," and our current experience tells us that the equivalent of $750,000 (US) in the year 2004 are resources well spent.

Summary and Conclusion

In this chapter, we address the use of portfolio learning and assessment to promote a pedagogy derived from constructivist assumptions about learning and knowledge, as well as how it is used for teaching, which furthers both. A discussion of the theoretical underpinnings is briefly presented. In that context, the historical background in research traditions is outlined, and relevant concepts such as deep and surface learning, as well as formative and summative evaluation, are explained. Categories of portfolios are addressed, and the way they are made to be both a work tool and part of an evaluation method provided a proper understanding of collaborative interchange in the learning community and surrounding environment. The Classfronter™ CMS implementation of supportive functionality is explained and exemplified step by step. Finally, we list some remaining challenges, on the assumption that at this stage equally critical as those of the technology are the institutional and pedagogical issues related to the relevant exploitation of that technology.

However, whereas the development of new educational practices must be emphasized, the technological artifacts are indeed crucial to innovative and modern pedagogy relevant to teaching and students in higher education in the first decade of the 21st century. It is our belief that if course management systems still keep the position as a major category of educational technology throughout the institutions of higher education, in years to come this position will be due to the ability of CMS creators to keep abreast with developments in pedagogy, work practices, and methods of knowledge production, and to provide groupware environments and tools to support deep learning and processes of educational revitalization in higher education. The issues discussed in this chapter point to some of these developments and the means to implement their support in terms of technology.

Acknowledgments

Thanks to Rino Skarpnord for assistance with the graphics, and to him, Helge Underhaug, and the rest of our colleagues in the Educational Technology Group. Thanks also to Berit Johnsen of the Section for Continuing and Distance Education for constructive criticism.

References

Akrich, M. (1994). The de-scription of technical objects. In Bijker & Law (1994). *Shaping Technology/Building Society*. Cambridge, MA: MIT University Press.

Ciborra, C. U. & Hanseth, O. (2000). Introduction. In Ciborra, Claudio, Braa, Cordella, Dahlbom, Failla, Hanseth, Hepsø, Ljungberg, Monteiro, & Simon (Eds.), *From control to drift: The dynamics of corporate information infrastructures.* Oxford, UK: Oxford University Press.

Dysthe, O. & Engelsen, K. S. (2003). Mapper som lærings-og vurderingsform. In O. Dysthe & K. S. Engelsen (Eds.), *Mapper som Pedagogisk Redskap: Perspektiver og Erfaringer* [*Portfolios as Pedagogical Tools: Perspectives and Lessons Learned*]. Oslo: abstrakt forlag.

Eco, U. (1979). *The role of the reader: Explorations in the semiotics of texts*. London: Hutchinson.

European Union. (2000). The Bologna Declaration on the European space for higher education: An explanation. Retreived June 25, 2004, from *http://europa.eu.int/comm/education/policies/educ/bologna/ bologna.pdf*

Hanseth, O. (2002). From systems and tools to networks and infrastructures — from design to cultivation. Towards a theory of ICT solutions and its design methodology implications. Retrieved June 25, 2004 from *http://www.ifi.uio.no/~oleha/Publications/ib_ISR_3rd_resubm 2.html*

Koschmann, T. (Ed.). (1996). *CSCL: Theory and practice of an emerging paradigm*. Mahwah, NJ: Lawrence Erlbaum Associates.

Latour, B. (1987). *Science in action: How to follow scientists and engineers through society*. Cambridge, MA: Harvard University Press.

Ludvigsen, S. (1999). Informasjon og kommunikasjonsteknologi, læring og klasserommet [ICT, Learning and the Classroom]. In *Bedre skole 2*, 1999, (pp. 61-68).

Mason, R. (2003). Successful online learning conferences: What is the magic formula? In P. Arneberg (Ed.), 2 *Læring i Dialog på nettet* [*Learning by Network Dialog*]. SOFF (National Agency for Flexible Learning in Higher Education) report 1/2003.

Nyborg, P. (2002). The quality reform of higher education in Norway: A national reflection of the Bologna Process. Retrieved June 25, 2004, from *http://www.see-educoop.net/education_in/pdf/q-reform-he-in-norway-oth-enl-t02.pdf*

Otnes, H. (2003). Arkivskuff eller læringsarena? Lærings- og dokumentasjonssjangre i digitale mapper [Archive or Learning Environment? Genres for learning and documentation in digital portfolios]. In O. Dysthe & K. S. Engelsen (Eds.), *Mapper som pedagogisk redskap: perspektiver og erfaringer* [*Portfolios as Pedagogical Tools: Perspectives and Lessons Learned*]. Oslo: abstrakt forlag.

Ramsden, P. (1988). *Improving learning: New perspectives*. London: Kogan Page.

Säljö, R. (1999). Learning as the use of tools: A sociocultural perspective on the human-technology link. In K. Littelton & P. Light (Eds.), *Learning with computers: Analysing productive interaction*. London: Routledge.

Vygotsky, L. S. (1978). *Mind in society: The development of higher psychological processes*. Cambridge, MA: Harvard University Press

Wenger, E. (1998). *Communities of practice learning, meaning and identity*. Cambridge, MA: Cambridge University Press

Wittek, L. (2002). Mapper som vurderings- og læringsredskap [Portfolios as tools for evaluation and learning]. Retrieved June 25, 2004, from *http://www.pfi.uio.no/uniped/gpm/mapper.html*

Wittek, L. (2003). *Mapper som lærings- og vurderingsform. Eksempler fra Universitetet i Oslo [Portfolios as Forms of Learning and Evaluation. Examples from the University of Oslo]*. Oslo: Unipub forlag.

Endnotes

[1]   The quality reform is a national instance of the current Bologna process aimed at restructuring and revitalizing European public higher education (European Union, 2000). In addition to reconfigurations of degree structures and other issues, the reform includes a strong pedagogical component, which involves proactive use of educational information and communication technologies (ICT) and digital media.

[2]   An open-edit-save functionality is developed for the purpose of editing Microsoft Office documents inside Classfronter™ instead of having to edit them outside Classfronter™ and re-import them.

[3]   The issue of "cultivation" of information infrastructures is most relevant for the present chapter. See Hanseth (2002).

Chapter XVII

Putting Course Management Systems Behind Us

Robby Robson, Eduworks Corporation, USA

Abstract

The course management systems developed in the mid-to-late 90s helped get instructors online and partially automated course administration services in ways that saved time and effort. But the course administration function is not central to the deeper problems of providing more universal access to learning and making learning more effective. Furthermore, service-oriented architectures are starting to dominate the information technology infrastructure landscape. This chapter discusses the author's personal history with developing a course management system and speculates how the functionality needed to support online learning is being taken apart and might be put back together.

Introduction

This chapter is about why universities once needed what are now called course management systems but do not anymore. It is about why and how they will be replaced by something more in line with modern technology and more germane to the goal of effective learning. It is about building technology to solve the right problems and it is about my own story, which is where I will start.

A Personal Story

In 1995, the United States had a problem with calculus instruction. Students were failing in droves, an emotional debate was raging over "traditional" versus "reform" calculus (Wilson, 1997), and everyone was tired of thick and boring textbooks.

A colleague[1] suggested a solution. Why not use the Web? With the Web, we could personalize instruction so that students could learn at their own pace, so that students could see examples relevant to their own interests, and so that instruction could follow both traditional *and* reform approaches. We could deliver calculus to working parents who couldn't come to campus and to students who couldn't function before noon. We could realize the vision that would later be described by Wayne Hodgins (2002) as being able to get "just the right stuff to just the right person at just the right time and place in just the right way"[2] (p. 64).

The idea was compelling. We soon found ourselves with funding to create a totally online first-term calculus course and, incidentally, to build the technology needed to make it work. And it was wonderful technology that we built (Bogley, Dorbolo, Robson, & Sechrest, 1996, 1997; Bogley & Robson, 1996). It was database-backed. We had a "quiz tool" with a sophisticated tree structure that allowed arbitrary levels of grouping among several different question types and that included randomization at each level. Our system allowed authors to create hyperlinks that would branch to different pages depending on the value of quiz scores. We had an engine that managed a special type of activity where one student's work would be shipped off to another student for comment and further work. We had a fully featured grade book. We had user types with different administrative privileges. We had a bulletin board and a place from which the instructor could send e-mail to class members. We even tried (without success) to get permission to integrate our grade book directly into our university's registrar system. And we had all that up and running in 1996.

What happened next is familiar to many innovators, especially in the academic realm. We had few adopters and learning results were good, but students and colleagues still greeted our methods with suspicion. We received some small degree of recognition,[3] but we ran into a brick wall when we started to talk with our university's technology transfer office. Politics intervened and our system joined dozens of other compatriots in the Land of Forgotten Technology. Why? Because *we did not have a course management system.*

Our technology ran on a separate server and could only be accessed by inserting appropriate links into the Web site for a course. We didn't have a shell of the type that has become the familiar interface to online course technology. In fact, we didn't want one. Our goal was to add interactive pedagogic functionality to Web pages and, separately, to automate some administrative functions. We intentionally left the development of content and structure to faculty authors, and we assumed that these authors knew how to create Web pages and modify HTML. In 1996, that was a bad idea.

What's the Problem?

In 1996, the problem that needed solving was that of getting the Web into the hands of faculty. Systems like WebCT™, TopClass™, CourseInfo™, and Web-Course-In-A-Box™[4] succeeded where we failed. By creating all-in-one environments, these products launched e-learning in the academic sector, and for that we should be grateful. But as we approach the second decade of online education, the Web, e-mail, and course management systems have deep penetration in college and university environments (Green, 2003). The question is no longer whether the Web will be used as an educational tool, but whether it will make a difference. "No significant difference" (Russell, 1999) is no significant progress.

But what would make a significant difference? How can technology best be used to bring more effective learning to more people? And how will we measure success? These are hard questions to answer, but we can at least look at what benefit is being derived from the current technology and at the underlying trends that will shape the future. With that as a backdrop, we can take a step back and ask whether the current solutions make sense and, if not, what would work better.

The Benefits of Course Management Systems

What do existing course management systems do and what are their benefits? The short answer is that they bundle a set of functionalities associated with the management and delivery of fairly traditional online courses. Their benefits are to increase access and reduce administrative overhead. For example, the Massachusetts Institute of Technology (2003) describes the benefits of its open-source Stellar™ course management system by saying:

> *The Stellar course management system supports teaching and learning on the Web. Instructors get an easy way to share class materials and take care of time-consuming administrative tasks. Students get round-the-clock access to materials, discussion boards, and online homework submission* (1st paragraph).

Similarly, Stanford's (2004) course management system, CourseWork™, lists its high-level advantages as:

1.   Web site management is simple and quick.
2.   CourseWork™ manages the distribution and collection of assignments.
3.   The system provides privacy and security.
4.   CourseWork™'s information management tools are quick and easy to use.
5.   A permanent record of course materials is always accessible.
6.   CourseWork™ has professionally maintained servers.

Course management systems have succeeded in making it easier to organize materials into courses and to handle some of the chores that are part of teaching or taking a course. These are gains in efficiency which, according to one study we have done, students also view as an educational benefit (CMS@WBW, 2003). But if online access and Web site management are the goals, then why purchase or maintain a system that also comes with chat, bulletin boards, quizzes, and other tools? And if it is the educational tools that are important, do current course management systems provide good ones? And if the real goal is "getting just the right stuff to just the right person at just the right time and place in just the right way," how much do we need to worry about course management at all?

Modularization

In analyzing any technology, it is important to understand the key trends that might influence its future. There is no lack of these for e-learning. The growing prevalence of mobile devices with wireless or cellular capabilities, the rise of gaming and simulation environments, the rapid expansion of broadband access, and the remarkable materials sciences and engineering advances that are uncannily extending Moore's law into the future – all of these will have a profound effect. But the trends with the most immediate impact on campus-based e-learning are service-oriented architectures and learning objects. These are both trends towards modularization, one for technology and the other for content. Together they point to a future that is different from the present. We will examine them in turn.

Service-Oriented Architectures

Educational institutions have become reliant on complex software systems that are increasingly interdependent and hard to get to work properly. These include systems that manage finances, personnel, facilities, student records, telecommunications, libraries, campus portals, and all that falls under the catch-all term of enterprise infrastructure. In this regard, educational institutions are no different than corporations or government agencies and, like their counterparts, educational institutions are turning to Web services and service-oriented architectures for relief. What were once complex and monolithic systems are now being viewed as consisting of separate components, each of which provides a set of services to other components, and all of which communicate with each other through a shared abstraction layer. Over time, these components and services are being separated so that they can be maintained and updated separately.

The implications for managing and delivering learning are clear. It no longer makes sense to support systems that bundle all the components of a learning environment into a single package. It makes far more sense to break the functionality currently offered by course management systems into separate services such as syllabus management, content management, content authoring, online assessment, online collaboration, record keeping and reporting, user authentication and authorization, and rights management. Even without potential gains in reliability and stability, doing so has two huge advantages.

First, much of the functionality currently offered by course management systems is not their natural dominion. For example, content management is being increasingly handled by institutional repositories and digital libraries (Crow, 2002; Lynch, 2003), record keeping and "single sign-on" are handled by student administration systems, and enterprise-wide directory services and online quizzing are offered by specialized assessment products that provide security, data analysis and adaptive testing. Second, a learning environment that consists of a selected set of services exposed through a portal offers more flexibility in choosing the components that work best in a specific educational context. This is the approach that is being taken by the Sakai Project and by the Joint Information Systems Committee, or JISC (Norton, 2004; Sakai, 2004), and it is a promising approach indeed.

Technical Standards

When we were developing our technology in 1995 and 1996, we provided pedagogic and administrative services by embedding links into Web pages. Not only did this address the wrong problem for the time, but it was also a primitive and clumsy method. Faculty who wanted to use a grade book, for example, had to paste an appropriately formatted URL into their course. This required a certain amount of technical savvy, and if the server moved or was shut down (as in fact happened), it was "game over."

In the intervening time, the ability to access externally provisioned functionality has improved dramatically, largely due to standards. Web services and service-oriented architectures rely on a slew of standards that first define grammars, syntax, and protocols for exchanging data and information and then define languages and semantics that can be used to exchange data and information of a specific type, such as financial transactions, authentication tokens, metadata, or the results of a learning experience.

That is not to say that the Web services framework is a panacea that makes all integration problems disappear. The protocols are general, and each community of practice must standardize on how it plans to exchange information that is peculiar to its requirements. Each community must come to a precise understanding of what its own data mean and of how to interpret data that are being exchanged with external systems. This understanding is part of the standardization process, and if the proper level of precision is not reached both in theory and practice, things won't work.

Fortunately, standardization of this type is nothing new for the learning technology community. As mentioned elsewhere in this book, significant effort has been put into technical specifications and standards that support interoperability between content and learning systems. These efforts predate service-oriented architectures but have started the modularization ball rolling by separating learning content from learning management systems and by defining information models for learning-related data and metadata. In addition, a set of related architecture projects, including the Learning Systems Architecture Lab learning and Web services descriptions (LSAL, 2004), the Open Knowledge Initiative (OKI, 2004), the JISC e-learning framework (JISC, 2004), and the IMS Global Learning Consortium abstract framework (IMS, 2004), have been working on factoring the functionality needed to support online learning in a college or university setting into a layered set of services.

Will We Have Modular Learning Environments?

Emerging standards and architectures point the way towards learning environments consisting of bundles of services, but we should not get carried away. Standards and architectures are not the same as working technology, and there are thousands of installations of course management systems that don't look at all like the architectural diagrams one finds on the Web sites of the projects cited above. Colleges and universities have established relationships with commercial vendors and have made investments in commercial and home-grown course management systems that will not be thrown out just because something new has come along. As Kenneth Green (2004) aptly observes, the market for course management systems "looks like a mature market with immature products" (3rd paragraph). Mature markets are characterized by evolution rather than revolution, and even if Web services are taking the rest of the world by storm, the academic community is capable of going its own way without being too concerned about fitting into the larger picture.

As a case in point, there has been relatively little uptake of SCORM™ (the Sharable Courseware Object Reference Model) or AICC (Aviation

Industry CBT Committee) guidelines by software vendors that serve the academic community, even though SCORM™ enjoys almost universal adoption in the commercial and government sectors.[5] This is not surprising since an underlying assumption in SCORM™ is that all learning functionality is separate and autonomous from the systems that manage it. In the SCORM™ model, a learning management system (or more accurately a run-time service) launches content into a learner's browser and exchanges data with the content, taking back control of the learner's browser only when instructed to do so by the content itself. There is no provision in SCORM™ for a learning management system to provide a proprietary set of functionality like a quiz or chat room. As far as SCORM™ is concerned, these are just other instances of content,[6] no different than a Flash™ movie or HTML page. Some of the basic tenets of SCORM™ are violated by the way that campus-based course management systems have evolved, and this has led to divergence in standards support between products for the academic and broader e-learning markets.

Nonetheless, the future of campus-based learning environments feels as though it will be a lot less bundled. The drive towards service-oriented architectures pervades across all information technology and is not simply something that applies to learning environments. Projects like OKI, Sakai, and the JISC framework come out of the academic community itself. Other developments, such as the spread of institutional repositories and portals, are making it less and less logical to support course management systems that offer specialized versions of more general functionality, and commercial course management systems are opening up to integration with external tools and services.[7] Given that, it cannot be long before we start to seriously consider what core functionality is really needed from existing course management systems and, more importantly, what functionality is needed to best address the problem of learning effectiveness.

With that in mind, it is time to examine one of most basic of assumptions behind existing course management systems, namely that their purpose is to manage courses.

Learning Objects and the Notion of a Course

Not surprisingly, the first attempts at using the Web as an instructional medium simply recast what was already being done in the classroom. Systems were built to put courses online. This is what my colleagues and

I set out to do in 1995 and what has mostly been done since then. We started with the paradigm of the course as the natural unit of instruction and are still stuck in it. But things are starting to change, and the name of the change is "learning objects."

A key feature of learning objects is that they can be reused, either in their entirety or by extracting some of their parts. The idea is that an instructor putting together an online course should be able find and use existing content rather than writing new content from scratch. Reusing online content mimics the way instructors use traditional texts, picking out a chapter here or using an exercise or an example there, and emphasizing the reusability aspects of learning objects gives them a comfortable feel that can help them move beyond the early adopters and into the mainstream. But once learning objects start to exist in any number, the need for organizing them into courses becomes less clear. From the perspective of the student, the problem that learning objects solve is not that of putting pieces of learning together into an instructional package but that of finding content that teaches what needs to be learned now. Why should a student have to do that inside of a course?

Learning Objects

Another key concept associated with learning objects is that of a learning objective. The classic learning object, as viewed by instructional designers, targets a single skill or concept and includes an assessment that can be used to measure or demonstrate mastery (Barritt & Lewis, 2000; Wagner, 2002). The targeted skill or concept is a very important piece of metadata associated with a learning object, often called an instructional objective or learning objective. Learning objectives are useful to students looking to fill particular gaps or trying to master particular techniques and are an essential part of the instructional design process.

College courses, however, are not organized according to learning objectives. They are typically organized into lectures, topics and assignments, a structure that is reflected in most existing course management systems. The topics and assignments, while pedagogic in nature, tend to indicate what will be covered or done rather than explicitly state what skills or concepts will be learned and how that learning is to be measured. In my own experience,[8] few instructors clearly identify learning objectives and even fewer use them as an organizing principle when designing a course, either for classroom or online use.

The learning object agenda is not only about reuse. It is also about how learning experiences are designed, how learning effectiveness is measured, and about enabling students to find the right content whether or not it is part of a course. The problems addressed by learning objects are the ones we would like to address, but they are not the ones that existing course management systems solve.

Where to Next?

In 1995, my colleagues and I struggled with the problem of how to use the Web to increase learning effectiveness, to get "the right stuff to just the right person at just the right time and place in just the right way." In retrospect, this is more of an information management problem than a course management problem. If we had it to do over again, we might concentrate more on developing excellent repositories and excellent content and less on making it easier for instructors to manage class rosters and provide discussion boards. We might try to think more "out of the course."

Nonetheless, the idea of aggregating online learning and administrative tools into a single environment was and remains a winner. If we want to unleash the learning possibilities offered by games, simulations, data sets and other forms of interactive and dynamic content, and if we want to add a means to assess and track learning outcomes, then we quickly come full circle to the notion of a Web-based learning environment that combines learning objects, learning tools, learning services, administrative tools, and administrative services. What has changed since 1995 is how such an environment can be architected and the requirements it must meet.

At the time when present course management systems were being developed, the fundamental requirement was to gently ease instructors and students into Web-based courses. That problem has been solved, and the next generation of online learning environments is being shaped by different problems. These newer environments must interoperate with other enterprise systems and be compatible with current technology trends. They must fit in with the agendas of the learning object and institutional repository communities and must meet demands for more specialized and more dynamic tools and services. They must improve access and educational effectiveness and must collect the data to prove it.

This is a tall order, but behind the scenes projects like Sakai and the JISC are taking steps that will help fill it. They have a realistic chance of leading to Web-based learning environments that are built on standards and into which a rich variety of tools and services can be integrated. Once these types of systems are in place, we will be able to find out what functionality is really important for learning and where and how course management should be handled. The journey has been long and is far from over, but there is a discernible point in the future where we might finally be able to address the problems we set out to solve almost 10 years ago. I, for one, am very much looking forward to that.

References

Architecture Lab. Retrieved August 22, 2004, from *http://www.lsal.cmu.edu/lsal/resources/services/index.html*

Barritt, C. & Lewis, D. (2000). Reusable learning object strategy: definition, creation process, and guidelines for building. Version 3.1. Whitepaper published by Cisco Systems. Retrieved August 22, 2004, from *http://www.reusablelearning.org/Docs/Cisco_rlo_roi_v3-1.pdf*

Bogley, W.A., Dorbolo, J., Robson, R. O. & Sechrest, J. A. (1996). New pedagogies and tools for Web-based calculus. *World Conference of the Web Society Proceedings*, 33-39.

Bogley, W. A., Dorbolo, J., Robson, R.O. & Sechrest, J. A. (1997). Pedagogic innovations in Web-based instruction. *Proceedings of the Ninth International Conference on Technology in Collegiate Mathematics*. Reading, MA: Addison-Wesley.

Bogley, W. A. & Robson, R. (1996). CalculusQuest Web Site. Available at *http://web.archive.org/web/19981205234615/iq.orst.edu/cq/*

CMS@WBW. (2003). Project CMS@WBW Website. Retrieved August 22, 2004, from *http://web.brandeis.edu/pages/view/Instructional/WBWInfo*

Crow, R. (2002). The case for institutional repositories: A SPARC position paper. The Scholarly Publishing & Academic Resources Coalition. Retrieved July 21, 2004, from *http://www.arl.org/sparc/IR/ir.html*

Green, K. (2003). Campus computing 2003, the 14th national survey of computing and information technology in American higher education. The Campus Computing Project.

Green, K. (2004). Sakai and the four C's of open source. *Syllabus*. March. Retrieved on August 22, 2004, from *http://www.syllabus.com/print.asp?ID=9030*

Hodgins, W. (2002). Are we asking the right questions? In *Transforming culture: An executive briefing on the power of learning*. University of Virginia Darden Institute. Retrieved on December 1, 2003, from *http://www.darden.edu/batten/clc/Articles/RightQuestions.pdf*

IMS. (2004). *Abstract framework*. IMS Global Learning Consortium. Retrieved August 22, 2004, from *http://www.imsglobal.org/af/index.cfm*

Joint Information Systems Committee (JISC). (2004). *JISC e-Learning programme: Technical framework and tools strand*. Retrieved August 22, 2004, from *http://www.jisc.ac.uk/index.cfm?name=elearning_framework*

Lynch, C. (2003). Institutional repositories: Essential infrastructure for scholarship in the digital age. *Association of Research Libraries Bimonthly Report*, February. Retrieved July 21, 2004, from *http://www.arl.org/newsltr/226/ir.html*

LSAL. (2004). *Learning and Web services descriptions*. Carnegie Mellon University Learning Systems.

Massachusetts Institute of Technology. (2003). Stellar™ course management system: Benefits. Retrieved August 22, 2004, from *https://stellar.mit.edu/features/benefits.html*

Norton, M. (2004). A comparison between the JISC and Sakai frameworks. April 5, 2003 - v. 3. Retrieved August 22, 2004, from *http://www.sakaiproject.org/tech/S040405N.pdf*

Open Knowledge Initiative (OKI). (2004). Open Knowledge Initiative Web Site. Retrieved August 22, 2004, from *http://web.mit.edu/oki*

Russell, T. (1999). The no significant difference phenomenon. International Distance Education Certification Center. Available at *http://www.nosignificantdifference.org/*

Sakai. (2004). Sakai Project Web Site. Retrieved August 22, 2004, from *http://www.sakaiproject.org*

Stanford University. (2004). Advantages: Why use CourseWork™? Retrieved August 22, 2004, from *http://aboutcoursework.stanford.edu/advantages.html*

Wagner, E. (2002). Steps to creating a content strategy for your organization. *eLearning Developers' Journal*, October 29. Retrieved December 5,

2003, from *http://www.elearningguild.com/pdf/2/102902MGT-H.pdf*

Wilson, R. (1997). "Reform calculus" has been a disaster, critics charge. *The Chronicle of Higher Education*, February 7. Available to subscribers at *http://chronicle.com/che-data/articles.dir/art-43.dir/issue-22.dir/22a00101.htm*

Endnotes

[1]   Bill Bogley, *http://oregonstate.edu/~bogleyw/*. Much of the subsequent work was inspired by Jon Dorbolo (http://oregonstate.edu/mediaservices/mspeople.htm) and John Sechrest (*www.peak.org/~sechrest/*).

[2]   The full quote is "just the right stuff to just the right person at just the right time and place in just the right way and with just the right context on just the right device and through just the right medium."

[3]   Including being one of five runners-up in the Paul G. Allen Virtual Education Awards for Online Courses given in 1998. The link to the awards has disappeared from the Web. See, however, *http://onlineacademy.org/acad/about_acad/conference/courses.html*.

[4]   CourseInfo became the course management system for Blackboard™, and Web-Course-In-A-Box was later acquired by Blackboard™. TopClass transformed into a learning content management system with a corporate orientation and remains as such today.

[5]   This statement about adoption is based on analysis of learning management and learning content management systems available (for purchase) from *www.brandon-hall.com*, features of course management systems listed on *www.edutools.com*, personal experience with various course management systems, and privately communicated results of surveys of e-learning technology vendors.

[6]   In SCORM™ 2004 these can be considered "activities," but the conclusion is the same.

[7]   For example, through Blackboard™ Building Blocks or WebCT™ PowerLinks.

[8]   Including two-and-a-half years as the person officially responsible for promoting outcomes-based education at Oregon State University from 1998 through the middle of 2000.

Section III

Next-Generation CMS

Chapter XVIII

Course Management Systems for Learning:
Future Designs

Barbara Ross, WebCT, USA

Abstract

Author Barbara Ross, co-founder and Chief Operating Office of WebCT, Inc., posits that in the future the "course" will become a decreasingly important construct in the "course management system." Building on a personal reflection on teaching and learning in higher education, she predicts an evolving focus on effective pedagogy will drive academic enterprise systems to support learning outcomes and assessment, a proliferation of digital learning objects, commercial and open source tool integration and an increasing focus on the student. In conclusion, she reminds skeptics of the changes in the last five years and looks forward to a bright, dynamic future.

Introduction

Long ago, in an epoch that evokes much nostalgia among aging baby boomers (and much eye-rolling among members of the generations that precede and follow them), I faced a dilemma common to college freshman both then and now. I had been shut out of a desired course and had a hole in my schedule that needed to be filled — fast — and preferably by something that didn't meet on Fridays or any earlier than 11:00 a.m. The friend of a sister of a guy in my dorm at the University of Pennsylvania was said to be heavily recommending a year-long course entitled American Civilization I, taught by a professor named Anthony N.B. Garvan. Dr. Garvan was reputed to be a great lecturer, just back from a sabbatical. The course had been opened on his return, and there were seats. It was supposed to be difficult (according to the mythology, 80 percent of the students received Cs or below), but worth it. I signed up, bought a spiral bound notebook for 69 cents at the campus bookstore (which sits beside me as I type this) and dutifully reported for class.

"Norsemen in Greenland!" Garvan bellowed in sonorous tones on the first day of class and then proceeded through a lengthy discourse on calamities and disappearing colonies in the New World from Greenland to Roanoke. At the time I took the course, Dr. Garvan had been delivering it for over twenty years. Legend had it that just to keep himself amused, he had once taught it Merlin-like — backwards, from the present day to Leif Ericsson.

The learning experience was everything that is sometimes derided by those who confuse the medium with the construct of the message. Garvan was nothing if not "the sage on the stage". There were 200 of us crammed into the lecture hall; the teaching assistant's sessions were worthless (or so as an 18-year-old I adjudged), and I am quite sure that the essay questions we laboriously answered in the blue exam books were never viewed by the great man himself.

For two semesters, Garvan talked about Cotton Mather, Benjamin Franklin, and Ulysses S. Grant. He explained the meaning of culture. We took notes in our spiral notebooks and read copiously from original sources. Spring came and finals rolled around. The lectures and the reading ended. The blank blue essay books were passed out one last time, and Garvan asked, in some elegant way I no longer recall, "What is an American?"

I wrote for two hours, and by the time I lay down my pen, something magical had occurred. In writing my answer, I reframed everything I had heard and read all year long, and understood at a different level than I had at any singular point in the course what Dr. Garvan was getting at. He had never told us straight out what his thesis was, but he had embedded it in everything he said and assigned, and in the reflection that his final question required, I constructed my own meaning. My answer was probably very close to his own, but he had never told me the answer to that central question. I built it myself out of the pieces he gave us, and that made it all the more meaningful.

And the process was transformative. To this day, whenever I have cause to think about that question — from discussions about bilingual education, to national security, to whether a marriage performed in one state will be recognized in another — I go back to the things I learned in that course as a touchstone for the larger context. And isn't that what education — not training, or skills transfer, but education — is all about?

Why Would You Ever Change a Course Like That?

Why would anyone change anything so magical? The academy is an essentially conservative place, but it is not immune to internal and external drivers for change. For example, if we look at American Civilization I of my day:

It was neither replicable nor scalable. When Dr. Garvan was on sabbatical, it simply wasn't given. Once 200 people had signed up and the lecture hall was filled, that was it for the year. Fine for then, but not for many of us now.

It was entirely sink or swim. I have no idea what percentage of my fellow students finally "got it" in the last hour of the last day of class. I think the stories of 80 percent of the students getting Cs or below were apocryphal, but I never deluded myself that anyone at the university cared if I passed or failed, stayed or left, "got it" or didn't. Again, fine for then.

It was solitary. Though some might argue this was the right model for figuring out the meaning of my own identity as an American, an argument at least equally persuasive might be made that I also would have benefited enormously by knowing how my classmates absorbed and processed the material throughout the course and answered that final question, especially given the diversity of experience and knowledge they brought with them into the room. This sharing also would have supported one of the central ideas of the course — that one of the things that makes us American is the way we are always rubbing up against and off on one another.

It was rare. In the rosy glow of the years between making our last student loan payments and writing the first tuition checks for our children, these transformative experiences are what we remember. But let's face it — it wasn't *all* that way. In a lecture hall not far from Dr. Garvan's, another professor (who shall remain nameless) had us buy his out-of-print book (republished by a vanity press), spent his lecture time *reading* to us from his book, and on the final exam asked us, "What does it say on page 279 of my book?" Though this example is extreme, in very few of my courses was there any obvious, clear set of educational goals and sound pedagogical ways to get us there — and watching my college-age children's experiences, I would say this is still the case.

It was delivered by a single professor and was the responsibility of a single department. Though American Civilization I combined history, art history, architecture, anthropology, political science, and other disciplines, it was provided under the aegis of a single department. Today, many institutions (and faculty and students) would see the benefit in taking a multidepartmental approach to such an offering.

It was delivered using technology appropriate to the time. The American Civilization I of my era made use of the technology of the day. We saw slides to help us compare and contrast American colonial chests with English ones. And at some point, when copying became cost effective, multiple copies of the out-of-print articles and original sources that we were assigned to read were made by the library — not *enough* ever, but multiples. We never questioned why we got to see the slides only once in the lecture class and never got to look at them again. We never questioned why we had to go hang around the over-heated reserve library, waiting for classmates to finish with those copies of the readings. These weren't just facts of our educational lives, but facts of our whole lives, and we accepted them. If, however, we had been made to take our lecture notes on slate by the light of oil lamps, we would have screamed bloody murder. And today, students often look on practices perfectly acceptable in my day as if they were akin to using those slates.

The Next Generation of Course Management Systems

The truth of the matter is that institutions shape course management systems — not the other way around. So in what directions are institutions driving course management systems? At WebCT, we have the privilege of working with institutions from around the world. On that basis, we believe that in the future:

- The course will continue to diminish as the singular organizational unit for the "course management system". In fact, much more flexible and powerful academic enterprise systems have already begun to expand and enhance the capabilities of the "traditional" (if eight years can be said to constitute a "tradition") course management systems.

- A new paradigm based on learning outcomes and assessment will emerge. Concomitant with it will come major efficiencies from authoring to student remediation and scaffolding to accreditation reporting.

- The shift away from the course paradigm and the proliferation of digital content will change profoundly the way institutions, libraries, faculty, and students find, acquire, customize, assign, interact with, and retain content.

- No longer course-bound, the academic enterprise system will continue to grow as the primary integrative technology in the learning space, knitting together campus infrastructure and teaching and learning tools from many sources, including open source. This integration will have the effect of automating non-value-added tasks for faculty, students, and administration — allowing them to focus on teaching, learning, and research.

- The student will become a much more critical constituent for the academic enterprise system — with new tools emerging to support their learning and social interactions in the system and to support the new devices with which they will arrive on our virtual or physical doorsteps.

The "course" will continue to diminish as the singular organizational unit for the "course management system". As long as institutions group students into courses and give grades and credits on that basis, the course will remain as an administrative structure, both on campus and within the learning system. However, even now, faculty, students, and administrators have strongly voiced a need to break down course walls. As more and more of their lives take place in digital formats, students want a central place (not course-bound) to store and work on their own reflections, research, and artifacts term-to-term while they are attached to the institution and beyond. This place combines the functions of a portfolio, a bookshelf, a file drawer, a resume, and a diary.

Faculty members have similar needs. They also want to team teach, break down disciplines, access, share, and reuse their own content and that of others, give partial credits, and run more amoeba-like collections of students, outcomes, and ideas that are unbounded by time or course. In addition, administrators need to be able to look across the institution to understand and document how it is supporting student and faculty achievement beyond course boundaries and grades.

New e-learning systems are already evolving to meet these demands; these new systems are called academic enterprise systems because of their integrative nature, enterprise architecture, and movement beyond course boundaries.

Learning outcomes will emerge as a new organizing principle. If the course is no longer the only or even the dominant organizing principle, what is? People can be the center of their own universe, and flexible roles and permissions allow them to be a student/faculty member/employee (and often all three) with all the right privileges. But what about content, interaction, and assessment? Learning outcomes become ways to link small, but instructionally meaningful, collections of content and interaction together that can then be grouped into larger collections to form courses (including alternative ways to meet objectives) and curricula. These collections can be reused for other courses and curricula, or outside of course/curricular boundaries for remediation, scaffolding, and ubiquitous performance support. Deans and advisors can look at student achievement across a curriculum, and schools and programs can roll up this information to capture efficient data for accreditation reviews and certifications.

The resistance to learning outcomes as an organizing principle has been entrenched in higher education. This may be due to prejudices and concerns about the early state of the art, where lower-level, skill-based, learning objectives were seen as easier to define and measure successful achievement. There is, however, no reason that learning objectives can't be attached to higher levels of learning. Students can be asked to demonstrate, apply, analyze, synthesize, evaluate, and create, either individually or in groups.

Another reason for the resistance to learning outcomes as an organizing principle may be that it is just so difficult given the current state-of-the-art technology to roll up learning outcomes with any degree of consistency or value. This is where academic enterprise system providers, working with leading institutional partners, can serve as critical enablers in terms of providing consistent, flexible, simple, and highly automated ways to describe the intersection of content, activity, and achievement. Capturing the data about cohorts of students that are already flowing into the database, as a part of the normal learning process, is the most viable, efficient way to support quality assessment and accreditation requirements. "Grafted on" solutions that ultimately create more work for faculty and institutional researchers, and don't systematically intersect with learning interactions, will prove unsustainable.

The move from courses to learning outcomes, combined with a well-established movement to digital content, will revolutionize course content and interactions. For hundreds of years, education has rewarded those people who could absorb and then create static linear representations of meaning on the printed page. It was the best system humans had for the collection and widespread communication of knowledge, and it has changed the world in ways perhaps more profound than anything else.

By the same token, as widespread access to other media has emerged, we have realized that writing paragraphs about the impact of a change in variables on an economic model, or describing what a heart murmur sounds like, makes no sense. This has also changed our view of what is valuable in learners. The ability to focus for long, solitary periods, "linearize" knowledge, and communicate in writing are still highly valued; however, the ability to multitask, work in interactive, problem-solving groups, synthesize information from diverse representations, and communicate in multiple media are equally important in academia and in life.

Over the last five years, academic library acquisition has shifted from almost entirely print to over 55 percent digital; yet all too often these assets, licensed at great expense, are under-leveraged, particularly by undergraduates. By searching for and then linking to library assets and assets from other content repositories at the right place (course, assignment, lesson, or learning object) and in the right way — as support for a single idea, a target reading list for a larger theme, or a predefined search to scaffold a research project — we can broaden and reinforce the use of trusted sources and teach our students how to do their own discovery in the future.

While library assets are critical, they are very often digital representations of static print, and usually serve a reference need only — they do not carry learning interactions or measurements of achievement. To fill this need, as well as the need for a greater variety of media, commercial publishers will step in. While academics and others will continue to contribute large amounts of content, it stretches credulity to believe that they can easily achieve the production values for video, animation, and games that today's students expect. It is also hard to believe that a $3.5 billion textbook industry will not transform itself to meet these expanding demands.

Institutions and course management system providers are not the only ones who depend upon the course today as the defining unit. Textbook publishers do as well and have worked hard to match books to the many flavors of course offerings. If, over the next five years, institutions (and academic enterprise systems) move away from the course as the defining unit of learning (as opposed to an administrative unit), publishers will make a change as well in their packaging and business models.

This transformation means that faculty will have the ability to select smaller units of learning based on learning outcomes and to put together just what they need. They may select assets that are licensed to their institutions or departments and passed along as fees, or paid for by students directly, just as they do now. The costs to the students should be lower in either case, as they will purchase only what they need and what the course requires, not the large compendiums designed to meet the needs of every course, as textbooks are used today. These collections of customized content assets — built to support a theory, theme, or pedagogical approach — may be wrapped, rebranded, and offered to other institutions. Departments and teaching teams may replace the sole author as the "brand name" for such collections.

For a small subscription fee, students will be able to move the digital assets that most interest them into their non-course bounded space, or ePortfolio, and keep them for learning, reference, and remediation throughout their academic careers and beyond.

The academic enterprise system will continue its integrative function, knitting together campus infrastructure and teaching and learning tools from many sources, including open source. The course management system or academic enterprise system has emerged as the primary integrative technology for teaching and learning at institutions around the world. Students and faculty alike expect to sign on to one system to find everything they need for teaching and learning — and they expect this to happen automatically, no matter how many times they drop or add courses. They expect tools or systems they use in their learning — no matter who developed or licensed them — to report their interactions and scores back to the academic enterprise system. They want grades and comments to be quickly viewable and reported back to the registrar's system automatically. The provost and institutional research department want all learning data, no matter what the source, to be captured in a central place so they can analyze the achievement of cohorts of students.

The integrative nature of the academic enterprise system will have the effect of automating non-value-added tasks for faculty, students, and administration, which will allow them to focus primarily on teaching, learning, and research. Students and faculty will expect support: including support for automatically integrated calendars and notification systems, support of workflow for multi-iterated assignments and documents, and support for more efficient group work interactions.

Successful academic enterprise systems in the future will provide common, modular integration frameworks based on open standards that will enable institutions, schools, departments, individual faculty, and individual students to chose and use the tools that support them best, either from a commercial provider or from the open source community.

The pace of technology change and the growing demands from students, faculty, administrators, and accreditors mean that we all must work together to meet our needs. There is no winning "go it alone" strategy for anyone.

The student will become a much more critical constituent for the academic enterprise system. While in some sense all of the work we do related to teaching and learning is for students, the exigencies of training faculty and changing the way we teach have been so central over the last five years that students have sometimes been considered only secondarily. Today we see a very limited number of institutions including students in course management system selection processes and very few solely "student-centered" features being required in requests for proposals (RFPs).

As greater automation, integration, and high-value content emerge, the student will become a much more critical constituent for the academic enterprise system — with new tools emerging to support learning and social interactions in the system. These tools will include productivity tools for managing time and workflow, tools for convenience that support portability and off-line work, tools for scaffolding learning and for coaching, tools for documenting independent work for the purposes of achieving credit, and tools to support even greater levels of group work.

In addition, academic enterprise systems will need to support the new devices that students bring with them. Ubiquitous as the phone, smaller than the tablet, cheaper than a paperback book, a new device that serves as your hard drive, communications center, media and game player, and commerce transaction manager will emerge. Students will use the same device to answer the survey in their political science course that they use to vote for the 2009 "American Idol".

We will need to embrace that device — just as we will need to embrace new ideas and new challenges — not just by continuing the evolution of our e-learning systems, but also by continuing the evolution of our teaching.

Conclusion

When Murray Goldberg, Sasan Salari, Carol Vallone, and I founded the companies that became WebCT, we were told by many people, investors and academic "thought leaders" alike, not to bother because academia would never change, because faculty would never touch technology, because students would never figure out how to use their computers or the Internet. But a group of dedicated, smart, risk-taking institutions proved the doubters wrong. In fact, they even surprised us a little with the speed and ardor of their embrace.

If we look at course management systems five years from now, we effectively double the real lifetime of these technologies on campus. Certainly in the last five years, more has changed in terms of teaching and learning than many people thought possible — but some of our hopes, dreams, and predictions have not come true.

There was, of course, a "course management system" in place when I took American Civilization I. There were systematic ways to get students into the course, assign a room to it, assign TAs and TA sections, get the right articles on reserve in the library, pass out, collect, and grade exams, and get the grades back to the registrar. And like today's course management systems, the systems in place for managing and delivering American Civilization I could be used for good or for evil. To paraphrase the famous sign in the Clinton War Room — IT'S THE PEDAGOGY, STUPID.

Over the last five years, I have been known, at times, to get discouraged about interest in the quality (and by quality, I mean measurable, demonstrable quality) of teaching and learning in post-secondary education and to wonder aloud if more than pockets of people cared about it at most institutions.

Over the last eighteen months, I have seen much cause for optimism. Interest in sound education with demonstrated outcomes is surging in the UK, emerging throughout the European Union and South Africa, moving to the forefront in Canada, rising throughout Asia, and cresting across Australia; it is even being exemplified by a singular, wonderful set of institutions, systems, and consortia in the exciting, complex, diverse, and fractious world that makes up higher education in the USA.

This movement to quality — real, demonstrable quality — is what will ultimately lift and drive the next generation of academic enterprise systems. Our job, as software vendors, will be to enable and support this process and to provide appropriate leadership in co-developing, with our customers, solutions to problems that today may seem too subtle or intractable to be solved. I can't wait to see it happen.

Chapter XIX

Future Directions of Course Management Systems

David Mills, ANGEL™ Learning, Inc., USA

Abstract

Course management systems will unquestionably become one of the most critical enterprise systems in higher education. This is because these systems are more closely aligned with the core mission of teaching and learning than any others. Although these systems have already undergone extraordinary transformation in just a few short years, we are at only the very beginning of the evolutionary process. It is critical that CMS vendors look to the students, educators, and administrators that interact with these systems to identify what new tools and features they need. Consequently, the next stage of innovation in course management systems should therefore focus more on features specifically related to promoting better and more efficient processes for teaching and learning online. More flexible administration options should make these systems easier to maintain. Emerging standards will continue to simplify communications and data exchange with other systems. Finally, the infusion of sound principles of instructional design and learning theory into the tools themselves promises to transform today's course management systems into tomorrow's expert systems for teaching and learning.

Introduction

Course management systems (CMS) have exploded onto the scene of higher education. In the late 1990s, the course management system was a fragile, loosely coupled set of Internet-based communication tools organized to support teaching a course. Each course had its own user accounts that, in most cases, were entered manually. The systems consisted of general communication and collaboration tools that were not in any way specifically tailored to online teaching and learning. Even with these limitations, however, course management systems have become one of the fastest growing enterprise systems ever.

Today's CMS evolution has been driven by user demand. Now, students and teachers can use the same user name and password to access all their courses from a single site. In most cases, the user name is even the same for all systems. Today's CMS are also expected to automatically integrate with other enterprise systems to synchronize course catalog and enrollment data. These advances have helped to catapult CMS adoption not only for distance education courses, but also for blended learning and to complement traditional classroom courses. In its current state, the CMS space has only tapped the surface of what these systems can offer. Now that the foundational issues of accounts and roster management are in place, future evolutions of CMS will be much more interesting. They will certainly become more integrated with other institutional systems. The benefits of automated synchronization of information are significant and tangible. They will also be engineered to be more specifically dedicated to the process of teaching and learning. But, for CMS technology to continue to grow, it must find ways to save time, save money, or offer tangible benefits for teaching and learning not otherwise attainable.

To answer the question of how next-generation CMS should or will be extended to add even more value, one must consider the stakeholders of these systems and clearly identify their needs. As the market and the community it serves evolve, active listening will become an increasingly important tool in designing these systems. Only by identifying the needs of each group of stakeholders will CMS technology be propelled forward in the necessary and appropriate direction. The primary stakeholders are students taking online courses or using the CMS as a resource for their traditional classes, faculty who use the CMS to both develop and teach their courses, and the information technology (IT) administrators who support these systems. To that end, the personas that follow attempt to provide a snapshot of each group of stakeholders, what motivates them, and some of the things they want and need from a course management system.

The Student

John is an 18-year-old freshman at Sunny College. The year is 2004, and John has grown up with technology. He has been using the Internet for both fun and school work since he was 10. Hardly a day goes by that John does not chat with his online buddies. He also enjoys online gaming where he is quite comfortable using the 17-button game pad control and simultaneously chatting with his virtual teammates about the virtual world they are conquering. When he is not gaming, John is either chatting online or using the Internet to research a class project. When John does not know a word, his first thought is to go online. Using a traditional dictionary does not even cross his mind. He is used to a world that provides him what he wants when he wants it. From on-demand movies to online access to his new bank account, the virtual world is an integral part of his life. John's parents are amazed at his ability to watch a television show, instant message (IM) with friends, and do his homework simultaneously.

John was amazed at the process he had to endure when he enrolled at Sunny College. He actually had to walk to three different buildings collecting and delivering paperwork. He could not believe what a waste of time it was. It took almost five hours to enroll in four traditional and one online course. Thankfully, John is told that from this point forward he will be able to enroll online.
On the first day of classes, John learned that two of his traditional classes would make heavy use of the CMS for quizzes and homework submissions. Another of his classes would be using a stand-alone Web site not hosted in the CMS.

It took nearly a week after classes started before John was given his individual sign-on user name and password. When he was finally signed on, only three of his courses showed up. At first, he thought something must have gone wrong with his registration. He then realized that only his classes with an online presence were listed.

As a result of the delay in getting his logon information, John was behind in his online course as well as the two courses that were using the CMS for quizzing and homework submissions. His instructors were accustomed to this, so they did not penalize him. However, it still made life difficult in the second week trying to complete two weeks worth of assignments while still getting acclimated to his classes.

All four of John's courses that used the Internet required that he check the course site every day for important announcements and assignments. This quickly became a tedious task because John had to actually log in to the CMS, enter each course, exit the CMS, and then go to the Web site for the course that was using a separate site. The entire process only took about ten minutes, but John quickly grew tired of repeating the steps every day. Moreover, after three weeks of doing this, only once was there an important announcement. As a result, John became more lax and only checked three times a week. This cost him dearly when one of his instructors posted a pop quiz that was only available for one day. While frustrating, it was clearly stated that students were supposed to check the site every day, so John had no recourse.

Navigating the course sites was also a problem. The course using a stand-alone Web site had a completely different navigation system than the courses using the CMS. Even the three courses using the CMS had completely different layouts. As a result, when John needed to find lecture notes or take a quiz, it took him much longer than it should have.

At one point in the semester, John missed a day of class due to illness. It was easy enough to get the lecture notes and assignments in his courses that had a course site. However, the course that had no site was a problem. He sent an e-mail to the instructor but had not yet received a response, and he did not know a soul in the class. While he had the lecture notes from his other courses, there were still a couple of things he did not understand. For his courses on the CMS, he simply sent an e-mail to his fellow students with his questions. However, in the course with a stand-alone Web site, there was no way to communicate with his fellow students.

In general, John was pleased that most of his courses had at least some online presence. However, he felt there was room for improvement. He would have liked to be able to contact his classmates in all of his courses. He was also frustrated by the expectations some of his teachers placed on his use of the course site. It seemed like an unfair burden having to spend ten minutes every day checking for new items just in case.

Analysis of the Student Experience

We can derive from John and his experiences several important details. Today's young adults have grown up in a world where they are immersed in technology every day. They are keenly aware of the productivity technology can provide and harsh critics when technology does not effectively solve a problem. These learners will likewise have very high expectations of what a course management system can and should offer them.

System Interoperability

John's initial registration experience points to a need for better integration among and between all of a school's enterprise systems. It also points to the need for standardized formats that allow data to be electronically exchanged between institutions easily, securely, and efficiently. Imagine the time, money, and frustration that would be saved if student records could be electronically transferred from a high school directly to a college or university. Agreeing to a set of schemas for data and communication protocols would make such a solution possible.

While high schools and higher education institutions will undoubtedly have different requirements and subsequently adopt different standards, this does not mean such transparency is impossible. For example, The School Interoperability Framework (SIF)[1] is a popular K-12 framework. Higher education has been drawn more to the specifications set forth by IMS.[2] However, agreeing to a simple mapping between these two standards will allow appropriate data to be electronically transferred. These standards are still in the early stages, and adoption is not yet widespread. Some of these initiatives will undoubtedly die off or become merged with others. Once it is clear which standards will prevail and more schools begin to adopt them, tremendous potential for interoperability will begin to be realized.

Single Point of Access

Many of John's problems stemmed from the fact that not all courses used the same system and, as a result, it was difficult to keep up with his courses. This also meant that communication tools that could have proven useful were not always available. These difficulties illustrate the benefits of having a single place students can go to access all their courses. This may be a function of the course management system or could be handled by another portal application adopted at the institution. In either case, all courses should be accessible from a single access point. Kentucky Virtual University (KYVU)[3] provides such a portal for their students. KYVU instructors choose from a number of course management systems. However, when the students log on, they see all of their courses listed under the "My Courses" section of their profiles. Selecting a course takes them directly to the course on the appropriate CMS without requiring additional authentication.

Learner Productivity

John's experiences also show that next-generation course management systems should focus on minimizing the effort it takes for students to keep up-to-date with their courses. The system should deliver the appropriate information, at the appropriate time, using an appropriate channel instead of requiring students to constantly log on to check. Much of this simply has to do with the way data are organized and presented within the system. For example, in many of today's course management systems, you must not only log on to the system, but actually enter each specific course to see calendar items, announcements, and course e-mails, and to check for new discussion forum postings or assignments. Learner productivity could be greatly enhanced if learners had easy access to a unified, top-level summary of these items outside their individual courses.

Figure 1.

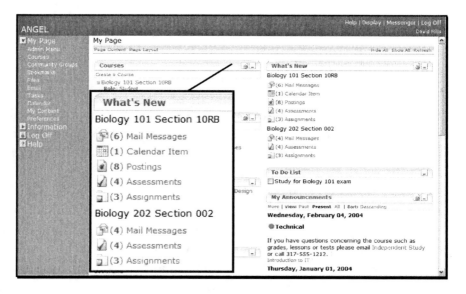

Figure 2.

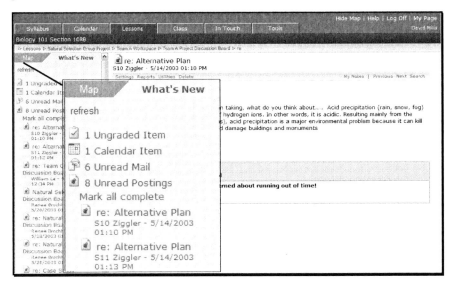

PDA Synchronization

This simple collation of information goes a long way toward making it easier for students to keep up with their courses. However, the portal page is only one medium for presenting such information. Personal digital assistants (PDAs) have become a valuable tool for both work and school. This same information could be synchronized with a learner's PDA to provide instant access to the information. With the explosion of wireless technologies, students could even access the items directly from their PDAs when necessity dictates. Automated e-mails or SMS (short message service) messages could also be sent to provide critical updates when appropriate. Of course, with so many communication channels, what is delivered, where, and when should ultimately be configurable by each individual learner.

The Instructor

Anne is a professor of biology who teaches 100-level and 200-level courses. Anne has been using the school's current course management system to post her syllabi and class notes. She taught an online course in 2002 but was disappointed. Creating the course was no small task. She had not anticipated the amount of time this would take and spent many late nights early in the semester putting her course together. She had expected to be able to easily import content from the publisher of the text she was using, but the publisher did not have content available for her CMS. Instead, she had to cut and paste, retype, and upload most of the files individually. Anne was sure she would find ample content on the Web to supplement the text. She was quickly disappointed when search after search resulted in useless materials. No doubt, there was appropriate content on the Web somewhere, but she could not find it. Anne asked a fellow biology professor who taught the same course online the previous semester if she could use some of his content. He was more than happy to oblige, but much of his content was created in the CMS system, and he could not figure out how to share it with her.

This was Anne's first attempt at creating an online course. She received no training about effective pedagogical approaches for online teaching. As a result, she fell into the same pitfall as countless others before her — ineffective and inappropriate use of the tools available. She added discussion boards, chat rooms, and more without really knowing how these tools should be used or what purpose they served.

Once Anne started actually teaching the course, she was overwhelmed by the amount of work it entailed. She had not realized how much time and effort it would be to keep up with the postings in all the discussion forums she had created. On top of that, the constant stream of mail was almost more than she could bear. Students seemed to expect her to respond immediately to every post. While Anne had dedicated a large portion of the overall grade to participation in forums, chat, and mail, she quickly realized that the reports the system provided allowed her to do little more than count the number of items each student had submitted. A qualitative review, though necessary, was not feasible given the time it would take.

Anne found having assignments submitted by e-mail was a welcome change, but the electronic drop boxes she had set up in her course had their own problems. It took far too many clicks to view and grade assignments. There was also no easy way to provide students with inline feedback to their submissions. Students also kept submitting work late, requiring her to go back and check drop boxes for assignments that were long since due.

Anne felt like she was letting her students down when she could not intervene quickly enough to get them back on track. Twice as many students dropped her online class as her traditional class, and teaching it consumed significantly more of her time. The lack of personal interaction made it difficult to identify students at risk. The fact that the reports available in the CMS were not well suited to the task of assessing students exacerbated the problem. Anne also grew tired of writing the same e-mail ten times for ten different students, and grading work submitted online by her students was a laborious task that required far too many clicks. In addition, some of her students had significant problems learning the CMS. Anne often felt more like a technical support person than she did a teacher.

At the end of the semester, Anne was disappointed to learn that her final grades could not be submitted through the CMS. Though all of her students' final grades were already in the online grade book, Anne was forced to transcribe them manually onto the official final grade submission form to provide to the registrar.

The next semester Anne opted not to teach any online courses. It was just too much work, and she did not feel she could adequately engage her students. Anne's experience online did, however, illustrate how effective the Internet can be for low-stakes assessments such as weekly quizzes. It was also a little easier to manage assignments submitted online instead of on paper. As a result, Anne chose to continue using electronic methods for homework submissions and low-stakes assessment even in her traditional courses. But when Anne completed an online section of one of her courses and wanted to re-use some of the items from that section in her next semester's traditional courses, she was disappointed to learn that the CMS had no easy way for her to re-use bits and pieces of the course. Her only option was to download the entire course as an archive on her computer and then import the entire course into each of her new sections. This was a painfully long process because the course had a number of high-resolution images of cells that were huge. The export file was nearly 200 megabytes compressed. It took her hours to transfer the materials into each new section and then delete two-thirds of what she had just imported.

Analysis of the Instructor Experience

Anne is representative of many of today's instructors. She is motivated to provide a rich learning experience for her students but feels hamstrung by the technology. As with the student experience, many instructor issues could be resolved simply by providing the appropriate data in the appropriate context. This task-oriented approach dictates that the system conform to the user and the task he or she is trying to accomplish.

Data Filtering and Presentation

Consider, for example, the data that is collected from an online quiz. Most of today's course management systems simply provide a listing of the submissions to the quiz and their respective grades. With such a view, it is extremely difficult to answer questions such as how many people scored less than 70, or who did worse on this quiz than they did on the last one? These data are far more useful when they are filtered and transformed to deal with the particular task at hand.

When instructors are ready to grade manually graded items such as essay questions or drop box submissions, all they really want to see are those items that have not yet been graded. Furthermore, if all the responses to a particular essay or drop box were grouped together, the task of grading would be that much easier. At some other point in time, an instructor will undoubtedly want to assess an individual learner. In this case, it would be beneficial to have all of the learner's quiz scores listed graphically, ordered by completion date, and compared to the class average as illustrated in Figure 3. With such a presentation, the instructor would immediately understand how the student has been performing. On the day following an exam, the instructor will undoubtedly want to see which students had trouble with the exam and are subsequently at risk. In this case, it would be helpful if the instructor could easily see a list of those students who did not perform at or above a specified threshold as depicted in Figure 4. Once identified, it is likely the instructor will want to contact these students, assign them some remedial content, or take another appropriate action.

All of the above cases deal with the same quiz data. However, by filtering the data and changing how they are presented, they become far more useful with far less effort. The ANGEL™ system contains a number of tools designed around this framework. The "Learner Profile" provides an easy way to assess individual learners, while the he "WhoDunIt" agent allows instructors to query for people who have or have not completed item X or scored at least Y on item Z and send an appropriate message. The "What's New" agent identifies submissions that need to be graded. Lastly, the "Actions and Triggers" framework allows the instructor to automate the delivery of messages, release of content, and more in response to user performance and interaction with the system.

While these tools are a great start, much more can be done. With the volumes of data CMS can handle, the potential exists for truly intelligent systems. Agents can be developed that understand the relationships between data elements, can derive information automatically, and make it available to the appropriate people at the appropriate time. When considering such solutions, it is important to balance the automation of the system with the autonomy of the instructor. Consider, for example a learner assessment agent. Instead of requiring the instructor to review the progress of all students in the course, such an agent could highlight those students who fall outside an acceptable range of performance on one or more items. But, what is an acceptable range of performance and who defines it? A reasonable guess would be to inform the instructor when a student scores below a 70 percent on an item. However, what if this is a

Figure 3.

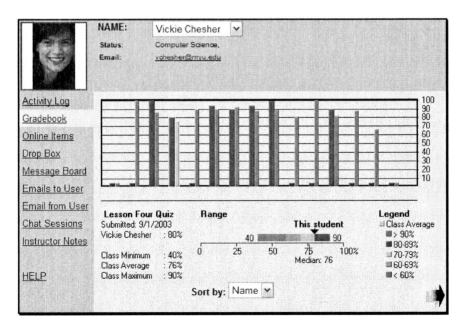

Figure 4.

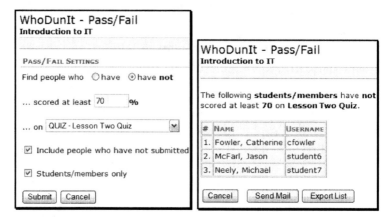

physics class and the mean score was a 40? Or, what if the instructor wants to intervene when a student scores anything less than an 80? These questions illustrate that, while it may be acceptable to make some default assumptions, those parameters should ultimately be configurable by the end user to meet his or her specific needs.

Features Specific to Teaching and Learning

Another issue in using CMS is illustrated by Anne's experience with the course drop box. For the most part, the tools available in today's course management systems were not originally designed for teaching and learning. As a result, many features that would be useful in a teaching and learning context are either underdeveloped or missing altogether. Consider, for example, threaded discussion tools. The ability to identify the type of message being posted, such as an assertion or rebuttal, is missing from most of these systems, though the benefit in a teaching and learning context is evident. Likewise, the ability to model different types of discussions such as "the hot seat" or "fish bowl" is either difficult or impossible. The current drop box functionalities in many of today's systems also have some deficiencies because they were modeled after the shared file spaces often used for such purposes before the advent of the CMS, rather than modeling the solution based on the actual work flow of homework submission and grading. As these systems mature, these tools will naturally become more specialized to the task of teaching and learning. Additionally, new tools will surely be introduced that facilitate other teaching and learning tasks.

Domain-Specific Tool Sets

It should also be recognized that some departments, such as mathematics and the languages, will need access to highly specialized tools. The next generation of course management systems will need to do a much better job at providing appropriate tool sets based on the type of course, its department, and other such criteria. Consider the following example. The math department has three advanced quizzing tools they want accessible in the CMS. The language department has two tools specifically for creating language exercises. The biology department has a virtual lab tool they want to integrate. None of these tools serves any practical purposes outside the context of their particular domains. If all of these tools are made available to all courses, the interface will be so crowded and confusing that faculty will quickly become frustrated. The other choice is not to integrate these tools at all, which would dramatically reduce the usefulness of the system for faculty in these departments. If the system can provide these tools only to those courses with which the department is associated, adoption could occur within these departments without affecting the usability of the system for others.

ANGELÔ has some support for this capability through its support for custom extensions, custom objects, and environment variables. Using these capabilities, the system can be customized so different options appear under the "Add Content" menu for a particular course. While the current capabilities make such customizations possible, more can be done to make these customizations practical. Imagine a system in which you could simply select the tools you wanted to use for a course from a categorized menu. In addition to domain-specific tools, tools that promote specific learning theories could be made available. Custom systems developed at the institutions could be seamlessly integrated. You could even set up your default preferences, so any course could be customized to your preferences with a single click. This may sound farfetched, but it is actually just around the corner. This level of customization is critical if enterprise-level course management systems are going to be adopted by departments with very specific needs.

System Interoperability

The inability of the CMS to export grades to the registrar system illustrates another area where the next-generation course management systems couldn't offer improvement. An institution should be able to easily and securely pass such data between its enterprise systems using standardized communication protocols and data structures. The IMS Enterprise specification currently offers support for representing much of the required data for such operations. New standards are also emerging for communication protocols to be used for the actual passing of data between systems. Web-based simple object access protocol (SOAP) services are at the core of most of these emerging standards.

Content Re-use

Re-use of content is yet another key area where future versions of course management systems can make great strides. Instructors managing multiple sections of a course are currently subjected to the task of manually replicating content across these courses. Semester transitions are another problem area in this respect. As richer content is developed, institutions increasingly want to share these resources across larger segments of the university such as departments, schools, or campuses. One example currently available in ANGELÔ is the ability to create question banks in a departmental resource library. These questions are then available for use on quizzes in any course offered by the department. In this way, the same questions can be made available to multiple sections of the same course or even altogether different courses. Projects such as Merlot (*www.merlot.org*) are currently developing global resource repositories of valuable content that could be used by these systems. Future systems must find ways to address these needs.

Course Management System Integration

Some vendors have opted to integrate resource sharing functionality in the CMS. While this solution may work for simple resources such as graphics, documents, and Web pages, it may prove problematic when dealing with more advanced resources such as quizzes and communication tools. Moreover, a solution based on a content management system will most likely never be able to support global repositories.

ANGEL™ currently supports a flexible resource library system that allows advanced resources such as quizzes, discussion boards, and even entire modules to be shared across course sections, departments, schools, campuses, or the entire system. Experience with this feature has helped to highlight where special consideration needs to be given when sharing such resources. For example, should library administrators be able to view and manage all responses to a quiz? What access to managing results should instructors have in a course that links to a quiz? Where should results be stored? When should results be purged and by whom? Unfortunately, the answer to all of these questions is that it depends. The details of responses to a course evaluation should most likely not be available to the instructors in the individual courses. Alternately, the results and submissions to a quiz should be managed by the individual course instructors, perhaps exclusively. The next generation of systems will need to be able to support such nuances to maximize the utility of such resources.

Library System Integration

Another way content re-use can be improved is by providing better integration with library systems. Some universities, such as Penn State, have been able to achieve tight integration between their course management system and their library system. In fact, in Penn State's case, librarians even use the CMS to author collections of resources for courses, departments, and schools. However, there are currently no accepted standards for generalizing such integration. Simply adopting a global authentication system such as Shibboleth® or Pubcookie would allow a much higher level of integration than is currently possible. While some course management systems, such as ANGELÔ, can be configured to use such a global authentication model, the value only comes when other systems support it as well.

Global Resource Sharing

In addition to better support for internal sharing of resources systems, better support for sharing resources globally is an inevitable requirement. This is really only now becoming possible, thanks to the emergence of standards that will allow interoperability of disparate systems. IMS has developed specifications for digital repositories and Web services that offer promise in this area.

Shibboleth[4] is a promising candidate for a global authentication and authorization solution. Other standards are emerging to help with intellectual property rights issues. As these and other standards become more widely adopted, the vision of secure global repositories will become a reality. Thanks to still other standards such as SCORM,[5] QTI,[6] and the IMS Learning Design[7] specification, it should be possible to share even the richest content in platform-neutral formats.

Digital Rights Management

Better support for digital rights management will be essential in promoting the re-use of content across boundaries of courses, departments, schools, and institutions. It is essential that the appropriate copyright and fair use information stay with an asset as the asset is used in these different contexts. Not only should systems preserve this information, they should be able to analyze it and act upon it accordingly when requests are received to view, reference, or copy the asset.

Infusing Instructional Design Principles into Content Creation Tool Sets

Just as the tools delivered by course management systems need to be designed more specifically for teaching and learning, so too should the tools and interfaces for creating the content. One example of this specification raised at the 2003 National Learning Infrastructure Initiative (NLII) focus session on next-generation course management systems is infusing instructional design principles and learning theory into the content creation tools themselves. This would undoubtedly result in the creation of better content by a majority of faculty. Just imagine — an instructor clicks the link to add a discussion forum to his or her course and is prompted with background information on effective use of forums and a series of questions about what he or she wants to accomplish. After answering these questions, a new discussion forum is created with appropriate settings. The instructor has learned about how to effectively use forums and has had the settings adjusted for his or her particular objective with a minimum of effort.

Now imagine the instructor needs to create a new forum for each of the twenty teams in the course. That useful information and series of questions will become very old in short order. Moreover, what learning theory should be used? Should this be up to the vendor? Should it be institutionally defined or be left up to the instructor? These questions illustrate that any such integration must be accompanied by a degree of flexibility. Instructors should have easy access to the assistance when they want it, but should not be burdened by it when they do not. Likewise, the environment should be flexible enough to support a variety of learning theories and allow wizards to be customized or extended as they see fit. An instructor could have the option of specifying his or her preferred learning theory and subsequently be directed to wizards that are consistent with that theory.

Recent releases of ANGEL$^{\hat{O}}$ provide the hooks for adding some such custom extensions. The "Add Content" page of the lessons section can be extended to include template and wizards sections. Moreover, which items are displayed under this section can be customized based on the course being accessed or the individual accessing the tool.

The IT Administrator

Frank has been a system administrator for 10 years. The university where Frank works has about 8,000 students and 500 faculty members. Frank started as a server administrator in the School of Business, where he maintained the departmental servers. The business school was an early adopter of course management software, and Frank handled all the details of maintaining the system. When the university decided to implement an enterprise course management system in 1999, Frank was transferred to IT services with a promotion and put in charge of the new enterprise initiative. While pleased with the promotion and honored to have been selected, Frank sometimes wonders if it was worth it. Frank never imagined there could be so many issues involved in maintaining a single system. Before the first class was added to the system, committee meetings were held for weeks trying to resolve issues related to the Family Educational Rights and Privacy Act, single sign on, account management, course catalog synchronization, and enrollment synchronization.

The registrar took a very strict interpretation of the act, commonly known as FERPA, and decided that students should not see other students unless they explicitly give their consent. Unfortunately, this capability was not possible with the CMS. As a result, the school had to disable all features that allow students to see fellow classmates.

Due to limitations of both the registrar system and the CMS, the process for synchronizing both course catalog and enrollment information is extremely complicated. Every night the system is synchronized with the latest course catalog and enrollment information from the student information system. Special handling is required for cross-listed courses, nonstandard schedule courses, and lecture/lab combination courses. A batch job extracts the necessary information from the student information system and writes it to text files. The files are then transferred to another machine where a scheduled script processes the files and imports the data into the CMS. The process is not pretty, but it works, usually.

The number of restores he has had to do to recover data accidentally deleted by instructors has frustrated Frank. Usually the problem is that an instructor accidentally removed a student from his or her course, which subsequently deletes all data associated with that student. Sometimes, it is an important discussion forum or quiz that has been deleted along with the associated responses. In either case, the recovery process takes far too long. Frank must restore an earlier version of the huge database to another system, log on to the course, export it, and import it back into the production system. If the deletion just occurred, the course is restored over the current production course. If the deletion happened some time ago, the restoration is done to an alternate course, and the instructor must manually transfer the appropriate information.

In addition to doing database restores, Frank spends a lot of time running custom reports for the provosts and deans of various departments. The system is very limited in its ability to retrieve the specific data he wants. As a result, Frank spends hours massaging and filtering the data in Excel to get it into an acceptable format. Frank knows he could extract the information he needs directly from the database, but the licensing prohibits this.

Many of the management and administration tasks that Frank does on the CMS could actually be done by other staff members. The problem is that the CMS does not allow Frank to specify that a user should have some administrative rights and not others. As a result, it is just too risky to give administrative rights to these additional staff members.

The start of a new semester is always frantic. There are always around 100 new accounts that, for whatever reason, are not correctly synchronized with the CMS. Frank also gets a number of support tickets from faculty and students about users not showing up in this section or that. Occasionally, this is a hiccup in the system. More often, users do not show up because they are not officially enrolled, they have not paid their tuition, or the instructor has simply not activated the course for student access. Another recurring theme is that the wrong instructor is listed as the faculty of record for a course. When this happens, the system enrolls the wrong instructor as an editor, and Frank is responsible for manually overriding to correct this situation.

The university policy is to archive courses that are more than two semesters old. This responsibility also falls on Frank. The system has some tools for archiving and deleting courses, but they could stand some improvement. The task is made much more complicated by the nonstandard schedule and open enrollment courses that are hosted on the system. Before Frank runs the scripts to delete old courses, he must manually review the list and remove these courses. Invariably, he misses one or two and ends up having to do a system restore to the courses.

Analysis of IT Administrator Experience

Frank's experience illustrates that there is room for improvement on the administration side of these systems as well. The FERPA issues make visible that each institution will have its own policies, procedures, guidelines, and requirements. Any enterprise system should adapt and conform to these requirements rather than require the institution to conform to the system. If the system is not flexible enough, institutions will choose not to use it, in whole or in part.

Support for Standards for Data Interchange and Communication

The issues surrounding the synchronization of the CMS with the registrar and other enterprise systems indicate the need for better support of standards for data interchange and communication. Several such standards exist, but many products have yet to support them. The IMS Enterprise specification is probably the most widely supported standard for exchange of these types of data. However, IMS has only recently begun addressing which communication channel systems should be used to send the data. As standards organizations extend these specifications and standards are more widely adopted, the data synchronization process will be significantly simplified.

Roster Synchronization

The reference to cross-listed courses highlights an important detail when dealing with this data. The data stored in the student information system and other registrar systems may not be in an optimal format for the content management system. Sometimes a course is cross-listed because it is offered under two or more departments. Other times the course is cross-listed because it is offered on both a standard track and an honors level. Combined lectures and labs are sometimes listed as a single section and other times are listed separately. These variances exist to support distinctions required by degree audit systems and the like. They are problematic when synchronizing the data with a CMS. If the cross-listing of a course is simply a matter of it being listed under two departments, it should most likely appear as a single course section in the CMS. However, if the course is listed as a standard track and an honors track, an instructor may choose to have these sections represented distinctly within the CMS. Likewise, a lecture/lab combination may need to be treated as a single section in the CMS or could potentially need to be treated as two separate spaces in the system.

CMS vendors must begin to address these tricky issues to minimize the customization required when implementing synchronization solutions. By dealing with these exceptions as part of the CMS rather than the synchronization process, the synchronization process is simplified to the point where standardized solutions are possible. The ANGELÔ Merged Roster Manager shown in Figure 5 is an example of this sychronization. This tool provides instructors the ability to treat multiple courses in the student information system as a single section in the CMS or create a new section in the CMS based on the enrollment information of multiple sections in the SIS data. For example, if 13 students are enrolled in a course under a standard track, and three are enrolled under the honors track, the instructor can configure the CMS to have all the students appear in a single course space. Moreover, as students are added or dropped in the standard or honors sections, the roster in the merged course is automatically updated. Alternately, if multiple lab sections share a common lecture, the instructor can create a common lecture section that is associated with one or more lab sections so a user enrolled in any lab section is automatically enrolled in the common lecture section.

The roster synchronization issue is just one example of a situation in which course management systems need to be more flexible and tolerant of exceptions

Figure 5.

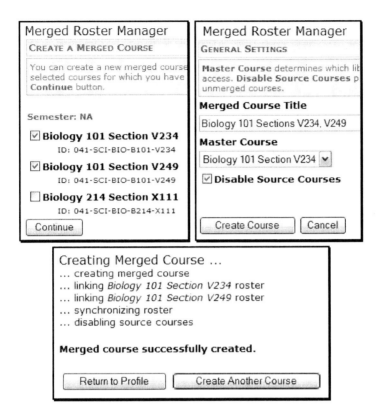

than other enterprise systems. Another example is allowing nonstudents to access a course. In a traditional classroom setting, when instructors want to use course assistants or invite guest lecturers to speak to the class, they do so at their own discretion. A course management system should be capable of affording this same luxury to instructors in the online world. Furthermore, systems should be able to support this level of flexibility regardless of whether the students in the course were added manually or through synchronization with another system. For the most part, the course management system is a consumer of integration data rather than a publisher. In the few exceptions to this rule, such as reporting of final grades back to the registrar system, the process should be structured to ensure that only valid entries are made back to the other system.

Data Recovery

Recovery of data is another area in which course management systems need improvement. Most enterprise systems restrict access to changing or deleting the data in the system to a very tightly controlled, highly trained group of users. How many people have rights to add or delete courses in the registrar system? How many people have rights to officially enroll or unenroll users in a course section? How many people have rights to delete a user's e-mail account? More than likely, the answer to each of these questions is very few. Contrarily, course management systems have hundreds of faculty only marginally trained on the system who have the ultimate power to delete content and remove users from a course. With some course management systems, the removal of a user from a course even deletes all of the submissions and data associated with that user. Course management systems need to consider this difference. Systems could flag items as deleted rather than physically deleting them and only purge the data when instructed by a system administrator. Alternately, systems could automatically back up data when appropriate, so data administrators or even course editors could restore the data with far less effort than is currently required.

Distribution of Administrative Responsibilities

Many of today's course management systems offer little or no flexibility with respect to the administrative features of the system. To allow institutions to effectively distribute responsibilities without exposing themselves to unnecessary risks, these systems need to allow much more granular control over the assignment of administrative features. For example, it should be possible to grant users the right to create and manage courses without also granting them administration rights. Likewise, these systems should support administrators at the campus, school, and department levels that have access to administrative tools for only the appropriate subset of users and courses.

Open Systems

Frank's issues with custom reports are directly attributable to the closed and proprietary nature of many of today's course management systems. In the future, course management systems should strive to be as open as possible.

There will always be unforeseen requirements or requirements that apply to such a small set of users they are not practical to implement. If vendors design course management systems in a manner that allows low-level access to the data they contain, institutions are empowered to address these issues on their own. By providing deeper access into the system, institutions should be able to develop custom-tailored solutions that meet their specific needs. In addition to low-level access, higher-level interfaces should be provided that allow customizations to be written in a manner that requires little or no modification when transitioning from one version of the software to the next.

Conclusion

Course management systems have rapidly evolved from fragile experimental systems to indispensable enterprise applications. Most of the enhancements to course management systems to date have been concerned with meeting the foundational requirements of an enterprise system. Now that these underpinnings are in place, course management systems can begin to focus on features specifically related to promoting better and more efficient processes for teaching and learning online. It is therefore critical that CMS vendors look to the stakeholders in these systems to identify what new tools and features are needed. Having considered the personas of John the student, Anne the educator, and Frank the administrator, it is clear much more can be done to accommodate these users.

Course management systems will unquestionably become one of the most critical enterprise systems in higher education. This is because these systems are more closely aligned with the core mission of teaching and learning than any others. Although these systems have already undergone extraordinary transformation in just a few short years, we are at only the very beginning of the evolutionary process. These systems will become more sophisticated as they are continually refined to meet the unique needs of teaching and learning. Infusion of sound principles of instructional design and learning theory into the tools themselves will help transform today's course management systems into tomorrow's expert systems for teaching and learning. Emerging standards will continue to simplify communications and data exchange with other systems. More flexible administration options should make these systems easier to maintain.

Endnotes

1   *http://www.sifinfo.org*

2   *http://imsproject.org*

3   *http://www.kyvu.org/home.htm*

4   *http://shibboleth.internet2.edu*

5   *http://www.adlnet.org/*

6   *http://www.imsglobal.org/question/index.cfm*

7   *http://www.imsglobal.org/learningdesign/index.cfm*

Chapter XX

From Course Management Systems to Open Frameworks and a Sustainable Ecology of Educational Systems

Vijay Kumar, Massachusetts Institute of Technology, USA

Jeff Merriman, Massachusetts Institute of Technology, USA

Abstract

We propose a trajectory for learning technology systems that represent a departure from closed, monolithic approaches, typically inherent in the design of these systems, to open, standards-based frameworks that can support diverse pedagogy and accommodate heterogeneous technology. Central to this vision is an architectural approach, illustrated by the Open Knowledge Initiative, which supports the development of sustainable educational tools and technology through enabling commoditization and community.

Introduction

We believe that course management systems as we know them are an idea whose time has come and gone. This statement of ours seems to fly in the face of the increasing use of course management systems (CMS) in higher education (Green, 2004). Indeed, the first years of the 21st century have seen a dramatic upsurge in the preoccupation with these "platforms" and systems for supporting course administration, class management, content posting, and communications.

But along with the data that marks the rise in the use of CMS come frequently expressed concerns about their cost and sustainability. Even more significant is the widely expressed recognition that these systems are not "educationally" useful beyond the relief from course administration drudgery that they provide.

We propose a trajectory for learning technology software that represents a departure from closed, monolithic approaches to open, standards-based frameworks that can support diverse pedagogy and accommodate heterogeneous technology implementations. Central to this trajectory is an architectural approach that supports the development of sustainable educational tools by enabling commoditization and community engagement. We will draw upon the design and development aspects of the Open Knowledge Initiative[1] in describing this architectural approach.

The Problem: A Push for a Different Perspective and Products

A look at the issues underlying the design and development of educational applications helps us understand some of the reasons for the limited educational value of these systems and their fragile viability. These issues include limited flexibility to meet changing academic needs, costly integration with the academic enterprise, and, even more importantly, reduced ability for institutions to share educational applications or to collaborate on their development. These limitations have been amply evident in CMS, a class of applications that have become commonplace in higher education. In this chapter, we use the terms CMS, learning management system (LMS), and virtual learning environment (VLE) interchangeably.

Commercial or even homegrown, institutional CMS products provide comprehensive tool sets but are typically designed to support general educational technology needs and not to meet the needs of sophisticated users or specialized use. As Hal Abelson (2002), professor of computer science at the Massachusetts Institute of Technology, noted, "While these systems present a low threshold for entry, the threshold for exit is steep." Course management systems have indeed been serving a very important function in that they have created a very low barrier to entry for universities and faculty mounting course material. However, technical design aspects limit the portability and interoperability of learning resources and consequently inhibit the kind of flexibility that leads to support of diverse pedagogy and sharing of learning materials. For example, the tight coupling of the user interface to learning components (as in a monolithic learning management system) constrains the ability for learning objects to be used in different contexts or to address different learning goals. With faculty becoming more sophisticated about the use of educational technology in teaching, something more is required. It is also not uncommon to hear faculty lament about the difficulty of incorporating simple or complex tools, that they have used successfully, into the CMS environment.

Even setting aside instructional effectiveness, most academic products on the market were initially conceived as solutions for departments, or even for single courses. Their underlying architectures did not anticipate the need to scale to many thousands of students and to smoothly integrate with student information, financial, human resources, and other institutional systems, or to easily incorporate new tools and functionality from a variety of sources.

Most critically, the price of CMS has been rising, not only for the software itself. Anecdotal evidence indicates that some campuses have written more lines of code to integrate campus systems with these products than there were lines of code in the vendor's system. The alternative massive, customized, in-house development brings with it not only cost, but also an increased risk of a system failure. It also induces reduced flexibility to adapt to changes in enterprise technologies, educational tools, and infrastructure services.

A Solution Strategy:
The O.K.I. Approach

It was this set of circumstances and observations that motivated us to launch the Open Knowledge Initiative (O.K.I.). The original expressed goal of the project was to address these issues by identifying, designing, and packaging "a set of Web-enabled learning components that [would] be of service to the widest range of educational environments" (OKI, 2000). O.K.I. aimed to create an open-source product providing LMS functionality that allowed easy and affordable customization, sharing of educational programs within and between institutions, and inexpensive integration into existing university infrastructure.

During the initial requirements-gathering efforts of O.K.I., considerable discussion and deliberation were devoted to how these ambitious project goals of enabling interoperable, flexible, and pedagogically relevant educational software could best be achieved. Input from numerous stakeholders validated the perception that higher education leaders were looking to reduce the cost and complexity of system integration while ensuring that their learning systems were built on a reliable, modular, and scalable foundation that would allow them to meet the diverse needs of teaching and learning. These leaders were also looking for a variety of avenues for acquiring and supporting such software. While some were eager to embrace open-source opportunities, others were more comfortable with solutions that relied entirely on products from the traditional commercial sector.

The need for educational technology to conform to emergent international learning technology specifications and standards was also generally acknowledged and reinforced throughout the requirements-gathering phase of the project. The standards of the day, however, were only designed to promote interoperability of learning content and other data used by educational software. The specifications and standards community had not addressed how to achieve portability of software within and among educational frameworks and enterprise systems. Therefore, even as these standards were gaining acceptance worldwide, it became clear early on that they were completely inadequate to meet the goals of O.K.I. in terms of application portability, interoperability, integration, and sharing.

This was not just a minor roadblock to achieving the goals of the higher education e-learning community; it was a canyon that had to be crossed. Without such standards, no open-source LMS, or other software for that matter, could do any better at meeting higher education's demanding requirements than had already been achieved. To have a lasting effect and to best address the requirements of the domain, it was decided that the primary project goal of O.K.I. must shift from delivering an open-source product providing LMS functionality to defining and promoting the appropriate architectural specifications and standards that could redefine the domain. This task would be far more difficult than the original one outlined in the proposal we submitted to the Mellon Foundation.[2] It would, however, offer the best hope for achieving far-reaching impacts on educational technology.

The primary goal of O.K.I., therefore, became the design and development of an open and extensible architectural specification for learning management systems and other educational software. From this foundation, it was hoped that O.K.I. would achieve far more than open-source code for traditional CMS functions by supporting an ecology for educational applications that would be transformational in its impact.

The Opportunity: A Pull Toward Innovation and Sustainable Educational Impact

To understand what will make CMS or equivalent educational technology platforms attractive, it is important to recognize the critical, catalytic role of faculty in spawning educational technology innovations. Innovation in the area of educational technology tools and techniques is largely driven by individual faculty developing solutions to address particular problems and opportunities, not by institutional edicts or large, golden visions of a better world. Many of today's educational software products, from simulations to sets of tools to facilitate computation and visualization, demonstrate this pattern.

An approach that allows these innovative products to be easily incorporated into a common platform to extend their value, and also make the development task more efficient, would leverage this tendency. The approach embraced by O.K.I. highlights several preferred and transformational attributes of educational applications. *Preferred attributes* include:

- Enabled support for diverse pedagogy.
- A shift in the locus of control in influencing design from systems administrators and technologists to academic clients.
- Enabled and supported choice by the users.
- Support proximity between *research* and *teaching/learning.*
- Sustainability, through pedagogical and technological diversity, and a pathway to commoditization.
- Coherence and efficiency in managing the content life cycle.

It is not difficult to identify useful features and functionality that these systems should provide. They are presented in the advertised list of features of several products in this space. They have also been described in reports from focus groups and institutional surveys that have been undertaken by projects such as O.K.I. and organizations such as Eduprise[3] and the Western Cooperative for Educational Telecommunications (WCET).[4]

However, beyond these, two critical attributes need to be considered in the design, development, and selection of these platforms for them to be attractive to education: *choice* and *sustainability.* Achieving these preferred attributes would require deconstructing the traditional LMS and adopting an architectural approach.

Choice

Enabling and supporting choice is an essential goal in light of some "givens" of the nature of technology and educational environments:

- Educational value is derived through multiple modes and diverse tools. For example, an instructor might want to support a class with a sophisticated simulation engine and a rather ordinary discussion list while administering tests on paper. Or a faculty member might want only online testing, but require tests that include complex mathematical notation and that integrate with client-based algebra software. Typically, current learning management solutions are all-in-one packages whose components offer a single level of functionality designed for widespread use.

- The technologies on which we build our infrastructure will necessarily change. In the near term, educational software frameworks must foster a marketplace of tools and content, both proprietary and open source, so that educational service providers in institutions of higher education can pick and choose the functionality that best meets the needs of their customers.

In the long term, this level of choice must be driven all the way to the customer. To achieve far-reaching impact, educational materials and software must become commoditized on a relatively granular level. Educators and students alike should have the ability to build, borrow, or buy functionality that offers them the most value. The tools, or applications, for teaching and learning should be as mobile as the people who use them, which requires that the concept of "learning management systems" must be completely rethought.

Initial work in this area — such as that of Advanced Distributed Learning[5] and its sponsorship of SCORM[6] and IMS[7] — have led to some common definitions and standards for data interchange. New specifications coming out of O.K.I. and elsewhere are providing the next level of interoperability and integration definitions required to build a flexible and viable e-learning marketplace. -

Sustainability

The key considerations for sustainability are cost, complexity, and enduring value. Heterogeneous innovation and technology change, both vital ingredients of a rich educational technology ecosystem, are challenging in terms of all these considerations. As already mentioned, the costs of integrating CMS with other enterprise systems is high. The approach embraced by O.K.I. is designed to mitigate these costs by embracing a component-based approach that relies on loose and lightweight but well-defined contracts to enable hooks to common infrastructure services.

The interface methods defined by O.K.I. support the ongoing integration of three general categories of software:

- *Learning applications* ranging from individual quizzing, authoring, and collaboration tools to suites of such tools that include course management and learning management capabilities.

- *Central administrative systems* such as student information, human resource, and directory management.

- *Academic systems,* including library information systems and digital repositories of research and educational materials.

The intent is to make it easier for campus and commercial developers to produce software that will work in higher education's infrastructures to satisfy diverse educational needs. By providing a stable, scalable base that supports the flexibility needed by higher education, O.K.I. offers an approach that may help us to produce and share high-quality courseware and to construct enterprise applications more cost-effectively and efficiently.

Beyond fine-grained application portability and modularity, which has been the focus of O.K.I., another challenge significantly impedes the ability of educational communities to quickly adapt to new and interesting models of educational engagement. Over the past few years, faculty have begun to push the limits of educational infrastructures, from end-user support to instructional systems and design to software development services. The information technology (IT) and educational technology units at our academic institutions are striving to find better and quicker ways to meet these demands. A growing requirement, one that continues to face significant bottlenecks, is the ability to rapidly develop new software applications in response to dynamically increasing sophistication among our clients. This is not to be confused with rapid prototyping, which involves creating demonstrations of expressed functionality. It has to do with rapidly developing robust enterprise applications that are ready for production deployment on short notice.

This requires technologies, methodologies, and processes that allow educational technologists to quickly and easily describe, develop, and assemble components into new applications and tools. It also requires tools that let faculty and students easily assemble and configure functionality without depending on skilled developers.

Untangling From the Web:
Beyond Browsers

LMS environments, with a few exceptions, typically refer to a Web-centered experience for managing, authoring, and delivering these functionalities. During the 1990s, browser-based computing eclipsed other software development activity. The dot-com boom was fueled by, and in turn fanned, the flames of the technologies of the Web, such as HTTP and HTML. The Web promised to integrate our computer experience into one window on the world — the browser. The Web also "channeled" educational technology, like almost every other domain of enterprise computing.

Reflecting on the past 15 years of educational technology, those of us whose educational technology careers pre-date the dot-com era will assert that educational technology didn't begin with the Web. Prior to HTTP, HTML, and browsers, there was a considerable amount of interesting and pedagogically relevant activity occurring with computers in teaching and learning. The heady early days of Mosaic and other early Web activity also brought the belief that the browser was the new operating system, solving most if not all of the problems posed by a diverse technological world — software distribution, version control, systems integration, systems distribution and so on. It appeared that the future of the computing experience had arrived. It was widely believed that the operating system, and enterprise systems for that matter, had been tamed and that, given time, all of the richness of full-blown desktop applications would be subsumed and improved upon by the Web. But this vision has not materialized. Many attempts have been made to push the limits of browsers with technologies such as Flash™ and JavaScript™ but with limited success.

The general software marketplace is already moving beyond the browser. Apple™'s iTunes™ is illustrative in this regard. While other contenders for the online music download market sought to leverage the "tried and true" browser approach, Apple™ realized that to best achieve technological "harmony," a new application was required. This new application needed to serve as the bridge between the client and resources on the Internet. Likewise, chat applications, like AOL Messenger™ and iChat™, are other examples of tools for which the preference is for a client-based, rather than browser-based, user experience.

The challenge today is to leverage a broad range of loosely coupled applications, browser or client-based, both commercial and open source, that are best suited for the function and context. But these tools must integrate with other educational applications, including those of the traditional LMS.

Towards a Sustainable Ecology

The ecological metaphor that is being increasingly invoked is indeed appropriate to describe the complex, interrelated interactions of sectors, products, and services for technology-enabled education. There are a few key interrelated considerations that we believe will advance the sustainability of this ecology, namely, commoditization and services, diversity in products and participants, and the enablement of innovation.

We should make it increasingly possible to take advantage of widely available "commodity" tools and render them relevant and useful in meeting the special needs of the educational context rather than building special products. Conversely, we should provide a pathway to commoditize products that are created to meet needs unmet by currently available tools.

The terms CMS, LMS, and VLE (virtual learning environments), like so many other computing-related terms, are artificial constructs. They refer simply to collections of functionality that have been identified as useful for supporting educational activity. These systems have come about not because there was some great need for a new breed of software application that would meet the "rigorous" demands of education. The typical LMS/VLE suite of functionality is, in fact, pretty mundane. It includes, primarily, applications for easily creating and aggregating content for consumption within an educational context — necessary, but hardly sufficient to be considered a platform for teaching and learning. In fact, the usefulness to the educational context is brought about by add-on applications including those for communication among teachers and learners in time-tested ways, such as chat rooms and discussion forums, tools for sharing and collaborating on documents, and applications for creating quizzes and tests for assessing the knowledge of the learner. More advanced systems offer applications for creating and managing workflows or learning pathways.

Few of these application objectives, if any, are especially new. Word processors, presentation tools, and Web site development tools have been around for quite some time, making it easier for the producers and aggregators of content to make that content available quickly and easily. Communications tools for chat and bulletin board environments have been around almost as long as the Internet itself, allowing for various forms of synchronous and asynchronous communication among people. The same can be said of personal organization software, which has allowed us to group people in our work and other activities for various purposes. Similarly, tools and infrastructure for collaboration including the peer-to-peer file systems introduced early on as AppleTalk™ services for Macintoshes and highly distributed file systems, such as Andrews File System™ have also been present.

The drawback of these widely available technologies from the perspective of educational relevance is that they do not readily integrate with the educational context in useful ways. The traditional CMS, by comparison, usually provides mechanisms for managing and grouping users of the system so that they can engage in the same educational context together. They also provide content repository functionality for managing learning assets in ways that allow for the educational value of the content to be described and realized. Consider, for instance, if popular, commercially available chat tools could directly leverage existing user data and security infrastructure and automatically create user groupings based on the enrollment in courses within an educational enterprise. As another example, what if Microsoft Word® or your favorite document editor opened files directly from an institutional digital repository of domain-specific content and stored edited files directly back into such repositories as easily as opening and saving files to a local hard disk. From campus security systems to digital libraries, from student information systems to enterprise calendaring and workflow, infrastructure services are quickly becoming available to realize a new level of systematized educational software, one that derives the educational context from the fabric of the overall computing environment and does not have to rely on special applications, including CMS.

The educational technology software of the future must be built from the perspective of enterprise infrastructure. It must be based on an open and modular framework that can be used by institutional developers and software vendors and that meets the needs of entire campuses, individual departments, and even single courses. And they must be based on international standards that are being used by formal educational systems around the world. The architectural approach advanced by O.K.I. is moving us to an era where commoditized, widely available software can readily become the tools of education that co-exist with other educational software and educational services. The long-term goal of such infrastructure efforts will be to link the community worldwide and provide easy access to the full range of intellectual resources such as library materials, research facilities, and colloquia. This kind of infrastructure will make it easy to communicate, follow coursework, conduct laboratory exercises, and collaborate online.

Promising education innovations are being developed through the participation of diverse agencies and sectors. Higher education, industry, and standards groups bring different contributions to the value chain and to the lifecycle of innovations, from research and development to ultimate commoditization, adoption, and diffusion. The architecture of these systems should leverage the participation and contribution of different actors based on the specific strengths that they bring to the overall effort.

A sustainable educational ecology requires this diversity of participants and products as well as the safety to innovate. This latter aspect can be lost or buried under ponderous treatment of technical and infrastructure considerations. In our treatment of the preferred attributes of the next generation of educational systems, we recommend an architectural approach as being central to delivering not only basic course administration functionality, but also to supporting and integrating exciting innovations, some developing tools and others content, that have implications for amplifying, extending, or even transforming educational practice. It is this work that will help to create a platform from which a new generation of learning technology and learning content can arise.

References

Abelson, H. & Kumar, V. (2001). *Proceedings – University Teaching as E-Business? Research and Policy Agendas*, Center for Studies in Higher Education, October 12. Available at *http://ishi.lib.berkeley.edu/cshe/projects/university/ebusiness/*

Advanced Distributed Learning (ADL). (2004). SCORM overview. Available at *http://www.adlnet.org/index.cfm?fuseaction=scormabt*

Green, K. (2004). Sakai and the four C's of open source. *Syllabus*. March. Retrieved August 22, 2004, from *http://www.syllabus.com/print.asp?ID=9030*

IMS Global Learning Consortium, Inc. (2004). About IMS. Available at *http://www.imsglobal.org/aboutims*

Open Knowledge Initiative (O.K.I.). (2000). From "The Open Knowledge Initiative – A Proposal to the Andrew W. Mellon Foundation. October. *http://www.okiproject.org*

Endnotes

[1]   *http://www.okiproject.org*

[2]   *http://www.mellon.org/*

[3]   *http://www.collegiseduprise.com*

[4]   *http://www.wcet.info/*

[5]   *http://www.adlnet.org/*

[6]   "SCORM describes that technical framework by providing a harmonized set of guidelines, specifications, and standards. Borrowing from work of other specification and standards bodies, ADL developed a model for creating and deploying e-Learning."

[7]   "The IMS Global Learning Consortium develops and promotes the adoption of open technical specifications for interoperable learning technology. Several IMS specifications have become worldwide de facto standards for delivering learning products and services."

Chapter XXI

Conceptualizing a New CMS Design

Ali Jafari, Indiana University-Purdue University
Indianapolis (IUPUI), USA

Abstract

This chapter discusses the characteristics and requirements for the Next Generation of Course Management System (CMS). The chapter begins with a survey of the current CMS systems elaborating on understanding the current CMS user interface design, understanding the next generation of CMS users, and understanding the forthcoming models for future courses and degree programs. The chapter concludes with painting a picture of the next generation of CMS software environment being characterized as offering smart services, featuring advanced controls, and offering comprehensive software environment.

Introduction

The CMS market continues to grow, and today it would be difficult to find a higher education institution not using CMS. CMS technology is steadily cultivating acceptance among educational institutions, especially those that offer distance learning courses and degree programs. The current system is substantially more user-friendly and sophisticated than the original systems introduced in the late 1990s, and the authoring and navigation schemes of most current systems are based on a template-based design.

In this chapter, I will endeavor to paint a picture of the next-generation of course management system, or CMS, a new software environment featuring a shrewd navigational scheme, a smart technology framework, and creative tool sets. The future of CMS promises to bring depth and color to what is now symbolically a rather flat, black and white system. Before I begin, however, I will posit my understanding of the current CMS technology and capabilities for both those CMS systems developed by commercial vendors and the home-grown systems developed internally within educational institutions.

Understanding the Current CMS User Interface Design: How It Happened and Why

The CMS was originally developed as a complement to classroom instruction, a Web-based software technology to connect students and instructors any-where, anytime. The initial systems, such as the early versions of WebCT™ in the late 90s, offered a basic series of communication and management tools. Instructors were expected to pick and package various tools to create the user interface by appropriately placing those choices on their course Web site. This development was welcomed by those who desired the freedom to design their own course Web site but was considered a challenge to those who lacked knowledge on how to design a course Web site and insight into how to develop a receptive user interface system.

The notion of the "pick-and-package" course Web site was soon replaced with easy-to-use, template-based designs present in most current systems, both vendor-created and homegrown. Oncourse, an enterprise course management system developed at Indiana University-Purdue University Indianapolis (IUPUI), was the first to introduce the template-based course management system, followed by the commercial Blackboard™ CMS system in the late 90s (Jafari, 2000). With such a template-based CMS system, when an instructor wishes to create a course Web site, he or she uses a simple, preconstructed template to load course content. Understandably, the introduction of the template-based course management system contributed significantly to the growth in popularity and success of CMS systems among end users, both instructors and students. Course Web site creation was abridged for instructors, and site use was simplified for students.

Many instructors, even those with just fundamental computer skills, find it unnecessary to take a training workshop or refer to a user's manual to learn how to create Web-based courses using this template-based system. The template system offers basic, self-explanatory tools conveniently placed under top-level tabs for easy posting of course content and also presents various communication, collaboration, and management tools. For instance, under the syllabus tab, the instructor can copy and paste a prewritten syllabus; under the communication tab, the major communication and collaboration tools such as course mail, message board, chat, and writing board, can be accessed. Other tools are strategically located under the various top-level tabs to manage the course, such as viewing access log, managing grade book, creating online quizzes, and the like.

In addition to offering this simple-to-learn and easy-to-use course authoring environment to instructors and course designers, the template-based course management system offers a straightforward user interface system to students. Once a student learns how to use the template within a course, the learned experience can be applied across the board in other CMS courses. The IT support providers in an institution also prefer the template-based CMS system because the help desk support personnel need only master and offer services for one type of navigation and user interface, the one offered by the CMS template.

In summary, the current template-based CMS system offers a practical course-authoring environment to instructors, while at the same time it offers a consistent user interface among all course Web sites for students, which parallels a reduction in need for help desk support.

Understanding the Users of the Next Generation of CMS

The users of the next generation of CMS may have one or more of the following major characteristics: advanced users, wireless learners, and impatient users. Each of these characteristics is explored in the following text.

Advanced Users

Today both students and instructors have more experience using the Web and Web-based software environments. As Web-based games become one of the most popular entertainment among K-12 students, the extensive time spent using a computer as the machine runs the software game offers the side benefit of encouraging an inherent understanding of the computer machine itself, its operating system, navigational tools, Internet, and the Web. Therefore, students are entering college with little or no need to take a technology literacy course as they likely did when CMS was introduced to the educational market. Instructors, as the second group of CMS users, are similarly more actively using the Web as they engage in online research and collaboration. Overall, users of the next generation of CMS are more computer and Web savvy, capable of using advanced software tools.

Wireless Learners

Cell phones, originally introduced as wireless phone technology, are now offering other services, including the functionality of instant messaging, Web surfing, and connectivity to the Internet and World Wide Web, introducing a new habitat for CMS users and heightening expectations of being wireless. No matter where you are or where you go, outside of your city or even your country, you can stay instantly connected via cell phone technology.

Wireless Internet that was initially available in some classrooms within limited brand universities is now within reach almost everywhere — at airports, shopping malls, hotels, conference centers, coffee shops, and, of course, homes. Again, this technology anticipates that the user no longer needs to go to a computer lab and log on to a desktop computer to get connected to the Web. To stay abreast with this technology, hardware designers face the challenge of making computers smaller — much smaller, such as to fit in a pocket — while offering full keyboard and multimedia capabilities.

Software designers face an even greater challenge: to offer the same functionality, they formerly offered services on a full-sized computer screen in a very small display with substantially less characters per screen and very limited keyboard functionality and ergonomics. This is a more daunting task to the CMS software developers because distance learning courses may include multimedia files that require a large display screen. For instance, a student may need to view a picture and a multiple-choice quiz, all on one screen. The navigation schemes of most current CMS technology are primarily designed for a full VGA computer monitor with a minimum of 800-by-600-pixel resolution and could not ergonomically run on a small PDA (personal digital assistant) or cell phone display.

Impatient Users

Information overload is causing computer users to be impatient users who must screen hundreds of e-mails or surf massive amounts of information and data sandwiched into Web sites, which leaves them less time to spend on other tasks. Consequently, the software environment of the next generation of CMS has to offer fast-to-navigate user interfaces that require fewer mouse clicks and less screen load time.

Current CMS, while offering easy-to-use interfaces, require many mouse clicks to complete a task. For example, reading, answering, and archiving e-mail messages within a CMS may take hundreds of mouse clicks, each requiring a screen load-up time that makes the user simply sit and wait. This becomes particularly annoying if the user has a slow or congested Internet connection.

Understanding the Next Generation of Course and Degree Offering Models

The current course design models are the traditional classroom-based model and the distance-learning model. The traditional classroom-based model is derived from the notion of having students come to campus to attend classes for a certain number of hours per week, per semester, to complete the requirements for a credit course. In contrast, the distance-learning model does not require students to come to campus and attend classes. As discussed in this section, a hybrid model that includes a combination of classroom attendance and distance learning propounds the possibility for students of the future to likely have the opportunity to receive education from multiple institutions as they pursue their degree program. For instance, a student attending a degree program within Institution X may take courses from other institutions, even campuses located in other countries, to complete degree requirements.

More Hybrid Courses

There is now a move toward the hybrid online course, a cross between the traditional classroom-based instruction and the totally online distance learning course offering. More faculty are becoming interested in reducing the in-classroom contact hours by putting more course content online using CMS tools. Students also prefer these hybrid courses mainly because there is less need to travel to campus for classroom attendance. This has become increasingly true among working students who find it inconvenient to drive to campus in the middle of the workday to attend a one-hour class, furthermore burning costly fuel and killing precious time unnecessarily.

More Inter-Institution Degree Programs

Imagine a student pursuing an engineering degree from his home college but completing some courses that are offered by out-of-state institutions via distance learning. Or, imagine a student in a foreign country who cannot easily obtain a U.S. visa to complete a degree program by attending a U.S. institution. In either case, the student could take a portion of the degree requirement courses from a home institution and complete the remainder from other institutions once institutional agreements were set up between the institutions to offer and to honor inter-institution courses.

Understanding New Add-On Tools and Feature Sets

The CMS as it stands today conveys methods for "course management," largely a Web-based authoring toolbox offering tools and services for instructors to put course content online and to manage the course environment. For students, CMS offers various communication, collaboration, and management tools permitting access to course content via the Web. However, CMS is not offering other related but important services to students and faculty. This section discusses four of the emerging new services as they relate to the next generation of CMS.

Lifelong ePortfolio

Over the last three years, the ePortfolio has received much attention (Greenburg, 2004). One of the most essential and demanded applications of an ePortfolio is to provide an environment for students to collect, select, and reflect upon their learning accomplishments, especially those achievements based upon their institution's principles of learning. Although the ePortfolio is often perceived as a toolbox and software environment separate from the CMS, CMS can and should play a major role toward the successful operation of an ePortfolio system and paradigm.

An anticipated functionality of the next generation of CMS, for instance, is the ability to port over and send student learning outcome documents and associated assessment data to the ePortfolio or student information system (SIS), using a central depositing file server that could maintain the files for future use, maybe for the life of a student. Because the CMS works on the notion of authentication and authorization, metadata certification tags can be attached to a student's learning documents and the CMS system could then transfer them to a central lifelong repository system (Jafari, 2004). For example, a term paper that a student has written for his English class, accompanied with assessment data such as a grade, a written assessment note from the course instructor, and class ranking, could be a good collection item for the student's ePortfolio.

Multimedia Transcript

As discussed in the previous section, the CMS can play a major role in the successful operation of the ePortfolio system. Once services such as the certified file-transferring services are obtainable by the next generation of CMS, the student information system can offer a new, more advanced transcript service which could be identified as the "multimedia transcript" or "electronic transcript." A typical college transcript today includes only a list of completed courses and accompanying grades in a printed format. The multimedia transcript, on the other hand, could include coursework artifacts in addition to the grade from each completed course. Artifacts could be comprised of, for example, a paper that a student wrote for a particular class, along with completed projects and assessment notes from the course instructor. The next generation of CMS could be very instrumental toward successful implementation of such a multimedia transcript.

Competency Assessment

Already launched in some institutions, competency assessment is increasingly being considered as a condition before a college degree is awarded to a graduating student. This implies that, in addition to passing required courses, students must achieve minimum levels of competency in communication, critical thinking, understanding our society and culture, and the like. The next generation of CMS can play a vital role in the realization of competency assessment. Once a student has developed projects or written papers that can substantiate proficiency, those supporting documents can be electronically transferred to a new software tool that can provide these services. That tool, a "learning matrix," can reside in an ePortfolio system, student information system, or in the next generation of CMS.

Understanding the Next Generation of CMS Software Developers

CMS is a relatively new software system currently being developed and marketed by commercial vendors, predominantly in the United States. There are budding CMS developers entering the field that hope to win a portion of the market for the next generation of CMS. One is the open-source community of CMS software developers within the higher education institutions. But other likely developers are the large software companies specializing in offering enterprise portal software environments and student information services, and those companies surely are eyeing the potential marketability and tremendous profitability of a successful CMS.

CMS Software Developer

The current CMS market is divided among three to four major CMS software companies, all offering very similar systems that have been optimized to offer full CMS services. These services typically provide the template-based authoring environment that affords a consistent look and feel among various courses developed within one system. The CMS can characteristically run as a totally stand-alone system or can link to various databases to offer dynamic creation and maintenance of new course sites, as well as automated accessibility to registered students and faculty of record.

The current commercial systems are complemented by robust business plans for solid growth and steady income, which is certainly welcome news to end users. A healthy business plan is the foundation upon which the best system is built to meet the requirements of future end users. However, the necessary economic stability can be challenging for new CMS developers seeking to establish a position in the market, especially the two potential groups discussed below.

Open-Source Collaboration

Over the last two years there has been enormous interest and much discussion among the higher education institutions to internally develop CMS modules, even to complete a CMS system and to share those developments among themselves, totally free or based on a membership fee (Wheeler, 2004). Only history will reveal if a substantial CMS market share can evolve within this community. Those institutions that have committed internal funding or raised soft money through research grants will have a better chance of survival using and maintaining an open-source CMS system than the smaller campuses with little or no research and development funding or internal technical resources.

With such limitations, the smaller and less-funded institutions will find it difficult to switch from a vendor-supported CMS package to a community-developed and maintained system that may not meet the reliability requirements of today's CMS, especially those being used for distance learning programs. The day-to-day operation and success of a distance learning program relies on the 24/7 dependability of the CMS engine. Should the CMS server go down, in effect, the entire campus closes and all classes are cancelled, similar to a snow emergency situation on a physical campus. Today, all CMS vendors guarantee technical services — and peace of mind — by assuring CIOs that their systems will meet better than a 99 percent reliability operation.

Viewing the open-source initiatives from a positive perspective suggests several exciting opportunities. Most importantly, researchers and scholars could participate in the advancement toward the next generation of the CMS and ultimately create a superior system for the simple reason that because they are also the end users, aware of their own teaching and learning needs and with a better understanding of the functional and technical limitations of current systems, they have freedom of input to develop the best system for themselves. Additionally, academic researchers would have the chance to use scientific methodology to test current systems and experiment with the benefits of new systems before marketing them commercially. This experimentation will prove more exciting as more researchers and scientists participate in the open-source CMS community rather than the limited participation of software developers within the IT departments of institutions.

Enterprise Portal Developer

As discussed earlier, the CMS of today is principally viewed as a course management toolbox that supplies services to faculty and students for their teaching and learning needs. Inside the CMS toolbox, we find a series of commonly used tools that may be already included in other campus tools and services such as the e-mail system and the file server, the two major CMS components. Logically then, the next generation of CMS may be a subset of a broader system, an integral component of a campus portal. Such a system, when developed and accepted within the marketplace, would certainly offer a more cost-effective solution to CIOs and a more usable and ergonomically sound system to faculty and students.

Painting a Picture of the Next Generation of CMS Software

After touching on the basic concepts for the next generation of CMS users, courses, and software, the author wishes to conclude this chapter by painting the big picture of the next generation of course management systems as it relates to the purposes of this book and specifically this chapter. Defining the next generation of a "thing" is based on a series of assumptions and speculations with various levels of accuracy. The presentation of this big picture does not result from funding nor scientific research methodology, but it is proposed to be debated and refined as the concepts are challenged or supported by visionary thinkers, technologists, and researchers in the field of course management systems.

The three major characteristics for the next generation of CMS are smart system, advanced controls, and comprehensive environment. Each of these characteristics is detailed in the following text and shown in the matrix depicted in Figure 1.

Smart System

A crucial element of the next generation of CMS is its capability to act smart — in other words, to offer intelligent services to each user according to his or her preferences and skill sets. Every user's situation is different, as evidenced by the skill level for using the software environment, the subject matter being taught in a course, and personal preferences to operate and interact with the software environment and the course content. Therefore, the next generation of the CMS must be a smart system, a new engine and framework that can think, reason, and ultimately make decisions based on the preferences of an individual user, be it learner or teacher (Jafari, 2002). This smart system must be able to learn, to monitor a user's routine interaction with the system, and the next generation of CMS will be able to intelligently react and respond to the individual user's needs.

The framework of the next generation of CMS can be designed to include an assortment of intelligent agents, each of which can be included as an add-on module to the CMS software environment to help end users, whether student or instructor, with learning, teaching, and day-to-day school work. Once such a system is developed, a user is no longer bound to the navigational scheme of the fixed template user interface as mandated by the current CMS design.

The smart characteristics of the next generation of the CMS thus make the software environment substantially more user-friendly since they offer the capabilities to completely customize the navigational scheme and user interface design according to the knowledge level of an individual. In addition, the new CMS is envisioned to introduce a course authoring feature such that, for example, a course designed as a 400-level course could be dynamically and intelligently redesigned to serve both undergraduate and graduate students.

Similarly, the smart characteristics of the next generation of CMS can offer comparable practices to that of a human teacher lecturing in the classroom. Once a human teacher realizes that students are not following his lecture, for instance, he offers examples or he switches to a lower level of discussion. Conversely, if that same instructor senses that the students have sufficiently grasped the subject matter, he has the advantage of progressing at an advanced pace. Through the use of an intelligent agent embedded within the next generation of CMS, a student may receive a different set of reading material and homework assignments based on learning progress evaluation. The agent offering this service would use an algorithm that has been scientifically developed by educational researchers and instructional designers.

Advanced Controls

The next generation of CMS technology will offer more options and controls to an individual user, both the instructors who act as the course authors and students as learners. Again, instead of being constrained by a fixed navigational scheme, the course instructors and course designers will have options for changing the navigational scheme according to some adjustable threshold. For instance, once a student user signs on, he or she may be directed immediately to a page to read a warning note or an announcement page because the system has realized that the user failed to complete certain assignments.

The next generation of CMS technology also will present advanced control services to system administrators and course authors; for example, a course can be configured to automatically transfer at the last week of the classes all the term papers submitted by students and graded by the faculty of record to a central certified file server where the paper will remain archived and cannot be changed after delivery.

Comprehensive Environment

The next generation of the CMS is not limited to merely "course management" services as the current CMS technology is designed to offer today. The many new or forthcoming services, such as the ePortfolio, multimedia transcript, and competency assessment mentioned in the earlier sections of this chapter will demand more functional and technical requirements to be integrated into the next generation of the CMS.

One may ask questions such as: Why in the future should an institution use multiple software systems to handle various "interrelated" teaching, learning, and SIS services? Why should there be three or more personal file servers, each existing within different systems — including CMS, personal homepage (PHP), and personal file server — used by each student? Why should the CMS use its own file manager system when every student in an institution is already offered a personal file server? Why do users have to authenticate into different software systems to take care of their day-to-day academic needs? Why can we not have a single comprehensive teaching and learning software environment for our students and faculty (like Microsoft Office®) that supplies a comprehensive toolbox to assist the average computer user with all of his day-to-day computer use? Why cannot all the functionality of the CMS be included and offered within a single campus portal environment offered by one vendor, where each tool uses a consistent user interface, navigational scheme, and single authentication (again, like Microsoft Office), with the institution paying but one licensing fee?

The prospect of such a system certainly envisions significant opportunities to current CMS vendors to enter into a bigger market, the campus portal business, while at the same time poses considerable pressure on those same vendors (Jafari & Sheehan, 2002). If they fail to enter the bigger market, they may face a loss of their current market share to a bigger software company that will include all of the CMS functionality within a single package of a portal software solution.

Next-Generation CMS Matrix

Figure 1 illustrates a two-dimensional matrix. The vertical column of the matrix lists the three primary characteristics of the next generation of CMS as perceived by the author and as discussed earlier in this chapter. The horizontal rows of the matrix list three perspectives: the users, the courses, and technology or the software.

The matrix of the next generation of CMS presented here can be perceived as both the summary and conclusion to this chapter. Additionally, it could suggest topics for future research work and papers and offer subjects for discussion and debates. The author certainly welcomes comments and challenges to his perception as presented in this chapter.

Figure 1. Matrix for the next generation of CMS

	Next generation of <u>users</u> V V V	**Next generation of <u>courses</u>** V V V	**Next generation of <u>software</u>** V V V
Smart System > > >	User-friendly system	Dynamically-customized courses according to users' personal settings	Intelligent software environment that knows users and their personal preferences
Advanced Controls > > >	User control operation	One course serving users with various levels of technical sophistication	Advanced distance learning and hybrid courses
Comprehensive Environment > > >	Multifunction tools and portal access	Transparent transformation of learning documents to other systems	Next generation of campus portal

References

Baylor, A. L. & Jafari, A. (1999). What are the possibilities of intelligent agents for education? Paper presented at the *International Conference on Technology and Education,* Tampa, Florida.

Greenberg, G. (2004). The digital convergence extending the portfolio model. *EDUCAUSE Review, (39),* 28-36.

Jafari, A. (2000). Development of a new university-wide course management system. In L. Petrides (Ed.), *Cases on Information Technology in Higher Education.* Hershey, PA: Idea Group Publishing.

Jafari, A. (2000). Optimizing campus Web sites: Is the portal approach a solution to improving campus Web site usability? *EDUCAUSE Quarterly Journal.* Available at *http://www.educause.edu/ir/library/pdf/EQM0026.pdf*

Jafari, A. (2002). Conceptualizing intelligent agents for teaching and learning. *EDUCAUSE Quarterly Journal.* Available at *http://www.educause.edu/asp/doclib/abstract.asp?ID=EQM0235*

Jafari, A. (2004). The "sticky" ePortfolio system: Tackling challenges and identifying attributes. *EDUCAUSE Review, (39),* 38-49.

Jafari, A. & Sheehan, M. (Eds.). (2003). *Designing portals: Opportunities and challenges.* Hershey, PA: Idea Group Publishing.

Jafari, A. & Baylor, A. L. (1999). *A technological learning environment of the future.* Paper presented at the 7th International Conference on Computers in Education, ICCE. Chiba, Japan.

Wheeler, B. (2004). Open source 2007: How did this happen? *EDUCAUSE Review, (39),* 12-27.

Chapter XXII

Next Generation:
Speculations in
New Technologies

Bryan Alexander, Middlebury College, USA

Abstract

Next-generation course management systems (CMS) are likely to take advantage of today's applications' structural and pedagogical limitations, supporting student and inter-collegiate collaboration. They should also be influenced by developments in social software and pre-existing information-sharing projects. CMS will reach out to the larger world to integrate with global informatics initiatives.

Introduction

The Internet will reveal the true hierarchy of good, because what is at stake is the essence of language: freedom. This hierarchy is complex: hyper-textual, interwoven, alive, mobile, teeming and spinning like a biosphere. (Pierre Levy[1])

Had Levy invented CMS, perhaps he would have imagined the now-available next-generation systems differently:

Catherine visits her course spaces after morning coffee, two hours before her first class of the day. Opening the main Web browser on her tablet, she scans her portal for today's information. Content feeds from sociology and French show activity, including an argument about Habermas (again), notes from the verb study group's leader, and three responses to her blog writing: one comment and two trackbacks to other blogs. But they aren't urgent this morning, so she marks them for later perusal. The morning class reading reappears, a chapter from Mary Shelley's last novel, with further comments and annotations attached, largely from her classmates. As she considers these collegial intertexts, a flurry of instant messages, or IMs, erupt alongside the reading. She greets several (two friends, a high school student with a question), then updates her away message to insist that she's "really busy studying." Switching over to her research project's feed, Catherine finds from video imagery and data streams that the Icelandic volcano has cooled slightly, and that her Swedish and Malaysian colleagues consider this well within their models. On a creative impulse, she grabs a screen capture of the caldera, adds it to her current video autobiography, and sets the editor to "rendering." She also copies the image to her course space profile, thinking it a dramatic yet economical way of representing herself and her geological interests. Maybe another volcanophile will inquire about joining her team — they really want a librarian this month.

This reminds her of her reading for the impending class. Catherine reflexively searches for commentary on The Last Man *(1826), adding to her personal wiki notes, then posting annotations with links to sources: a London professor's semantic analysis (both data set and commentary) and a Toyko high school class's discussion with some interesting reactions. Her trackbacks to their Web sites might trigger follow-up IMs, e-mails, or posts to her blog. Thinking about how this will look to future readers within the learning object her professor assures her the class discourse will become, she revises her prose to a more scholarly pitch, then races out the door, tablet under her arm.*

During the discussion, Catherine builds out loud on a point she made in course space. While conversation moves on, she takes notes but copies class notes on her earlier topic into a spin-off space, add links from her professor and fellow students, pastes in a copy of her earlier wiki and annotation comments, links to a social search query for two keyword combinations, then saves the new entity in an encrypted folder for later development. It might be the materials for a paper. Just before the end of class, Catherine notices that her video editor has finished rendering her updated film, so she uploads the entire clip to her blog, checks its permissions ("use freely, with acknowledgment") and awaits comments from friends around the world.[2]

As we've seen throughout this book, the current generation of CMS has grown rapidly, succeeding in being adopted across higher education with impressive speed. In order to apprehend the CMS landscape, it is important to consider the dynamics of that success in order to examine each application's formal features. Extensive adoption stems from several factors, each of which strikes at the heart of campus informatics. To begin with, compared with many other digital tools used for various purposes in higher education, CMS are relatively easy to support. Although stories about slow customer response are widespread, the software does not require external training (compare with Oracle™ geographic information system tools, or Director™), massive installation processes (compare Banner™), or complex interactions with rapidly changing software and hardware environments (such as digital video). Additionally, CMS have been embraced not by early adopters, but also by the broad technological middle of campuses, generally, extending the reach of computer-mediated teaching and learning, a major instructional technology goal.

These CMS have also taken the lead for a major external reason, in that they serve as shields from the copyright struggles currently raging throughout the United States and intervening in many levels of campus life. The Digital Millennium Copyright Act (DMCA), which came into effect in 2000, poses a restriction on fair use (itself enshrined in the 1976 Copyright Act) in its blanket prohibitions of unauthorized access through anticircumvention technologies.[3] At the same time, the Motion Picture Association of America (MPAA) and, especially, the Recording Industry Association of America (RIAA) have fostered a climate of copyright wariness, and sometimes fear, with their subpoenas and take-down campaigns aimed at colleges. Yet the leading CMS offer a rare bright spot in this gloomy landscape by taking advantage of the TEACH Act (2002). This law allows a fair use defense for educational use of digital materials, so long as such usage occurs within a closed classroom environment. That is, materials can be copied under fair use intent if they are accessible only to a class's students and instructor, and only for the duration of that class (a semester or equivalent), and if outsiders (the rest of the Web and world) are blocked by technological means, such as a decently strong login and password system.[4] The leading CMS do precisely that, providing a shielded, single-class space, requiring minimal effort on the part of instructors. In a sense, these CMS articulate a specific copyright stance, using TEACH to protect accessed content by supporting a "walled garden."

Such informatics structures necessarily embody pedagogical principles, which also tie into the success of CMS. Unlike the classic decentralizing, antiauthoritarian pedagogy of computer-mediated teaching, where the sage on the stage gives way to the guide on the side, Blackboard™ retains that sage's position. CMS make it very easy for an instructor to upload documents, such as a syllabus or readings; put another way, CMS enable the hierarchical transmission of information, from expert to learner. The reverse flow is also present in the form of drop boxes. The broadcast model of learning is what these are about, rather than any collaborative or nonauthoritarian one. Students are not encouraged to be content creators or participants in the construction of learning materials, based on the shape of the interface; their participation is limited to dropping off work in the instructor's box, posting to discussions, and checking the grade book. Peer learning and collaboration approaches are available through discussion tools (themselves traditional forms, dating back to the Daedalus software in education, or UseNet and the first list servers in the Internet), but these remain relatively underused. As Glenda Morgan put it in her 2003 ECAR study:

> *Faculty look to course management systems to help them communicate easily with students, to give students access to class documents, and for the convenience and transparency of the online gradebook... Fifty-nine percent of faculty surveyed reported that their communication with students increased as a result of using the CMS. This communication is broadcast in nature, from the faculty member to the student.*

Morgan's study also notes that student demand for CMS rarely played a role in faculty decisions to adopt it. We should note that, at the same time, those students have already adopted other tools for communicating with each other, and that those are not broadcast, but peer-to-peer, such as instant messaging and file-sharing applications. Students are already living a collaborative digital environment but not through leading CMS.

Collaboration is also underplayed between classes. As the TEACH-compliant password protection restricts the online environment to a single class, it also produces a speed bump for sharing between classes. Multiple sections of the same large class can collaborate, much as students share the physical space of a large lecture hall. But communication between different classes on the same campus is difficult, and even more problematic between campuses, especially as different CMS are in play. It is difficult for an intercampus class, or a virtual program, to work through these tools. Blackboard™'s founder aims for a global reach for education (Pittinsky, 2003) but within the segmentations of classes.

It is important to note the pedagogical implications of these thickened digital barriers between classes. While they don't prevent students from browsing the Web (Carmean & Haefner, 2002), they nevertheless present an interface speed bump to reaching the full, open Web of Tim Berners-Lee's vision. That creator of the Web sought easy and direct connections between users and the world of documents, where technological mediation would be enabling rather than shaping and restrictive. The screen of WebCT™, its presentation of options, and the emphasis on a separate space lead the user to focus on materials available within that framework. The larger implication of this barrier is not that it is an obstacle to move from CMS to the Web, but that it is very hard to reach from the Web into a CMS. As a default, materials within this form of virtual class are not accessible to the outside world. Although it might be construed as a radical shift or regression, this is not a pedagogical innovation, as it recalls the medieval origins of the university of creating a safe, secluded zone for study, followed by the residential campus' sense of focused learning.

Leading CMS also appear something other than radical when we consider concurrent cybercultural developments. The rise of visually rich, interactive games and simulations, especially in the massively multiplayer online sense, has led to the creation of large virtual worlds, some with global reach (e.g., EverQuest™, Star Wars Galaxies™). Collaborative social software has blossomed into a multilevel movement, including social networking tools (Friendster™, Orkut™, LinkedIN™, Flickr™), publication technologies (blogs, wikis), and Web applications and standards (trackback, RSS). Peer-to-peer (p2p)-oriented technologies and practices have threatened business models and altered the norms of collaboration, from Napster to BitTorrent™. Large data sets continue to grow in size and applications, while searchability and metadata remain problematic. Learning objects persist as a focus for digital material production, usage, and sharing. This complex, dynamic mix of technologies and practices has shaped the generation entering colleges and using CMS, while offering many different approaches to the administrative, pedagogical, and communicative problems CMS attempt to solve. We can draw on cyberculture to get a sense of possible futures for courseware.

At the largest level, consider the notion of cyberinfrastructure. In 2003, the National Science Foundation's (NFS) Advisory Committee for Cyberinfrastructure released *Revolutionizing Science and Engineering through Cyberinfrastructure*, which describes the developing complex system linking scientists and their students as they taught and researched:[5]

> *Like the physical infrastructure of roads, bridges, power grids, telephone lines, and water systems that support modern society, "cyberinfrastructure" refers to the distributed computer, information and communication technologies combined with the personnel and integrating components that provide a long-term platform to empower the modern scientific research endeavor.*

Rather than articulating a series of classroom and lab spaces organized conservatively, this report instead relies on an advanced sense of information-based networks, along the lines of Pierre Levy's global intelligences, or Berners-Lee's vision of a world of researchers sharing their documents. These networks share a variety of heterogeneous objects across multiple platforms, from digital video to simulation runs, handheld devices to distributed computing. The concept of cyberinfrastructure enables the organization of this vast array of objects into a dynamic field for teaching and learning. The widespread interest in this paradigm has led to a follow-up study for other disciplines, the Mellon Foundation-funded Commission on Cyberinfrastructure for the Humanities & Social Sciences, which is in progress at the time of this writing.[6]

This approach offers several levels of interaction with CMS. First, there is the sense that CMS might participate in such a structure. The problem becomes importing fluid content into these class spaces and being able to expose and publish CMS content to the wider infrastructure. Second, given the collaborative nature of the NSF's model, partly driven by the collaborative tendencies of the sciences, the challenge becomes building CMS capable of communication across class barriers. Third, the emphasis on collaboration also raises the problem of interoperability between applications and systems—that is, how does a FirstClass™ class talk with a Blackboard™ one? Fourth, one wonders about the information habits learned in a now traditional CMS, which focus on content presented to the learner, rather than materials sought out or constructed. Can such a learner dive into a planetary cyberinfrastructure, or would he or she suffer a literacy gap requiring acculturation and training (Lynch, 2003)?

A similarly grand or architectonic approach is that of information ecology. This springs largely out of the knowledge management field, and is predicated on developing strategies for sharing information and knowledge effectively within a group. Information can be explicit, as in documents, as well as implicit, in the sense of knowledge rarely voiced or shared. The ecological element involves considering a community's information as a dynamic, interrelated, holistic system, where multiple agents play multilevel roles, producing, sharing, and consuming information.[7] Not so open and wide-ranging as the NSF's cyberinfrastructure, the information ecology model nevertheless shares its heterogeneity. Davenport and Prusak (1997) argue that this model includes politics, behavior and culture, staffing, materials, practical processes, and information architecture. In this context, traditional CMS are small, closed systems, each constituting its own ecology, largely withdrawn from the information ecosystem of a campus, discipline, or, more broadly, academe. How will future course management tools approach the larger levels of information ecologies? Will students' skills in information fluency, honed within the microenvironments of classes, apply when seeking implicit knowledge in larger environments?

A more recent[8] approach to organizing social information at the macro level is the social software movement, which encompasses technologies, practices, and the general sense of improving our ability to collaborate by using digital networks.[9] The roots of this approach include social network analysis (SNA), which analyzes and maps out connections between people in social, informational contexts. The most popular application of SNA is the "Kevin Bacon game," where players seek to build connections between Hollywood people and the hard-working actor. Networks display uncanny similarities across a variety of venues, from virus propagation to news story coverage to the operations of terrorist organizations, which helps us understand human interaction more precisely and proactively (Barabasi, 2002; Watts, 2003). For example, we now have a working body of knowledge about mapping informal social connections that cut across the grain of formal organizational structures. We understand the spread of stories across a population better, knowing to look for a certain proportion of connecting "hubs" rather than "spokes." Social network applications, structured in part by SNA insights, have emerged and grown dramatically in the past year and seek to connect people for politics (Meetup, used most notably with the Dean and Clark presidential campaigns), friendship and dating (Friendster™, Orkut™), and business (LinkedIN™) (Boyd, 2003). Other technologies have affiliated with social software, including collaborative writing tools such as blogs and wikis.[10]

Social software has already been repurposed for campus needs. On the social level, TheFaceBook has appeared as a Friendster™ for college campuses.[11] In terms of courseware, a growing number of classes have used wikis and blogs as virtual classrooms. Such tools enable nearly all pedagogical functions found in CMS: document presentation, discussion, and communication. They add many other affordances, depending on the implementation. For example, wikis allow users to edit others' documents directly, which is valued by some writing classes (Rick, Guzdial, et al., 2002).[12] Blogs can support discussion postings from beyond the classroom, allowing students to upload their multimedia work while encouraging hyperlinking to the full Web, building a more porous class boundary.[13] Blogs as CMS offer a different culture than that supported by Blackboard™ or WebCT™, one that is more collaborative and less hierarchical (Long, 2002). In one sense, then, social software tools are alternatives or competitors to leading CMS, supporting different pedagogies and support models. In a different, more prospective sense, upcoming CMS could build in social software functionality. One could imagine a campus-wide discovery tool, *a la* LinkedIN™, where members of the campus community could present their interests and connect with the similarly minded. Faculty could develop an alternative method for soliciting class interest beyond the registrar. Over time, a blog-based CMS would create archives of previous classes, which could serve as learning objects for subsequent iterations of that class or related ones, distributing learning over time as well as space.

Remaining at this higher level of analysis, and considering the preceding set of contemporary movements in digital informatics, it is clear that boundary issues are critical for the development of CMS. While the leading examples of the form are very conservative in forming barriers around the classic classroom, other aspects of cyberculture are transforming what academic boundaries have meant. Classroom, community sector (library, IT, faculty, student, administration, and so on), and academic discipline all connect in different ways under the cyberinfrastructure paradigm, when considered part of the same information ecology, or when students join instructors in blogging. Separate campuses and educational sectors (state school, research I, small liberal arts, community college, for-profit) begin to see cross-fertilizations by these practices. A community college student, a research I librarian, and a faculty member at a large state school can end up reading and posting to the same blog, learning together. Similarly diverse populations already make use of Massachusetts Institute of Technology's OpenCourseWare (Diamond, 2003). If we speculate on what forms such collaborations can take, some form of CMS could emerge to encompass and support them. Anxieties around border-crossing[14] might be alleviated by a powerful, flexible, and accessible application. Indeed, one possible reason for the rapid adoption of Blackboard™ and WebCT™ might be their refusal to challenge these borders, rendering them even more palatable.

We have some precedents for organizing hybrid groups around information-centric needs. The Internet has contained discussion forums since the 1970s, with the advent of Usenet and list servers. Their organizational innovations are deeply underrated, given the long-term, sustained successes of both, and especially Usenet, in bringing together very heterogeneous populations from many nations for the purpose of conversation. More recently, as noted above, social networking tools continue in this vein, using innovative approaches to connect people for business, friendship, and romance. Perhaps it is time for a Learnster™ or LinkedEdu™ CMS, where teachers and would-be learners could present themselves and discover each other, and then find ready-at-hand the collaborative tools for extending learning.

Gilles Deleuze and Felix Guattari (1987) offer a powerful metaphor for describing the conceptual shift suggested above by opposing the games of chess and go. In the western classic, pieces possess carefully demarcated roles, ranked in specific hierarchies. Their spatial positioning shapes the board and its early movements quite reliably. In contrast, the Japanese game's pieces are entirely equal at start, all with precisely the same capabilities. It is only when played onto a similarly unmarked board that new patterns and connections become apparent, emerging from patterns and formations iterated through play. The entire board can be revised and transfigured at a stroke, in contrast with chess' unfolding, gradual nature. Our current CMS, like chess, neatly map out specific hierarchical positions and roles, separated carefully by class and campus. New CMS might operate like go, connecting across the board, driving new formations and organizations.

At the same time, it is important to distinguish between connection and collaboration, discovery and follow-up operations. While the Internet is quite good at announcing projects, successful projects are less common, as a glance at SourceForge will indicate. We do know of a series of collaborative projects that have succeeded to various levels. The Wikipedia, for example, is now a large, collaboratively edited encyclopedia, where any user can edit any of the more than 300,000 entries.[15] Despite its openness to vandalism, the site's community and content have persisted. In the gaming world, alternate reality games (ARGs) have grown in recent years, as teams of players distributed around the world combine to solve complex puzzles pieced together into narratives. Players conduct Web research, translate texts in foreign languages, apply steganography, analyze video, decrypt codes, and build multiple, searchable archives for their work, along with social practices for welcoming new players. The Beast, a promotion for the film *A.I.*, is the most recognized of these games.[16]

Beyond textual collaborations, distributed pedagogy has gradually emerged, despite the various setbacks for distance learning. For example, the Associated Colleges of the South's Sunoikisis project, a "virtual classics" department, supports teaching, research, and study abroad for nearly a dozen liberal arts colleges. Faculty lecture to other schools' classes, students compare notes with classmates in different states, and teams across two time zones learn archaeology before coalescing at a dig in Turkey.[17] Proving that new forms of CMS can grow to meet new pedagogical needs to support inter-campus classes, the ACS built its own open-source CMS, the Course Delivery System, which readily integrates classes on two physically separate campuses. In terms of research, the China Filtering Project distributed data-gathering around the world to assess China's network strategy.[18]

Taken together, these information-centered collaborations demonstrate ecological responses to information needs, combining multiple digital tools around a social, purposeful nexus. Each enables multiple positions along a continuum of participation and textual production, with participants reading, writing, or both to various levels. Mechanisms appear to explain the process, from archive presentations to staged participation levels. In a sense, all of this is what an institution of higher learning has done for decades, from the admissions process through college archives — and now CMS. From another perspective, the invention and fluidity of online information collaborative describes potential forms for new CMS.

A deeper challenge to current CMS is to address self-organizing learning. How does a campus link its preferred courseware to a group that emerges to study a topic on its own, such as a reading group, a film club seeking to expand its knowledge, or a religious exploration? More importantly, how does a CMS grapple with self-organization within pre-existing institutions? Small group work within a class, for instance, can be a dramatically effective practice for participants, yet that success remains locked behind a WebCT™ password, hidden from the Web, and possibly inaccessible after time passes, depending on the campus. Beyond that class, CMS could grow to support connections between students in different classes sharing similar interests, as noted above; a greater challenge is to link over time and between classes. Such connections are hard to make in a face-to-face, nondigital environment, and become even more difficult as a campus size increases. Yet social software and collaborative information practices surely offer guides to opening pathways between two students — one in 1999, the other in 2004 — interested in the later Byzantine Empire in the Balkans. Web-presented archives, searchable postings, and collaborative filtering could add to our abilities to interconnect members of our communities. Portals can, in theory, support such functions at the cost of some intensive dataveillance, which gives rise to privacy and process concerns.

Further, a full course format might not be the best mode for such connected students. One response to this may be found in Middlebury College's Segue CMS, which allows users to create content pages in various formats, including class, blog, Web site, and research project.[19] Users can spin off from one format to another, launching a blog from a class, a research project from a Web site, and so on. While Blackboard™ and WebCT™ speak in terms of modularity, perhaps the next step for CMS includes a deeper modular function, where CMS pieces can be disaggregated and reassembled by users.

Along these lines, then, may be found an alternative approach to the copyright problems. As we noted above, traditional CMS afford a solution to digital fair use, at least in the United States, by using the class restriction to create a TEACH Act shield. This has been one reason for the widespread adoption of these CMS. But an alternative response to intellectual property struggles has emerged over the past several years, in favor of shared content. There is a growing openness to alternative intellectual property systems, such as the GNU code license and the burgeoning Creative Commons.[20] Despite limitations due to the extension of copyright terms in 1998, the public domain has been increasingly celebrated.[21] Shouldn't the next generation of CMS be able to partake of the Creative Commons, such as by allowing the publication of a class under a CC license? Moreover, could a new CMS support sharing copyright-free content across campuses, including public domain materials, as well as works created for sharing? WebCT™'s Vista™ might offer a seed for this, with its ability to share content between the same class on networked campuses. Students who want to gain exposure for their creative works, for example, could make them available through a CMS network. Expanded collaboration tools could then facilitate feedback, along with the creation of derivative and follow-up works.

So many options for functional growth in CMS suggest changes in their architecture, or the creation of radically different ones. Perhaps a CMS could follow in the path of the peer-to-peer collaboration tool Groove and be based on shared document spaces.[22] Instead of broadcasting content to students, a class would consist of materials shared between students and instructors, passed back and forth, modified and grown. This would free up modularity in that exported documents could be shifted to other p2p spaces, allowing students and instructors to repurpose the materials or archive them for personal use. Encrypting content should reiterate the TEACH copyright shield, creating a safe space for learning. Focusing on p2p relationships should drive the development of a more collaborative tool set within such a CMS, including by now familiar options such as image sharing, profile searching, instant messaging, co-browsing, and co-authoring pages. Truly extensible design would allow these tools to be disaggregated at will and repurposed for new functions, depending on the learner.

Turning from the class to the world suggests a different architecture based on exposure to the Web. While CMS have boomed, multiple projects have developed and connected for improving the searchability of educational content. The Open Archives Initiative, for example, has been working with repository projects to expose content to spiders, while discussing metadata standards to improve discovery.[23] IMS has been developing and promulgating standards for sharing information.[24] CMS could play a role in giving feedback to these movements, as their work often ends up aimed at class content and experience. Moreover, CMS should have much to gain by working to enhance the incorporation of, and access to, such materials within the class environment. Additionally, these large projects could serve as venue to win greater exposure for class content, produced by any members of the college community. Collaborative informatics projects constitute a complex network already in process, and collaborating with them could help connect students with the larger networks of the world.

That world has advanced in many ways since CMS first made their way into our classrooms and campuses. Paying attention to those developments and their ambitions is a powerful way to imagine the next generation of courseware, especially as it addresses common issues and dynamics. The risks are large, especially as the world's defensive tendencies manifest in a growing drive for walled gardens, between fears of copyright, terrorism, and compromised privacy. Yet the chance to expand teaching and learning, to deepen our communities of knowledge, and to play a role in the growth of global networks for collaboration demonstrates the powerful situation and potential of CMS. Given their present success, we should imagine their next iterations boldly.

References

Barbasi, A.L. *(2002)*. *Linked.* New York: Perseus.

Boyd, S. *(2003)*. Are you ready for social software? *Darwinmag*, March. Available at *http://www.darwinmag.com/read/050103/social.html*

Carmean, C. & Haefner, J. (2002). Mind over matter: Transforming course management systems into effective learning environments. *Educause Review*, November/December. Available at *http://www.educause.edu/ir/library/pdf/erm0261.pdf*

Davenport, T. H. & Prusak, L. (1997). *Information ecology: Mastering the information and knowledge environment.* New York: Oxford University Press.

Deleuze, G. & Guattari, F. (1987). *A thousand plateaus: Capitalism and schizophrenia*, B. Massumi. (Trans.). Minneapolis: University of Minnesota Press. Originally published as *Mille plateaux* (Paris: Éditions de minuit, 1980).

Diamond, D. (2003). MIT everywhere. *Wired*, September. Available at *http://www.wired.com/wired/archive/11.09/mit_pr.html*

Levy, P. (2000). *Collective intelligence: Mankind's emerging world in cyberspace.* R. Bononno (Trans.). New York: Perseus.

Long, P. (2002). Blogs: A disruptive technology coming of age? *Syllabus*, October. Available at *http://www.syllabus.com/article.asp?id=6774*

Lynch, C. (2003). Life after graduation day: Beyond the academy's digital walls. *Educause Review*, September/October, 12-13. Available at *http://www.educause.edu/ir/library/pdf/erm0356.pdf*

Morgan, G. (2003). Faculty use of course management systems. *ECAR Key Findings*. Available at *http://www.educause.edu/ir/library/pdf/ecar_so/ers/ers0302/ekf0302.pdf*

Nardi, B. & O'Day, V. L. (1999). *Information ecologies: Using technology with heart* (2nd ed.). Cambridge: MIT.

National Science Foundation. (2003). Revolutionizing science and engineering through cyberinfrastructure. Available at *http://www.communitytechnology.org/nsf_ci_report/*

Pittinsky, M. S. (2003). *The wired tower*. New York: Financial Times.

Rick, J., Guzdial, M., Carroll, K., Holloway-Attaway, L. & Walker, B. (2002). Collaborative learning at low cost: CoWeb use in English composition. Paper published in the *Proceedings of CSCL*, Boulder, CO. Available at *http://newmedia.colorado.edu/cscl/93.pdf*

Watts, D. J. (2003). *Six degrees: The science of a connected age*. New York: Norton.

Endnotes

[1] *http://webnetmuseum.org/html/en/reflexion/reflexion_levy_seoul_en.htm*

[2] A fine introduction to Trackback is at *http://www.movabletype.org/trackback/beginners/*. The Creative Commons Web site, *http://creativecommons.org/*, offers a good survey of alternative copyright permissions. The full text of *The Last Man* is available at *http://www.rc.umd.edu/editions/mws/lastman/*.

[3] *http://www.educause.edu/issues/issue.asp?Issue=DMCA*

[4] The TEACH Act toolkit is probably the Web's best resource for this law. Find it at *http://www.lib.ncsu.edu/scc/legislative/teachkit/*.

[5] *http://www.communitytechnology.org/nsf_ci_report/*

[6] *http://www.acls.org/cyberinfrastructure/cyber.htm*

[7] *http://en.wikipedia.org/wiki/Information_ecology* has a good, hyperlinked discussion. Cf also Nardi and O'Day (1999).

[8] Arguably, social software is a conservative movement, in that it recapitulates older visions of computer-mediated collaboration. JFC Licklider is perhaps the leading historical figure for this, from his visionary published work ("Man-Computer Symbiosis," 1960, and "The Computer as a Communications Device," 1968) to his crucial role in funding the initial Internet research from the Advanced Research Projects Agency (ARPA) during the 1960s.

9   The Many-to-Many blog is a fine source of information and news on social software. Find it at *http://www.corante.com/many/*.

10   In a valuable and influential article, Clay Shirky argues that most Internet technologies can be repurposed for social software needs, including e-mail. Read the article at *http://www.shirky.com/writings/group_politics.html*.

11   *http://thefacebook.com/*

12   For example, Denham Gray's human-computer interaction class (*http://www.voght.com/cgi-bin/pywiki?HciSummer*) or Georgia Tech's campus-wide wiki, CoWeb (*http://c2.com/w2/bridges/CoWeb*).

13   For example, Barbara Ganley's 2003 Irish literature class (*http://wl.middlebury.edu/irishf03/*). *http://www.weblogg-ed.com/* is an excellent blog for keeping up with this approach.

14   See Gloria Anzaldua's work, most notably *Borderlands/La Frontera* (San Francisco, CA: Spinsters/Aunt Lute, 1987).

15   *http://en.wikipedia.org/wiki/Main_Page*

16   See *http://www.nytimes.com/2001/05/03/technology/03GAME.html?searchpv=site01*. *http://unfiction.com* is a fine resource for information and collaboration.

17   *http://www.sunoikisis.org/* and *http://www.nitle.org/tr_lm_segue_cds.php*

18   *http://cyber.law.harvard.edu/filtering/china/test/*

19   *http://segue.middlebury.edu/index.php?&action=site&site=segue* and *www.nitle.org/tr_lm_segue_cds.php*

20   *http://www.creativecommons.org/*

21   *http://www.law.duke.edu/cspd/* is one leading academic focus of public domain study.

22   *http://www.groove.net/home/*

23   *http://www.openarchives.org/*

24   *http://www.imsglobal.org/*

Glossary of Terms

This glossary is taken in part from the glossary prepared for the 2003 EDUCAUSE Learning Initiative (ELI), formerly known as the National Learning Infrastructure Initiative (NLII), focus session on next-generation CMS by Patricia McGee and revised for this book.

A

Accessibility Compliance: Meeting the standards that allow people with disabilities to access information online. Persons with disabilities (e.g., the blind) use a device to "read" the screen (edu•tools, n. d.).

Active Learning: Learners make deliberate choices and actions about what and how they acquire knowledge typically through case studies, reflection, role-play, simulations, etc.

Activity: An objective-driven task that the learner engages in independently or with others and which may or may not result in a product or be assessed.

Adaptive Learning: Allows a learner to make choices within the learning environment about modality preferences (e.g., visual, text, audio, animation, etc.) and structure of learning (e.g., linear, structured, hierarchal, nonlinear, random-accessed)

Adult Learning Theory (andragogy): Stipulates that adults need to know the reason they are learning something, learn through experience, see learning as problem solving, and learn most readily when they can immediately apply what they learn (Knowles, 1984).

Analysis (Bloom's Taxonomy): The breaking down of material into its component parts so its organizational structure and component parts can be understood (Anderson & Krathwohl, 2001).

Application (Bloom's Taxonomy): The learner's use of learned material in new situations. The learner can use and make an abstraction of the material in a concrete context (Anderson & Krathwohl, 2001).

Assessment: The process used to systematically evaluate a learner's skill or knowledge level (ASTD, n. d.).

Assignment: In general, the output of an activity that results in a product that will be turned in for assessment.

Asynchronous Learning: Learning in which interaction between teachers and students occurs in different times and locations.

Authentic Assessment: Learners perform real-world tasks that demonstrate their ability to apply skills and knowledge in such a manner that their learning can be documented.

Authentic Problems: Curriculum-based scenarios or situations drawn from the real world and used to allow the learner to make connections between theory and practice through application and analysis.

B

Blended Learning: Learning events that combine both online and face-to-face instruction.

Bookmark: A saved location that is stored in a browser for easy and quick retrieval, or a previously accessed resource.

C

CAI (Computer-Assisted Instruction): The computer is a medium of instruction, for tutorial, drill, and practice, simulation, or games. CAI is used for a variety or purposes but most often for introductory learning or remediation.

Case Study: A scenario-based problem for intensive examination, judgment, assessment; provides students practice in applying their analytical and presentation skills and theoretical knowledge. May be constructed by the instructor or learner from real-world events or hypothetical situations.

Cognitive: Mental operations that involve perceptions, judgments, memory, and reasoning (LeFrançois, 1991).

Collaborative Learning: Two or more learners interact as a group to develop a consensual answer that may or may not reflect an absolute or recorded truth but, rather, what the group agrees upon to be a rational and reasonable answer.

Community: A group of individuals who have shared needs, interests, or requirements and who interact and communicate using technology. Online communities encourage and support member-based rules, rituals, and norms (NLII, n. d.).

Competency-Based Instruction (CBI): A learner-centered approach to learning in which the student progresses as specific skills are mastered as indicated by well-defined competencies.

Comprehension (Bloom's Taxonomy): Interpreting, explaining, or translating information (Anderson & Krathwohl, 2001).

Concept Map: A visual representation of the relationships between concepts, such as categorical, hierarchal, causal, quantitative, similarity/dissimilarity, etc. (West, Farmer & Wolff, 1991)

Conceptual Framework: Organizational posits that illustrate the beliefs, values, and philosophies of an initiative, organization, or body of work.

Constructivism: A philosophy of learning drawn from the work of Dewey, Piaget, and Vygotsky in which learners actively engage in learning experiences that have meaning and relevance to them, acquire knowledge through interacting with content and others, and negotiate meaning through this interaction (TIP, n. d.).

Content: The facts, concepts, and/or generalizations (rules, principles, procedures, and processes) that form the basis of information and knowledge to be learned. Content may be in the form of text, audio, video, animation, and/or simulation.

Context: Situated information and/or environment that have specific characteristics that may not be transferable to other contexts.

Contextual: Information situated within individual, culture, time, place, and other events.

Control: The degree to which an end user (learner or instructor) can make decisions, choices, or changes within a learning context having to do with communication, activities, or interface interaction.

Cooperative Learning: Learners work together in a common effort (typically with assigned roles) to achieve a common learning objective.

Curriculum: A set of courses, modules, or other organized learning experiences that constitute a complete, cohesive, and coherent program of study.

D

Deeper Learning: Occurs when students can acquire knowledge in a manner that is enjoyable, without undo stress or discomfort, and with a dedication that is compelling (DiSessa, 2000).

Digital Drop Box: Learners submit assignments directly to the instructor within a CMS.

Disconnected User: Someone who is not logged into a system and therefore not present.

Discovery Learning: A learner-initiated and instructor-supported or technology-supported process through which the learner explores, queries, and browses to determine answers.

Discussion: Interactions among individuals in which there is reciprocal communication that can be one-to-one, one-to-many, many-to-many, in the present, or occurring over time.

Distributed Learning: Learner and instructor are separated by time and space and interactions are mediated through information communication technologies (ICTs).

Diverse Learners: Learning abilities that are non-uniform and vary by learner characteristics such as culture, learning preferences, cognitive abilities, gender, age, and non-academic responsibilities.

E

Engaging: The design of representations, activities, and tasks that add sensory modalities, interactions, and/or communication options that allow the learner to do more than read text.

Evaluation, Content (Bloom's Taxonomy): The learner makes judgments based on knowledge of the material about the value of its methods and materials for some specific purpose. Judgments can also be based on supporting evidence (Anderson & Krathwohl, 2001).

Evaluation, Learning: Specific tasks, devices, or strategies used to determine the effectiveness of a learning activity.

Expectations: What the student and teacher anticipate about their technical and learning experience.

Exploration: Students learn most about a particular subject when they learn how to build knowledge for oneself through discovery.

F

Facilitator: An instructor, peer, or assistant who observes and may participate in course activities in order to solve technical, logistical, or interaction problems and to encourage and provide feedback as the learner learns.

Feedback: Information that responds (preferably immediately) to a learner's completion of assignment or task.

Field Trips: Learner moves into a new environment (virtual or real) to examine or experience artifacts, events, or people.

Formative Assessment or Evaluation: Ongoing feedback provided to the learner about his or her progress towards achieving a learning goal or objective. Formative assessment supports learner knowledge acquisition as well as provides motivation.

G

Game: A simulated decision-making scenario in which an individual player or a group of players follow predetermined rules and use tokens to achieve an objective or payoff.

Goal: A broad statement of purpose for a course of instruction that does not specify how learning will be accomplished.

Group Work: The capacity to organize a class into groups and provide group workspace that enables the instructor to assign specific tasks or projects.

H

Higher-Order Thinking: Cognitive skills that operate at top levels of Bloom's Taxonomy: Analyze, Evaluate, Create (Anderson & Krathwohl, 2001).

I

Independent: To make decisions on one's own judgment and reasoning.

Individualized Learning: Providing the learner multiple learning paths to meet one objective (CAST, n. d.).

Instructional Design: The process of conceptualizing and creating a series of activities, assignments, and assessments to achieve specific objectives and goals.

Instructivist: A theory of teaching in which the learner is a passive recipient of information (Reynolds, Mason, & Caley, 2002).

Intellectual Property Rights: Involves the legal and ethical rights of the creators of instructional materials (may include faculty, designers, students, etc.) and how they may control the use, replication, distribution, and access of their materials.

Interactive: A student action triggers an event from which the student makes a new decision and facilitates a new action.

Interface Design: The environment in which the content developer or instructional designer functions

Interface, User: The environment in which the learner, instructor, or guest manipulates the learning material.

J

Journaling: The learner captures ideas over a stated time period; it can be archived in multiple media formats and kept private or shared publicly.

Just-in-Need: Learners are able to access the information or support they need exactly when they need it.

Just-in-Time: Learners are able to access the information or support they need exactly when they want it.

K

Knowledge Types (Bloom's Taxonomy):

> **Existing**: Recall or identification of previously learned material.

> **Factual**: Identification of empirically documented events.

> **New**: Concepts and/or facts to be examined and fit within existing knowledge structures (Anderson & Krathwohl, 2001).

L

Learner: Any user who accesses or uses resources to gather information, acquire skills, or construct knowledge.

Learner Independence: The amount of self-control a learner is permitted to explore and evaluate new knowledge.

Learner Options: The variety of events, tools, and strategies offered to a student on a given topic.

Learner Preference: Conditions, tools, or resources that a learner may prefer but not require in specific learning activities that facilitate learning.

Learning: The acquisition of knowledge or skill acquired by experience, instruction, or study information which results in new or improved skills, knowledge, behaviors, and/or attitudes.

Learning Content Management System (LCMS): A system in which the content is separated from the organizational and interface structures. Instructional development tools are a part of the LCMS, unlike a content management system.

Learning Object: Any digital resource that can be used and reused to support a learning objective.

Learning Objective: A statement that describes what the learner should be able to do by the end of a learning activity or task. Typically, learning objectives are written as measurable and behavioral outcomes and are often used as an advanced organizer for the learner to focus on desired knowledge acquisition.

Learning Strategies: Procedures, routines, or memory devices that a learner uses to remember and recall information (LeFrançois, 1991). Examples include outlining, note taking, study groups, etc.

Learning Style: A learner's preferred mode, strategy, or design to learning that may include studying, thinking, or processing information.

M

Metacognition: Thinking about how one thinks, which includes connecting new information to what one already knows, deliberately selecting thinking strategies, and intentionally monitoring thinking while evaluating thinking processes (LeFrançois, 1991).

Metadata: Metadata is descriptive information about a learning object that is not visible to a user of an object for "purposes of description, administration, legal requirements, technical functionality, use and usage, and preservation" (Baca, n. d., p. x). Metadata is designed to help users and managers locate, organize, access, and use objects differently.

Module: Groups of readings, activities, tasks, and assignments that are organized around a central topic or theme.

N

Navigation: Systems, menus, or directions provided to users so they can explore, locate, and proceed to different parts of a learning environment through a series of events and requests.

O

Objective-Driven: Learning experiences that are designed to achieve a specific learning objective.

Organization: The manner in which a curriculum and a learning environment is structured to provide coherent and readily accessible lessons, feedback and support, and interaction and communication.

Outcome: The goal of instruction.

Outline: A text summary that is broken down into main ideas and listed in a numerical or bullet format.

Output: See End Product

Ownership: A feeling or acknowledgment that a user has proprietary and intellectual control of what he or she has created.

P

Pedagogy: Methods, strategies, and activities of teaching.

Peer-to-Peer: Any interaction or communication between two learners.

Performance-Based Outcomes: Learner outcomes that are observable, demonstrated products or behaviors based on standards.

Portal: A dynamic and personalizable Web interface that connects a user to services, people, and functions of their choosing. Examples include chat rooms, courses, records or management systems, e-mail, etc.

Portfolio: A collection of learner artifacts and articulation of beliefs that illustrate and document learning over a period of time.

Practice and Reinforcement: Activities, tasks, and feedback provided to the learner by the instructor or the technical system throughout the initial learning experience (LeFrançois, 1991).

Pre-Assessment: A survey, questionnaire, interview, or other device that allows the instructor to assess the entry-level knowledge and abilities of a learner.

Prescriptive Learning: A process in which only coursework that matches a learner's identified skill and knowledge gaps is offered to him or her, with the goal of making the learning experience more meaningful, efficient, and cost-effective (ASTD, n. d.).

Procedural Knowledge: The steps taken to complete a process.

Public Viewing: A choice that a learner or instructor can make within a technology-based learning environment that allows general access to material.

R

Real-World Problem Solving: Learning that is situated around an event, case, problem, or scenario. Students collaborate to study issues of a problem while also striving to create viable solutions.

Reciprocity: A response from an individual or system that complements an initial action or returns one in kind.

Reflection: The cognitive processes that take place when a learner thinks about something that has happened in the past.

Repository, Digital: A searchable database that houses digital artifacts such as learning objects.

Retrieval: Recalling information stored in long-term memory (LeFrançois, 1991).

Role Play: A teaching strategy in which learners act out characters in order to try out behaviors, practice interactions, communicate for a desired outcome, or solve a problem.

S

Scaffolding: The instructor, or a more advanced peer, supports a learner as he or she constructs knowledge.

Self-Assessment: Process by which the learner determines a personal level of knowledge and skills through metacognition or testing.

Self-Directed: The learner determines such things as content, process for learning, outcomes, etc.

Self-Paced Instruction: The learner determines how quickly to complete tasks, activities, or a course of study.

Simulations: Highly interactive applications that allow the learner to model or role-play in a scenario. Simulations enable the learner to practice skills or behaviors in a risk-free environment (ASTD, n. d.).

Situated Context: A situation that is defined and bound in a particular and specific set of beliefs that includes expectations, operations, and assumptions (LeFrançois, 1991).

Social: Any interaction or communication with another person or group of people.

Social Learning: Occurs in a learning experience in which participants observe and adopt the behaviors and attitudes of other group members (LeFrançois, 1991).

Standards: Set specifications for packaging and instructional design that are designed to ensure accessibility, interoperability, reusability, and durability (IMS, n. d.).

Student-Owned: Intellectual materials and/or a print, electronic, or artifact created by a learner.

Summative Assessment of Evaluation: Formal and definitive events (such as quizzes, tests, or written/designed products) that document the learner's degree of mastery of a learning goal or objective.

Syllabus: A text document that describes and explains course goals, topics, activities, assignments, schedule, and resources.

Synchronous Learning: A real-time online learning experience in which all participants present at the same time and interact.

Synthesis (Bloom's Taxonomy): Putting all of the pieces of the material together to form a new application of the whole (Anderson & Krathwohl, 2001).

T

Tasks: Specific and discrete actions taken by the learner within an activity.

Teaching: Directed by an expert or more knowledgeable peer, teaching intends to increase or improve knowledge, skills, attitudes, and/or behaviors in a person to accomplish a variety of goals.

Team Learning: Active learning in which group members assume specific roles in order to achieve an outcome.

Template: A set of predetermined elements that are used to replicate a design set for media (e.g., text, Web page, etc.), assignments (e.g., paper, project, etc.), or instructional elements (e.g., syllabus, glossary, calendar, etc.).

Training: A process that aims to improve knowledge, skills, attitudes, and/or behaviors in a person to accomplish a specific job task or goal. Training is often focused on business needs and driven by time-critical business skills and knowledge, and its goal is often to improve performance (ASTD, n. d.).

Transformative Assessment: The purposeful gathering and use of data to ensure that the application of findings and the dissemination of results will substantially change and enrich the learning experience (Brown, 2004).

U

Units: An instructional plan for a set of learners for a course of study smaller in scope than a course. Units typically include goals, objectives, activities, tasks, and assignments with forms of formative and summative assessment.

V

Virtual Field Trip: Involve participant interaction within a remote site that is accessed through technology. Unlike real-world field trips, virtual field trips can easily be repeated, can allow learners to proceed at their own pace and to their own depth, can allow them to visit a location they may not be able to physically visit, can provide a risk-free environment, and can provide expert resources.

References

American Society for Training & Development (ASTD). (n.d.). Learning Circuit's Glossary [online]. Available at *http://www.learningcircuits.org/glossary.html*

Anderson, L. W. & Krathwohl (Eds.). (2001). *A taxonomy for learning, teaching, and assessing: A revision of Bloom's Taxonomy of educational objectives.* New York: Longman.

Baca, M. (n. d.). Introduction to metadata: Glossary [online]. Getty Standards Project. Retrieved December 12, 2004, from *http://www.getty.edu/research/conducting_research/standards/intrometadata/4_glossary/index.html*

Brown, G. (2004). Technology and assessing for transformation: Lessons learner, part 2. Paper presented at the *Teaching with Technology Conference.* Denver, CO.

Center for Applied Special Technology (CAST). (n.d.). Universal design: A framework for individualized learning. Retrieved December 12, 2004, from *http://www.cast.org/udl/index.cfm?i=571/*

DiSessa, A. (2000). *Changing minds: Computers, learning and literacy.* Cambridge, MA: MIT Press.

edu•tools. (n.d.). Glossary [online]. Available at *http://www.edutools.info/course/help/glossary.jsp*

IMS Global Learning Consortium, Inc. (n.d.). Specifications [online]. Available at *http://www.imsglobal.org/specifications.html*

Knowles, M. (1984). *The adult learner: A neglected species* (3rd ed.). Houston, TX: Gulf Publishing.

LeFrançois, G. R. (1991). *Psychology for teaching* (7th ed.). Belmont, CA: Wadsworth Publishing Co.

National Learning Infrastructure Initiative (NLII). (n.d.). Virtual communities of practice [online]. Available at *http://www.educause.edu/Virtual CommunitiesOfPractice/2604*

Reynolds, J., Mason, R., & Caley, L. (2002). *How do people learn?* London: Chartered Institute of Personnel Development.

Theory Into Practice (TIP) Database. (n. d.). The theory into practice database [online]. Available at *http://tip.psychology.org/index.html*

West, C. K., Farmer, J. A., & Wolff, P. M. (1991). *Instructional design: Implications from cognitive Science.* Boston: Allyn & Bacon.

About the Authors

Patricia McGee is a faculty member in the instructional technology program in the College of Education and Human Development at the University of Texas at San Antonio (USA). Two successive summers as a faculty member of the American Society for Engineering Education (ASEE) U.S. Navy Research with the Joint Advanced Distributed Learning (ADL) Co-Laboratory provided a foundation for her work as a 2003 EDUCAUSE Learning Initiative (ELI), formerly known as National Learning Infrastructure Initiative Fellow, researching and writing about learning objects and next-generation course management systems. As director of a Preparing Tomorrow's Teachers to Use Technology Program (PT3) and Microsoft/Innovative Teaching grant, she contributes to campus-wide technology initiatives. She also develops, teaches, and studies online courses. Currently, she is leading an open-source ePortfolio project in her college, as well as conducting research about pedagogy within course management systems and institutional learning object development and policy making. Patricia earned a PhD in curriculum and instruction with a concentration in instructional technology from the University of Texas at Austin.

Colleen Carmean is the information technology director of instructional and desktop support for Arizona State University (USA) at the West campus. She teaches applied computing, is responsible for faculty development and support initiatives in technology at her campus, and is currently on the teaching and technology editorial board for MERLOT. As a EDUCAUSE Learning Initiative (ELI), formerly known as EDUCAUSE Learning Initiative (ELI), formerly known as National Learning Infrastructure Initiative Fellow in 2002, Colleen researched learner-centered practices in higher education. She earned her master's degree from the University of Arizona, earned her bachelor's degree from the University of Illinois, and studied at the University of Paris, Sorbonne, where she received a baccalaureate in civilization.

Ali Jafari has initiated, directed, and served as the conceptual architect for two highly successful course management systems, Oncourse and ANGEL. Oncourse is currently serving all campuses of Indiana University, and ANGEL is commercially available through the CyberLearning Labs, a for-profit company he cofounded in 2000. Ali is currently the director of the Indiana University-Purdue University Indianapolis (IUPUI) CyberLab and professor of computer and information technology in the School of Engineering and Technology at IUPUI (USA). Since 1986, he has worked as a software designer, system engineer, technology architect, professor, and researcher. Ali's research interests include interface design, agent-based learning environments, intelligent user interfaces, and, most recently, Internet portals.

****

Xornam Apedoe is currently completing her PhD in instructional technology at the University of Georgia (USA). While completing her BSc Honors Psychology degree at the University of Alberta, Canada, Xornam worked as an instructional technology assistant, providing support for psychology faculty and graduate students, developing multimedia resources, and conducting research on the use of technology in teaching introductory psychology. Xornam's current research interests include the use of technology (such as online discussions and digital libraries) to enhance and enrich the learning experience for students in large undergraduate classes, and the relationship between instructors' conceptions of teaching and their technology use.

Bob Bender, professor emeritus of English at the University of Missouri-Columbia (USA), also served there as faculty liaison with information and access technology. In addition to teaching courses in English literature and women's studies, as director of special degree programs, he was responsible for almost all undergraduate interdisciplinary programs at UM. Since 1995, he has taught a variety of Web-based "paperless" courses to effectively engage students in computer-mediated writing. He has published widely in the fields in which he has taught and more recently on technology and teaching. Currently, he is a Fellow with the EDUCAUSE Center for Applied Research.

Marwin Britto is currently the director of the Educational Technology Center and a faculty member at Central Washington University in Ellensburg, Washington (USA). He received a PhD in instructional technology from the University of Georgia in Athens, Georgia. His involvement with course management systems (CMS) began in 1997, and since that time he has had experiences with CMS as a student, instructional designer, support staff, instructor, trainer, and consultant. His current primary research interests include evaluation instruments of Web-based instruction, technology integration in teacher education programs, and the use of wireless technologies to promote and support K-12 learning.

Gary Brown directs the Center for Teaching, Learning and Technology (CTLT) at Washington State University (USA). He has designed, developed, and assessed innovative projects across the curriculum. He has conducted assessments in the costs of educational technologies and recently received, with his CTLT colleagues, the National University Telecommunications Network (NUTN) award for best research on faculty motivation and perceptions of the efficacy of online learning. Gary is a National Learning Communities Fellow, and a co-principal investigator on a Fund for the Improvement of Postsecondary Education (FIPSE)-funded critical thinking project. Gary has been a leader with the EDUCAUSE Learning Initiative (ELI), formerly known as National Learning Infrastructure Initiative and EDUCAUSE and the Teaching, Learning, and Technology Group of the Transformative Assessment Project. Gary edits the assessment section for *The Technology Source*, serves on the advisory board of the Higher Education Knowledge & Technology Exchange (HEKATE), and directs the CTLT Silhouette Project, which serves Flashlight Online for the TLT Group.

Richard Caladine has coordinated the Learning, Innovation and Future Technologies (LIFT) program of the Centre for Educational Development and Interactive Resources (CEDIR) at the University of Wollongong, Australia, since 2001. The aim of this program is to enhance teaching and learning through staff development opportunities in the application of current and future technologies to learning and teaching. Richard, through LIFT, has successfully introduced a number of new learning technologies to teaching and learning. These include CUPID (Collaborative, User-Produced Internet Documents) and eduStream, a system for the automated recording, processing, and distribution of learning materials via the Internet.

Amy Campbell (M.S., University of Michigan) is the senior academic technology consultant in the Duke University Center for Instructional Technology (USA). Amy consults with faculty on effective uses of technology in teaching and learning. She is the Duke Blackboard learning system project manager and recently hosted the 2004 Blackboard Southeast Users Conference at Duke.

Nada Dabbagh is an associate professor of instructional technology in the Graduate School of Education at George Mason University (USA). She teaches courses in instructional design, Web-based instruction, applied psychology, and technology integration. Nada received her doctorate in instructional systems from the Pennsylvania State University in 1996. Her main research interests are task structuring in online learning environments, problem generation and representation in hypermedia learning environments, and supporting student self-regulation in distributed learning environments. Nada has published many journal articles and book chapters in each of these research areas and most recently a book entitled *Online Learning: Concepts, Strategies, and Application.*

Samantha Earp (M.A., Indiana University) is the director of foreign language technology services at Duke University (USA). She is a former editor-in-chief of the International Association of Language Learning Technology (IALLT) *Journal of Language Learning Technologies* and a national trainer for the American Council of Teachers of Foreign Languages and Houghton Mifflin's Teach with Technology professional development series.

Jennifer Gurrie has been studying online teaching and learning for several years, both through her personal interest as well as through her job as senior product manager for a major e-learning software vendor. In this position, she has the privilege of working with many faculty and students who are immersed in online learning environments.

Jesko Kaltenbaek is currently a research assistant at the Freie University of Berlin (Germany) while completing his PhD in media psychology. He is a member of a commission of experts for the selection of a learning management system (LMS) and course management system (CMS) for the Freie University of Berlin. Since 2002, he has been teaching a variety of Web-based courses. He is also juror for several prices of multimedia. Furthermore, he has supervised and evaluated several e-learning and notebook projects in Germany. Jesko's current research interests include implementing and supporting e-learning and blended learning in universities and companies and the usage and effects of media by children and adults.

Vijay Kumar is assistant provost and director of academic computing at the Massachusetts Institute of Technology (MIT), USA. Through these roles, he influences the Institute's strategic focus on educational technology and promotes the effective integration of information technology in MIT education. Vijay provides leadership for units engaged in delivering infrastructure and services to support educational technology activities at MIT, including the Academic Computing in Information Services and Technology unit and MIT's Academic Media Production Services (AMPS). Vijay is the principal investigator of O.K.I (Open Knowledge Initiative), an MIT-led collaborative project to develop an open architecture for enterprise educational applications.

Jon Lanestedt holds the position as manager of the Educational Technology Group, a unit within the University of Oslo Center for Information Technology (Norway). In this capacity, he has played a major role in the strategic planning and implementation of the institution's digital learning infrastructure. Lanestedt has a master of arts, as well as formal studies in informatics and project management, and has been professionally involved in the educational application of digital technology for a number of years, both in academia and in the publishing industry.

Joan K. Lippincott is the associate executive director of the Coalition for Networked Information (CNI), USA, a joint project of the Association of Research Libraries (ARL) and EDUCAUSE. Joan held positions in the libraries of Cornell, Georgetown, George Washington University, and State University of New York at Brockport, as well as in the Research and Policy Analysis Division of the American Council on Education. She has written articles and made presentations on such topics as networked information, collaboration among professional groups, assessment, and teaching and learning in the networked environment. Joan received her PhD in higher education policy, planning, and administration from the University of Maryland.

Youmei Liu earned an Ed.D. in instructional technology at the University of Houston (USA), where she works as an instructional designer in the Office of Educational Technology and University Outreach. She is also an adjunct faculty member teaching an advanced Web technology course at UH. She provides faculty training and support related to online course design and instructional delivery. Her research interests include faculty development, integration of multimedia components and learning objects in course design, and online assessment.

Cyprien Lomas is a researcher in the faculty of science at the University of British Columbia (Vancouver, Canada) and a 2004 NLII Fellow. His work explores and supports the teaching and learning of science with and without technology. Recent projects have included using guided inquiry and simulations to prepare students for chemistry labs, creating biological image learning objects, and implementing writing, reflection, and ePortfolios in a first-year science course. Cyprien is interested in using technology to enhance social interactions and community development in learning environments.

Phil Long is a senior strategist for the Academic Computing Enterprise at the Massachusetts Institute of Technology (USA), and director of learning outreach for the MIT iCampus Outreach Initiative. He provides direction in applying MIT information services and technology resources to support the integration of technology into the curriculum. He leads the MIT iCampus Outreach Initiative, freely disseminating MIT-developed educational technology tools that complement the OCW distribution of MIT educational content. Phil's professional activities are numerous, including serving on the Syllabus Conference board, past chair of the Advisory Committee on Teaching and Learning of the NLII, MIT's DSpace Policy Committee, the NMC Project Horizon technology advisory task force, Steven's Institute of Technology WebCampus board, the U.S. Army Distance Learning Subcommittee, and many others. Phil is also a senior associate with the TLT Group, the AAHE technology affiliate. Phil enjoys running and birding and maintains his fragile mental state through an avid dedication to sailing.

Jeff Merriman is currently senior strategist for academic computing at the Massachusetts Institute of Technology (USA) and project director of the Open Knowledge Initiative. Jeff has spent much of his career building and promoting various kind of technology infrastructure for higher education. As director of academic computing at Stanford University, he brought the notion of "wired campuses" into the forefront by networking all of Stanford's graduate and undergraduate residence halls, leading an aggressive effort that began in 1987. Jeff also founded the annual ResNet Symposia series. In 1998, Jeff helped to form Stanford's Academic Computing program and became director of the school's academic computing technology group.

David Mills is the vice president, chief technology officer, and cofounder of ANGEL™ Learning, Inc. (USA). David has served as the chief architect of the ANGEL LMS since the technology's conception at the Indiana University-Purdue University Indianapolis (IUPUI) CyberLab, where he served as associate director. David is recognized for his vision in the field of education technology. He is credited with producing the first large-scale, enterprise LMS. Prior to CyberLearning Labs, David also served as an associate professor in the Computer Technology Department at IUPUI and president of Meehan Mills Software, a Web-based software development company focused on teaching and learning. David holds a bachelor of science in computer technology from Purdue University.

Lynne O'Brien (PhD, University of Delaware) is director of instructional technology at Duke University (USA) and led the creation of Duke's Center for Instructional Technology. Lynne came to Duke from Brown University, where she was a faculty member and manager of instructional computing services. At Duke, she is especially interested in promoting collaboration and information sharing across schools and in helping faculty use technology to support innovative and effective teaching strategies.

Ulrich Rauch directs the development and implementation of integrated technologies in the Faculty of Arts at the University of British Columbia (UBC) in Vancouver, Canada. He combines his experience as an instructor with his perspective on e-learning to develop strategies for the use of new media in teaching, learning and research. Ulrich's current interests include initiatives such as the development of open-source educational technology tools for instructors, staff, and students and the participation in the creation of an envisioned "Media Lab", which would provide research and development space for the Arts in Vancouver. Ulrich holds a PhD in Sociology from UBC and loves to engage in a critical analysis of new technologies in the workplace, in education, and in public life.

Robby Robson is president of Eduworks Corporation (USA), chair of the Institute of Electrical and Electronics Engineers (IEEE) Learning Technology Standards Committee, and principle investigator for the National Science Digital Library Reusable Learning Project. He has been involved in designing and implementing Web-based learning technology since 1995, including several academic online learning environments and commercial software designed for Global 2000 companies. Robby received a doctorate in mathematics from Stanford University in 1981, and currently holds adjunct positions in mathematics at Oregon State University and in computer science at Dalhousie University. His resume and publication list can be found at *www.eduworks.net/robby*.

Barbara Ross launched Universal Learning Technology, Inc., which later became WebCT, Inc. (USA), with founder and CEO Carol Vallone in 1995. Her responsibilities include developing strategies and providing operational management for marketing, support, services, and partnerships. Barbara has worked for over 20 years at the nexus of information, technology, and learning. She has a liberal arts degree from the University of Pennsylvania, which prepared her well for her future endeavors, even though nothing she has done in her career actually existed while she was in school.

Steven Shaw is an associate professor at Concordia University in Montreal, Canada, where he is also director of the graduate programs in educational technology. He has almost two decades of experience in developing, implementing, and evaluating training, performance support, and e-learning solutions in a variety of corporate and educational settings in North America and Europe. He is also chief learning officer of Eedo Knowledgeware Corp., a firm recognized as a leader in the field of learning content management systems and knowledge management tools.

Mona Stokke is a senior executive officer in the Educational Technology Group, a unit within the University of Oslo Center for Information Technology (Norway). Stokke holds a master's degree in pedagogy, and her current professional focus is on faculty development related to the educational uses of digital media. Stokke has previously held academic positions as teacher of pedagogy at the Norwegian Military Academy and has professional experience as an editor and educational adviser for digital productions in the publishing industry.

Vicki Suter currently leads iCohere's (http://www.icohere.com) higher education business development and client services activities, consulting with educational institutions, nonprofits and associations focused on community-oriented collaboration. She also develops, designs and facilitates online conferences and workshops, and helps design and support online communities of practice. Previously, as Director of NLII Projects for EDUCAUSE, for six years, she provided vision and leadership for a wide range of initiatives and projects for professional development of faculty and staff in the use of technology for teaching and learning. Her research interests include virtual communities of practice and transformation of higher education. Prior to that, she worked in academic computing in higher education for more than 15 years. She received her M.B.A. from the University of California, Davis, holds an undergraduate degree in economics, and is currently a doctoral student in the Graduate School of Education and Psychology at Pepperdine University in the US.

Frank Tansey is technology consultant as well as a co-editor of eLearning Dialogue, a bi-weekly electronic newsletter. He was the former project administrator for CaliforniaColleges.edu, an intersegmental Web site project involving the University of California, the California State University, California Community Colleges, the Association of Independent California Colleges and Universities, and the California State Department of Education. Prior to that, he was a member of the founding management team for the IMS Project of the EDUCAUSE Learning Initiative (ELI), formerly known as National Learning Infrastructure Initiative (EDUCAUSE) that evolved into IMS Global Learning Consortium. These two activities followed a career as a university administrator, the most recent as associate vice president for enrollment services at Sonoma State University. Frank survives by living in the middle of California's wine country.

Vivek Venkatesh is a doctoral student in the educational technology program at Concordia University in Montreal, Canada. He possesses graduate fellowships from both Concordia University as well as the *Fonds québecois de* *recherche sur la société et la culture*. His research interests include exploring how individuals self-assess their performances on ill-structured tasks as well as in the development and evaluation of topic map engines in corporate and postsecondary educational settings.

Van Weigel is professor of ethics and economic development at Eastern University in St. Davids, Pennsylvania, USA (*vweigel@eastern.edu*). He earned a PhD in ethics and society from the University of Chicago and is the author of *A Unified Theory of Global Development* (1989), a *Choice* Outstanding Academic Book, and *Earth Cancer* (1995). Van's most recent book, *Deep Learning for a Digital Age: Technology's Untapped Potential for Higher Education* (Jossey-Bass, 2002), explores how faculty can help students develop skills in research, problem solving, critical thinking, and knowledge management by using Web-based collaboration tools. John Seely Brown, formerly the chief scientist of Xerox and director of the Xerox Palo Alto Research Center, describes the book as "a visionary but also pragmatic view of what is possible in facilitating deep learning with today's and tomorrow's digital technologies", and *University Business* (April 2002) characterizes it as "an intriguing blend of theory regarding the possible future of education".

Index

Designing Instruction for Technology-Enhanced Learning

Patricia Rogers
Bemidji State University, USA

When faced with the challenge of designing instruction for technology-enhanced education, many good teachers find great difficulty in connecting pedagogy with technology. While following instructional design practices can help, most teachers are either unfamiliar with the field or are unable to translate the formal design process for use in their own classroom. *Designing Instruction for Technology Enhanced Learning* is focused on the practical application of instructional design practices for teachers at all levels, and is intended to help the reader "walk through" designing instruction for e-learning.

The goal of *Designing Instruction for Technology Enhanced Learning* is to pool the expertise of many practitioners and instructional designers and to present that information in such a way that teachers will have useful and relevant references and guidance for using technology to enhance teaching and learning, rather than simply adding technology to prepared lectures. The chapters, taken together, make the connection between intended learning outcomes, teachings strategies, and instructional media.

ISBN 1-930708-28-9 (h/c) • US$74.95 • 286 pages • Copyright © 2002

> "Most often, when forced to use new technologies in teaching, teachers will default to a technology-enhanced lecture method, rather than take advantage of the variety of media characteristics that expand the teaching and learning experience."
> –*Patricia Rogers, Bemidji State University, USA*

It's Easy to Order! Order online at www.idea-group.com or call 1-717-533-8845 ext.10!
Mon-Fri 8:30 am-5:00 pm (est) or fax 24 hours a day 717/533-8661

Idea Group Publishing

Hershey • London • Melbourne • Singapore • Beijing

An excellent addition to your library